Lecture Notes in Computer Science 6191

Commenced Publication in 1973
Founding and Former Series Editors:
Gerhard Goos, Juris Hartmanis, and Jan van Leeuwen

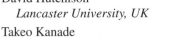
T0092414

Astrid M.L. Kappers
Jan B.F. van Erp
Wouter M. Bergmann Tiest
Frans C.T. van der Helm (Eds.)

Haptics: Generating and Perceiving Tangible Sensations

International Conference, EuroHaptics 2010
Amsterdam, July 8-10, 2010
Proceedings, Part I

 Springer

Volume Editors

Astrid M.L. Kappers
Helmholtz Institute, Utrecht University
Padualaan 8, 3584 CH Utrecht, The Netherlands
E-mail: a.m.l.kappers@uu.nl

Jan B. F. van Erp
TNO Human Factors
PO Box 23, 3769 ZG Soesterberg, The Netherlands
E-mail: Jan.vanErp@tno.nl

Wouter M. Bergmann Tiest
Helmholtz Institute, Utrecht University
Padualaan 8, 3584 CH Utrecht, The Netherlands
E-mail: w.m.bergmanntiest@uu.nl

Frans C.T. van der Helm
Delft University of Technology
Mekelweg 2, 2628 CD Delft, The Netherlands
E-mail: F.C.T.vanderHelm@tudelft.nl

Library of Congress Control Number: 2010929194

CR Subject Classification (1998): H.1.2, I.6, C.3, H.5, I.2.6, I.2

LNCS Sublibrary: SL 3 – Information Systems and Application, incl. Internet/Web and HCI

ISSN   0302-9743
ISBN-10 3-642-14063-7 Springer Berlin Heidelberg New York
ISBN-13 978-3-642-14063-1 Springer Berlin Heidelberg New York

springer.com

© Springer-Verlag Berlin Heidelberg 2010
Printed in Germany

Typesetting: Camera-ready by author, data conversion by Scientific Publishing Services, Chennai, India
Printed on acid-free paper   06/3180

Preface

Welcome to the proceedings of EuroHaptics 2010. EuroHaptics is the major international conference and the primary European meeting for researchers in the field of human haptic sensing and touch-enabled computer applications. We were proud to have received more submissions for presentations, demonstrations and special sessions than ever before. This shows that the topic and the conference's quality and approach appeal to an increasing number of researchers and companies.

We received more than 200 submissions for oral and poster presentations, demos and pre-conference special workshops. A team of 25 associate editors and 241 reviewers read the submissions and advised the four volume editors. We owe the associate editors and reviewers many thanks. We accepted 43 submissions as oral and 80 as poster presentations, 7 pre-conference workshops were approved and more than 20 demos could be experienced 'hands-on' during the conference. The proceedings contain all oral and poster presentation papers. No distinction between the two presentation types was made because selection was not on the basis of submission quality but on relevance for a broad audience. We were proud to add three distinguished keynote speakers to the conference program: Mark Ernst, Rosalyn Driscoll and Patrick van der Smagt.

Besides the authors, presenters and reviewers, we would like to express our gratitude to our supporting organizations, The Netherlands Organisation for Applied Scientific Research TNO, VU University Amsterdam, Utrecht University and Delft University of Technology, and to our sponsors, especially our four gold-level sponsors: Force Dimension, Engineering Systems Technologies, TNO and Moog.

Traditionally, EuroHaptics aims at a multidisciplinary audience from (scientific) fields such as neuroscience, perception and psychophysics, rendering and software algorithms, hardware development and applications. To further increase the multidisciplinary approach, we adapted a new setup for the conference program by organizing the sessions across and not along scientific disciplines. We hope that this will further increase the crosstalk between the disciplines involved in haptics, which we consider a prerequisite for the further development of the field. Reading through the proceedings will show you that the field is already maturing rapidly and has a bright future ahead.

Finally, it is my honor and pleasure to acknowledge the Organizing Committee and acknowledge their roles in making EuroHaptics 2010 a memorable event: Astrid Kappers (Program Committee Chair, editor), Wouter Bergmann Tiest (editor, proceedings coordinator), Jeroen Smeets (local host, treasurer), Peter Werkhoven (sponsors), Frans van der Helm (editor), Tom Philippi (webmaster, treasurer) and Anne-Marie Brouwer (demos and social program).

Jan van Erp

Organization

Organizing Committee

Jan van Erp (Chair)	TNO Human Factors, Soesterberg, The Netherlands
Jeroen Smeets	VU University, Amsterdam, The Netherlands
Astrid Kappers	Utrecht University, Utrecht, The Netherlands
Frans van der Helm	Delft University of Technology, Delft, The Netherlands
Peter Werkhoven	Utrecht University, Utrecht, The Netherlands
Wouter Bergmann Tiest	Utrecht University, Utrecht, The Netherlands
Anne-Marie Brouwer	TNO Human Factors, Soesterberg, The Netherlands
Tom Philippi	Utrecht University, Utrecht, The Netherlands

Editors

Astrid Kappers (Editor-in-chief)	Utrecht University, Utrecht, The Netherlands
Jan van Erp	TNO Human Factors, Soesterberg, The Netherlands
Wouter Bergmann Tiest	Utrecht University, Utrecht, The Netherlands
Frans van der Helm	Delft University of Technology, Delft, The Netherlands

Associate Editors

David Abbink	Delft University of Technology, The Netherlands
Cagatay Basdogan	Koç University, Turkey
Seungmoon Choi	Pohang University of Science and Technology, South Korea
Göran Christiansson	SKF Engineering & Research Center, The Netherlands
Herman Damveld	Delft University of Technology, The Netherlands
Knut Drewing	Justus-Liebig-Universität Gießen, Germany
Abdulmotaleb El Saddik	University of Ottawa, Canada
Berthold Färber	University of the Bundeswehr, Munich, Germany
Manuel Ferre	Universidad Politécnica de Madrid, Spain
Antonio Frisoli	PERCRO, Scuola Superiore S. Anna, Pisa, Italy
Martin Grunwald	Universität Leipzig, Germany
Matthias Harders	ETH Zürich, Switzerland
Vincent Hayward	Université Pierre et Marie Curie, Paris, France
Thorsten Kern	Continental Corporation, Germany
Abderrahmane Kheddar	CNRSUM2 LIRMM, Montpellier, France

Dong-Soo Kwon	KAIST, Daejeon, South Korea
Ki-Uk Kyung	ETRI, Daejeon, South Korea
Karon MacLean	University of British Columbia, Vancouver, Canada
Mark Mulder	Delft University of Technology, The Netherlands
Haruo Noma	ATR Media Information Science Labs, Kyoto, Japan
Miguel Otaduy	URJC Madrid, Spain
William Provancher	University of Utah, Salt Lake City, USA
Chris Raymaekers	Hasselt University, Belgium
Jeha Ryu	Gwangju Institute of Science and Technology, South Korea
Jeroen Smeets	VU University, Amsterdam, The Netherlands

Reviewers

Jake Abbott	Oliver Braddick	Marc Ernst
Marco Agus	Jean-Pierre Bresciani	Thomas Ertl
Hyo-sung Ahn	Stephen Brewster	Paul Evrard
Fawaz Alsulaiman	Andrea Brogni	Ildar Farkhatdinov
Mehdi Ammi	Etienne Burdet	Irene Fasiello
Hideyuki Ando	Gianni Campion	Mark Fehlberg
Michele Antolini	Ozkan Celik	Peter Feys
Hichem Arioui	Pablo Cerrada	Alessandro Formaglio
Angelo Arleo	Jongeun Cha	Antonio Frisoli
Carlo Avizzano	Elaine Chapman	Ilja Frissen
Mehmet Ayyildiz	Hee-Byoung Choi	Yukio Fukui
José Azorín	Seungmoon Choi	Ignacio Galiana
Sarah Baillie	Göran Christiansson	Fabio Ganovelli
Soledad Ballesteros	Q. Chu	Marcos García
Karlin Bark	Salvador Cobos	Pablo García-Robledo
Kenneth Barner	Edward Colgate	Carlos Garre
Jorge Barrio	Chris Constantinou	Roger Gassert
Cagatay Basdogan	Koen Crommentuijn	Christos Giachritsis
Gabriel Baud-Bovy	Andrew Crossan	Frederic Giraud
Massimo Bergamasco	Herman Damveld	Brian Gleeson
Wouter Bergmann Tiest	Joan De Boeck	Pauwel Goethals
Antonio Bicchi	Nienke Debats	Daniel Gooch
Marta Bielza	Barbara Deml	Florian Gosselin
Hannes Bleuler	Massimiliano Di Luca	Burak Guclu
Juan Bogado	Andrew Doxon	Hakan Gurocak
Raoul Bongers	Knut Drewing	Gabjong Han
Monica Bordegoni	Christian Duriez	Sung H. Han
Gianni Borghesan	Mohamad Eid	Gunter Hannig
Diego Borro	Abdulmotaleb El Saddik	Riender Happee
Martyn Bracewell	Satoshi Endo	Matthias Harders

Mitra Hartmann
William Harwin
Wataru Hashimoto
Christian Hatzfeld
Vincent Hayward
Thomas Hazelton
Andreas Hein
Morton Heller
Denise Henriques
Constanze Hesse
Jim Hewit
Sandra Hirche
Hsin-Ni Ho
Robert Howe
Barry Hughes
Inwook Hwang
Jung-Hoon Hwang
Rosa Iglesias
Ali Israr
Miriam Ittyerah
Hiroo Iwata
Caroline Jay
Seokhee Jeon
Li Jiang
Lynette Jones
Christophe Jouffrais
Georgiana Juravle
Kanav Kahol
Lukas Kaim
Marjolein Kammers
Idin Karuei
Sebastian Kassner
Thorsten Kern
Dirk Kerzel
Shahzad Khan
Abderrahmane Kheddar
Sang-Youn Kim
Yeongmi Kim
Roberta Klatzky
Alois Knoll
Umut Kocak
Ilhan Konukseven
Gabor Kosa
Katherine Kuchenbecker
Tomohiro Kuroda
Yoshihiro Kuroda

Hoi Kwok
Dong-Soo Kwon
Ki-Uk Kyung
Mung Lam
Patrice Lambert
Piet Lammertse
Anatole Lécuyer
Susan Lederman
Vincent Levesque
Ming Lin
Robert Lindeman
Claudio Lo Console
Javier López
Karon MacLean
Charlotte Magnusson
Florence Marchi
Davide Mazza
Thorsten Meiß
Christopher Moore
Konstantinos Moustakas
Winfred Mugge
Masashi Nakatani
Marko Nardini
Fiona Newell
Günter Niemeyer
Verena Nitsch
Farley Norman
Ian Oakley
Shogo Okamoto
Marcia O'Malley
Sile O'Modhrain
Keita Ono
Jun Oohara
Miguel Otaduy
Martin Otis
Krista Overvliet
Miguel Padilla-Castaneda
Karljohan Palmerius
Jaeheung Park
Jinah Park
Jerome Pasquero
Volkan Patoğlu
Ricardo Pedrosa
Angelika Peer
Myrthe Plaisier
Daan Pool

Dane Powell
Carsten Preusche
Roope Raisamo
Markus Rank
Jyri Rantala
Jacqueline Rausch
Chris Raymaekers
Stéphane Régnier
Miriam Reiner
Gerhard Rinkenauer
Gabriel Robles De La Torre
Andreas Röse
Emanuele Ruffaldi
Jee-Hwan Ryu
Jeha Ryu
José Sabater
Eva-Lotta Sallnäs
Roopkanwal Samra
Krish Sathian
Joan Savall
Thomas Schauß
Stefania Serafin
Sascha Serwe
Shahin Sirouspour
Lynne Slivovsky
Massimiliano Solazzi
Edoardo Sotgiu
Jonas Spillmann
Mark Spingler
Christoph Staub
Arno Stienen
Hong Tan
Jean Thonnard
Nikolaos Tsagarakis
Brian Tse
Dzmitry Tsetserukou
Costas Tzafestas
Sehat Ullah
Ana Rita Valente Pais
George Van Doorn
René van Paassen
Dennis van Raaij
Lode Vanacken
Emmanuel Vander Poorten
Iason Vittorias
Frank Wallhoff

David Wang
Carolina Weber
Joel Carlos West
Eleonora Westebring-Van
    der Putten

Maarten Wijntjes
Alan Wing
Raul Wirz
Mark Wright
Juli Yamashita

Gi-Hun Yang
Hiroaki Yano
Yasuyoshi Yokokohji
Mounia Ziat

Table of Contents – Part I

Mass, Force, and Elasticity

Teleoperation

Novel Approaches

Table of Contents – Part II

Texture and Surfaces

Virtual Reality

Grasping and Moving

Performance and Training

PART I
Mass, Force, and Elasticity

Efficient Bimodal Haptic Weight Actuation

Gunter Hannig[1] and Barbara Deml[2]

[1] Universität der Bundeswehr, Werner-Heisenberg-Weg 39, 85577 Neubiberg, Germany
gunter.hannig@unibw.de
[2] Otto-von-Guericke-Universität Magdeburg, Universitätsplatz 2, 39106 Magdeburg, Germany
barbara.deml@ovgu.de

Abstract. In virtual environment scenarios the physical object property *weight* is rarely provided for operators due to its extensive technical complexity.

This paper addresses two approaches that both rely on pseudo-haptic feedback and that enable an efficient display of weight: *pneumatic* and *control/display* feedback. The former offers the substitution of proprioceptive weight perception by asserting well-defined pressure levels to the operatorís wrist while the latter feedback mode encodes weight by visually altering the motion of the virtual hand compared to the real hand movement. Two experiments (A and B) were conducted in order to derive Stevens' functions that express the relationship between objective feedback settings and subjective weight perception. Additionally, a conjoint analysis (experiment C) was carried out that quantifies the weight of each single feedback modality in simultaneous feedback conditions. Finally, the results of user ratings regarding the quality of the bimodal feedback are presented.

Both displays prove to be of value as the majority of human test subjects report haptic perceptions without any real haptic stimulation.

Keywords: Pseudo haptic feedback, weight perception, haptic feedback, pressure sleeve, pneumatic feedback, control/display ratio, CDR, virtual reality, psychophysical scaling, conjoint analysis.

1 Introduction

In teleaction scenarios, a human operator usually controls a robot which is located at a remote environment. In order to do so efficiently, the operator needs feedback of his actions at this remote location, be it visual, auditory, haptic or any combination thereof. In the best case the operator would get exactly the same quality and quantity of feedback as he can perceive in everyday life [1].

Scientists and engineers are still working on getting as close as possible to this perfect teleaction system: haptic feedback quality catches up with already high quality visual and auditive systems; multi-degree of freedom actuators [2] or exoskeletal solutions [3] allow force feedback; surface roughness is simulated by miniature voice coils [4], vibrating dc-motors [5] or pin displays [6], to name just a few.

In this paper an alternative approach for simulating the weight of an object is presented: instead of relying on complex, heavy, and expensive hardware the potential of pseudo-haptic feedback and substitution is used. Pseudo-haptic feedback does not

A.M.L. Kappers et al. (Eds.): EuroHaptics 2010, Part I, LNCS 6191, pp. 3–10, 2010.

provide any *real* haptic cue but it makes use of the fact that human haptic perception is also influenced by appropriate visual and auditive stimuli (see section 2.1). The pneumatic device substitutes the cues normally gathered by arm and shoulder proprioception for pressure receptors located around the wrist (see section 2.2). In section 3 three experiments are presented that deal with the human perception of these new feedback modalities; in section 4 the results are discussed against the background of immersive virtual or telepresence scenarios.

2 Haptic Feedback Rendering

Both approaches of simulating weight feedback are described in detail below. Operators are equipped with a head mounted display[1] that is tracked by a Flock of Bird device[2]. Besides, a P5 data glove[3] is used, but only the finger bending is assessed. The tracking of the hand is provided by a second Flock of Bird sensor. The technical set-up is shown in figure 1.

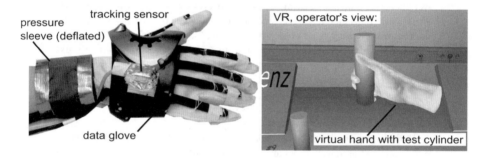

Fig. 1. Data glove (left) and virtual hand with a test cylinder (right)

2.1 Pseudo-Haptic Weight Feedback (Control/Display)

The idea behind pseudo haptic feedback is to make use of a human's ability of interpretation: although when lifted, a virtual object may not have any physical weight at all, it may feel heavy if the object's movements correspond to physical laws: Normally, a heavy item is lifted more slowly than a light one. So based on the acceleration or the speed of motions a human may form an implicit hypothesis on the weight of an object when it is picked up.

Biocca et al. [7] could demonstrate this cross-modal phenomenon (visual to haptic transfer) by implementing a snap-to-spring algorithm into a virtual environment and thus inducing a feeling of physical force without providing any real haptic actuation. Dominjon et al. [8] show that the visual cues that are given to subjects while weighing two virtual balls influence their discrimination ability. The faster the balls move the lighter they seem. Similar results of pseudo-haptic feedback can be found for the perception of roughness [9] and for the spatial interpretation of actually flat surfaces [10].

---

[1] Cybermind Visette 45; 1280x1024 pixel, 60Hz.
[2] Ascension Technology Corp.; ERT set-up used.
[3] Essential Reality.

In general, the ratio between the movement of the real hand and its virtual visual display determines the strength of the effect. A *"control/display ratio"* (CDR) below one means that the object's movements are displayed faster than they are commanded (which again is perceived as lighter or smoother), whereas a ratio larger than one results in a decelerated behaviour (which is perceived as heavier or rougher). A CDR value of one is a neutral setting as both real and virtual movements match perfectly and no pseudo-haptic feedback is provided.

Within this work pseudo-haptic weight feedback is implemented by altering the hands' tracking data along the vertical z-axis: the Flock of Bird tracker feeds the data of the hand position into the VR program[4]. Here, the position data is downsampled to 60 Hz and the virtual hand is moved with this rate, too. Once an object is lifted the position data stream is expanded by interpolating further vertical position data in between already existing data; the position on the horizontal plane is not altered and it is displayed as tracked. The higher the simulated weight is, the more additional z-positions are inserted. As the position data is still processed with a constant 60 Hz, a FIFO (First-in-First-out) memory is filled and it can only be reduced again if the operator stops lifting the virtual object (a small deadband is provided) or if it is released. So the operator perceives the z-reactions of the virtual hand as decelerated compared to the commanded movements and thus, it is assumed to induce an impression of pseudo-weight.

2.2 Pneumatic Weight Feedback

The substitution of force or torque feedback by visual stimuli (e.g. force arrows) has been used successfully in minimally invasive surgery scenarios [11]: instead of stimulating operators haptically, they receive force or tactile feedback that is encoded visually. Just the same, auditive substitution has been proven to be beneficial for some micro assembly tasks [12]. Especially, when enhancing haptic actuators or when auditive and visual cues are combined a positive effect of sensory substitution can be expected.

In this domain a novel concept is the sensory substitution of proprioceptive weight perception by applying pressure around an operator's wrist. In this part of the hand, the proprioceptors cannot be stimulated without relying on "bulky" actuators [2][3]; however, it is easier to stimulate the epidermal Merkel cells [13] by applying pressure: depending on the 'weight' that is to be displayed a pressure sleeve is filled with air compressing the wrapped wrist to various degrees (see fig. 1 left). By two valves, a manometer, and an air pump the pressure level can be controlled in real time depending on the actions in the virtual environment. The control currents of the valves as well as the manometer's measurement voltage are linked to a Sensory 262 IO Card that is controlled by a Simulink model. Via TCP/IP connection the model receives trigger events from the VR in real time and sets defined pressure levels based on the values of a look-up table.

3 Experiments

Three experiments were conducted: in the experiments A and B psychophysical functions, for both the pseudo-haptic and the pneumatic feedback, were calculated; experiment C focuses on the analysis of the bimodal weight feedback.

---

[4] Blender v2.49 GameEngine.

3.1 Psychophysical Scaling of Pseudo-Haptic Weight Feedback (Exp. A)

The Stevens' function [14] for the pseudo-haptic weight feedback is derived by the magnitude estimation technique. The function is defined as

$$\psi\,(I) = k * I^a \tag{1}$$

where the subjective magnitude of the weight perception ψ equals the product of a constant k and the objective stimulus magnitude I to the power of a. The exponent a defines the shape of the function and it has to be determined empirically.

Design of Experiment A
Five different CDR values (2, 3, 4, 5, 6) have to be rated in a paired-comparisons test. As experimental stimuli, plain grey cylinders (see fig. 1 right) are used and pseudo-weight feedback is displayed as soon as they are lifted. In each trial two cylinders are to be compared concerning their weight: one of them constitutes as a reference cylinder, which has a fixed CDR value of 2 (i.e. the lightest of all CDR settings apart from the neutral setting 1) and the other cylinder reveals the five different CDR values. To assure a similar weighing movement, the stimuli have to be raised up to a fixed height, which is indicated by a sound signal. All participants are allowed to use their own quantification scale, but they are reminded to keep it consistent throughout the experiment. No further instruction of how to interpret the feedback is given. The presentation of the stimuli is randomized. In total, 20 subjects ($\emptyset$ = 27.4 ± 8 years) took part in this experiment.

Results of Experiment A
The median values of all ratings are plotted on a log/log scaled coordinate system (see fig. 2 left). The data can be fitted well by a regression line (R^2 = .886). Thereby, the most interesting value is the exponent (a_A = 1.36) as it quantifies the relationship between the CDR value and the perceived weight: the perception of weight rises fast with increased CDR values (see figure 2 left).

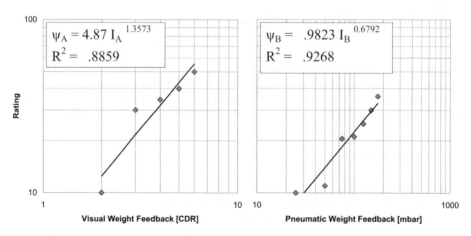

Fig. 2. Stevens' functions as derived in the experiments A (left) and B (right); log/log scale

3.2 Psychophysical Scaling of Pneumatic Weight Feedback (Exp. B)

Within the second experiment the perception of the pneumatic weight feedback is regarded and again the exponent a of the Stevens' function is determined.

Design of Experiment B
Just as in the experiment A, magnitude estimation is used here, too: test cylinders have to be lifted and they have to be compared to a reference cylinder. The pneumatic weight feedback of the test cylinders refers to 25, 50, 75, 100, 125, 150, and 175 mbar; the pressure level of the reference cylinder is set to 25 mbar. Again, all stimuli are presented in a randomized order and the experiment was carried out by 20 participants ($\phi = 26.3 \pm 7.7$ years).

Results of Experiment B
The median values are calculated for each pressure setting over all participants and trials. Just like in experiment A, the participants' ratings are plotted on a log/log scale against the objectively measured pressure values. Again, a regression line reveals a good fit ($R^2 = .927$); the exponent ($a_B = .679$) implies that the perception of weight rises much slower than the pressure of the sleeve (see figure 2 right).

3.3 Conjoint Analysis of Bimodal Weight Feedback (Exp. C)

Whereas meanwhile the psychophysical approach is rather widespread in the field of haptic display design, conjoint measurement is relatively new to this area of research. Commonly, this statistical procedure is used in marketing research in order to analyse how complex products are experienced by customers [15]. It decomposes products and assesses how important their various single elements are perceived. As products (or more generally speaking, stimuli) are typically composed of a set of different attributes that all have several distinct features (e.g. a product X with a certain colour, price, size, and flavour) a whole range of possible stimuli combinations is available. Paired comparisons of all attribute combinations have to be rated by human participants that lead to an overall ranking of all stimuli. Subsequently this ordinal ranking is used to estimate a metric value of usefulness for each attribute and these estimates are then aggregated over all participants to derive a representative result. As stated above, this method is widely used in marketing research but it is also applicable for multi-modal feedback analysis: the impact of each feedback modality on the overall percept can be extracted and quantified accordingly. Stimuli that are explored under multi-modal haptic feedback condition (e.g. weight information provided by pneumatic and pseudo-haptic feedback at the same time) have to be ranked by subjects regarding their perceived characteristics (e.g. ranking from the lightest to the heaviest stimuli). This ranking is the basis of a monotone analysis of variance, which provides a rating of usefulness for every modality that the feedback is composed of (e.g. pneumatic and pseudo-haptic visual cues); thus quantifying how each modality contributes to the overall percept.

Design of Experiment C
Four different pneumatic settings (25, 75, 125, and 175 mbar) and four CDR values (2, 3, 4, and 5) are combined so that in total 16 bimodal stimuli (e.g. 25 x 2, 25 x 3, …, 175

x 5) are presented in this experiment. In order to derive a subjective ranking of weight the participants have to classify these stimuli in rather rough categories first, namely *light, medium or heavy*. For this purpose one cylinder after the other is presented and has to be examined. Thereby, only pseudo-haptic and pneumatic weight feedback is given but no further information or explanation of how the feedback works is provided. After all 16 stimuli have been sorted, they are presented once more in order to give the test subjects the possibility to rearrange them if desired. Next the participants are instructed to rank the stimuli within each category from the lightest to the heaviest by paired comparisons. Thus, finally every participant has ranked all 16 stimuli according their weight. The data of 34 participants ($\varnothing = 26.8 \pm 7.4$ years) were recorded. Besides, a questionnaire was answered by everyone at the end of all trials.

Results of Experiment C
The ratings of the participants reveal a high variance. As an immediate aggregation of the data might bias the outcome a ward cluster analysis is done first. Two groups disperse very early and display a strong partition of data. Figure 3 shows both the mean values and the standard deviations of these two groups: whereas the first cluster (N = 14) relies mainly on CDR feedback (69%) and to a lesser degree on pneumatic cues (31%), the second cluster (N = 20) shows the opposite behaviour pattern (CDR cues: 18.4%, pneumatic cues 81,6%). The error bars span the range of ± 1 standard deviation.

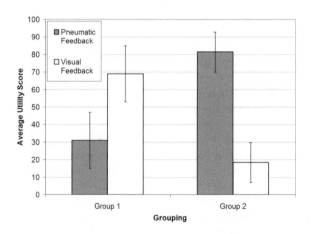

Fig. 3. Utility values of each feedback, grouped after cluster analysis

The questionnaire assesses the participants' attitude towards several aspects of bimodal weight perception. The majority (93.1 %) actually perceived a sense of weight even though they were not instructed as to how to interpret the feedback provided. The fact that 82.7 % rated this feedback as being *average* or *well* highlights the adequacy of our new feedback proposal. When comparing pneumatic and CDR feedback latter seems to be slightly less intuitive: 31 % judge CDR to be irritating with 48.3 % finding it helpful.

4 Discussion

Experiments A and B have delivered details as to how human operators perceive different magnitudes of pseudo-haptic and pneumatic feedback: the exponent of a_A = 1.35 for CDR based weight feedback reveals that perceived intensities aggravate faster than the corresponding objective weight. Like sucrose taste or warmth perception of small areas [14], little increases of upper CDR values lead to big perceptual changes. The pneumatic feedback approach shows a contrary effect: with an exponent of a_B = .68 small increases of high pressure feedback values intensify the percept only little while in low pressure ranges the perception of weight is rather sensitive, comparable to the sensation of brightness of a point source or vibrations on a finger [14]. Based on these results as well as the fact that both weight displays can be combined into one system easily it might be worth considering supplying pneumatic feedback for displaying light objects while providing CDR feedback for heavy stimuli.

In experiment C the participants displayed a split pattern of favourizing either one or the other feedback modality. The averages reported show to what extent a single modality influences the percept of each group. In both cases the participants' responses can be lead back to a combination of pneumatic as well as CDR feedback. The reason for such a split-up may be found in diverging feedback preferences when redundant haptic as well as visual cues are provided. The group membership can be ascertained perfectly by a single item classification task: do they perceive an item with CDR = 1 and pressure = 175 mbar to be light ($\rightarrow$ group 1) or heavy ($\rightarrow$ group 2). This would also allow to identify the personally most suitable feedback in case a single modality feedback is sufficient.

On the basis of the presented experiments the usefulness of both feedback modalities seems to be evident. While being technically simple virtual objects can be provided with weight properties to increase the immersion of virtual or telepresence scenarios. Especially in settings that require mobility these new techniques may be alternatives to current multi-DOF actuators.

This research was funded by the German Research Center, SFB 453, TP I7.

References

1. Pongrac, H.: Gestaltung und Evaluation von virtuellen und Telepräsenzsystemen an Hand von Aufgabenleistung und Präsenzempfinden. Dissertation. UniBw, Neubiberg (2008)
2. Buss, M., Lee, K.K., Nitzsche, N., Peer, A., et al.: Advanced Telerobotics: Dual-Handed and Mobile Remote Manipulation. In: Advances in Telerobotics: Human System Interfaces, Control, and Applications. STAR. Springer, Heidelberg (2007)
3. Schiele, A.: Case study: The ergonomic exarm exoskeleton. In: Pons, J.L. (ed.) Wearable Robots: Biomechatronic Exoskeletons, pp. 248–255. J. Wiley & S. Ltd, Chichester (2008)
4. Murray, A.M., Klatzky, R.L., Khosla, P.K.: Psychophysical Characterization and Testbed Validation of a Wearable Vibrotactile Glove for Telemanipulation. Presence: Teleoperators & Virtual Environments 2, 156–182 (2003)
5. Hannig, G., Deml, B., Mihalyi, A.: Simulating surface roughness in virtual environments by vibro-tactile feedback. In: IFAC Symposium - Analysis, Design and Evaluation of Human-Machine Systems, Seoul, Korea (2007)

6. Yang, G.-H., Kyung, K.-U., Srinivasan, M., Kwon, D.-S.: Development of Quantitative Tactile Display Device to Provide Both Pin- Array-Type Tactile Feedback and Thermal Feedback. whc, 578–579 (2007)

7. Biocca, F., Kim, J., Choi, Y.: Visual Touch in Virtual Environments: An Exploratory Study of Presence, Multimodal Interfaces, and Cross-Modal Sensory Illusions. Presence: Teleoperators and Virtual Environments, 247–265 (2001)

8. Dominjon, L., Lécuyer, A., Burkhardt, J.-M., Richard, P., Richir, S.: Influence of control/display ratio on the perception of mass of manipulated objects in virtual environments. In: Virtual Reality Proceedings VR 2005, pp. 19–25. IEEE, Los Alamitos (2005)

9. Hannig, G., Deml, B.: Scrutinizing pseudo haptic feedback of surface roughness in virtual environments. In: VECIMS - IEEE International Conference on Virtual Environments, Human-Computer Interfaces and Measurement Systems (2008)

10. Lécuyer, A., Burkhardt, J.-M., Etienne, L.: Feeling Bumps and Holes without a Haptic Interface: the Perception of Pseudo-Haptic Textures (2004)

11. Hagen, M., Meehan, J., Inan, I., Morel, P.: Visual clues act as a substitute for haptic feedback in robotic surgery. Surgical Endoscopy 22(6), 1505–1508 (2008)

12. Petzold, B., Zaeh, M., Faerber, B., et al.: A study on visual, auditory, and haptic feedback for assembly tasks. Presence: Teleop. and Virtual Enviro. 13(1), 16–21 (2004)

13. Maricich, S.M., Wellnitz, S.A., Nelson, A.M., Lesniak, D.R., et al.: Merkel Cells Are Essential for Light-Touch Responses. Science 324(5934), 1580–1582 (2009)

14. Stevens, S.S.: On the psychophysical law. Psychological Review 64(3), 153–181 (1957)

15. Backhaus, K., et al.: Multivariate Analysemethoden, 10th edn. Springer, Berlin (2006)

The Contribution of Proprioceptive and Cutaneous Cues in Weight Perception: Early Evidence for Maximum-Likelihood Integration

Christos Giachritsis, Rachel Wright, and Alan Wing

Behavioural and Brain Sciences Centre, School of Psychology, The University of Birmingham,
Edgbaston, Birmingham, B15 2TT, UK
C.Giachritsis@gmail.com, {R.Wright.1,A.M.Wing}@bham.ac.uk

Abstract. When manipulating an object we use weight information in order to apply an effective grip to prevent it from slipping as well effective arm muscular force to maintain a desirable distance from the ground. In such task, the main sources of weight information that we use may come from cutaneous and proprioception feedback. Even though the contribution of these two cues has been partially demonstrated, there is no evidence about their relative importance in weight perception. Here, we conducted a weight discrimination experiment using a 2IFC constant stimuli procedure to investigate the role of cutaneous and proprioceptive feedback in weight perception. The participants judged weights using both proprioception and cutaneous cues, proprioception-only cues and cutaneous-only cues. Preliminary results showed that performance deteriorates when either of these cues is missing. There is also an early indication that the two cues may be integrated on the basis of maximum likelihood estimation (MLE).

Keywords: Weight Perception, Proprioception, Cutaneous, Psychophysics, Maximum Likelihood Estimation.

1 Introduction

Effective object manipulation during displacement, which may also involve obstacle avoidance, or precise penetration of surface using a probe, or assembly of fragile objects, requires accurate weight perception. This is because weight information will allow the actor to adjust grip force and arm muscle forces in order to sustain a secure grip, maintain a safe distance from a surface or apply a desirable force during contact with a surface. Cutaneous and proprioceptive signals including skin pressure, grip fore and muscular activity, have been shown to contribute to weight perception [1, 2]. For example, objects with rougher surface texture or geometry allowing effortless grip are perceived to be lighter than objects with smoother texture or geometry resulting in strenuous grip since both require application of greater grip forces to secure object from slipping resulting in greater 'sense of effort' [3-5]. Other studies have shown that the state of the muscles (e.g., paresis, anesthesia) as well as the level of muscular activity (e.g., fatigue, changes in arm weight, posture) may affect 'sense of

A.M.L. Kappers et al. (Eds.): EuroHaptics 2010, Part I, LNCS 6191, pp. 11–16, 2010.

effort' and weight perception [6-9]. Therefore, loss, impairement or restriction of cutaneous and/or proprioceptive feedback seems to affect our ability to accurately perceive the weight of an object.

However, it is still unclear what is the relative importance of cutaneous and proprioceptive signals in weight perception and how the central nervous system (CNS) may integrate them to produce a unique weight percept. McCloskey [1] studied the contribution of cutaneous feedback but did not address the exclusive contribution of the proprioceptive cue. Here, we carried out a preliminary study to investigate the relative importance of these two cues. We used a weight discrimination paradigm that tested sensitivity to weight changes using proprioception and cutaneous, proprioception-only or cutanenous-only feedback.

2 Methods

2.1 Participants

Three students (undergraduates and postgraduates) and two members of from the University of Birmingham, aged between 22 and 39, volunteered to take part in the study. The students were paid for their participation.

2.2 Stimuli and Apparatus

Nine weights ranging from 226-290g were placed in nine wooden boxes weighted 42g each, thus, providing an actual testing range from 268-332g. Thus, the *standard* (STD) stimulus was 300g and the step size 8g. The top of the boxes was fitted with a grip block which was 23mm wide (the grip aperture), 25mmm deep and 30mm tall. The sides of the grip block were covered with a medium sandpaper (100 grade) to allow effective grip (Figure 1).

2.3 Set up and Procedure

Three conditions were tested: *proprioception* and *cutaneous* cues were available (PC), *proprioception* only (P) and *cutaneous* only cues were available (C) (Figure 1). In the PC condition, the participants freely lifted the weights as in everyday activities. In the P condition the finger pads were covered with plastic cylindrical sections to prevent the use of cutaneous sheer forces caused by friction due to downward load forces. The participants lifted the weights in exactly the same way as in condition PC. In the C condition, a 'grip rest' was used to prevent the participants from using proprioceptive feedback either from the arm muscles or the finger joints. The grip was also padded to eliminate use of secondary pressure cutaneous cues.

The participants were sitting in front of a table in a relaxed position and kept their eyes closed thought the experiment. They used precision grip of their right hand to lift/hold the weights. A 2IFC paradigm with constant stimuli procedure was used to find the discrimination thresholds. In each condition there were three phases: (i) sense test/std weight, lift (ii) sense std/test weight, (iii) verbally report which was heavier. While in the PC and P conditions sensing involved active lifting for about 100mm and then return it to the table, in the C condition the experimenter had to place the weight between participants grip and then ask them to close the grip and judge the weight. Each weight was tested twelve times resulting in 108 trials per condition. Each condition was testing in a different session, trials ware randomized and the presentation order of STD and test stimuli was balanced.

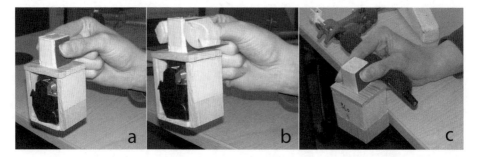

Fig. 1. Illustration of the three different conditions used in the experiment: (a) *proprioception* and *cutaneous* feedback (PC), (b) *proprioception* feedback, and (c) cutaneous feedback (C)

3 Results

Individual data were fitted with the commonly used psychometric function

$$\psi(x;\alpha,\beta,\gamma,\lambda) = \gamma + (1 - \gamma - \lambda)F(x;\alpha,\beta) \tag{1}$$

where α is location of the function on the x-axis, β is its slope, γ is the lower and $1-\lambda$ the upper bound of the function [10]. Here, the location and slope of the function were determined by the cumulative Gaussian function. Performance in each condition was measured in terms of the *discrimination threshold* (T) defined as half the difference between the point at which 20% of the weights were perceived as lighter than the standard weight and the point at which 80% of the weights perceived as heavier than the standard weight; that is $T=(T_{80}-T_{20})/2$.

Figure 2 shows the average performance under the three conditions. Performance in the PC condition was better than in P or C conditions which were very similar. Moreover, the standard deviations of the P and C Gaussians were 50% (σ_p=27.41) and 67% (σ_c=30.43), respectively, greater than the standard deviation of the PC function (σ_{pc}=18.27).

This large differences in variability of performances between the condition PC and the conditions P and C may indicate that the two cues could be integrated on a basis of maximum likelihood estimation (MLE). The MLE rule states that the combined PC estimate has lower variance than the P or C estimate [11]. Since the variance is related to threshold, the relationship between the discrimination thresholds in the three different conditions is

$$T_{pc}^2 = \frac{T_p^2 T_c^2}{T_p^2 + T_c^2}. \tag{2}$$

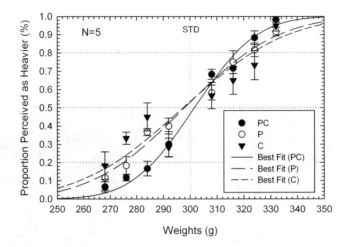

Fig. 2. Overall performance in the three conditions and best-fit cumulative gaussian. The symbol ● represents performance in PC condition, the symbol ○ represents performance in P condition and the symbol ▼ represents performance in the C condition. Error bars represent standard error.

Figure 3 shows the predicted discrimination threshold for the PC condition and the observed overall discrimination threshold for the conditions PC, P and C. In conditions P and C, discrimination thresholds tend to be higher than in PC indicating that a deterioration of performance when only the proprioception or cutaneous cues are available. In addition, it can be seen that the observed PC discrimination threshold is predicted well by the ME model.

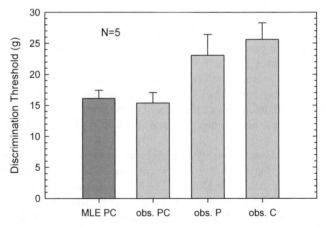

Fig. 3. Predicted PC and observed PC, P and C discrimination thresholds based on 80% accurate judgments. The observe PC threshold is similar to the MLE prediction. Error bars represent standard error.

Repeated measures ANOVA showed that there was an overall statistically significant effect on JND ($F_{(2,8)}$ = 4.892, p=0.41). Following paired t-tests showed significant JND differences between the PC and P ($T_{(4)}$ = -3.121, p=0.36) and PC and C ($T_{(4)}$ = -3.808, p=0.19) but not between P and C. There was no statistically significant effect on PSE.

4 Discussion

Previous research has shown that proprioception and cutaneous cues seem to contribute to weight perception without assessing their relative importance [1]. The present study has provided preliminary results showing that restricting the proprioception or cutaneous feedback when lifting an object with precision grip tends to reduce sensitivity to weight changes. Discrimination thresholds tend to be lower when participants can have access to both proprioception and cutaneous weight signals than when either of the two is missing. Furthermore, there is early indication that the integration of both cues could be based on a MLE rule.

Even though there was no difference between the P and C conditions, participants reported that they found it more difficult to judge the difference of weights in the C condition. One plausible explanation could be the difference in the apparent weight between the C and P conditions. Since there was not lifting involved in the C condition, the apparent weight was approximately equal to the actual weight. However, in the P condition the apparent weight was a positive multiple of the actual weight since it was accelerating against gravity due to lifting forces. There is evidence that acceleration and deceleration during lifting may improve weight perception with real [12] and virtual weights [13]. Nonetheless, the results also indicate that absence or restriction of cutaneous feedback seems to result in a deterioration of weight sensitivity. This may be one of the reasons that in some applications of virtual weights sensitivity without cutaneous feedback has been shown to decrease by a factor of five [14]. It is very likely that the acceleration and deceleration during lifting may affect the contribution of cutaneous feedback since skin deformation could increase due to greater sheer forces applied to stabilize a faster moving object. Further research is needed to access whether manipulation of apparent weight can improve performance with cutaneous-only feedback.

Acknowledgments. This work was funded by the European Commission under the IMMERSENCE Integrated Project of the Sixth Frame Program (IST-4-027141-IP).

References

1. McCloskey, D.I.: Muscular and cutaneous mechanisms in the estimation of the weights of grasped objects. Neuropsychologica 12, 513–520 (1974)
2. Brodie, E.E., Ross, H.E.: Sensorimotor mechanism in weight discrimination. Percept. Psychophys. 36(5), 477–481 (1984)
3. Flanagan, J.R., Wing, A.M., Allison, S., Spenceley, A.: Effects of surface texture on weight perception when lifting objects with a precision grip. Percept. Psychophys. 57(3), 282–290 (1995)

4. Flanagan, J.R., Wing, A.M.: Effects of surface texture and grip force on the discrimination of hand-held loads. Percept. Psychophys. 59(1), 111–118 (1997)
5. Flanagan, J.R., Bandomir, C.A.: Coming to grips with weight perception: Effects of grasp configuration on weight heaviness. Percept. Psychophys. 62(6), 1204–1219 (2000)
6. Gandevia, S.C., McCloskey, D.I.: Effects of related sensory inputs on motor performances in man studied through changes in perceived heaviness. J. Physiol. 272, 653–672 (1977)
7. Gandevia, S.C., McCloskey, D.I.: Sensations of Heaviness. Brain 100, 345–354 (1977)
8. Ross, H.E., Brodie, E.E., Benson, A.J.: Mass-discrimination in weightlessness and readaptation to earth's gravity. Exp. Brain Res. 64, 358–366 (1986)
9. Wing, A., Giachritsis, C., Roberts, R.: Weighing up the value of touch. In: Pye, E. (ed.) The Power of Touch, pp. 31–34. Left Coast Press, Walnut Creek (2007)
10. Wichmann, F.A., Hill, N.J.: The psychometric function: I. Fitting, sampling, and goodness of fit. Percept. Psychophys. 63(8), 1293–1313 (2001)
11. Ernst, M.O., Banks, M.S.: Human integrate visual and haptic information in a statistically optima fashion. Nat. 415, 429–433 (2002)
12. Brodie, E.E., Ross, H.E.: Jiggling a lifted weight does aid discrimination. Am. J. Psychol. 98(3), 469–471 (1985)
13. Hara, M., Higuchi, T., Yamagishi, T., Ashitaka, N., Jian Huang Yabuta, T.: Analysis of human weight perception for sudden weight changes during lifting task using a force displaying device. In: 2007 IEEE Int. Conf. Robot. Autom., Roma, pp. 1808–1813 (2007)
14. Giachritsis, C., Barrio, J., Ferre, M., Wing, A., Ortego, J.: Evaluation of weight perception during unimanual and bimanual manipulation of virtual objects. In: World Haptis 2009 Third Jt, EuroHaptics Conf. Symp. Haptic Interfaces Virtual Environ. Teleoperator Syst., Salt Lake City, USA, March 2009, pp. 629–634 (2009)

The Shape-Weight Illusion

Mirela Kahrimanovic, Wouter M. Bergmann Tiest, and Astrid M.L. Kappers

Universiteit Utrecht, Helmholtz Institute
Padualaan 8, 3584 CH Utrecht, The Netherlands
{m.kahrimanovic,w.m.bergmanntiest,a.m.l.kappers}@uu.nl

Abstract. In the present experiment, we investigated the influence of the shape of 3-dimensional objects on haptic perception of weight. A systematic shape-weight illusion was found when subjects compared a tetrahedron to a cube: a cube was perceived as being heavier than a tetrahedron of the same physical mass and volume. However, when subjects compared a sphere to a tetrahedron or to a cube, some subjects perceived the sphere as heavier than the other objects, while other subjects perceived the sphere as being lighter. These results indicate that the influence of shape on haptic perception of weight is not mediated only by the perceived volume, as would be predicted from previous studies, but that some subject dependent factors are involved.

Keywords: Weight, Size, 3-D shape, Touch, Haptics.

1 Introduction

When a human observer wants to lift or to move an object, weight information is necessary for the determination of the force that has to be applied in order to perform efficiently the required manipulation of that object. The initial weight percept can be biased by different physical object properties. For example, when human observers compare two objects of the same mass but of different size, they perceive the smaller object as being heavier. This is known as the size-weight illusion [1]. Dresslar [2] and Ellis [3] proposed that weight perception is also influenced by the shape of objects. To study this illusion, Dresslar used a set of objects that were made of sheet lead. They were all of the same unreported area and weight. Their shape varied from regular figures, such as a circle or a square, to irregular cornered figures. The objects could be explored unrestricted. On the other hand, Ellis used a set of solid objects with the same weight (350 g) and volume (132 cm³). The objects were rectangular cuboids with different dimensions and cylindrical objects with different lengths and diameters. The objects were explored in separate visual, haptic and bimodal conditions. The exploration was restricted to a four-finger/opposing-thumb grasp and the subjects were allowed only to lift the objects in a vertical motion.

These two studies revealed contradictory results. Dresslar showed that objects that appeared to be the *smallest* or of the most compact form were judged to be the heaviest. In contrast, Ellis showed that the *largest* objects were perceived to be the heaviest. Regardless of which of these results is more convincing, it is more important to question if these experiments are an appropriate way of measuring the shape-weight illusion. The main problem that we have with Dresslar's study is that the objects varied

A.M.L. Kappers et al. (Eds.): EuroHaptics 2010, Part I, LNCS 6191, pp. 17–22, 2010.

only along two dimensions. On the other hand, Ellis used 3-dimensional objects, but the exploration was restricted in such a way that mainly the width of the objects was perceived. The present experiment was designed to omit these problems, and to study the possible existence of a shape-weight illusion in a more appropriate way. We used a set of cubes, tetrahedrons and spheres, which could fit in the hand when explored. Subjects were blindfolded and the exploration was not restricted, encouraging the subjects to perceive shape, volume and weight of the objects as thoroughly as possible.

The bias for the shape-weight illusion can be predicted from the size-weight [4] and the shape-size [5] illusions. Ellis and Lederman [4] investigated a purely haptic size-weight illusion and showed that a doubling of the volume of cubes with the same physical weight resulted in a 26 % decrease of their estimated weight. If we assume that this relationship holds for the whole range of volumes and weights, then it can be written as

$$\frac{W_{new}}{W_{old}} = \left(\frac{V_{new}}{V_{old}}\right)^{-0.43}, \qquad (1)$$

where W is the perceived weight and V the perceived volume of objects. Kahrimanovic et al. [5] demonstrated the occurrence of a shape-size illusion when subjects compared differently shaped objects. A tetrahedron was perceived as being larger than a cube or a sphere of the same volume, and a cube was perceived as larger than a sphere. The measured biases are shown in the second column of Table 1.

If the shape-weight illusion is mediated by the perceived size of objects, as proposed by Dresslar [2], then we can predict that a sphere will be perceived as heavier than a cube or a tetrahedron of the same physical mass, and that a cube will be perceived as heavier than a tetrahedron. The magnitude of these biases can be predicted by substituting the biases found in Kahrimanovic et al. [5] for the ratio V_{new}/V_{old} in Equation (1). The biases predicted from these studies are shown in the third column of Table 1. On the other hand, if the shape-weight illusion is not mediated by the perceived volume, as proposed by Ellis [3], then the biases will be in the opposite direction and/or their magnitude will deviate from the expected magnitude. The present study will investigate these possibilities.

Table 1. Predictions for the shape-weight illusion. The magnitude of the biases indicates the relative difference between the physical volumes/weights of two differently shaped objects that are perceived as equal in volume/weight. The biases are expressed with respect to the first mentioned object in each object-pair. The direction of the bias shows which object is expected to be perceived as lighter/heavier if objects of the same physical weight are compared.

Condition	Magnitude of the bias		Direction of the bias	
	Shape–Size [5]	Shape–Weight (prediction)	Dresslar [2]	Ellis [3]
▲ - ●	32 %	- 11 %	▲ < ●	▲ > ●
▲ - ■	11 %	- 4 %	▲ < ■	▲ > ■
■ - ●	21 %	- 8 %	■ < ●	■ > ●

2 Methods

2.1 Subjects

Eight subjects participated in this experiment. Subjects 2, 3, 6, 7 and 8 were male and subjects 1, 4 and 5 were female (mean age 20 years). All subjects were strongly right-handed, as established by Coren's handedness test [6].

2.2 Stimuli and Procedure

Tetrahedrons, cubes and spheres were used as stimuli (see Fig. 1). They were made of brass and their mass ranged from 16.8 to 117.6 g, in steps of 8.4 g. The volume of the objects co-varied consistently with their mass. Hence, the volume ranged from 2 to 14 cm³, in steps of 1 cm³. These stimuli are the same as those used in our previous paper on the effects of shape on volume perception [5].

The stimuli were placed in the centre of the hand palm of blindfolded subjects (see Fig. 1). The subjects were instructed to enclose the stimuli, thereby perceiving their 3-D shape and volume. During enclosure, they were allowed to perform an up and down movement with the hand, in order to perceive the weight. These instructions were based on the stereotypic exploratory procedures associated with the perceptual encoding of these object properties [7]. The subjects were instructed to maintain the same exploratory procedure during the complete experiment. The period of exploration was not restricted, but was often just a few seconds. After exploration of the first stimulus, this stimulus was replaced by a second stimulus, which was explored in the same way as the first one. The order of the reference and comparison stimuli was randomized. The participants judged which of the two explored stimuli was heavier.

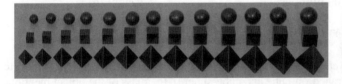

Fig. 1. On the left: the stimulus set. On the right: stimulus placed on the hand of the subject.

2.3 Conditions

The experiment consisted of 9 conditions; 3 object-pairs (tetrahedron-sphere, tetrahedron-cube, cube-sphere) and 3 reference-weights (small, medium, large). The reference weights were for the tetrahedrons 25.2, 42 and 58.8 g, for the cubes 33.6, 50.4 and 67.2 g, and for the spheres 42, 58.8 and 75.6 g. These references were the same as in the study on haptic volume perception [5]. The conditions were performed within 3 sessions. Object-pair was randomized between sessions and reference-weight was randomized within sessions. For each combination of object-pair and reference-weight, each shape was the reference stimulus in half of the trials and test in the remainder. For each reference, 35 trials were performed, resulting for each subject in a total of 210 trials per session and 630 trials for the complete experiment. On average, 2 hours per subject were needed to perform all the conditions.

2.4 Data Collection

The data were collected by way of a computer-driven 1-up-1-down staircase procedure (see Fig. 2A). For each object-pair by reference-weight combination, two staircases were intermingled, each starting at one end of the stimulus range, i.e. at 16.8
and 117.6 g. For each stimulus combination, the fraction was calculated with which
the subject selected the test stimulus to be heavier than the reference stimulus. This
calculation was performed for all test weights. A cumulative Gaussian distribution (f)
as function of the physical mass (x) was fitted to the data with the maximum-
likelihood procedure [8], using the following equation:

$$f(x) = \frac{1}{2}\left(1 + \mathrm{erf}\left(\frac{x - \mu}{\sigma\sqrt{2}}\right)\right),$$ (2)

where σ is a measure of the discrimination threshold, and μ a measure of the Point of
Subjective Equality (PSE). This point indicates the physical weight of the test stimulus
that is perceived to be of the same heaviness as the reference stimulus (see Fig. 2B).

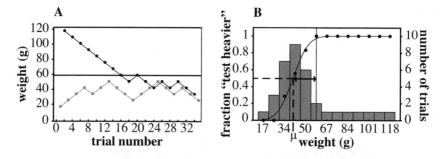

Fig. 2. (**A**) An example of the staircase. (**B**) The psychometric curve fitted to the data.

Relative biases were calculated from these data. For each matched object pair (tetrahedron-sphere, tetrahedron-cube and cube-sphere), the mass of the object mentioned
first was subtracted from that mentioned second and expressed as a percentage of the
mass of the object mentioned first. Hence, the magnitude of these biases indicated the
relative difference between the physical weights of two differently shaped objects that
are perceived as equal in weight. These relative biases were used for the statistical
analysis.

3 Results

Fig. 3 shows the individual and average perceptual biases for the different object
comparisons. The biases from the different reference-weights are taken together, since
no significant effect of reference-weight was measured ($F_{2,14} = 3.7$, $p = 0.08$). A t-test
revealed only significant biases for the tetrahedron-cube comparison ($t_7 = -9.3$, $p <
0.001$). The left part of the figure shows that these biases are consistently negative,
with an average of about -18 %, SE 2 %. A negative bias in this condition means that

a cube is perceived as being heavier than a tetrahedron of the same volume. The analysis revealed that the average biases in the other conditions were not significantly different from zero (t_7 = -0.4, p = 0.7 and t_7 = 0.8, p = 0.4 for the tetrahedron-sphere and cube-sphere comparisons respectively). However, we cannot ignore the large individual differences in these conditions. As the middle and right parts of Fig. 3 demonstrate, the sphere is perceived as being either heavier (negative bias) or lighter (positive bias) than a tetrahedron or a cube of the same physical mass. This pattern is consistent within subjects.

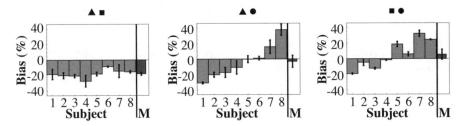

Fig. 3. Individual and mean data (M) for the different conditions. The subjects are ordered from the subject with the most negative bias to the most positive bias in the tetrahedron-sphere condition. The error bars for the individual subjects represent the standard deviations, and for the average data they represent the standard errors of the mean.

4 Discussion

The present study demonstrates that the weight of a tetrahedron is consistently under-estimated compared to the weight of a cube with the same physical mass and volume. The average bias in that condition was -18 %. The direction of the bias corresponds to the prediction from the study by Dresslar [2], who showed that (2-D) objects that appear smaller are perceived to be heavier. The magnitude of the measured bias is larger than the predicted bias of -4 % (see Table 1). This indicates that the shape-weight illusion cannot be explained only on the basis of a direct influence of perceived volume on perceived weight. This conclusion is supported by the large individual differences observed in the tetrahedron-sphere and cube-sphere compari-sons. Ellis [3] concluded that, instead of perceived volume, the profile area (defined as the area of the largest face) is the best predictor for perceived weight. However, the influence of the profile area may be triggered by the restriction of the exploration strategy to a four-finger/opposing-thumb grasp. In our experiment, the exploration was not restricted and each subject could select its own strategy, which probably caused the large individual differences. An interesting observation is that the individ-ual differences in the direction of the bias are only observed in the conditions includ-ing a sphere. This may be caused by the variation in the size of the object's area that is in contact with the skin during exploration. This contact area for a sphere is smaller when the hand is stretched out than when it is cupped. How far the hand is cupped could differ between subjects. For a tetrahedron or a cube the contact area did not differ because of a flat base. This may be a relevant point to investigate in further experiments.

The present study emphasizes that we cannot ignore the influence of an object's shape on weight perception, since large perceptual biases are observed. Nevertheless, with these results we cannot explain the shape-weight illusion in detail, and more research is needed to understand this phenomenon. A comprehensive understanding of these effects can be important for different problems of more applied nature. As we noted in the introduction, a proper estimation of the weight of objects is necessary for the determination of the force that has to be applied in order to manipulate the object efficiently. This object could also be, for example, a handle of a machine. For the construction of such handles, it is necessary to consider the factors that could influence the perception and action of a human operator. The shape of objects seems to be one of them.

Acknowledgments. This research was supported by a grant from The Netherlands Organization for Scientific Research (NWO).

References

1. Murray, D.J., Ellis, R.R., Bandomir, C.A., Ross, H.E.: Charpentier (1891) on the size-weight illusion. Perception & Psychophysics 61, 1681–1685 (1891)
2. Dresslar, F.B.: Studies in the psychology of touch. American Journal of Psychology 6, 313–368 (1894)
3. Ellis, R.R.: Haptic weight illusions with and without vision. Unpublished doctoral dissertation, Queen's University Kingston, Ontario, Canada (1996)
4. Ellis, R.R., Lederman, S.J.: The role of haptic versus visual volume cues in the size-weight illusion. Perception & Psychophysics 53, 315–324 (1993)
5. Kahrimanovic, M., Bergmann Tiest, W.M., Kappers, A.M.L.: Haptic perception of volume and surface area of 3-D objects. Attention, Perception & Psychophysics 72, 517–527 (2010)
6. Coren, S.: The left-hander syndrome. Vintage Books, New York (1993)
7. Lederman, S.J., Klatzky, R.L.: Hand movements: A window into haptic object recognition. Cognitive Psychology 19, 342–368 (1987)
8. Wichmann, F.A., Hill, N.J.: The psychometric function: I. Fitting, sampling, and goodness of fit. Perception & Psychophysics 63, 1293–1313 (2001)

Force-Based Calibration of a Particle System for Realistic Simulation of Nonlinear and Viscoelastic Soft Tissue Behavior

Bektas Baybora Baran and Cagatay Basdogan

College of Engineering, Koc University, Istanbul, Turkey, 34450
{bekbaran,cbasdogan}@ku.edu.tr

Abstract. We present a new approach for realistic visio-haptic simulation of nonlinear and viscoelastic behavior of an organ tissue using a particle model. The spring and damper coefficients of the particle model are calibrated using a derivative-free optimization technique such that its behavior mimics the behavior of a corresponding finite element (FE) model. In our approach, we first conduct static indentation and stress relaxation experiments on the FE model to record a) force versus displacement and b) force versus time responses of the surface nodes, respectively. We then use these data sets to calibrate the spring and damper coefficients of the particle model such that its force response is similar to that of the FE model. To test the feasibility of our approach, we compare the static and dynamic behavior of the particle model to that of the FE model under the influence of gravity.

Keywords: Viscoelasticity, soft tissue behavior, surgical simulation, particle system.

1 Introduction

The particle system approach is a widely used mesh-free method in simulating soft tissue behavior [1]. The coefficients of springs and dampers in a particle system must be tuned individually to accurately mimic the response of the corresponding physical system. However, the integration of measured material properties of a soft tissue into a particle system is a highly challenging task.

Only a few studies in the past attacked the problem of parameter identification for a particle system. In [2], the authors establish a link between discrete mass-spring models and the classical theory of elasticity. In [3], a genetic optimization algorithm is used to determine the topology of the mass-spring system. In [4], a 2D mass-spring-damper system is trained to behave like a nonlinear FEM. A more advanced approach is taken in [5]. By using a layer of 2D linear springs and dashpots supported by non-linear springs in parallel, the dynamical deformations of the human thigh is simulated. In [6], a method is introduced to derive analytical expressions for the spring coefficients of a particle model based on a reference FE model.

This paper presents a novel approach for the realistic particle-based simulation of hyper-viscoelastic organ behavior. Most of the earlier studies in this area have focused

A.M.L. Kappers et al. (Eds.): EuroHaptics 2010, LNCS 6191, Part I, pp. 23–28, 2010.

on matching the visual response of a particle model to that of the corresponding FE model, but not the strain- and time-dependent force responses. In our approach, we first perform characterization experiments with a FE model of an organ mesh in virtual domain: strain- and time-dependent force responses of a set of nodes selected on the surface are measured through static indentation and stress relaxation experiments, respectively. Then, a particle model is constructed from the same geometric mesh. Each particle in our model is connected to its neighbors by a Maxwell Solid (MS), made of 3 springs and 2 dampers (N = 2). Finally, the same characterization experiments are performed on the particle model to estimate the spring and damper coefficients of each MS via a set of novel optimization algorithms such that the haptic response of the particle model successfully imitates that of the FE model.

2 Numerical Model of the Particle System

To model the viscoelastic relaxation behavior of a soft tissue, the most basic force model is the Standard Linear Solid (SLS). The SLS is a special case of Generalized MS model when only one Maxwell arm (a spring and a damper in series) is used. In our studies, we have observed that SLS is still insufficient to model the relaxation response of soft tissues [7]. This is due to the fact that the measured force relaxation response of soft tissues is typically governed by multiple exponential decaying functions having different time constants and a single time constant is not capable of modeling the actual response. For this reason, we use a MS model with two Maxwell arms (N = 2) (Fig. 1).

In addition to modeling the viscoelastic force response, we modify the original MS model to simulate the strain-dependent force response of soft tissues. This is achieved by replacing the linear spring responsible from the static response in the original MS model with a strain-dependent nonlinear spring. Hence, the spring coefficient K_∞ in the MS model (Fig. 1) is written as a function of strain as:

$$K_\infty(\varepsilon) = K_0 + a.\varepsilon + b.\varepsilon^2$$

This representation enables us to model the strain-dependent nonlinear material properties of the organ.

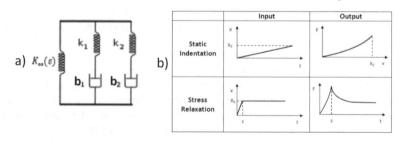

Fig. 1. a) Maxwell Solid with two Maxwell arms, b) The force response of the Maxwell solid model to static and ramp and hold stimuli

To calculate the force response of particles in our particle model in real-time, Verlet time integration method is chosen, which is explicit and conservative in the long run. We use the following scheme for the calculation of the forces on each connector joining two particles to each other via the MS model ($N = 2$):

$$F^t = K_\infty(\varepsilon).\Delta x^t + \sum_{i=1}^{2} F_{maxwell\_arm\_i}^{\ t}$$

$$F_{maxwell\_arm\_i}^{\ t} = \frac{k_i.b_i}{k_i.\Delta t + b_i}\left((\Delta x^t - \Delta x^{t-1}) + F_{maxwell\_arm\_i}^{\ t-1}/k_i\right)$$

Here Δx^t is the difference between the current connector length and its original length, and Δt is the time step used for the integration.

3   Calibration of the Particle System

We construct our deformable FE model in this study by inputting the Mooney-Rivlin parameters for hyperelasticity and the Prony parameters for viscoelasticity to ANSYS, which were obtained from the experiments performed on pig liver [7]. In order to calibrate the particle model such that its haptic response resembles to the FE model, we first identify a set of test points on the surface of the geometric mesh used for both models. We then perform static indentation and stress relaxation experiments with the FE model using these test points in ANSYS and record their a) force versus displacement and b) force versus time responses.

The calibration of the springs and dampers of the particle system is achieved in two sequential optimization steps using the recorded force data. In the first step, a unique set of parameters for all connectors (i.e. $K_0, a, b, k_1, b_1, k_2, b_2$), is determined by considering the force-responses of all test points in the optimization. This step is called global tuning and helpful to determine the initial values of parameters. In the second step, starting from the initial values determined in the first step, we fine-tune the parameters of each connector by considering the individual response of its nodes. This step is called local tuning. In both steps, the optimization of the parameters is achieved using Nelder-Mead derivative-free optimization method.

More specifically, the nonlinear strain-dependent material parameters of our particle model for each connector (i.e. K_0, a, b), are obtained from the force versus displacement responses of the test points under the static loading (Fig. 1). Since the indentation rate during a static loading is very slow, all time-dependent effects contributing to the force response are negligible. Hence, the force response during static loading is governed by the strain-dependent nonlinear spring $K_\infty(\varepsilon)$ only. An analogy is possible for the stress relaxation test and hence the related material parameters are k_1, b_1, k_2, b_2. The viscoelastic force relaxation response of each test point is governed by the two time constants in our MS model ($\tau_1 = b_1/k_1, \tau_2 = b_2/k_2$). Hence, the hyperelastic material parameters K_0, a, b are optimized first using the recorded static indentation data and then the viscoelastic material parameters k_1, b_1, k_2, b_2 are optimized using the recorded stress relaxation data. To optimize the parameters of the particle model, a cost function is defined as:

$$G_{cost\_j} = \sum_{i=1}^{N}(F_{ref\_i} - F_{sim\_i})^2 \, , G_{Total\ Cost} = \sum_{j=1}^{M} G_{cost\_j}$$

Here, F_{sim} represents the force response generated by the particle model and F_{ref} represents the reference force response obtained from the FE simulations performed in ANSYS. N is the number of data samples taken from the response curves, and M is the number of test points used for the optimization.

The goal of the optimization process is to find a single set of material parameters that minimize $G_{Total\ Cost}$. However, we observe that it is not possible to obtain a set of optimum material parameters that satisfy the individual force responses of all the test points in one-step optimization. For this reason, in the global tuning step, all the connectors are assumed to have the same values of material parameters and an initial set is obtained. In the local tuning step, using this data set as the initial guess, we further improve the quality of the fit by fine-tuning the material parameters of each connector. The optimization is performed locally by modifying only the connectors that are in the first degree neighborhood of the test points.

4 Results

To demonstrate our approach, we compared the static and dynamic behavior of a particle model of a liver mesh to that of the corresponding FE model under the influence of gravity. The liver mesh consists of 887 tetrahedral elements, 269 nodes, and 1358 connectors. A total of 31 test points on the mesh surface were used to calibrate the particle model. The test points were chosen such that all the connectors on the mesh surface were considered in the optimization calculations. It took about 8 hours to complete the calibration process in a dual-core Pentium PC, each having 3 GHz CPU. In figures 2a and 2b, the results of the global and the local optimizations are shown for a surface node under static loading (i.e. static compression test) and ramp and hold loading (i.e. stress relaxation test). In both cases, the global tuning returns a nearby solution and then the local tuning increases the quality of the fit by locally modifying the parameters of individual connectors. The convergent behavior of the cost function as a function of the increasing number of optimization iterations is shown in figures 2c and 2d for the global tuning step. To give an idea about the variation in the material parameters of connectors as a result of the two-steps optimization process, the values of K_0 and the time constant τ_1 are plotted for each connector in figures 2e and 2f.

The static and dynamic responses of the particle model under the influence gravity were compared to that of the FE model. For this purpose, some of the nodes at the bottom surface of the liver mesh were fixed (zero displacement) and the free nodes of the liver were allowed to move under the influence of gravity (Fig. 3). The comparison for the static response is given in Fig. 3c. For the comparison of dynamic response, the surface node that is on the far right side of the liver mesh was selected (Fig. 3d) and changes in its displacement with respect to time were compared (Fig. 3e).

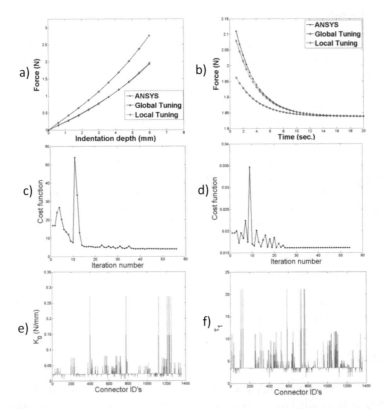

Fig. 2. The results of the global and the local optimizations for a surface node under a) static loading and b) ramp and hold loading. The evolution of the cost function during the global optimization for c) the static indentation and d) the stress relaxation tests. The variations in e) the nonlinear spring coefficient K_0 in static indentation and f) the time constant ($\tau_1 = b_1/k_1$) in stress relaxation over the connectors.

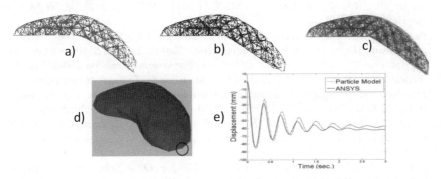

Fig. 3. a) The comparison of the static responses for the gravity test: a) the solution obtained from ANSYS, b) the solution obtained from the calibrated particle model, and c) both solutions in the same view. d) The node chosen for the comparison of dynamic response, e) The dynamic displacement of the chosen node under the influence of gravity (note that the dynamic simulation shown in the graph for 3 seconds is executed by the particle model in 1.3 seconds).

5 Conclusion

A parameter estimation technique for a particle system that simulates the complex nonlinear and viscoelastic behavior of a soft organ tissue was presented. The earlier studies on parameter estimation of particle based systems are limited to the estimation of linear or nonlinear material coefficients to simulate the static response and not the time-dependent viscoelastic response. Here, it is important to emphasize that the popular Voigt connector (a spring and a damper in parallel) is not capable of modeling the "true" viscoelastic "relaxation" response of a soft tissue though it is frequently used in particle models developed to simulate the behavior of deformable objects in computer graphics. Also, the earlier studies have mostly focused on matching the visual response of a particle model to that of the reference FEM model. In our approach, we focused on matching the hyper-viscoelastic force response. Since our calibration is based on the force response rather than the visual one, the developed particle model can be more easily integrated with a haptic device for displaying realistic force feedback to a user during the simulation of surgical procedures.

Acknowledgements

The Scientific and Technological Research Council of Turkey supported this work under the contract MAG-104M283.

References

1. Basdogan, C., Sedef, M., Harders, M., Wesarg, S.: Virtual Reality Supported Simulators for Training in Minimally Invasive Surgery. IEEE Computer Graphics and Applications 27(2), 54–66 (2007)
2. Etzmuss, O., Gross, J., Strasser, W.: Deriving a Particle System from Continuum Mechanics for the Animation of Deformable Objects. IEEE Transactions on Visualization and Computer Graphics 9(4), 538–550 (2003)
3. Bianchi, G., Harders, M., Székely, G.: Mesh topology identification for mass-spring models. In: Ellis, R.E., Peters, T.M. (eds.) MICCAI 2003. LNCS, vol. 2878, pp. 50–58. Springer, Heidelberg (2003)
4. Pezzementi, Z., Ursu, D., Misra, S., Okamura, A.M.: Modeling Realistic Tool-Tissue Interactions with Haptic Feedback: A Learning-Based Method. In: 16th Symposium on Haptic Interfaces for Virtual Environments and Teleoperator Systems, Reno, pp. 209–215 (2008)
5. d'Aulignac, D., Cavusoglu, M.C., Laugier, C.: Modeling the Dynamics of the Human Thigh for a Realistic Echographic Simulator with Force Feedback. In: Taylor, C., Colchester, A. (eds.) MICCAI 1999. LNCS, vol. 1679, pp. 1191–1198. Springer, Heidelberg (1999)
6. Lloyd, B.A., Székely, G., Harders, M.: Identification of Spring Parameters for Deformable Object Simulation. IEEE Transactions on Visualization and Computer Graphics 13(5), 1081–1094 (2007)
7. Samur, E., Sedef, M., Basdogan, C., Avtan, L., Duzgun, O.: A Robotic Indenter for Minimally Invasive Measurement and Characterization of Soft Tissue Behavior. Medical Image Analysis 11(4), 361–373 (2007)

Haptic Perception of Viscosity

Wouter M. Bergmann Tiest[1], Anne C.L. Vrijling[2], and Astrid M.L. Kappers[1]

[1] Helmholtz Institute, Utrecht University, The Netherlands
{w.m.bergmanntiest,a.m.l.kappers}@uu.nl
[2] Royal Dutch Visio, National Foundation for the Visually Impaired and Blind, Huizen,
The Netherlands
annevrijling@visio.org

Abstract. Viscosity is a liquid's resistance against flow. Using a discrimination experiment, the human ability to distinguish between different viscosities was measured over the range of 200–20,000 mPa·s. Eight blindfolded subjects stirred pairs of different silicone oils using a wooden spatula and had to indicate the "thicker" of the two. The viscosity of the liquids was measured seperately using a rheometer. Weber fractions for discrimination ranged from 0.3 at high viscosities to almost 1 at the lowest viscosity. For the higher viscosities, discrimination could be described as Weber-like, but for the low viscosities, there seemed to be a floor effect for the absolute threshold. The characterisation of the discrimination threshold as a function of viscosity is of fundamental interest in perception research, but also of practical value for designers of haptic devices capable of displaying viscosity.

Keywords: Kinaesthesia, Dynamic touch, Thresholds, Liquid, Weber fraction.

1 Introduction

The viscosity or "thickness" of a liquid is a property that can be easily perceived haptically, as is noticable in the everyday context of stirring in a pot on the stove. But for certain professionals, such as dough-makers or cooks, being able to accurately judge viscosity is of great importance. Medical professionals should be able to correctly judge the viscosity of texture-modified liquids that they prescribe to patients with orpharyngeal dysphagia. These patients have a delayed swallow initiation and benefit from thickened liquids that enter the pharynx slowly [1]. The cited study showed that information on the product packaging was insufficient to reliably characterise the liquid's viscosity, whereas clinicians could perfectly discriminate between different viscosities by stirring the liquids or by taking a sip. The importance of being able to rely on somesthetic perception is clear.

Physically, viscosity is the internal resistance of a liquid against shear force. It is expressed as the ratio between *shear stress* and *shear rate*. Shear stress is the amount of force applied in the direction of shear per unit area (in N/m^2 or Pa). Shear rate is the gradient perpendicular to the force of the liquid's moving speed (in m/s/m or s^{-1}). Viscosity is thus expressed in units of Pa·s. Water has a viscosity of 1 mPa·s. The relationship between physical and perceived viscosity has been investigated for silicone

A.M.L. Kappers et al. (Eds.): EuroHaptics 2010, Part I, LNCS 6191, pp. 29–34, 2010.

liquids stirred with a rod [2]. This relationship could be described by a power law with an exponent of 0.43. For manually stirred solutions of gum in water, the power law exponent was found to be 0.33 [3]. In that same study, a very similar exponent of 0.34 was found for orally perceived viscosity, but the absolute viscosity was judged to be somewhat higher in the mouth compared to stirring with the finger.

Concerning *discrimination* of different viscosities, early work was performed by Scott Blair and Coppen using balls of bitumen that were handled under water [4]. They found a Weber fraction of about 0.3 for 80 % correct discrimination. This was at a very high viscosity of about 10^8 mPa·s. It is unknown if the same Weber fraction holds for lower viscosities. Orally, the discrimination of viscosity has been tested using seven mixtures of corn syrup and water, each differing a factor of about three in viscosity from the next, in the range from 3 to 2240 mPa·s [5]. All could be identified above chance level except the fifth (202 mPa·s). The fact that even with a difference in viscosity of a factor of ~ 3, mistakes were made indicates that at least for oral perception, which was found to be quite comparable to manual perception [3], the Weber fractions for these lower viscosities could be quite a bit higher than the value of 0.3.

Discrimination of the "viscosity" of a mechanical system (the ratio between force and moving speed) has been investigated in a matching experiment using computer-controlled electrical motors for the range from 2 to 1024 N·m/s [6]. Weber fractions ranged from 0.3 at the highest viscosity to 0.8 at the lowest. Although this type of viscosity is different from that of a liquid, and is expressed in different units, the Weber fraction at the high-viscosity end might be compared to and is found to be equal to that reported by Scott Blair and Coppen [4]. This raises the question whether Weber fractions for discrimination of the viscosity of liquids show a simular upward trend for lower viscosities. It is the aim of the present paper to investigate this dependence of Weber fractions on viscosity. This is done by performing discrimination experiments with silicone liquids in the range from 78 to 31,000 mPa·s.

2 Methods

2.1 Subjects

Eight healthy adult subjects (5 male, age range 20–30 yrs, mean 24 yrs) participated in the experiment. All subjects were strongly right-handed as determined by the Coren test [7]. All subjects gave their informed consent before participating in the study. They were paid for their time.

2.2 Stimuli

A set of 29 distinct viscosities, ranging from 78 mPa·s to 31,000 mPa·s were created by mixing silicone liquids of standard viscosity (AK series, Wacker Chemie AG). The mixing ratios were determined from a diagram provided by the manufacturer. The diagram displays a weight percentage scale which indicates the amount of high and low viscosity silicone liquids that have to be mixed to obtain the desired intermediate viscosity. The density of the silicone liquids ranged from 9.6×10^{-4} kg/m^3 to 9.7×10^{-4} kg/m^3. 250 ml of each mixture was poured into containers of 8 cm diameter and 8 cm height.

To determine their exact viscosity, the blended stimuli were measured with a rheometer (Physica Modular Compact Rheometer 300, Anton Paar GmbH). This measuring system uses a cone-and-plate geometry (CP-50-1), with a cone angle of 1.001° and a diameter of 49.95 mm. The total volume of the space between cone and plate is 0.57 ml. The rheometer is equipped with a Peltier plate temperature unit that controls the temperature of 25°C over an extended time. Rotational measurements were performed in which the shear rate was set to 100 s^{-1} and decreased to 0.1 s^{-1} in 10 steps. The total measurement time of a stimulus is 100 s. The torque necessary to obtain the applied velocity is measured and converted to a shear stress by multiplying with a constant factor. From these data, the viscosity was calculated at each shear rate. The calculated viscosities did not differ more than 1 % between the different shear rates. This means that within this range, the stimuli behave as Newtonian liquids. The calculated viscosities were averaged over the shear rates.

The stimulus set was made up out of 5 ranges of viscosity each consisting of a reference stimulus and 6 test stimuli. The choice of the reference viscosities was based on the Weber fractions reported by Jones and Hunter, which were fairly constant at high viscosities, but increased with decreasing viscosity [6]. For this reason, we had a dense spacing of reference stimuli at low viscosities, and only few reference stimuli at high viscosities, see table 1. On a logarithmic scale, the spacing of the test stimuli was symmetric around the reference stimulus and equidistant within a range: there was a constant ratio between the viscosities of subsequent test stimuli within a range, as shown in table 1. These ratios were chosen such that the reference stimulus and the most viscous test stimulus within a range differed by a factor of about 2.5 times the value of expected Weber fractions based on pilot experiments.

Table 1. Viscosities of the reference stimuli for the 5 ranges

Range	Reference stimulus (mPa·s)	Ratio between subsequent test stimuli
1	199	1.51
2	449	1.44
3	938	1.35
4	1853	1.30
5	16060	1.25

2.3 Procedure

The subjects were blindfolded and comfortably seated at a table perpendicular to the experimenter, see figure 1 (left). The subject was presented with pairs of stimuli. A pair always contained a reference stimulus and one of the accompanying test stimuli. At the beginning of the experiment the subject was informed that the task would be to stir both liquids and indicate which of each pair was the more viscous, explained as the "thicker". The subject had to use the dominant hand (in all cases the right hand) to stir with a wooden spatula (150 × 20 × 1.8 mm, with rounded ends). Subjects were allowed to go back and forth between the stimuli, but this was not encouraged. The 6 pairs of stimuli of each of the 5 ranges were presented 10 times in a pre-established random order, different for each subject, for a total of 300 trials. These were performed in two

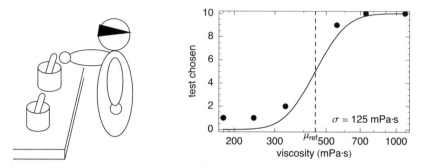

Fig. 1. Left: A schematic illustration of the setup. **Right:** A representative example of data points and the psychometric function that was fitted to these data points. On the horizontal axis is the viscosity on a logarithmic scale. On the vertical axis is the number of times that the test viscosity was chosen to be the more viscous. σ is the difference between the 50 % and the 84 % point.

sessions of about 50 minutes and one session of 25 minutes, either on different days or with sufficient time in between. No feedback was given during the sessions.

2.4 Analysis

Psychometric curves were determined by plotting the number of times that each test stimulus was chosen as a function of its viscosity (μ) on a logarithmic scale. In a pair where the test stimulus has lowest viscosity within the range, the test stimulus is expected to be chosen in none of the 10 trials to be the thickest. In a pair where the test stimulus has the highest viscosity within the range, the test stimulus is expected to be chosen in all 10 of the trials to be the thickest. In between, there is a transition from 0 to 10, the slope of which is a measure for the discrimination threshold. The psychometric curves were determined for each range and for each subject. The curves have a characteristic sigmoid shape, which is often approximated by a cumulative Gaussian distribution [8]. The discrimination threshold is then defined as the difference between the centre of the distribution (50 % point) and $-\sigma$ or $+\sigma$ of the underlying Gaussian distribution, corresponding to the 16 % and 84 % points, respectively. However, when the discrimination is expected to be described by a constant Weber fraction, one should not expect the thresholds (16 % and 84 % points) to lie at an equal absolute distance to the left or to the right of the centre, but at an equal *relative* difference. That is, the ratio between the 16 % and 50 % points should be equal to the ratio between the 50 % and 84 % points. A sigmoid function that satisfies this condition is given by

$$f(\mu) = 5 + 5\,\mathrm{erf}\left(\frac{\log \mu / \mu_{\mathrm{ref}}}{\sqrt{2}\log(\sigma/\mu_{\mathrm{ref}} + 1)} \right).$$

Here, μ_{ref} is the viscosity of the reference stimulus and $\sigma/\mu_{\mathrm{ref}}$ is the Weber fraction. On a logarithmic scale, this function looks symmetrical. The function was fitted to the data of all subjects in all ranges. Figure 1 (right) shows a representative example of how the function fits the data.

3   Results

The Weber fractions and absolute thresholds averaged over subjects are shown in figure 2. From about 2,000 mPa·s, the thresholds show Weber-like behaviour, but at lower viscosities, the thresholds are much higher than would be expected from Weber's law. A repeated measures ANOVA on the Weber fractions showed a significant effect of range ($F_{4,28} = 15$, $p = 8.8 \times 10^{-7}$). Bonferroni-corrected post-hoc tests showed that the Weber fraction for the lowest range (199 mPa·s) differed significantly from all others ($p \leq 0.017$) except for the third range (938 mPa·s, $p = 0.057$). There were no significant differences between other Weber fractions.

Since the behaviour is clearly not Weber-like, we will have a look at the absolute thresholds as depicted in figure 2, right. For these also, a repeated measures ANOVA showed a significant effect of range ($F_{1.1,7.5} = 39$, $p = 2.8 \times 10^{-4}$, Greenhouse-Geisser corrected value). Bonferroni-corrected post-hoc tests showed that only the thresholds from the highest range (16060 mPa·s) differed significantly from the others ($p \leq 0.005$); the lower four ranges are not significantly different from each other.

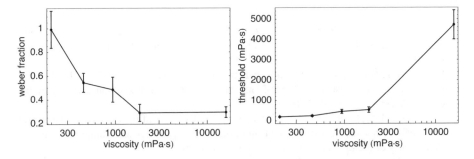

Fig. 2. Weber fractions (left) and absolute thresholds (right) averaged over subjects as a function of reference viscosity. The error bars indicate the standard error of the sample mean.

4   Discussion and Conclusions

One striking result is that the Weber fractions for the higher viscosities (0.29 ± 0.07, SE) agree very well with those reported by Scott Blair and Coppen [4] and Jones and Hunter [6], even though those values were measured in very different ways. Scott Blair and Coppen used balls of bitumen which were handled directly by the subjects, whereas in the present experiment the subject interacted with the stimulus through a rigid probe. In that sense, the situation is perhaps more like that of Jones and Hunter, where subjects moved a rod to and fro. In that experiment, like the present one, there was an increase in Weber fractions for decreasing viscosity. Unfortunately, the two types of viscosity (of a liquid and of a mechanical system) cannot be directly compared, so we cannot check whether the dependence on viscosity is the same.

Below about 2,000 mPa·s, the absolute thresholds do not seem to depend on viscosity. Apparently, there is a floor effect which does not allow the resolution of viscosity perception to keep pace with viscosity itself. This does not coincide with a similar floor effect in the perception of movement or force, so it is unlikely that the floor effect is caused by limitations in force discrimination, as has been shown earlier [6]. Viscosity perception is therefore not simply an integration of movement and force perception, but (to some extent) a perceptual continuum in its own. By this we mean that viscosity is considered to be a perceivable quantity in itself, and not (subconsiously) calculated from other, more basic cues.

To conclude, we find a non-Weberlike dependence of discrimination thresholds on viscosity, which transforms into Weber-like behaviour above 2,000 mPa·s. This will enable designers of haptic interfaces to save on bandwidth during the display of low viscosities, because human perception is relatively inaccurate in that range.

Acknowledgements. This work was supported by a grant from the Netherlands Organisation for Scientific Research (NWO). We thank ing. Emile Bakelaar (dept. of chemistry) for his assistance with the rheometer measurements.

References

1. Steele, C.M., Van Lieshout, P.H.H.M., Goff, H.: The rheology of liquids: A comparison of clinicians' subjective impressions and objective measurement. Dysphagia 18(3), 182–195 (2003)
2. Stevens, S.S., Guirao, M.: Scaling of apparent viscosity. Science 144, 1157–1158 (1964)
3. Christensen, C.M., Casper, L.M.: Oral and nonoral perception of solution viscosity. Journal of Food Science 52, 445–447 (1987)
4. Scott Blair, G.W., Coppen, F.M.V.: The subjective judgements of the elastic and plastic properties of soft bodies; the "differential thresholds" for viscosities and compression moduli. Proceedings of the Royal Society 128 B, 109–125 (1939)
5. Smith, C.H., Logemann, J.A., Burghardt, W.R., Carrell, T.D., Zecker, S.G.: Oral sensory discrimination of fluid viscosity. Dysphagia 12(2), 68–73 (1997)
6. Jones, L.A., Hunter, I.W.: A perceptual analysis of viscosity. Experimental Brain Research 94(2), 343–351 (1993)
7. Coren, S.: The left-hander syndrome: the causes and consequences of left-handedness. Vintage Books, New York (1993)
8. MacMillan, N.A., Creelman, C.D.: Detection theory: a user's guide. Cambridge University Press, Cambridge (1991)

Multi-sensorial Interface for 3D Teleoperations at Micro and Nanoscale

Nicolas Venant[1,3], Antoine Niguès[2,3], Florence Marchi[2,3], Michal Hrouzek[4], Fabio Comin[3], Joël Chevrier[2,3], and Jean-Loup Florens[1]

[1] ICA, INPG, 46 av. Félix Viallet, 38 031 Grenoble Cedex, France
[2] Institut Néel, CNRS/Université Joseph Fourier,
25 avenue des Martyrs, BP 166, 38042 Grenoble cedex 9, France
[3] ESRF, 6 rue Jules Horowitz, BP 220, 38043 Grenoble cedex 9, France
[4] Small Infinity, 6 rue Jules Horowitz, BP 220, 38043 Grenoble cedex 9, France
Jean-Loup.Florens@imag.fr

Abstract. This paper presents the design of a new tool for 3D manipulations at micro and nanoscale based on the coupling between a high performance haptic system (the ERGOS system) and two Atomic Force Microscope (AFM) probes mounted on quartz tuning fork resonators, acting as a nano tweezers. This unique combination provides new characteristics and possibilities for the localization and manipulation of (sub)micronic objects in 3 dimensions. The nano robot is controlled through a dual sensorial interface including 3D haptic and visual rendering, it is capable of performing a number of real-time tasks on different samples in order to analyse their dynamic effects when interacting with the AFM tips. The goal is then to be able to compare mechanical properties of different matters (stiffness of soft or hard matter) and to handle submicronic objects in 3 dimensions.

Keywords: Atomic Force Microscope (AFM), ERGOS Force-Feedback transducer, Haptic Interface, Nanomanipulator, Real-Time, Tuning-Fork.

1 Introduction

Consistent improvements of nanotechnologies have opened the way to the possibility of manipulating, modifying or measuring single nano-objects with very high efficiency. However, those actions still represent an important challenge [1,2], often linked to the different set of rules that govern the nano world at variance with macro world (adhesion forces larger than gravity, for example) [3,4]. In such unusual world "easy" actions can turn in very difficult tasks, like drinking a glass of water in a weightlessness spaceship. This paper deals with the development of a 3D multi-sensorial interface nanomanipulator using the ERGOS haptic system (bandwidth over 10kHz for a maximum force of 50N). This high performance haptic device is coupled with two nanometric tips glued on resonant quartz tuning forks as nanoforce sensors/ actuators. This unique and innovating combination between a haptic device and a dynamic force sensor provides new opportunities for nanomanipulation in comparison to a classical AFM cantilever. Used in static mode, conventional AFMs used in nanotweezers mix mechanically the two

A.M.L. Kappers et al. (Eds.): EuroHaptics 2010, Part I, LNCS 6191, pp. 35–42, 2010.

functions of action and force detection. To the contrary, the tuning fork can distinguish these two functions thanks to its high spring constant and the very small oscillations necessary for the detection (see Sect. 3).

Thanks to our custom-made interface, teleoperations in 1D, 2D and 3D are available via the coupling of real measurements with basic virtual information.

2   Description of the Multisensorial Haptic Interface

For teleoperation action at the micro and nanoscale, the user controls the position of one or two AFM probes (see Fig. 1) through a multisensorial interface. Indeed, the experimentalist could choose to perform action with a single nano-finger or two nano-fingers. To perform the micro-nano task, two complementary interfaces are available: haptic rendering (described in detail below) and visual rendering based on an optical objective mounted on a CCD-camera.

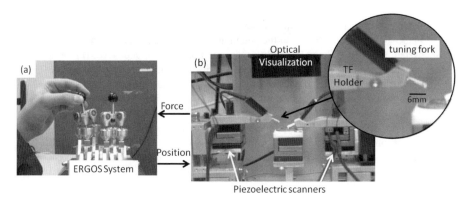

Fig. 1. (a) User space: 3D Joysticks from ERGOS system; (b) Task space: tuning fork AFM probes mounted on 3D piezoelectric scanners (MiniTritor from *PiezoJena System*)

The haptic system is an ERGOS interface composed of two 3 degrees of freedom Joysticks allowing each 3 translational motions in XYZ reference [6]. The full workspace of the slave robot (the 3D piezoelectric scanner) is a cube of $40\mu m$ side. Thus, a similar workspace geometry has been selected for the haptic system: a cube of 2 cm side for each joystick is mapped into the working space of the 3D piezoelectric scanner via a tuneable scaling factor that can vary the micro-cube side from less than $1\mu m$ to $40\mu m$. To create this cubic workspace, we imposed virtual boundaries by applying elastic forces to the joystick when it reaches a point of the cube surface in order to make the user feeling a wall. The stiffness of those elastic forces must be high enough to clearly define the inner working space. Given the variety of tasks and samples, this virtual environment must be flexible. So, the virtual environment parameters can be modified at will via the dashboard screens of the real-time software (programmed in Labview language). As an example the user can choose a rectangular, a flat or an arbitrary 1D direction as workspace or just freeze the joystick in one point. This virtual environment provides the basic virtual guides to assist the user in his/her action tasks.

3   Quartz Tuning-Fork as a Force Sensor/Actuator

Quartz Tuning Fork (TF) resonators replaces silicon cantilever in those atomic force specific applications where optics free detection is required [7]. Indeed, the main advantages of the TF are: (1) a compact ergonomics, quite compatible with other set-up (SEM, Scanning Electron Microscope, for example), (2) a high spring constant K (around 45kN/m versus few N/m for standard AFM cantilever) that eliminates the position hysteresis of the tip when it gets in contact with the surface (the snap on and off is avoided). From a haptic point of view this high spring constant is a key issue to avoid the limitation due to the actuator stiffness in the force measurement and its haptic rendering with an AFM cantilever.

The use of a TF can allow to work in liquid environments [8], necessary for applications in biology.

The TF is used in dynamical mode: it is excited with sinusoidal signals close to the resonance frequency ($\omega_0 \approx 32kHz$), and it behaves as an harmonic oscillator. When an interaction occurs between the tip and the surface, the resonance frequency is modified. The frequency shift is measured with a Phase Locked Loop (PLL). Considering just small oscillations, the frequency shift Δf is related to the force gradient as [9]:

$$\Delta f = \frac{\omega_0}{2K} \frac{\partial F}{\partial z} \tag{1}$$

where $\frac{\partial F}{\partial z}$ is the gradient of the tip-surface force along the Z direction.

The relationship between the force gradient and the z component F_z of the force between the tip and the sample can be approximated by the equation [10]:

$$F_z = A \frac{\partial F}{\partial z} \tag{2}$$

where A is the oscillations amplitude. The amplitude A depends on the intensity of the TF exciting signal. In practice, a PI controller maintains A constant (by adjusting the intensity of the exciting signal) leading to a proportional relationship between the force and the frequency shift:

$$\Delta f = \frac{\omega_0}{2KA} F_z \tag{3}$$

Nevertheless, those approximations hold as long as the oscillation amplitude A is small compared to the average tip-surface distance (one order of magnitude lower). This condition fits with typical experimental conditions where A is about few angstroms while the average tip-surface distance is about few nanometers.

The force feed-back is then calculate via a linear equation:

$$F_{feedback} = C \cdot \Delta f + D \tag{4}$$

where C and D are tuneable parameters adjusted to the sensitivity required by the experimentalist and the stability of the system (see Sect. 4).

This force is a 1D force and should naturally be applied in the Z direction to correspond to the TF measurement. We performed our 1D experiments in this configuration.

However, for 2D manipulations, a different configuration has been chosen. The $F_{feedback}$ is applied on the *three* directions of the user space. The direction of the force is imposed to be the opposite to the motion but does not correspond to real 3D force measurement in the task space as the TF can only measure force in 1D. In this condition, the user detects the contact whatever the direction he is moving on but he cannot distinguish the direction of the interaction force between the tip and the sample. Thanks to this configuration, a 3D haptic recognition of the sample has been achieved (see Figure 4, Section 5).

To overcome the lack of a complete information about the interaction, we plan to develop a virtual nanoscene associated to the real one. The virtual nanoscene will allow to simulate the associated force fields, and can be used in parallel with the teleoperation measurement in a Augmented Reality configuration. Via this configuration, the lateral force can be eventually evaluated. A similar approach have been already implement by others groups [11].

A second approach relies on the possibility of a dual excitation of the TF arms: the first in the vertical and the second in the lateral direction. From the resulting double information on the tip-sample interaction, a 3D reconstruction of the force field can be computed based on the approach implemented by Onal and Sitti [12] for a contact mode configuration with an AFM cantilever.

4 Real Time Control

The system setup supports two independent calculation systems as illustrated in Fig. 2. They are connected by an analogue signal (Frequency Shift).

The first system is a PLL from the commercial *Nanonis* electronics that is composed of a *National Instruments* FPGA card running at 5MHz. It controls the tuning-fork oscillations and measures the frequency shift (see Sect. 3). We notice here that the entire Nanonis Electronic System can also be configured to restitute classical AFM images.

The second element is a DSP card from *Sheldon Instruments*. This card links the master and slave robots, it has been programmed in LabView via QuView librairies supplied by *Sheldon*. The card is equipped with Input-Output channels of 16bits resolution at a sample rate of 10kHz. To run in Real-Time configuration the algorithm also runs at 10kHz (single point mode).

Our system presents the ideal properties for the transparency of the set actuator/haptic interface: a high stiffness transducer, a high speed Real-Time control loop and a high quality features haptic device (ERGOS system, mechanical bandwidth over 10kHz). This configuration assures that the user controls the tip through a rigid stick, thus making the reproduction of fast nano-phenomenons and hard-contact rendering possible.

The drawback is the increase of instabilities of the haptic interface. The problems of stability in haptic macro and nano-manipulation should not be underestimated due to the sensibility and time delays of the force sensor and the huge dynamics of the interaction stiffness between the tip and the sample. In the present work, the easiest solution has been implemented: we use a linear transformation to reproduced the nano interaction force on the haptic device (see Equ. 4). The amplification gain (C in Equ. 4) is manually adjustable and has to be chosen carefully in order to avoid any instability.

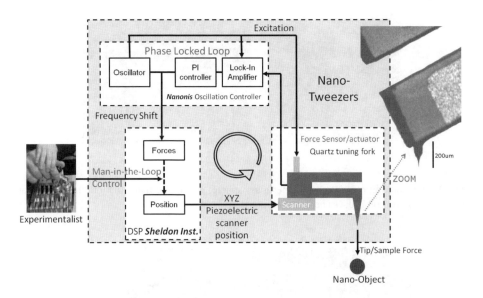

Fig. 2. Real-Time Control Loop: Oscillation Controller from *Nanonis System* and a DSP card from *Sheldon Instruments* to implement the man-in-the-loop control

This parameter is sample and task dependant. The D parameter in Equ. 4 is used to balance the static error (natural drift) of the Δf.

Better solutions to preserve the passivity of the system are under examination.

5   Experimental Results

Teleoperation experiments have been carried out in air at room temperature to validate the contact detection in 1D or 3D using well characterised samples.

3D Basic Teleoperation Mode: Grabbing of a Microsphere

A glass microsphere of $20\mu m$ (diameter) has been successfully pushed, grabbed and held above the surface with the two tip system via visual rendering and joystick control (Fig. 3) but without force feedback. At the end, the user can maintain the micro-objet above the surface for several minutes.

2D Basic Teleoperation Mode: Manipulation of a Microsphere

A latex sphere of $2\mu m$ of diameter has been moved by one tip, using a 3D force feedback in the user space. This 3D force, built on the user's motion (see Section 3) enables to explore haptically the sample. After the sphere has been haptically localized (Fig. 4(a)), it has been moved on the surface for few microns without damage (Fig. 4(b)).

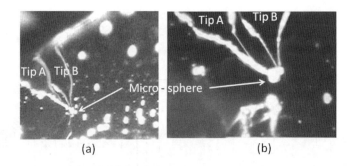

Fig. 3. Manipulation of a 20μm diameter glass sphere: during the manipulation, the sphere has been pushed; (a) grabbed; (b) held over the surface

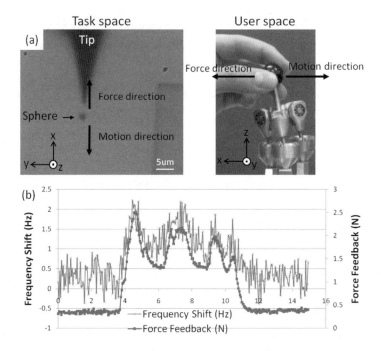

Fig. 4. Manipulation of a 2μm latex sphere: (a) the sphere has been haptically "felt" via a 3D force feeback and then pushed for few microns along the surface; (b) Frequency Shift and Force Feedback signals in function of time (s) during the displacement of the sphere

Despite the easiness to manipulate the sphere with 3D force feedback, a strong limitation still persists: the micro-object is manipulated by a 3D displacement of the tip, but the complete picture of the interaction is still unknown as only the Z component of the force is measured.

1D Teleoperation: Exploration of the Sample Elasticity

The interaction force between a tip and a PDMS circular membrane (soft sample) has been probed and the corresponding force on the haptic device recorded (Fig.5). Thanks to the high spring constant of the TF, the frequency shift variation could be attributed only to the sample deformation. This experiment cannot be realised with an AFM cantilever due to the limited cantilever stiffness.

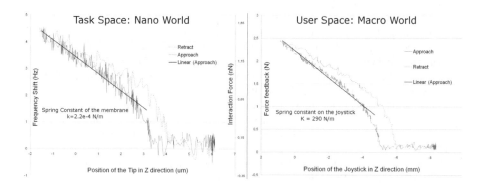

Fig. 5. Approach-Retract Curve over a PDMS (polydimethylsiloxane) circular membrane with the haptic interface manipulator. Membrane diameter and thickness: 5*mm*; 10*μm*.

6 Conclusion

The set of experiments validates the efficiency of the dual independent probes as a gripping micro/nano-prehensor and its coupling with a Real-Time haptic interface. All the experiments have been accomplished several times with good repeatability and no need of particular dexterity. In addition, this work demonstrated the relevance of frequency shift measurements in the task space to transfer them in force information in the user space. This result paves the way for the nanomanipulation in dynamic mode with rigid micro-transducer.

In the next step, a more complex simulated nano environment will be implemented to provide additional virtual information like realistic 3D force field and visual surface rendering.

Acknowledgments. Curie Institut, Paris, for providing PDMS samples.

References

1. Aruk, B., Hashimoto, H., Sitti, M.: Man-Machine Interface for Micro-Nano Manipulation with an AFM Probe. In: IEEE-NANO 2001, pp. 151–156 (2001)
2. Xie, H., Haliyo, D.S., Regnier, S.: A versatile atomic force microscope for three-dimentional nanomanipulation and nanoassembly. Nanotechnology (2009)

3. Marliere, S., Urma, D., Florens, J.L., Marchi, F.: Multi-sensorial interaction with a nano-scale phenomenon: the force curve. In: Proceedings of EuroHaptics 2004, Munich, Germany, June 5-7, 2004, pp. 246–252 (2004)
4. Saeidpourazar, R., Jalili, N.: Towards fused vision and force robust feedback control of nanorobotic-based manipulation and grasping. Mechatronics 18, 566–577 (2008)
5. Sitti, M.: Survey of Nanomanipulation Systems. In: IEEE-NANO 2001, pp. 75–80 (2001)
6. Florens, J.L., Lucianni, A., Cadoz, C., Castagne, N.: ERGOS: Multi-degrees of Freedom and Versatile Force-Feedback Panoply. In: Proceedings of EuroHaptics 2004, Munich, Germany, June 5-7, pp. 356–360 (2004)
7. Scheler, T., Rodrigues, M., Cornelius, T.W., Mocuta, C., Malachias, A., Magalhes-Paniago, R., Comin, F., Chevrier, J., Metzger, T.H.: Applied Physics Letters 94, 23109 (2009)
8. Lee, L., Schaller, R., Haber, L.H., Saykally, R.J.: High Spatial Resolution Imaging with Near-Field Scanning Optical Microscopy in Liquids. Anal. Chem. 73(21), 5015–5019 (2001)
9. Barbic, M., Eliason, L., Ranshaw, J.: Femto-Newton force sensitivity quartz tuning fork sensor. Sensors and actuators. A. Physical 136, 564–566 (2007)
10. Rensen, W.H.: Tuning Fork Tunes, Exploring new scanning probe techniques, p. 31 (2002)
11. Vogl, W., Ma, B.K.L., Sitti, M.: Augmented Reality User Interface for an Atomic Force Microscope-Based Nanorobotic System. IEEE Transactions on Nanotechnology 5, 397–406 (2006)
12. Onal, C.D., Sitti, M.: Teleoperated 3-D Force Feedback From the Nanoscale With an Atomic Force Microscope. IEEE Transactions on Nanotechnology 9(1) (2010)

Classifying Torque, Normal Force and Direction Using Monkey Afferent Nerve Spike Rates

Stephen James Redmond[1], Ingvars Birznieks[2], Nigel H. Lovell[3],
and Antony W. Goodwin[4]

[1] School of Electrical Engineering and Telecommunications, University of New South Wales,
Sydney, Australia
[2] Prince of Wales Medical Research Institute, Sydney, Australia
[3] Graduate School of Biomedical Engineering, University of New South Wales,
Sydney, Australia
[4] Department of Anatomy and Cell Biology, University of Melbourne, Australia
{s.redmond,ingvars.birznieks,n.lovell}@unsw.edu.au,
a.goodwin@unimelb.edu.au

Abstract. In this study, tactile afferents in monkey fingertips were mechanically stimulated, using a flat disc shaped probe, with several magnitudes of torque, in clockwise and anticlockwise directions. In order to prevent slip during the stimulation event, a sufficient normal force was also applied, with three different magnitudes tested. Recordings were made from afferents innervating the glabrous skin covering the entire distal segment of the finger. A Parzen window classifier was used to assess the capacity of tactile afferents to discriminate, concurrently and in real-time, the three stimulus parameters; namely, background normal force, torque magnitude and direction. Despite the potentially confounding interactions between stimulus parameters, classification accuracy was very high and was improved even further by selecting subsets of best performing afferents.

Keywords: tactile sensing, afferent, Parzen window, classifier, torque, force.

1 Introduction

Tactile sensory afferents provide critical information to the biological control system which governs the movement of primate hands and limbs.

Grasping, lifting and rotating delicate objects become particularly difficult in the absence of tactile sensory input [1]. During simple object manipulation, tactile afferents encode critical manipulative parameters like the grip force, or normal force, applied to the object to prevent slip; the load force applied to lift or move the object, and the torque. Torque is ubiquitous in everyday tasks and arises when an object's centre of mass does not align with the vector of force application [2, 3]. Sensorimotor mechanisms controlling the effects of torque have been investigated in human experiments employing a two finger opposition grip [4-6] and in tasks where objects are held in a multi-finger grasp [7-11].

A.M.L. Kappers et al. (Eds.): EuroHaptics 2010, Part I, LNCS 6191, pp. 43–50, 2010.
© Springer-Verlag Berlin Heidelberg 2010

Smooth self-paced object manipulation and coordination of fingertip forces is largely achieved by predictive strategies based on internal representations which must be updated by sensory input [12]. When errors or unpredictable events occur, the adequate reaction can only be triggered by sensory input.

Our task was to investigate how such information is encoded. Although it is not understood exactly how the brain decodes this information, it is still possible to apply statistical classification or pattern recognition models to these data, to observe how the information is encoded throughout the population; whether the brain uses this information in a mathematically equivalent manner to that of the derived classifier model is currently a matter of speculation.

In this study, the monkey fingertips were mechanically stimulated, using a flat disc-shaped probe, with several magnitudes of torque, in both a clockwise and anti-clockwise direction. In order to prevent slip during the stimulation event, a sufficient background normal force was also applied, with three different magnitudes tested. The stimuli were applied to the centre of the monkey finger pad. Recordings were made from afferents innervating the glabrous skin covering the entire distal segment of the finger in order to obtain a representative sample of the entire population response [13].

A Parzen window classification model was applied to the data ensemble to investigate how accurately the various stimulus attributes, of normal force, torque and direction, were encoded in the afferent nerve responses. The challenge of this study was to find a solution to how interactions between numerous stimulus features may be disentangled in real-time, as timing is an exceptionally important component of this process.

2 Methods

2.1 Neural Recordings

Recordings of afferent nerve responses were made from three anesthetized *Macaca nemestrina* monkeys, with approval from the University of Melbourne Ethics Committee and conforming to the National Health and Medical Research Council of Australia's Code of Practice for non-human primate research. The animals weighed from 4.5 to 7.6 kg.

Surgical anesthesia was induced and standard procedures were used to isolate and record from single cutaneous mechanoreceptive afferents in the median nerve [14]. Established criteria were employed to analyze: the responses of each afferent to static and rapidly changing stimuli; and the receptive field size [15]. Hence, each single fiber was categorized as a slowly adapting type I (SA-I), fast-adapting type I (FA-I), or fast-adapting type II (FA-II) afferent. All responding SA-I and FA-I afferents innervating the glabrous skin of the distal phalanx of digits 2, 3 and 4 were included in this study; FA-II afferents did not demonstrate a reliable response. Calibrated von Frey hairs were used to determine the location of each receptive field.

Digits were affixed by splaying the digits and embedding the dorsal aspect of the hand in plasticine up to the mid-level of the middle phalanges, with the distal phalanges stabilized by gluing the fingernails to small metal plates, each of which was firmly fixed to a post embedded in the plasticine. The glabrous skin of the distal phalanges did not contact the plasticine, thereby allowing the fingertip to deform as it might if it was actively pressed against a surface (see Methods in [13]).

2.2 Stimulation Procedure

2.2.1 Stimulator

A custom-made mechanical stimulator, controlled using LabVIEW 5 software (National Instruments, Austin, TX), was used to apply concurrent normal force and torque forces. A six-axis force-torque transducer (Nano FT; ATI Industrial Automation, Apex, NC) measured the applied forces. The respective resolutions of the transducer to force and torque were 0.0125 N and 0.0625 mNm. The stimulus applicator was a flat circular surface (diameter 24 mm) covered with fine grain sandpaper (500 grade).

2.2.2 Application of Torsional Loads

The stimulus was applied to the center of the flat portion of the volar surface of the fingertip. Digits 2, 3 and 4 were used. The direction of the normal force was aligned at right angles to the skin surface and positioned so the rotational axis of the torque was aligned with the chosen application location, defined above.

Three normal force magnitudes were employed: 1.8, 2.2 and 2.5 N. The three torque magnitudes were: 0.0, 2.0, 3.5 mNm. Torque was applied in both clockwise and anticlockwise directions, giving rise to 18 ($3\times3\times2$) force/torque/direction combinations. The following passages describe the order in which the various stimuli were applied.

For each normal force, all torques were applied in ascending order. Once all torques were applied for a given normal force, the normal force was increased and all torques were reapplied. This was repeated until all three normal forces had been applied for all three torques. This entire process was repeated six times, after which the entire procedure was repeated six more times with the torque applied in the opposite direction. In summary, there were 18 different stimulation combinations, each applied 6 times in total, giving 108 different training examples for the classifier model (described later), when the responses of all afferents were considered as a simultaneously acquired ensemble.

For each individual application of force and torque, the procedure was as follows. Normal force was ramped up over a 0.2 s loading phase; the normal force was maintained for a 3.6 s plateau phase, before a 0.2 s retraction phase removing the normal force. The torque was superimposed on this constant normal force, commencing 1 s after the plateau phase of the normal force had begun. The torque loading phase lasted 0.5 s, with the maximum torque then maintained at a constant value for 1.5 s, before being unloaded over a 0.5 s duration. Hence, the normal force was completely retracted 0.1 s after the unloading of the torque force.

2.3 Attribute Discrimination Using Afferent Populations

2.3.1 Feature Vector Ensemble

As described above, there were 18 stimulus combinations comprising: three normal forces (1.8, 2.2 and 2.5 N), three torque magnitudes (0.0, 2.0 and 3.5 mNm) and two directions (clockwise and anticlockwise). Each combination of force, torque and direction was applied six times leading to 108 training patterns, which may be presented to the classifier (described below).

The responses (spike counts) of the ith stimulus event, $i \subset \{1,...,108\}$, from each of the K afferents in a population may be considered as an ensemble of simultaneously acquired data, which can be cast into a K element feature vector, $\mathbf{x}_i = [x_{i1}, x_{i2}, ..., x_{ik}, ..., x_{iK}]$, where x_{ik} is the total number of action potentials (spikes) elicited by a single afferent within a chosen analysis window starting at the onset of the torque force (the analysis window duration will be discussed below).

Combining the feature vectors for the 58 SA-I afferents and 23 FA-I afferents, generates a 108×81 feature matrix.

2.3.2 Classifier Model

The tool used to investigate the discriminative power of the information encoded in the afferent spike counts was a Parzen window classifier. The purpose of the classifier is to assign the multi-dimensional feature vector, $\mathbf{X}_i$, occurring from a stimulus event, to a particular class, ω, in a Bayesian optimal sense [16].

For example, in the case of classifying normal force there are three classes $\omega \in \{1.8, 2.2, 2.5\}$ N. Separate independent classifiers are designed for the different classification tasks of normal force, torque and direction. Let us use the classifier for normal force as an example.

The *a posteriori* probability densities for each of the three normal force classes were estimated using the set of rows, τ, of the feature matrix (described above) corresponding to the events when the given normal force class was applied, assuming the *a priori* probabilities are equal; that is no normal force is more likely to occur than any other. The probability density for normal force class ω at point $\mathbf{X}_i$ in the feature space is estimated as:

$$g_\omega(\mathbf{x}_i) = \sum_{j \in \tau} \left[\frac{1}{(2\pi)^{\frac{d}{2}} r^d} \exp\left(\frac{\|\mathbf{x}_i - \mathbf{x}_j\|^2}{r^2} \right) \right] \tag{1}$$

The radius variable r serves to adjust the smoothness of the nonparametric density estimation by changing the width of the radial basis function. A value $r=1$ was used, after each afferent response has been normalized across all training vectors, by removing the mean and dividing by the standard deviation. d is the number of afferents used in the discrimination task, which defines the dimension of the feature space. A discrimination task decision is made by labeling the event as belonging to the class ω

which maximizes Eq. (1); that is, the unknown test vector $\mathbf{X}_i$ is assigned to the most likely class ω.

2.3.3 Cross-Fold Validation
A leave-one-out cross-fold validation procedure was used to obtain an unbiased estimate of classification performance [16]. A single test vector was removed from the training data and the remaining 107 vectors were used for training. The withheld vector was then reintroduced for testing. This process was repeated 108 times, withholding a different row vector from the feature matrix each time for testing, and training with the remaining 107 rows. The results presented below represent the percentage of these 108 rows which were correctly classified.

2.3.4 Temporal Analysis Window
To observe how the classification accuracy develops over the time course of the torque application, the afferent responses (which constitute the entries in the feature vector – described above), are calculated as the total number of spikes evoked since the start of the torque loading phase until the specified time under investigation, increasing in 10 ms steps.

2.3.5 Afferent Selection
A greedy backwards feature selection algorithm was utilized to search for the optimum subset of afferents, from the available pool of 81 afferents. The procedure starts by including all afferents in the classification process. The performance of the current subset of selected afferents, as defined by the classification accuracy, is calculated. Next, the afferent whose exclusion provides the greatest increase (or the least decrease) in accuracy is removed from the current selected subset. This sequential removal is repeated until there are no afferents remaining in the selected afferent subset. The intermediate subset of afferents which gave the best classification accuracy is returned as the best subset found. This feature search procedure is performed to optimize the performance at 350 ms after the application of torque is initiated, using the spike count over this entire 350 ms duration. Since torque magnitude and direction are easily decoded using all afferents at 500 ms (the end of the torque loading phase), there is no advantage to optimizing performance at 500 ms or later (c.f. Fig. 1 (a), (c) and (e)).

3 Results

Fig. 1 (a), (c) and (e) show plots of classification accuracies as they evolve after the torque force is applied, and also includes the first 0.2 s of the torque plateau phase from 500–700 ms. At each time point a new classifier is retrained, using the total number of spikes evoked up to that point, and using the afferent subsets found during optimization at 350 ms. For comparison, the classification performance using all afferents, without afferent subset selection, is also shown. Fig 1 (b), (d) and (f) are the normalized positions of the afferents in the finger pads after scaling to a standard template; the origin is taken as the centre of the tip of the distal finger segment. The different afferent types (SA-I and FA-I) are also plotted.

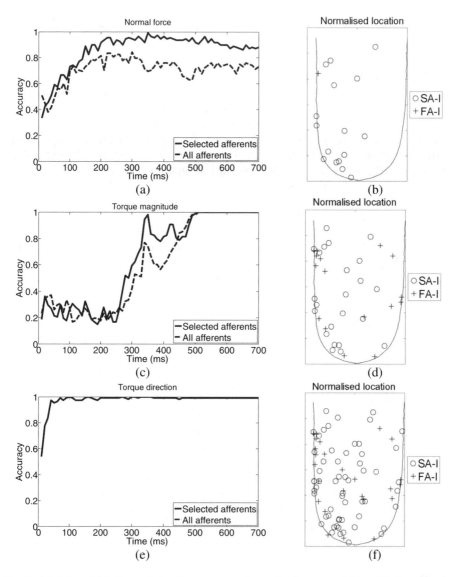

Fig. 1. (a), (c) and (e) show plots of accuracy, estimated using cross-fold validation, versus time, using all afferents (dashed line) and the best selected subset (solid line) chosen using a feature subset selection search. (b), (d) and (f) show the corresponding normalized positions of the selected afferents for optimized accuracy at 350 ms after the application of torque began, with a finger outline superimposed.

At 350 ms the accuracies for normal force, torque magnitude and torque direction, when using all 81 available afferents were 69.4%, 74.0% and 100.0%, respectively. The corresponding values when afferent selection was employed were 99.1%, 98.2% and 100.0%, respectively.

4   Discussion

The results indicate that even with this small population of 81 afferents, 100% classification accuracy is attainable after 500 ms for torque magnitude and direction classification tasks, with good performance in the discrimination of normal force, showing that the various stimulus attributes can be disentangled from the population response. In fact, Fig 1 (b) shows that 100% accuracy is maintained from approximately 500 ms for torque magnitude. Fig 1 (c) shows the same accuracy is reached at around 100 ms for torque direction.

Afferent subset selection provided a significant improvement for normal force and torque magnitude classification, with only sixteen SA-I afferents and one FA-I afferent retained to achieve the improved performance for normal force. (While not plotted here, optimizing performance at 500 ms achieves 100% accuracy for normal force discrimination.) In contrast, when subset selection is applied during the training of the torque direction classifier, all 81 afferents are retained, as 100% accuracy had already been reached by 350 ms. It is evident from Fig 1 (d) and (f) that the selected afferent locations are distributed across the finger pad, which makes some intuitive sense, as discrimination of torque and direction are tasks that require analysis of the differential responses across the population.

The analysis performed here has some advantage over the central nervous system, in that it is provided with the stimulus start time, and the analysis window expands from that instant. In reality there would be no event marker for the onset of the torque and a fixed width sliding analysis window (whose width must be optimized) would be used. In addition, future work will analyze the discriminative power of SA-I and FA-I afferents independently.

5   Conclusion

A supervised classification paradigm has been applied to the evoked responses of afferent mechanoreceptors in the monkey finger pad to investigate the ability of such a machine learning approach to disentangle the multiple concurrent stimulus factors such as normal force, torque magnitude and torque direction. The results indicate that 100% accuracy is possible within approximately 350 ms of the application of torque using only a subset of mechanoreceptors.

Acknowledgements. This research was supported by the Australian Research Council (ARC) Thinking Systems grant TS0669860.

References

1. Flanagan, J.R., Bowman, M.C., Johansson, R.S.: Control strategies in object manipulation tasks. Curr. Opin. Neurobiol. 16, 650–659 (2006)
2. Johansson, R.S., Westling, G.: Roles of glabrous skin receptors and sensorimotor memory in automatic control of precision grip when lifting rougher or more slippery objects. Exp. Brain Res. 56, 550–564 (1984)

3. Kinoshita, H., Bäckström, L., Flanagan, J.R., Johansson, R.S.: Tangential torque effects on the control of grip forces when holding objects with a precision grip. J. Neurophysiol. 78, 1619–1630 (1997)
4. Goodwin, A.W., Jenmalm, P., Johansson, R.S.: Control of grip force when tilting objects: effect of curvature of grasped surfaces and of applied tangential torque. J. Neurosci. 18, 10724–10734 (1998)
5. Wing, A.M., Lederman, S.J.: Anticipating load torques produced by voluntary movements. J. Exp. Psychol. Hum. Percept. Perform. 24, 1571–1581 (1998)
6. Johansson, R.S., Backlin, J.L., Burstedt, M.K.O.: Control of grasp stability during pronation and supination movements. Exp. Brain Res. 128, 20–30 (1999)
7. Burstedt, M.K.O., Flanagan, R., Johansson, R.S.: Control of grasp stability in humans under different frictional conditions during multi-digit manipulation. J. Neurophysiol. 82, 2393–2405 (1999)
8. Flanagan, J.R., Burstedt, M.K.O., Johansson, R.S.: Control of fingertip forces in multi-digit manipulation. J. Neurophysiol. 81, 1706–1717 (1999)
9. Latash, M.L., Shim, J.K., Gao, F., Zatsiorsky, V.M.: Rotational equilibrium during multi-digit pressing and prehension. Motor Control 8, 392–404 (2004)
10. Shim, J.K., Latash, M.L., Zatsiorsky, V.M.: Prehension synergies in three dimensions. J. Neurophysiol. 93, 766–776 (2005)
11. Shim, J.K., Park, J., Zatsiorsky, V.M., Latash, M.L.: Adjustments of prehension synergies in response to self-triggered and experimenter-triggered load and torque perturbations. Exp. Brain Res. 175, 641–653 (2006)
12. Nowak, D.A., Glasauer, S., Hermsdörfer, J.: Grip force efficiency in long-term deprivation of somatosensory feedback. Neuroreport 14, 1803–1807 (2003)
13. Birznieks, I., Jenmalm, P., Goodwin, A.W., Johansson, R.S.: Encoding of Direction of Fingertip Forces by Human Tactile Afferents. J. Neurosci. 21, 8222–8237 (2001)
14. Goodwin, A.W., Browning, A.S., Wheat, H.E.: Representation of curved surfaces in responses of mechanoreceptive afferent fibers innervating the monkey's fingerpad. J. Neurosci. 15, 798–810 (1995)
15. Vallbo, A.B., Johansson, R.S.: Properties of cutaneous mechanoreceptors in the human hand related to touch sensation. Hum. Neurobiol. 3, 3–14 (1984)
16. Duda, R.O., Hart, P.E., Stork, D.G.: Pattern Classification, 2nd edn. John Wiley & Sons, Chichester (2001)

A New Coupling Scheme for Haptic Rendering of Rigid Bodies Interactions Based on a Haptic Sub-world Using a Contact Graph

Loeiz Glondu, Maud Marchal, and Georges Dumont

IRISA/INRIA Rennes
Campus de Beaulieu
35 042 Rennes, France
{lglondu,mmarchal,gdumont}@irisa.fr

Abstract. Interactions with virtual worlds using the sense of touch, called haptic rendering, have natural applications in many domains such as health or industry. For an accurate and realistic haptic feedback, the haptic device must receive orders at high frequencies, especially to render stiff contacts between rigid bodies. Therefore, it is today still challenging to provide consistent haptic feedback in complex virtual worlds. In this paper, we present a new coupling scheme for haptic display of contacts between rigid bodies, based on the generation of a sub-world around the haptic interaction. This sub-world allows the simulation of physical models at higher frequencies using a reduced quantity of data. We introduce the use of a graph to manage the contacts between the bodies. Our results show that our coupling scheme enables to increase the complexity of the virtual world without having perceptible loss in the haptic display quality.

Keywords: Haptic Rendering, Rigid Bodies, Contacts, Coupling Scheme.

1 Introduction

Haptic rendering offers the possibility to make a human user interacting with a virtual object as if it was a real one, using the sense of touch. However, in order to haptically render stiff contacts between rigid bodies, a high refreshment frequency must be maintained in order to ensure a stable and accurate interaction [5]. Therefore, it is often considered to create two processes in haptic rendering applications: one for the physical simulation, and another one for the haptic rendering. The simulation process extracts at its rate a so-called intermediate representation [1] from the virtual world. This intermediate representation is a simplified and local model of the world that is exploited by the haptic process to generate orders at frequencies allowing good haptic rendering quality.

There are different models used for intermediate representation in the literature. Some authors proposed to use the Jacobian of forces with respect to a displacement of the tip of the haptic device [4]. An other approach consists in extracting a simplified geometry from the virtual world, around the interaction area. The nature of the geometry can be a single plane [1], a set of planes [7], parametrized surfaces [3], set of nearest triangles [8], or other data for collision detection [6]. Finally, multiresolution

A.M.L. Kappers et al. (Eds.): EuroHaptics 2010, Part I, LNCS 6191, pp. 51–56, 2010.

approaches have been proposed for deformable bodies, where a part of the body mesh that is close to the tip of the device is extracted, and simulated at different rates, using different levels of details [2]. A linearized version of deformation simulation can also be used in the haptic process [4]. More recent work has been proposed in [9] to deal with haptic display of bodies having complex geometries. The geometry is dynamically simplified in a sensation preserving way around contact points.

Most of the methods have been developed in order to allow haptic interactions with deformable bodies. However, contacts between rigid bodies are simulated using different models, and need higher haptic frequency. Therefore, the methods proposed for deformable bodies can not be applied to rigid bodies. In this paper, we present a multiresolution approach for haptic rendering between rigid bodies. The main idea of our new coupling scheme is to dynamically extract a subset of the global world and to build a second physical world as an intermediate model. We call this second physical world the *haptic sub-world*. As presented in Section 2, the haptic sub-world is built from a limited number of carefully selected bodies, and can therefore be simulated at a higher frequency into the haptic process, as depicted on Fig. 1. The results presented in Section 3 show that our coupling scheme enables to increase the complexity of the global world without any perceptible alteration of the haptic display.

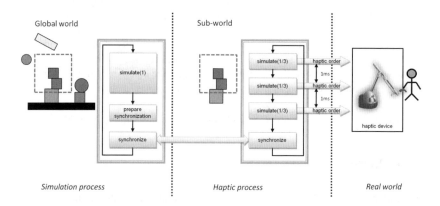

Fig. 1. Haptic-sub world main algorithm. The simulation process simulates the global world once with a time step of dt, while the haptic process simulates for example 3 times its haptic sub-world using a time step of $1/3 \times dt$ (we call the ratio between the time steps the *simulation ratio value*, noted r_{sim}). At the end of the haptic cycle, the two worlds are synchronized, exchanging bodies positions and efforts information.

2   The Graph-Based Haptic Sub-world Coupling Scheme

We define the haptic sub-world as a subset of the bodies of the world that is simulated at a frequency allowing a good haptic rendering. We noticed that during the interactions, only the bodies that are directly or indirectly in contact with the proxy (the body linked to the haptic device) can influence it. Therefore, we define the haptic sub-world based on the graph of contacts between the bodies. Let us define β, the set of bodies of the global world and $p \in \beta$ represents the proxy. If we suppose that we have a function called $contact : \beta \times \beta \rightarrow \mathbb{R}$ that provides the number of contacts occurring between a pair of bodies, then we can define the graph $G = (\beta, \mathcal{V})$, where an edge $v = (b_1, b_2)$ from the edges set $\mathcal{V} \subset \beta \times \beta$ exists only if there is a direct contact between b_1 and b_2, i.e.:

$$\forall b_1, b_2 \in \beta, \, contact(b_1, b_2) \geq 1 \Rightarrow (b_1, b_2) \in \mathcal{V} \tag{1}$$

From the graph G, we define $\mathcal{H} = (\beta_h, \mathcal{V}_h), \beta_h \subset \beta, \mathcal{V}_h \subset \mathcal{V}$ as the connected subgraph of G that contains p (the proxy). Fig. 2 shows an example of how the graph $\mathcal{H}$ is obtained.

In practice, we only need the graph $\mathcal{H}$ (the connectivity information of the other bodies in G is useless for our purpose). Therefore, we designed an algorithm that progressively builds the graph $\mathcal{H}$ over the simulations, starting from the proxy and the bodies that are directly in contact with it.

From this definition, a body can belong to the haptic sub-world only if it has a (direct or not) contact with the proxy. However, a haptic cycle is needed before a body is added to the sub-world. Therfore, we anticipate all potential contacts by bringing bodies close to the proxy even if there is no contact with it (Paragraph 2.1). Also, we must limit the complexity of the haptic sub-world to preserve the haptic frequency (see Fig. 2, card house). However, if the graph is limited, it may exist contacts between the two worlds, and we must manage the exchange of energies to avoid loss of physical plausibility (Paragraph 2.2).

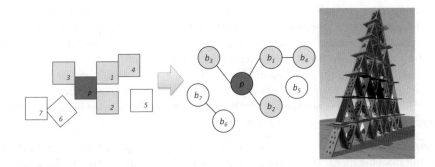

Fig. 2. The graph G (middle, containing all nodes) defines the contact configuration of the bodies of the global world. The colored connected components of the graph containing the proxy (in red) form the graph $\mathcal{H}$ (containing only colored nodes) of the bodies that compose the haptic sub-world. The card house (right) illustrates the haptic sub-world composed of colored cards extracted from the proxy (red card).

2.1   Building the Haptic Sub-world

A body close to the proxy is a body that can be reached by the proxy in less than two haptic cycles. Indeed, the linear velocity of the proxy has a limit v_{max} defined by the mechanical constraints of the haptic device. For a given fixed haptic frequency rendering f, and a chosen simulation ratio value r_{sim}, the maximum displacement p_{max} of the proxy during two haptic cycles is $p_{max} = \frac{r_{sim}}{f} \times v_{max}$. Assuming that the size of the proxy bounding cube side is c_{size}, then we define a boundary cube with a side size of $c_{size} + 2 \times p_{max}$ centered around the proxy that represents the limit of close bodies. All the bodies intersecting the boundary box are added into the sub-world to avoid the loss of physical information.

2.2   Building the Graph and the Interface

As previously mentioned, using a haptic sub-world with a small number of bodies enables to perform a parallel simulation at high rates for the haptic rendering concerns. However, it is possible that the haptic graph $\mathcal{H}$ has too many nodes (we may have $\mathcal{H} = \mathcal{G}$, the global graph), and in that case, the sub-world looses its sense. To ensure a fixed haptic frequency, we limit the propagation of the graph to a maximum number of bodies. We define an interface that manages the energy exchanges between the global world and the haptic sub-world when the graph is limited. Different exchanges are controlled:

Efforts Coming from the Global World. We define border bodies as bodies of the haptic sub-world having a contact with a body of the global world (*e.g.* the yellow cards on Fig. 2). During the simulation of the global world, we store non-penetration impulses applied at these contacts and apply them on border bodies at each simulation step of the haptic cycle.

Border Friction. To include friction at border, we create a "friction point" constraint at each border contact where an impulse is applied. This constraint imposes the body point to stay along the contact normal line. If a big enough tangential effort is applied, the constraint is freed. The threshold is determined using Coulomb friction model. Namely, knowing the normal impulse magnitude i applied at border contact and the coefficient of friction μ at that point, the intensity threshold used for the perpendicular effort is $\mu \times i$. Sliding friction is not applied, but approximated by the fact that the friction point constraint is updated at each synchronization.

Efforts Coming from the Haptic Sub-world. In order to propagate the normal actions coming from the haptic sub-world to the global world, we simply impose the positions of the bodies of the haptic sub-world to their equivalent body in the global world. For tangential efforts, we store at each friction constraint the sum of impulses applied to maintain the constraint, and apply them on each body of the global world that has a contact with border bodies.

3   Results and Evaluation

Our tests and experiments have been performed on PC running on Windows XP, equipped with 2 processors Intel Pentium D (3.4 GHz) and 2 Go RAM. The haptic device used is a 6 DOFs Virtuose 6D35-45 (Haption company, France). The graphic card for display is a NVidia Quadro FX 3450. We used Havok physics software (http://www.havok.com)

for collision detection and rigid body simulation (the solver complexity is $O(n)$, n being the number of constraints). We used a third process to manage visual rendering in order to increase computation time performances.

3.1   Same Haptic Frequency for More Complex Scenes

The simulation process has r_{sim} haptic periods of time to simulate its world and prepare the synchronization (see Fig. 1). Namely, the number of bodies allowed into the global world is approximatively equal to the number of bodies allowed into the haptic sub-world multiplied by r_{sim}. For example, on our configuration, using a value of 10 for r_{sim} enabled us to perform satisfying haptic rendering in virtual worlds containing more than 500 cubes at a frequency of 1kHz. Without our method, this frequency can be maintained only for scene containing less than 50 cubes.

3.2   Accuracy Measurements

We performed accuracy measurements based on the velocity of the bodies on scenes containing up to 250 bodies, and about 2000 contacts. We measured that the sub-world method generates a loss of energy of 6% in the worst case (compared to the simulation without sub-world), using a simulation ratio value of 8. This loss of energy is due to the approximations and filters applied during the haptic cycle in order to avoid energy gain, that could lead to instability. Even if these approximations increase with r_{sim}, we experienced that the haptic feedback remains the same for the user, even with high r_{sim} values (> 10).

3.3   Comparison with Other Coupling Methods

We implemented and compared the haptic feedback obtained with our method to other coupling schemes between the physical simulation and haptic rendering: the direct coupling, the interpolation of position and a static sub-world coupling. With a direct coupling, a stable and accurate haptic rendering is obtained, but the complexity of the virtual world is limited. With the interpolation method, the efforts returned by the haptic device are stored during the haptic cycle, and are then applied all at a time during synchronization. This behavior produces artifacts and decreases the stability of the haptic feedback, even for small values of r_{sim} (under 4). Using a static sub-world, we no longer simulate the haptic sub-world: it is freezed and all objects are fixed. The position of the proxy is imposed into the simulation process at each synchronization. This produces a stable simulation, but the late integration of the action of the proxy produces annoying vibrations artifacts. Using our sub-world method, we can increase the complexity of the virtual world while avoiding the artifacts produced using the interpolation or the static sub-world methods.

4   Conclusion

In this paper, we presented a new coupling scheme based on a haptic sub-world principle with the use of a graph to manage the contacts between rigid bodies. The scheme allows to couple the physical simulation of rigid bodies and haptic rendering, and enables to increase the complexity of the virtual world without having perceptible loss in haptic rendering quality. We also presented an interface that manages the exchanges of energy between the sub-world and the global world when contacts remains between the two worlds. With our coupling scheme, we have been able to perform 1kHz and satisfying haptic rendering in scenes containing more than 700 cubes with many contacts.

Future work will be focused on the use of our method as a tool for haptic rendering applications. We also project to validate it on user-based scenarized scenes. Also, we think it is possible to use our coupling scheme to perform several haptic displays together from the same global world without loss of computation time performance.

References

1. Adachi, Y., Kumano, T., Ogino, K.: Intermediate representation for stiff virtual objects. In: Proceedings of VRAIS 1995, pp. 203–210 (1995)
2. Astley, O.R., Hayward, V.: Real-time finite-elements simulation of general visco-elastic materials for haptic presentation. In: Proceedings of IEEE/RSJ International Conference on Intelligent Robots and Systems, pp. 52–57 (1997)
3. Balaniuk, R.: Using fast local modelling to buffer haptic data. In: Proceedings of Fourth PHANTOM Users Group Workshop (1999)
4. Cavusoglu, M.C., Tendick, F.: Multirate simulation for high fidelity haptic interaction with deformable objects in virtual environments. In: Proceedings of IEEE ICRA, pp. 2458–2465 (2000)
5. Colgate, J.E., Stanley, M.C., Brown, J.M.: Issues in the haptic display of tool use. In: Proceedings of IEEE/RSJ International Conference on Intelligent Robots and Systems, pp. 140–144 (1995)
6. Davanne, J., Meseure, P., Chaillou, C.: Stable haptic interaction in a dynamic virtual environment. In: Proceedings of IEEE/RSJ International Conference on Intelligent Robots and Systems, pp. 2881–2886 (2002)
7. Mark, W.R., Randolph, S.C., Finch, M., Verth, J.M.V., Taylor II, R.M.: Adding force feedback to graphics systems: Issues and solutions. In: Proceedings of SIGGRAPH, pp. 447–452 (1996)
8. Mendoza, C., Laugier, C.: A solution for the difference rate sampling between haptic devices and deformable virtual objects. In: Proceedings of International Symposium on Robotics and Automation (2000)
9. Otaduy, M.A., Lin, M.C.: Sensation preserving simplification for haptic rendering. In: Proceedings of SIGGRAPH, pp. 72–83 (2005)

A New Multi-DOF Haptic Device
Using a Redundant Parallel Mechanism

Jumpei Arata, Norio Ikedo, and Hideo Fujimoto

Nagoya Institute of Technology, Gokiso-cho, Showa-ku, Nagoya 466-8555, Japan
{jumpei,cig17510,fujimoto.hideo}@nitech.ac.jp

Abstract. In recent years, parallel mechanisms have been widely introduced to haptic devices for advantageous benefits such as a high rigidity, a high output force, a high accuracy and a high backdrivability by its multi-legged structure and fixed actuators on the base. On the other hand, multi-DOF haptic devices including rotational motions are getting important in recent years as haptic applications have grown more diverse as typified by a surgical training system. However, realizing a multi-DOF haptic device within a wide range of rotational working area by using parallel mechanism is a challenging work. In this paper, a 6 DOF (3 translations, 2 rotations and 1 passive rotation) parallel mechanism D-8 is presented to overcome this challenge.

Keywords: haptic device; parallel mechanism, redundant mechanism.

1 Introduction

In recent years, parallel mechanisms have been widely introduced to haptic devices. In general, parallel mechanisms have advantages on a high rigidity, a high output force, a high accuracy and a high backdrivability by its multi-legged structure and fixed actuators on the base. In an impedance type haptic device, the performance of haptic sensations and operability are depending on its kinematic structure. Therefore, parallel mechanisms can be effectively used for such purpose. On the other hand, multi-DOF haptic devices including rotational motions are getting important in recent years as haptic applications have grown more diverse as typified by a surgical training system. However, realizing a multi-DOF haptic device within a wide range of rotational motions by using parallel mechanism is a challenging work. As multi-DOF parallel mechanisms which have rotational and translational DOF, HEXA[1], Stewart platform[2] have been presented. However, it is known that the working area of rotational motions is limited in these mechanisms. Vituose 6D[3] is also a haptic device using a multi-DOF parallel mechanism with a limited working area of rotations (35° in pitch, yaw and roll). To overcome this drawback, redundant parallel mechanisms have been presented. Asano presented a 6 DOF haptic device with a redundant parallel mechanism of 9 motors[4]. Haptic wand (Quanser, US.) realized a 5 DOF motions (3 translation motions and 2 rotational motions) by 6 motors[5]. In this paper, a new redundant parallel mechanism D-8 is presented for a new haptic device. By introducing D-8 into a haptic device, it is possible to realize a wide range of rotational working area within the advantages of parallel mechanism.

A.M.L. Kappers et al. (Eds.): EuroHaptics 2010, Part I, LNCS 6191, pp. 57–64, 2010.

2   Mechanism

D-8 was developed by using the advantageous features of our previously presented DELTA-R (formerly called as DELTA-4) [7] mechanism. In this chapter, the overview of the developed mechanism is introduced.

2.1   DELTA-R

The overview of DELTA-R mechanism is shown in Fig.1. DELTA-R is a redundant parallel mechanism, which realizes translational 3 DOF motions by four fixed motors on the base plate. The kinematics of DELTA-R consists of a base plate, an end-effector and a pair of arms. Each arm consists of two parallelograms ($P1_i$ and $P2_i$). (The suffix $i = 1, 2$ represents a pair of arms.) Link 5 is a T shape linkage bar, which connects parallelograms $P1_i$ and $P2_i$ in each arm. 2 DOF motions are given by the motors attached on the joints $J1_i$ and $J2'_i$ in each arm. Two arms are fixed on the base plate with the allocation angle θ_i from X axis around Z axis of the reference frame O. The end-effector is attached on the tips of two arms by the joint $J4_i$ on the parallelogram $P2_i$. The connections between the end-effectors and the two parallelograms by $J4_i$ give a motion constraint in parallel between the end-effector and the base plate. By having the motion constraint, it is possible to maintain the posture between the end-effector and the base plate in parallel, and finally the DELTA-R can obtain the translational 3 DOF motions with its redundant mechanism.

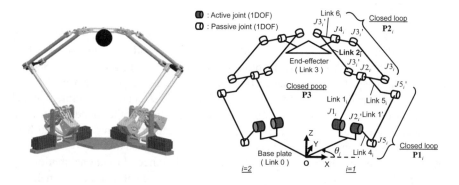

Fig. 1. Overview of the DELTA-R mechanism

2.2   D-8

D-8 is an extension of DELTA-R mechanism. The overview of the D-8 mechanism is illustrated in Fig.2. D-8 realizes a 6 DOF motions (3 translational motions, 3 rotational motions with a passive roll joint) by 8 motors. In the D-8 structure, an end-effector bar is held by a pair of DELTA-R mechanisms, which are located in face-to-face. As DELTA-R has a working distribution on its front of the structure, the face-to-face configuration of a pair of DELTA-R realizes a desirable mechanical access to the end-effector from the

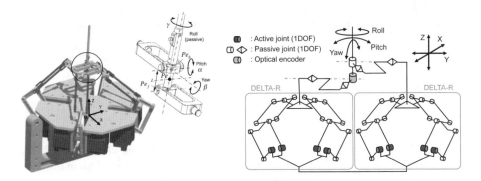

Fig. 2. Overview of the D-8 mechanism

both sides. The end-effector is held by two 3 DOF passive joints in serial. Therefore, differential motions of a pair of DELTA-R mechanisms generate a 2 DOF rotational motions (pitch and yaw). In this manner, it is possible to realize a wide range of working area in its rotation angles of pitch ($\pm 65°$) and yaw ($\pm 90°$). As a roll joint is realized by a passive joint in D-8, there is no limitation of working area in the roll angle. In addition, as same as general parallel mechanisms, all motors can be fixed on a base part in the D-8 mechanism. Therefore, it is possible to introduce the advantageous features of parallel mechanisms to the structure.

2.3 Kinematics of D-8

The structure of D-8 consists of a pair of DELTA-R mechanism, which are interconnected by a 3 DOF joint to the end-effector. Therefore, the translational motions are generated in the case that a pair of DELTA-R moves in a same direction, and the rotational motions (pitch and yaw) are generated by differential motions of a pair of DELTA-R. The center of rotational motions (pitch, yaw and roll) $\boldsymbol{Pe}$ is located on a middle point between the endpoints of each DELTA-R mechanism ($\boldsymbol{Pe}_f$ and $\boldsymbol{Pe}_b$). A roll motion is given by a passive joint on the end-effector.

Forward Kinematics. The end-effector of D-8 is supported by a pair of DELTA-R mechanisms by the points $\boldsymbol{Pe}_f$ and $\boldsymbol{Pe}_b$. Therefore, as these points can be given by using the kinematics of DELTA-R, the end-effector point $\boldsymbol{Pe}$ can be given as follows:

$$\boldsymbol{Pe} = \frac{\boldsymbol{Pe}_f + \boldsymbol{Pe}_b}{2} \tag{1}$$

For the rotation angles of pitch (α) and yaw (β), first, a unit vector between $\boldsymbol{Pe}_f$ and $\boldsymbol{Pe}_b$ can be given as:

$$\boldsymbol{z}_e = \frac{\boldsymbol{Pe}_b - \boldsymbol{Pe}_f}{L} \tag{2}$$

Then the rotation matrix of end-effector is given by using a homogeneous transformation matrix $^{pe}\boldsymbol{T}_e$, based on a reference frame $\boldsymbol{\Sigma}_{pe}$ with its origin at $\boldsymbol{Pe}$. From the rotation matrix $^{pe}E_e$ in $^{pe}T_e$, the unit vector of Z axis a can be given, which equals to the unit vector z_e in (1). Thus, in the case $z_e = a$, α and β can be obtained as follows:

$$a = \begin{bmatrix} a_x & a_y & a_z \end{bmatrix}^T$$

$$\alpha = \arctan\left(-\frac{a_y}{a_z}\right) \tag{3}$$

$$\beta = \arcsin(a_x) \tag{4}$$

Inverse Kinematics. ^ePe_b is a vector from the origin O_{pe} to the end-effector of DELTA-R Pe_b in the local frame Σ_{pe} with its origin at O_{pe}. As ^ePe_b is a rigid link in the kinematics, $|^ePe_b| = L/2$. Therefore, ^ePe_b can be obtained by using α and β as:

$$^ePe_b = \begin{bmatrix} \frac{L}{2}S_\beta & -\frac{L}{2}S_\alpha & \frac{L}{2}C_\alpha \end{bmatrix} \tag{5}$$

From (5), the vector ^0Pe_b in the reference frame Σ_0 can be given as:

$$^0Pe_b = \begin{bmatrix} P_{xb} & P_{yb} & P_{zb} \end{bmatrix}$$
$$= \begin{bmatrix} P_{ex} + \frac{L}{2}S_\beta & P_{ey} - \frac{L}{2}S_\alpha & P_{ez} + \frac{L}{2}C_\alpha \end{bmatrix} \tag{6}$$

Likewise, ^0Pe_f in the reference frame Σ_0 can be given as:

$$^0Pe_f = \begin{bmatrix} P_{xf} & P_{yf} & P_{zf} \end{bmatrix}$$
$$= \begin{bmatrix} P_{ex} - \frac{L}{2}S_\beta & P_{ey} + \frac{L}{2}S_\alpha & P_{ez} - \frac{L}{2}C_\alpha \end{bmatrix} \tag{7}$$

Therefore, ^0Pe_b and ^0Pe_f can be obtained from $Pe = [P_{ex}\ P_{ey}\ P_{ez}]$, α, β.

3   Implementation

Fig.3 shows the developed prototype of D-8. The prototype is installed on an armrest, which the tilt angle is adjustable from 0° to 30° for different users. The working area of D-8 mechanism can be defined as the cross over area of a pair of DELTA-R mechanisms. The working area of translational motions is illustrated in Fig.5. The working area of rotational motions are ±65° in pitch and ±90° in yaw in all working area. As DELTA-R mechanism does not have singularity point in its working area[7], D-8 mechanism does not have singularity point. The size of the prototype is 400 mm in height, 395 mm in width and 395 mm in depth (not including the armrest). Eight AC servo motors (SGMPS-02AC, Yasukawa Electric Corporation, Japan) are implemented on a fixed base. The motors are implemented in direct-drive for realizing a high backdrivability. As the specifications of the AC servo motors, rated power, rated torque, rated speed, resolution and inertial moment are 200 W, 0.637 N-m, 3000 rpm, $131072(2^{17})$ and 0.263×10^{-4} kgm^2 respectively. By using these motors, the maximum output force of the prototype (continuous) is 16 N in translations and 240 N-mm in rotations. More detailed specifications of the prototype are shown in Table 1. As a passive roll motion, an optical encoder (MEH-9-1000PC, Harmonic Drive Systems Inc., Japan) was implemented. The resolution of the encoder is 1000 pulse/rev. The electric wiring was put

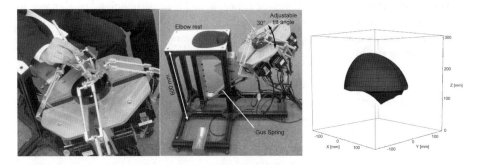

Fig. 3. Overview   **Fig. 4.** Armrest configuration   **Fig. 5.** Working area

Table 1. Mechanical specifications of the prototype

Working area	Translation: $100 \times 100 \times 100$ mm
	Rotation: Pitch $\pm 65°$ and Yaw $\pm 90°$
Output force	Translations: continuous 16 N in X, Y and Z axes
	Rotations: continuous 240 N-mm in pitch(α) and yaw(β)
Resolutions	Liner 0.01 mm, Angler 0.01 deg
Dimension	Height 400 mm, width 395 mm, depth 395 mm

through inside of the mechanical links. In this implementation, the motors were controlled by VxWorks 5.5.1 in the control frequency of 1 kHz. For impedance type haptic devices, it is important to output a desired force without having a force sensor feedback. Therefore, only the inverse kinematic model and Jacobian are used for calculating the torque of each motor for displaying the force on the prototype.

4 Evaluations

Evaluation tests were conducted to clarify the mechanical characteristic of D-8 mechanism on the prototype in a quantitative manner.

4.1 Accuracy of Display Force

Experimental Setup. The output force was measured in 5 points, 1(0, 0, 200), 2(-50,-50,200), 3(50,-50,200), 4(50,50,200) and 5(-50,50,200), in the reference frame O. The translational force and rotational force was displayed in each axis, X, Y, Z, α and β. The translational force was varied from 0 to 4 N, and the rotational force was varied from 0 to 0.1 N-m. A 6 axes force sensor (IFS-50M31A25-I25, Nitta Corporation, Japan) was positioned in each point by setting a sensor jig to measure the display force. The generated force was calculated only by the kinematic model and the measured force was not fed back to the controller.

Experimental Result. A representative experimental results (in point 1) are shown in Fig.6. From these results, the force was displayed in 0.056 N of average error (0.13 N of maximum error) in translations, and 0.0018 N-m of average error (0.0043 N-m of maximum error) in rotations. On the other hand, a "crosstalk" force was observed between X-Y axes at the maximum 0.18 N in X axis and 0.38 N in Y axis in translational force output. As a reason of the crosstalk, it is supposed to be a distortion of the mechanical structures. However, the amount of the crosstalk is relatively small comparing the output force. Therefore, from these results, it is shown that the prototype has a capability of accurate force display.

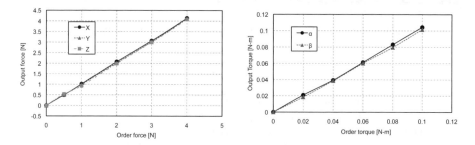

Fig. 6. Results of accuracy of display force test (left: in translations, right: in rotations)

4.2   Rigidity

Experimental Setup. Fig.7 shows the overview of the experimental setup. The end-effector was fixed at the center of working area (at point 1 of the previous test) by fixing all active joints during the measurement. The load was gradually applied from 0 to 5 N in every 1 N. Then the load was gradually unloaded in every 1 N in the same manner in X, Y and Z axes. Optotrak Certus (Northern Digital Inc., US.) [9] was used for the position measurement by putting optical markers on the prototype.

Experimental Result. The experimental result is shown in Fig.8. The points on the graph represent the average of the measurements of 5 sec in 100 Hz. The range of the mean error was less than 0.02 mm. The experimental result revealed that the rigidity of the prototype of X, Y and Z axes are 7.00, 5.43 and 4.71 N/mm respectively. In general, it is challenging to realize a rigid mechanism with a multi-DOF structure. As a multi-DOF haptic device using a serial link mechanism, PHANTOM Premium 3.0[8] realized a rigidity of 1.0 N/mm. Therefore, from the result, an advantageous performance of the D-8 mechanism on the rigidity was shown.

4.3   Resistance Force in Free-Hand Motion

Experimental Setup. A force sensor (Nitta Corporation, IFS-50M31A25-I25) was attached on the end-effector, and grabbed by a operator to measure the resistance force (Fig.9). A free-hand circular motion (in X-Y, X-Z and Y-Z planes) in approximately 80 mm/s was performed by the operator. In this test, the effect of gravity was compensated by using the AC servo motors.

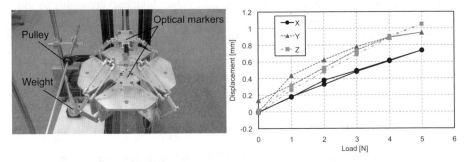

Fig. 7. Setup of rigidity test

Fig. 8. Results of rigidity test

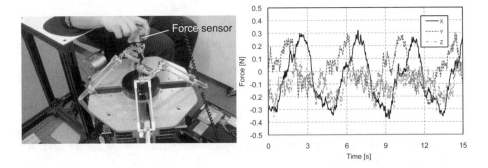

Fig. 9. Setup of resistance force test

Fig. 10. Result of resistance force test (in X-Y)

Experimental Result. From the experimental record, the average speed of the input motion was 78.5 mm/s. Fig.10 shows the experimental results in the X-Y plane as a representing result. The resistance force was observed periodically in the results. As the peak value was observed in the point, where the operator changed the direction, the main causes of the resistance force can be regarded as an inertia force and a static friction of motors and joints. The maximum resistance force was observed as 0.37 N, 0.37 N and 0.60 N in X, Y and Z axes respectively. From these results, it was revealed that the the prototype has a significantly high backdrivability.

5 Conclusions

In this paper, a new multi-DOF haptic device using a redundant parallel mechanism D-8 was presented. D-8 is an extension of DELTA-R mechanism, which is a translational 3 DOF redundant parallel mechanism, proposed in our past study. In the D-8 mechanism, an end-effector is held by a pair of DELTA-R mechanisms, which are located in face-to-face. The most advantageous feature of D-8 mechanism comparing the past presented studies is a wide range of rotational working area within the multi-DOF structure. In addition, D-8 realizes advantages of general parallel mechanisms in haptic devices such as a high rigidity, high output force, a high accuracy and a high backdrivability by introducing its redundant mechanism. Evaluation tests were conducted on the prototype of D-8 mechanism. The experimental results of an accuracy test and a rigidity test revealed the advantageous features of D-8. Moreover, it was shown that the backdrivability of D-8 was significantly high. Therefore, from these results, the effectiveness of the presented mechanism was positively shown.

Acknowledgments

A part of this study was funded by NEDO P08006 "Intelligent Surgical Instruments Project", Japan.

References

1. Pierrot, F., Uchiyama, M., Dauchez, P., Fournier, A.: A New Design of a 6-DOF Parallel Robot. J. Robotics and Mechatronics 2(4), 308–315 (1991)
2. Stewart, D.: A Platform with Six Degrees of Freedom. Proc. of the Institution of Mechanical Engineers 1965-1966, 180(1)15, 371–386 (1965)
3. Haption, http://www.haption.com
4. Asano, T., Yano, H., Iwata, H.: Basic technology of simulation system for laparoscopic surgery in virtual environment with force display. In: Medicine Meets Virtual Reality, Global Healthcare Grid, Studies in Health Technology and Informatics, vol. 39, pp. 207–215. IOS Press, Amsterdam (1997)
5. Quanser, http://www.quanser.com/
6. Hayward, V.: Toward a seven axis haptic device. In: Proc. of the IEEE/RSJ Int. Conf. of intelligent Robots and Systems, pp. 133–139 (1993)
7. Arata, J., Kondo, H., Sakaguchi, M., Fujimoto, H.: A haptic device DELTA-4: kinematics and its analysis. In: Proc. world Haptics, pp. 452–457 (2009)
8. SensAble Technologies, http://www.sensable.com/
9. Optotrak Certus, http://www.ndigital.com/medical/certus.php
10. Clavel, R.: Conception d'un robot parallèle rapide à 4 degrés de liberté. Ph.D. Thesis, EPFL, Lausanne, No.925 (1991)

Estimation of Normal and Tangential Manipulation Forces by Using Contact Force Sensors

Ignacio Galiana, Marta Bielza, and Manuel Ferre

Universidad Politécnica de Madrid, Centro de Automática y Robótica (UPM-CSIC)
José Gutiérrez Abascal 2, 28006 Madrid, Spain
{ignacio.galiana,marta.bielza}@etsii.upm.es, m.ferre@upm.es

Abstract. This article describes the design and development of a lightweight, adjustable end-effector for different haptic interfaces that estimates normal and tangential forces felt by the user during virtual object manipulation. This thimble was specially designed to provide information about the computed force exerted to the user when manipulating a virtual object with a haptic interface by using four contact force sensors (contact force sensors only measure the force component normal to its active area). Likewise, the aim of this paper is focused on the mechanical design, which relies on developing an adjustable mechanical tool non-finger-size dependant.

Keywords: Force-Sensing resistors, Force measurement, Haptic devices, manipulation forces, force estimation, contact force sensors.

1 Introduction

Haptic interfaces provide the user force information from virtual environments, this force is reflected to the user and is usually calculated based on fingertip's penetration with virtual objects according to Hooke's law with damping. In recent years, haptic interfaces have received a lot of attention; they have found their way into applications, such as medical training, rehabilitation, virtual prototyping, telesurgery, telemaintenance as well as manipulation [1]. Some of these tasks require at least two points of contact to recreate the action of pushing, squeezing or grasping different objects and adjustable end-effectors that fit properly to the user's hand/finger are needed to facilitate precise manipulation of the environment.

The use of multi-finger haptic devices increases the realism of the manipulation, and recreates the virtual object interaction in a more natural and easy way.

Measuring computed forces that represent user interaction with virtual objects can be used for haptic data segmentation based on force and position measurements, this approach is very challenging because of the interdependency of the data [2].

In this paper, a lightweight end effector that estimates normal and tangential forces by using contact force sensors is described. In section 2, the calibration of the contact force sensors, the mechanical set-up of the thimble is described and its precision is calculated. In section 3, an example of haptic data segmentation for complex scenarios is described.

A.M.L. Kappers et al. (Eds.): EuroHaptics 2010, Part I, LNCS 6191, pp. 65–72, 2010.

2 Sensorized Thimble

As a new alternative to haptic interface's end-effectors, a sensorized thimble has been designed in order to allow direct interaction between the user's fingers and the computed virtual environments.

The geometry of this Thimble is very similar to the human finger in order to obtain similar touch responses. It is cone-shaped, narrow at the top and a little thicker at the bottom where the distal phalanx bounds the beginning of the middle phalanx in a real finger.

The thimble has been designed so that it can be easily adjusted to different finger sizes. For that purpose, the design includes a system of screws that can be tight to both sides of the finger, maintaining it safely locked during the haptic interaction. The pressure added by the screws interferes with the perception of the user; this pressure should be enough to lock the finger but not so much so as to stress the user.

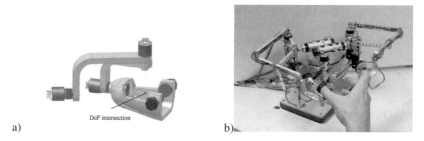

a)   b)

Fig. 1. a) Gimbal with three DoF that intersect at the same point. b) Designed thimble as an end effector of a multi-finger haptic device.

The thimble is attached to a gimbal system with three rotational axis that intersect in the user's fingertip as shown in Fig.1. This configuration assures that only forces are reflected to the user.

2.1 Flexiforce Sensors

In order to estimate forces felt by the user, four Flexiforce sensors provided by the company Tekscan Inc [3] were added to the thimble that has been previously described. These sensors were selected due to its thinness (0.2 mm),lightweight, and performance specifications, particularly its repeatability which is +/- 2.5%. Besides, they were found very cost effective for these applications compared with other products in market. The sensor model used is A201-25, which has a range from 0 to 11 kgf (0 to 25 lbf).

The Flexiforce sensor is an ultra-thin and flexible printed circuit. The active sensing area is a 0.375'' diameter circle located at the end of the sensor. This sensor acts as a variable resistor in an electrical circuit. When the sensor is unloaded, its resistance is very high (greater than 5Meg-ohm) and when a force is applied to the sensor, the resistance decreases.

The electronic circuit used was the one recommended by the manufacturer, which is shown in Fig.2.

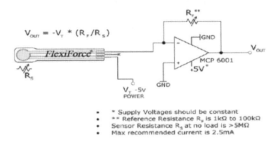

- * Supply Voltages should be constant
- ** Reference Resistance R_r is 1kΩ to 100kΩ
- Sensor Resistance R_s at no load is >5MΩ
- Max recommended current is 2.5mA

Fig. 2. Electronic circuit used for each sensor

2.1.1 Contact Force Sensors Calibration

To calibrate the selected sensors, the first thing that had to be taken into account is that force should be applied in a homogeneous way over the active sensing area of the sensor; to assure this a "sandwich configuration" was used, this consists on two sheets of metal of the same diameter that this active area as shown in Fig.5.c.

This calibration has been done using the Flexiforce force sensor and a high-accuracy ATI [4]. This sensor depicted in Fig.3. measures the 6-dimensional force components (forces/torques) using a monolithic transducer with silicon extensiometric gauges, obtaining excellent noise immunity.

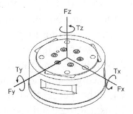

Fig. 3. ATI sensor and axis

The sensors were located so that a normal force applied to the Flexiforce sensor was measured in the z-axis of the ATI sensor. This way, the calibration was done using a least squares polynomial interpolation between the force measured by the ATI sensor and the voltage obtained in Flexiforce circuit. The resulting polynomial interpolation for the Flexiforce calibration was:

$$F(V)=0.0557V^7 - 0.9616V^6 + 6.5957V^5 - 22.9525V^4 + 42.9525V^3 - 41.9706V^2 + 22.0111V + 0.0648 \tag{1}$$

The results obtained from the Flexiforce and the ATI sensors were very similar in a range from 0 to 18 N (Fig.4.). This maximum force is usually enough when talking about haptic interfaces.

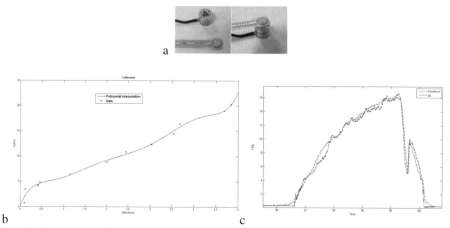

Fig. 4. a) Set-up for calibrating the contact force sensor. b) Least squares polynomial interpolation of the data. c) Comparison between Flexiforce and ATI outputs.

2.2 Sensors in the Thimble

The goal of adding the calibrated sensors to the thimble is to be able to estimate not only normal forces but tangential too (contact force sensors only measure the force component normal to its active area) while manipulating objects with haptic interfaces. To achieve this objective, four Flexiforce sensors were added to the Thimble. The position of the sensors inside the thimble was chosen strategically so that during the experiments one sensor measures the normal force exerted to the object and some other measures the tangential force applied, this disposition is shown in Fig.5. d. In order to make sure that the whole forces felt by the user are transmitted to the sensing area of the sensors (with the sandwich configuration), four fingerprint-shaped metal sheets were added to the design, as shown on Fig.5 c.

Including the sensors, the total weight of the thimble is 30 gr., which is very convenient for haptic applications. Low weight implies a device with lower inertia, and, consequently, less interference with the perception of the virtual world. In haptic interfaces, high inertia can lead to instabilities and reduce the minimum force that the user is able to feel [5],[6].

The first thing that had to be considered was that sensors located at the finger sides measured not only the force applied, but also the pressure used to fix the finger to the thimble; deformations that appear in the finger when pressing a surface also increased the pressure applied to the sensors located at these positions (Fig.6.a). According to the symmetrical position of the finger sides in the thimble, the fixing pressure and finger deformations make the same force over both lateral sensors. This way, the solution was to subtract one measure to the other, getting, as a result, the real force applied to the object. For instance, when pressing a surface in a normal direction (Fig.6.a), the sensor located at the bottom of the finger should be the only one that measures force, thus force measured by sensors 2 and 3 (sensors located at the finger sides) is mainly due to deformations in the finger, but as was stated before is the same in both of them (The result after subtracting will be close to 0 N).

To illustrate this distortion on the measures, a cylinder that was known to weight 4.5N was lifted horizontally using two thimbles as shown in Fig.5.b; with this disposition, the sensor located under the fingertip should measure the force applied in the normal direction to the cylinder, while the tangential force should be estimated by the sensor located at the upper finger side and should be equal to half of the total weight of the cylinder (because there were two thimbles). The results of this experiment are shown in Fig.6.b; the highest force value is the one measured by sensor 1 (corresponding to the normal force exerted by the user). The real tangential force is the subtraction of the two measures of the lateral sensors. The total weight obtained is 4.3-2= 2.3N, which is a good approximation for half of the weight of the cylinder. As a conclusion, we can state that the measure that was obtained is correct and equal to what was expected.

Fig. 5. a) Developed thimble and position of the sensors inside the thimble. b) Experiment measuring forces when grabbing a cylinder (upper view). c) Flexiforce and mechanical. d) CAD design.

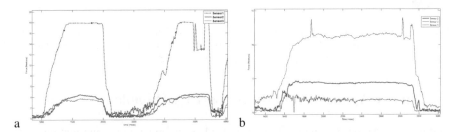

Fig. 6. a) Forces when pressing a surface with the thimble. b) Forces when grabbing and lifting the cylinder with the disposition shown in Fig.5.

2.3 Precision of the Designed Thimble

To check the quality of the estimation of normal and tangential forces with the designed thimble, a thimble that contained both the ATI and the contact force sensors was designed (Fig.7). With this new design, the thimble was adjusted and force was applied in different directions. When comparing the estimation of forces using the contact force sensors with the data obtained with the high precision sensor, it was noticed that, when varying the force, the flank of the signal measured by the Flexiforce and the one measured by the ATI sensor were very similar. This information can be useful for some applications in haptic interfaces such as task segmentation.

The error between the estimated value and the measured value is +/-1.43N in a range from 0 to 20 N; this is a tolerable deviation for some applications that we are designing.

To check the precision in the detection of flanks of forces, an approximation of the first derivative was calculated for the forces measured by the ATI sensor and for the contact force sensors. This derivative function was estimated for the discrete values obtained by the sensors using the following expression:

$$DF/Dt=(F_i - F_{i-500})/\Delta t \tag{2}$$

The standard deviation of the difference between both first derivate responses was equal to +/- 0,166 N/sec. As it was introduced, the precision of the estimation of manipulation forces is much more precise for flank detection than for obtaining exact values of normal and tangential forces.

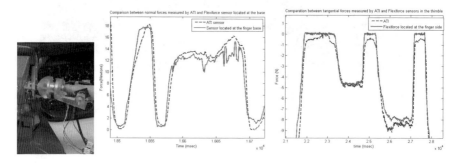

Fig. 7. a) Thimble with ATI and Flexiforce sensors. b) Comparison between normal forces measured by ATI and Fexiforce located at the finger base. c) Comparison between tangential forces measured by ATI and Fexiforce located at the finger sides.

3 Example Application of the Sensorized Thimble

Getting information of forces felt by a user when grabbing and manipulating a complex object may facilitate the design of a virtual model of that same object. For this purpose, in this experiment, forces that a user feels when manipulating a real bottle with water are recorded with the thimble that incorporated contact force sensors.

As shown on Fig.8, the normal force applied to the bottle is estimated by sensor 1 (sensor located under the fingertip), and the tangential force is estimated by sensor 3 (the sensor located at the upper finger side). The tangential force when grabbing the bottle in a vertical position should be, as in the lifting of the cylinder, equal to half of the total weight of the bottle with the water in it. As the bottle is tilted it can be noticed how the tangential force decreases. If the bottle is in a horizontal position, the tangential force estimated is 0N. From this position, if the tilting continues, the sensor that measures the tangential force is no longer the sensor 3, but sensor 2 (this sensor is now the one located on the upper finger side). If the bottle is returned to its vertical state, the tangential force is the corresponding to half of its weight; we can see that the weight has decreased, this is because the bottle was open and some fluid was spilled.

In this experiment, the sensorized thimble can give useful information about task segmentation, and this information can be very useful to know what forces should be applied to the user and know what task is he performing at any time when manipulating this complex object. In Fig.8 an example of task segmentation is shown, first, the user approximates to the bottle (A), when the user is in the correct position, he grabs the bottle (B) until he is able to lift it (C), after that he holds the bottle vertically (D), and starts tilting (E) until the bottle is in an horizontal state, he continues to tilt the bottle and tilts it back to the horizontal state (G), after that, he holds the bottle vertically again and releases it over a table (I).

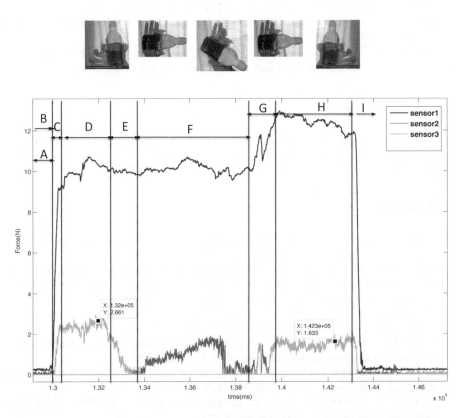

Fig. 8. Forces measured when manipulating a bottle with water in it. Task segmentation: A: Approximating the bottle. B: Starts to grab the bottle. C: Grabbing the bottle. D: Grabbing the Bottle vertically. E: Tilting the bottle to a horizontal state. F: Continue tilting the bottle, and tilting it back to a horizontal state. G: Tilting the bottle back to a vertical position. H: Grabbing the bottle in a vertical state. I: The user releases the bottle.

4   Conclusions

In this article, the design of a sensorized end effector for haptic interfaces is presented. This Thimble-sensor can estimate normal and tangential forces by using contact force sensors (contact force sensors only measure forces applied in the normal direction) located at strategic points in the thimble.

Flexiforce contact force sensors have been calibrated obtaining an error of +/-0,3N by using the so-called "sandwich configuration" that ensures that the load is uniformly distributed over the active sensing area of these sensors.

The thimble has been developed to increase the immersion feeling of the user within virtual environments. It incorporates four contact force sensors placed on strategic points to estimate normal and tangential forces during manipulation. The precision of this thimble-sensor is +/-1,43N in a range from 0 to 15 N. This sensor-thimble has been included to the MasterFinger-2 [7] haptic interface providing direct interaction of the user with virtual environments by using its index and thumb fingers facilitating the realization of precision manipulation.

The information obtained with this thimble-sensor can be used to do task segmentation that can be useful when performing complex manipulations.

Acknowledgement

This work has been partially funded by the European Comission under the "IMMERSENCE" (FP6-IST-4-027141), Spanish Ministerio de Ciencia e Innovación under the project "TEMAR"(DPI 2009-12283) and formación de personal investigador (RR01/2009) UPM.

References

1. Peer, A., Buss, M.: A New Admittance-Type Haptic Interface for Bimanual Manipulations. IEEE/ASME Transactions on Mechatronics 13(4) (August 2008)
2. Stefanov, N., Peer, A., Buss, M.: Role Determination in Human-Human Interaction. In: Third Joint Eurohaptics Conference and Symposium on Haptic Interfaces for Virtual Environment and Teleoperator System, Salt Lake City, USA (2009)
3. Flexiforce Sensor, http://www.sample.co.kr/flexiforce/ssbmanual.pdf
4. ATI Sensor, http://www.ati-ia.com/products/ft/sensors.aspx
5. Daniel, R.W., McAree, P.R.: Fundamental limits of performance for force reflecting teleoperation. Int. Journal of Robotics Research 17(8), 811–830 (1998)
6. Shull, P.B., Niemeyer, G.: Force and position scaling limits for stability in force reflecting teleoperation. In: Proc. of IMECE 2008 (October 2008)
7. Monroy, M., Oyarzabal, M., Ferre, M., Campos, A., Barrio, J.: MasterFinger: Multifinger Haptic Interface for Collaborative Environments
8. Monrroy, M., Ferre, M., Barrio, J., Eslava, V., Galiana, I.: Sensorized thimble for haptics applications. In: Proc. of IEEE ICM 2009, Spain (2009)
9. García-Robledo, P., Ortego, J., Barrio, J., Galiana, I., Ferre, M., Aracil, R.: Multifinger haptic interface for bimanual manipulation of virtual objects. In: IEEE Congress on HAVE 2009, Italy (2009)

Modeling and Experimental Studies of a Novel 6-DOF Haptic Device

Zhouming Tang and Shahram Payandeh

Experimental Robotics Laboratory, Simon Fraser University
8888 University Drive, Burnaby, BC, Canada, V5A 1S6
zta3@sfu.ca, shahram@cs.sfu.ca

Abstract. This paper presents modeling and experimental studies of a new type of haptic device which combines the spherical parallel and the serial configurations. The paper presents an overview of our design and then outlines the procedure for mapping the force/moment vector acting on the stylus coordinate frame of the device to its joint torque. The paper then demonstrates the experimental studies of the new haptic device. Results demonstrates the performance of the kinematic mapping of the device and compares the computed haptic force feedback with the measured force/moment data at the stylus of the device. Interaction with a test-based virtual environment further demonstrates the actual performance of the device.

Keywords: Haptic device, spherical parallel/serial configuration, kinematic modeling, force modeling, experimental studies, haptic force feedback.

1 Introduction

Haptic interfaces are electro-mechanical devices that provide users with the sense of contact forces information while interacting in virtual or remote tele-operation environment. The essential objective of haptic interfaces is to match between the forces and displacements given by user and those of the virtual or remote tele-operation environment. As such, this requires the haptic device to have large workspace, low friction and inertia properties of its moving parts and high stiffness and precision. In addition, in order to maintain the global stability of the closed-loop system, a passive computational/control environment is required [1] - [3].

Various 6-DOF haptic devices have been designed commercially and also at various research institutes. For example, the PHANTOM Premium 1.5/6-DOF and 3.0/6-DOF devices from SensAble Technologies Inc [4] and the Freedom 6S device from MPB Technologies Inc [5] are designed mostly based on serial robot configuration with relatively large workspace. The Omega-6 and Delta-6 devices from Force Dimension [6] are designed based on combination of two 3-DOF parallel robot configuration. In addition to the commercialized devices, other types of 6-DOF haptic devices have been investigated at various research institutions. S.S. Lee and J.M. Lee [7] present a general-purpose 6-DOF haptic device featuring a parallel combination of three serial manipulators. The performance of the device is evaluated by examining the force feedback at the

A.M.L. Kappers et al. (Eds.): EuroHaptics 2010, Part I, LNCS 6191, pp. 73–80, 2010.

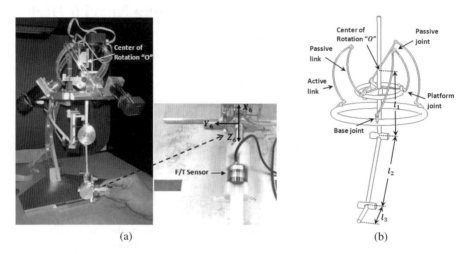

(a)   (b)

Fig. 1. The 6-DOF haptic device: (a): the prototyped 6-DOF haptic device; (b): the kinematic configuration of hybrid parallel/serial haptic device

handle giving step and sinusoidal inputs. In addition, a force reflection along the trajectory of motion generated by the operator is presented to demonstrate that the device is able to serve as motion generator. G. Carbone and M. Ceccarelli [8] propose a serial-parallel robot manipulator for medical applications. It is composed of a commercially available 3-DOF serial robot and a prototype of 3-DOF parallel manipulator. The serial mechanism is responsible for positioning since it possesses larger workspace while the parallel mechanism is responsible for performing the actual surgery. In this paper, we introduce modeling and experimental studies of a novel design hybrid 6-DOF haptic device for surgical training application.

2   Overview of the 6-DOF Haptic Device

Figure 1a) depicts the prototype of the haptic device while Figures 1b) show its kinematic configuration. The spherical parallel mechanism part of the device is composed by three identical kinematic chains where each has 3 revolute joints. In this configuration, the moving platform is supported by both active parallel spherical mechanism and by passive spherical joint located at the center of rotation. The active part controls the orientation of the mobile platform while the passive part supports the static weight of the robot and the resultant user interaction force on the mobile platform. As a result, the center of platform can move along the geodesic paths on a sphere having a fixed redial distance about the center of rotation "O". A rigid link l_1 (Figure 1b) is connected to the moving platform which is the supporting base of the serial manipulator. The two intersecting joint axes at the end of l_2 is the wrist of the device where the stylus is attached to and also where the force/moment transducer can be mounted. Figure 2 depicts the approximation of the reachable workspace of the device. The current dimensions of the workspace, l_1, l_2, l_3 and l_4, are 146mm, 128mm, 449mm and 261mm respectively. Overall, the combination

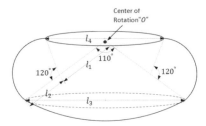

Fig. 2. Approximation of the reachable workspace

of the parallel spherical and serial configuration has following advantages: 1) location for the actuators are away from the moving platform; 2) larger workspace for the end-effector through the connecting link to the platform. Previously, we have presented the forward and inverse kinematic models in [9] and [10]. In this paper, we experimentally evaluate and verify the kinematic and force/torque correspondences.

3   Force Mapping

In this paper, we propose a two-step approach to solve for actuator joint torques given the desire force and moment at the end-effector. First, we determine the joint torques of serial mechanism and the resultant moment vector exerted at the mobile platform. Then, we solve for the actuator joint torques of the spherical parallel mechanism given the torque vector exerted at the coordinate of the mobile platform. An inward iteration method introduced in [11] is utilized to solve for the joint torques of the serial robot in terms of the torque/moment exerted on the end-effector. Referring to Figure 3a), we denote the desire force and moment acting on the end-effector as F_6 and M_6 respectively, where F_6 is $[F_{x_6}, F_{y_6}, F_{z_6}]^T$ and M_6 is $[M_{x_6}, M_{y_6}, M_{z_6}]^T$. The torques of actuator joint 6, 5 and 4 (τ_6, τ_5, τ_4) are expressed as shown in equation (1), where s_6 and c_6 represent $\sin(\theta_6)$ and $\cos(\theta_6)$ respectively. The expression for the moment vector acting on the platform, M_p, is not presented in this paper due to the space constraint [10].

$$
\begin{aligned}
\tau_6 &= M_{z_6} \, , \\
\tau_5 &= -s_6 M_{x_6} - c_6 M_{y_6} \, , \\
\tau_4 &= -s_6 M_{x_6} - c_6 M_{y_6} - 128 c_5 (c_6 F_{x_6} - s_6 F_{y_6}) + 128 s_5 F_{z_6} \, ,
\end{aligned}
\tag{1}
$$

Having obtained the moment vector acting on the platform, the actuating torque of the three spherical parallel joints (τ_1, τ_2, τ_3) can be obtained by solving the extended Jacobian matrix of the spherical parallel mechanism [12] as shown in equation (2). The extended Jacobian is $(B^{-1}A)R$, where matrix A and B are obtained based on the passive joint axes ($W_i, i = 1, 2, 3$), platform joint axes V_i and base joint axes U_i of each kinematic chain of the spherical parallel mechanism; matrix R maps the angular velocities of the mobile platform to the Euler angular velocities.

$$
\tau = B^T (AR)^{-T} M_p \, ,
\tag{2}
$$

where, $A = \left[(W_1 \times V_1)^T, (W_2 \times V_2)^T, (W_3 \times V_3)^T \right]^T$, $B = diag(U_i \times W_i \cdot V_i)$.

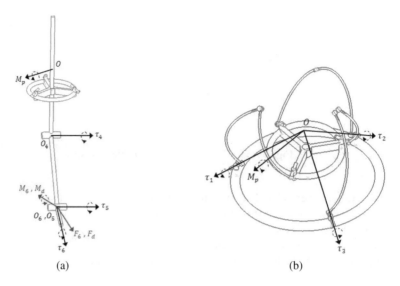

(a)   (b)

Fig. 3. Force mapping of the haptic device: (a): force mapping from the end-effector to joint 6, joint 5, joint 4 and the mobile platform; (b): force mapping from the mobile platform to joint 1, joint 2 and joint 3

4   Experimental Studies

4.1   Kinematic Correspondence

Kinematic correspondence is aimed to examine the forward kinematic models of the haptic device. For example, determining the position of the stylus of the haptic device when the user moves it along an arbitrary trajectory which for examples starts and terminates at the physical home position of the device. In this case, while the user manipulate the haptic device, the kinematic correspondence system collects the six joint angles, determines the position and orientation of the stylus reference coordinate system based on the forward kinematic model, and renders the corresponding graphic configuration of the haptic device in real time. Three sets of joint angles S_1, S_2 and S_3 recorded at 1st, 1500th and 2500th sample respectively are utilized to examine the forward kinematic model as shown in Table 1.

The three sets of joint angles are used in the forward kinematic model to solve for the position and orientation of stylus coordinate frame at the corresponding selected

Table 1. List of joint angles at the three selected samples (S_1 is recorded at the 1st sample, S_2 is recorded at the 1500th sample and S_3 is recorded at the 2500st sample)

	θ_1	θ_2	θ_3	θ_4	θ_5	θ_6
S_1	42.19°	47.76°	45°	−13.65°	−81.49°	0°
S_2	64.14°	59.65°	42.03°	−28.74°	−78.23°	−42.37°
S_3	35.33°	27.64°	49.57°	−59.6°	−87.42°	−95.41°

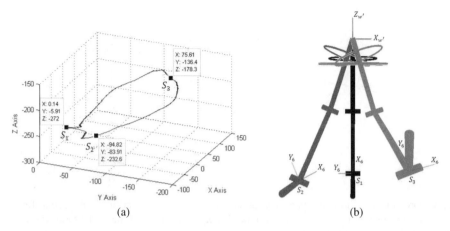

(a)   (b)

Fig. 4. Kinematic correspondence experiment results: (a): real time records of the trajectory of the end-effector; (b): graphical display of the haptic device

sample. The resulting forward kinematic solutions are described in equation (3). For example, $_6^{W'} T_{S_i} (i = 1,2,3)$ represents the forward kinematic solution of the S_i sample.

$$
_6^{W'} T_{S_1} = \begin{bmatrix} 0 & -1 & 0 & 0.15 \\ -0.16 & 0 & -0.99 & -5.9 \\ 0.99 & 0 & -0.16 & -272.02 \\ 0 & 0 & 0 & 1 \end{bmatrix}, _6^{W'} T_{S_2} = \begin{bmatrix} 0.89 & -0.44 & -0.07 & -94.81 \\ 0.13 & 0.41 & -0.9 & -83.93 \\ 0.42 & 0.8 & 0.43 & -232.58 \\ 0 & 0 & 0 & 1 \end{bmatrix}, _6^{W'} T_{S_3} = \begin{bmatrix} 0.96 & -0.17 & -0.2 & 75.62 \\ 0.08 & 0.9 & -0.41 & -136.44 \\ 0.25 & 0.38 & 0.89 & -178.28 \\ 0 & 0 & 0 & 1 \end{bmatrix}.
$$

(3)

Figure 4a) presents the trajectory of the end-effector recorded through the manipulation in real time. This figure is able to verify the position solution of the forward kinematic model. In order to verify the orientation solution of the forward kinematic model and to visualize the physical change of the device along the trajectory, three graphic representations of the device are depicted in Figure 4b). These three graphic representations are overlapped by aligning the $\{W'\}$ frame. In addition, they are black, gray and light gray colored which correspond to device configuration at S_1, S_2 and S_3 respectively.

4.2 Force Correspondence Experiments and Results

Six experiments are designed, each of which takes the desired force or torque value at the stylus as input, determines the corresponding six actuator joint torques and renders the force feedback accordingly. Specifically, the first four experiments take the desire force magnitude of 1 N along $\pm Z_6$ axis and $\pm Y_6$ axis respectively. The last two experiments take the desire torque magnitude of 1 Nm along $\pm X_6$ axis restively. These six experiments are chosen to present the characteristics of the force and torque correspondence of the haptic device in present state. The actual measured force and torque results are collected from the F/T sensor which is mounted at the end-effector as shown in Figure 1a).

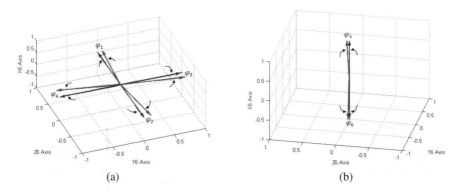

(a)   (b)

Fig. 5. Force mapping test results at the end-effector: (a): direction errors of the actual force vectors with respect to the desire force vectors; (b): direction errors of the actual torque vectors with respect to the desire torque vectors

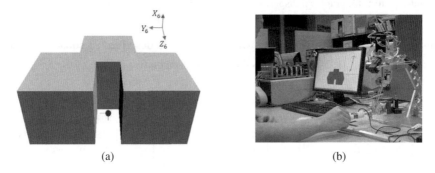

(a)   (b)

Fig. 6. Interaction with virtual walls: (a): the virtual environment; (b): user interact with virtual environment

Figure 5a) and Figure 5b) show the desire force or torque vectors and the normalized actual measured force or torque vectors of the six experiments. The vectors of red color are the normalized actual measured force or torque vectors while the vectors of blue color are the desire force or torque vectors. The direction errors between the desire and actual force or torque vectors are denoted by $\varphi_1, \ldots, \varphi_6$. The values of these angles are $4.29°, 6.91°, 7.85°, 11.43°, 2.11°$ and $1.32°$ respectively. The relatively significant error occurs when the desire force vectors are along positive or negative Y_6 axis. This can be attributed to the posture of the user holding the force sensor.

Having established the force correspondence system, we present some preliminary results when the haptic device interact with virtual environment. Figure 6a) exhibits the virtual environment of this experiment, the blue cursor represents the stylus; the red, green and blue lines on the cursor represent the X, Y and Z axes of the stylus; the three sides of the vertical notch which are located at the back, left side and right side of the end-effector, represent three virtual walls. A spring model with the stiffness coefficient of 1 N/mm is applied to model the virtual wall. Since we have not yet included any damping or passivity control mechanism into the haptic interface, the stiffness coefficient

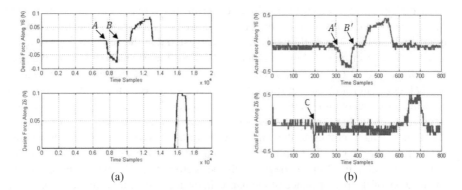

(a)   (b)

Fig. 7. Computed and measured haptic force results when interact with virtual walls: (a): the desire force along Y_6 axis (upper portion) and Z_6 axis (lower portion); (b): the actual force along Y_6 axis (upper portion) and Z_6 axis (lower portion)

is selected at relatively low level. In this experiment, as depicted in Figure 6b), the user moves the stylus of the haptic device starting from the physical home position and then makes contact with the virtual walls located on the left side, the right side and back side sequentially. The desire force is computed and recorded at 1 KHz while the actual force from the F/T force sensor is collected at 40 Hz. Figure 7a) shows the desired force along Y_6 axis (upper portion) and Z_6 axis (lower portion), while Figure 7b) depicts the actual measured force along Y_6 axis (upper portion) and Z_6 axis (lower portion).

The results reflect the three contact events. For example, the first contact event takes place at the left side virtual wall at between 7.62 second and 8.98 second, and the expected reaction force is along the negative Y_6 direction. This can be observed between A (7626th sample) and B (8985th sample) of the desire force plot along Y_6 axis (sampling rate is 1 KHz) in Figure 7a) and between $A^{'}$ (310th sample) and $B^{'}$ (386th sample) of the actual force plot along Y_6 axis (sampling rate is 40 Hz) in Figure 7b). The 0.15 second time delay of the actual force display is noticed according to the time difference between A and $A^{'}$. This can be attributed to the delays from varies different components in the haptic control loop (i.e. quantization delay and amplifier delay) and the serial communication with F/T controller. The magnitude of the actual force display is proportional to the amplifier gain (which is assigned to be 5 in this experiment). This can be observed by comparing the Y axis scale of the desire and actual force plots in Figure 7a) and 7b). The user can be active during the manipulation, which affects the results of the actual measured force. For example, a jitter of the force along Z_6 axis occurs at 5 second which corresponds to C (200th sample) of the actual force plot along Z_6 axis in Figure 7b). This is caused by the user dragging the stylus away from the physical home position.

5 Discussion and Conclusion

In this paper, the design of the proposed 6-DOF haptic device was reviewed. The force mapping of the hybrid structure haptic device was presented. The kinematic correspondence and force correspondence experiments were presented to evaluate the displacements and forces/torques correspondence given by user and those applied to the virtual environment. The preliminary results suggested that the actual force exerted at the hand of the user reflected the computed or desired force. The results also indicated time delay (about 0.15 seconds) which can be attributed to the serial communication with F/T controller and the various different delays in the haptic control loop, such as quantization delay and amplifier delay. The significance of such delay effect and secondary overlaid high frequency associations will be elevated as a part of the future user studies. It is hypothesize that such effect can be masked through the impedance model of the user, e.g. [13]. Comprehensive workspace analysis and comparison with existing commercialized haptic devices will be performed in the future. Furthermore, enhancement of the performance of the haptic interface will be investigated. For example, feed-forward compensation of the friction and inertia of the haptic device can be established to improve the force/torques correspondence.

References

1. Diolaiti, N., Niemeyer, G., Barbagli, F., Kenneth Salisbury Jr., J.: Stability of Haptic Rendering: Discretization, Quantization, Time Delay, and Coulomb Effects. IEEE Transactions on Robotics 22(2) (2006)
2. Adams, R.J., Hannaford, B.: Stable Haptic Interaction with Virtual Environments. IEEE Transactions on Robotics and Automation 15(3) (1999)
3. Hannaford, B., Ryu, J.: Time-Domain Passivity Control of Haptic Interfaces. IEEE Transactions on Robotics and Automation 18(1) (2002)
4. SensAble Technologies Inc., Specifications for PHANTOM Premium 3.0/6 DOF Haptic Interface (January 6, 2006),
   http://www.sensable.com/haptic-phantom-premium-6dof.htm (accessed: January 26, 2010)
5. MPB Technologies Inc, http://www.mpb-technologies.ca/ (accessed: January 26, 2010)
6. Force Dimension, http://www.forcedimension.com/products (accessed: Januaruy 26, 2010)
7. Lee, S.S., Lee, J.M.: Design of a general purpose 6-DOF haptic interface. Mechatronics 13, 697–722 (2003)
8. Carbone, G., Ceccarelli, M.: A serial-parallel robotic architecture for surgical tasks. Robotica 23, 345–354 (2005)
9. Tang, Z., Payandeh, S.: Design and modeling of a novel 6 degree of freedom haptic device, whc. In: World Haptics 2009 - Third Joint EuroHaptics conference and Symposium on Haptic Interfaces for Virtual Environment and Teleoperator Systems, pp. 523–528 (2009)
10. Tang, Z., Payandeh, S.: Kinematic Modeling and Solution of a Class of Hybrid Spherical/Serial Manipulator, Technical report, Experimental Robotics Lab, Simon Fraser University (2009), http://www.sfu.ca/~zta3/papers.html
11. Craig, J.J.: Introduction to robotics mechanics and control, 3rd edn. Pearson Prentice Hall, Upper Saddle River (2005)
12. Birglen, L., Gosselin, C.M.: SHaDe, A New 3-DOF Haptic Device. IEEE Transactions on Robotics and Automation 18(2) (2002)
13. Payandeh, S., Dill, J., Zhang, J.: A Study of Level-of-Detail in Haptic Rendering. ACM transaction for Applied Perception 2(1), 15–34 (2005)

Inertial Force Display to Represent
Content Inside the Box

Yuichiro Sekiguchi[1], Satoru Matsuoka[2], and Koichi Hirota[1]

[1] Graduate School of Frontier Sciences, University of Tokyo,
5-1-5 Kashiwanoha, Kashiwa, Chiba 277-8563, Japan
sekiguchi@media.k.u-tokyo.ac.jp, smatsuoka76@gmail.com,
k-hirota@k.u-tokyo.ac.jp
http://www.media.k.u-tokyo.ac.jp/hirota/
[2] Department of Mechanical Engineering, University of Tokyo,
7-3-1 Hongo, Bunkyo-ku, Tokyo 113-8656, Japan

Abstract. By shaking a box, we can estimate content inside. Relationship between force that is applied to the box and resulting motion of the box is considered to be a clue to the estimation. In this paper, we implement 4 physical models consist of a box and contents, and evaluate users' discrimination ability between different models and parameter of each models.

Keywords: force-motion relationship, inertial force display, haptics rendering.

1 Introduction

By shaking a box, we can estimate nature (e.g., solid, liquid, or powder) and quantity of content inside the box. In this type of estimation, the sensation of motion and sensation of force are playing an essential role. For example, total weight of the box and the content may be perceived by the sensation of force, and information on dynamic aspect of the content is acquired by force-motion relationship while shaking the box.

According to the wide spread of handheld devices, vibrators and acceleration sensors become very common functions for those devices. The acceleration sensor enables interactions using device motions, such as shaking, tapping, and titling, and vibrators also enables to output haptic signals to user. Thus, using these sensors and actuators, it is possible to construct interactions using force-motion relationship. And there are some research activities on these type of interaction[1][2].

In this paper, we discuss about the information transfer capability using this force-motion relationship scheme. We use previously proposed force-motion relationship device[3] to represent 4 physical models and evaluate the discrimination ability between these models. And we also evaluate the threshold for discrimination for the parameters of these models.

2 Related Works

According to advancement and downsizing of computers, a variety of wearable and handheld force feedback devices have been investigated. HapticGEAR is a wearable

A.M.L. Kappers et al. (Eds.): EuroHaptics 2010, Part I, LNCS 6191, pp. 81–86, 2010.

force feedback device that is grounded to a part of the user's body and present inter-nal force using some wire-based mechanism[4]. Yano et al proposed a handheld device based on Coriolis force. That actively changes the direction of rotation axis of fly-wheel, and generates Coriolis force[5]. Amemiya et al proposed a handheld device that displays pseudo force sensation using reciprocal motion of a mass[6]. Most of these researches are focusing on presentation of the sensation of force and torque, and used to display the direction information: furthermore they are not discussed approaches or framework to represent force-motion relationship.

There are some researches on haptic device that have focused on the aspect of in-formation transfer via force-motion relationship. Our previous work proposed a device that virtually feedbacks colliding impact using two solenoids. This represents collisions caused by shaking the box containing some contents[1]. The study also carried out an that evaluate user's ability to discriminate the number of balls in a box by shaking de-vice. Williamson et al implemented a more sophisticated device that is based on similar idea using vibrotactile sensations[2]. Both of these researches are focused on the only one model, a box containing some balls inside. Yao et al implemented a apparatus that represent a rolling stone inside the tube[7]. This work is similar to our work in repre-senting the model of the device's content. Our interests are expanding the number of representable models and the user's ability to discriminate those models.

3   Device Implementation

3.1   Inertial Force Display

Inertial force display is a device that present reaction force when a mass is accel-erated. Previously, we propose a device with one degree-of-freedom pendulum-type mechanism[3]. This device senses the motion by the acceleration sensor and swings the weight by motors. And this device is hanged from the 1.5m above to limit the de-vice movement on one axis. Figure 1 shows the control system(left) and the device image(right).

We applied a Kalman filter algorithm because of the acceleration sensor has much noise. The Kalman filter estimates the status of the device. State variables are $[\theta^*, \dot{\theta}^*, F^*]$,

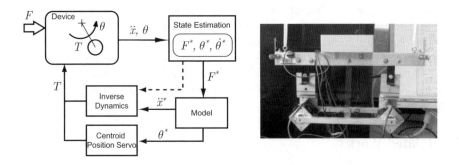

Fig. 1. Control system (left) and prototype device(right)

observable variables are $[\theta, \ddot{x}]$, and a control variable is $[T]$. In some cases the position of weight is displaced due to the lack of motor output power. We employ the servo mechanism for the device's centroid position to avoid this problem.

3.2 Representational Models

Figure 2 shows the 4 models we implemented.

Rigid body model does not have an inner contents. The weight of this model equals to the device's weight.

Pendulum model represents a box has a pendulum inside. The weight of the box is M_b and the weight of pendulum is M_w. The total weight of this model is also same to the devices'. The length of pendulum (l) is also changeable.

Spring-dumper model represents a box contains a weight connected to the box's wall by spring and dumper. The sum of M_b and M_w equals to the device's weight. The spring constant k and the damping coefficient c are controllable.

Box-contents model represents a box contains a solid object. The sum of M_b and M_w also equals to the device's weight. The contained object moves the box's inner space and bounces when collides with the box's inner wall. The elastic coefficient e and the friction coefficient C are controllable.

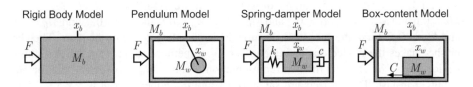

Fig. 2. Images of representational models

4 Experiment

4.1 Identification of Models

We evaluate the users' ability of model discriminations by using 4 models described in figure 2. First, the device represents one model and the subject shakes the device at most 10 seconds. Then, the device represents another (or sometimes same) model and he or she shakes the device at most 10 seconds. Finally he or she answers the two represented models are same or different. The pair of models are represented random order, and each pair is represented once. Thus, we done $4 \times 4 = 16$ trials for each subject. The number of subjects is 8 and all subjects are college students without background of haptics. Before experiments, we explain about the 4 physical models to subjects.

The figure 3 shows the results of discriminations. The precision value for each pair is the number correct answer of all subjects divided by the number of all trial for the pair. The precision at the pendulum model and spring-damper model is 0.813, and 0.938 at the rigid body model and pendulum model. No one is wrong at other pairs.

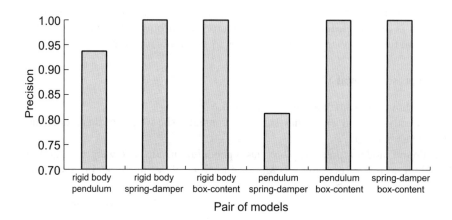

Fig. 3. Precision of model discrimination

4.2   Identification of M_w Difference

We evaluate the discrimination ability for the model parameters. First, the proportion of M_b and M_w is evaluated. 5 patterns of weights pair are used. $M_b = 0.5$ and $M_w = 0.9$, $M_b = 0.6$ and $M_w = 0.8$, $M_b = 0.7$ and $M_w = 0.7$, $M_b = 0.8$ and $M_w = 0.6$, and $M_b = 0.9$ and $M_w = 0.5$. First, the subject shakes the device displaying one of the pairs. Then he or she shakes the device displaying another (or sometimes same) pair. After shaking device, he or she answers the two representation is same, M_w is bigger in first, or M_w is bigger in last. The subjects are same to 4.1 and the nuber of trial is $5 \times 5 = 25$ in random order.

The left of figure 4 shows the results of discriminations for difference of M_w. The precision value is calculated for each M_w difference. For example, the difference in a pair of $M_w = 0.5, M_b = 0.9$ models and $M_w = 0.7, M_b = 0.7$ model is 0.2. Thus, the number of pairs with 0.2 difference is 3. The discrimination rate for differnce 0.2 is calculated in dividing the number of correct answer by the total number of answers. (In this case, the total number of answers are 3 pairs $\times$ 2 orderings $\times$ 8 subjects = 48.) If the difference is less than 0.3 kg, the discrimination rates are less than 0.6. In the case of the difference is 0.4 kg, the discrimination rate becomes 0.875.

Thus it is able to say the user could discriminate the difference if the difference of M_w is bigger than 0.4 kg. The possible value of M_w is from 0 kg to 1.4 kg. Therefore, the pendulum model able to display 4 different parameter settings. For example, M_w is 0.1 kg, 0.5 kg, 0.9 kg, and 1.3 kg.

We also evaluate for the spring-damper model same way. The right of figure 4 shows the results for the spring-damper model. If the difference is bigger than 0.2 kg, the discrimination rates becomes bigger than 0.80. Thus, the spring-damper model able to display 7 different parameter setting. For example, M_w is 0.1 kg, 0.3 kg, 0.5 kg, 0.7 kg, 0.9 kg, 1.1 kg and 1.3 kg. The spring coefficient $k = 50[N/m]$ and dumping coefficient $c = 1.0[kg/s]$ are used.

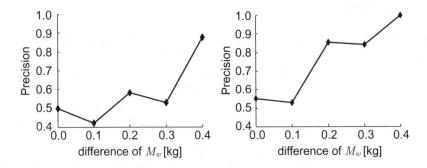

Fig. 4. Precision of weight difference discrimination

These results shows that the spring-damper model is more easy to discriminate than the pendulum model. It is assumed that the peak of reactive force is delayed in spring-damper model because of damping factor, and the delay time becomes bigger if the M_w becomes bigger.

4.3 Identification of Damping Factor Difference

We evaluate the discrimination ability for damping factor in spring-damper model. We prepare 6 patterns of damping factor settings, such as $c = 0, 2, 4, 6, 8, 10$, and evaluate discrimination precision in the same way with 4.2. We use $M_w = 1.0[kg], M_b = 0.4[kg], k = 50[N/m]$. It is difficult to explain the defference in dumping factor. Thus, subjects had some practices when they hearing the explanation of each model at begining of the experiment.

The figure 5 shows the results of discriminations for difference of c. The discrimination rate becomes 0.6 in difference equals 2. In other cases, the discrimination rate becomes higher than 0.7. The discrimination ratios for the damper factor are higher than it for M_w. We think this is because the difference of the damper factor shifts the delay of the peak of reactive force.

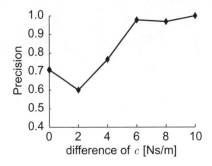

Fig. 5. Precision of damper factor difference discrimination

5 Conclusion

In this paper, we discuss about the representation of models consists of a box and a content. The experiment results show the user easily discriminate the each models, and the user is sensitive to the spring-damper model than the pendulum model. These results are useful when designing an interface using haptic interactions. Changing physical model is more recognizable than changing physical parameters. Thus, in the case of showing the number of arriving mails, changing the model according to the number increase would be a good way. And when using the parameter changing, time delay in force-motion relationship makes users' discrimitation better.

Our future work is to explore more parameters and more models. The elasticity and friction parameters in box-content model and fluid model are the first step. Through those approach, we try to reveal the effective models and parameters for haptics interfaces.

References

1. Sekiguchi, Y., Hirota, K., Hirose, M.: The Design and Implementation of Ubiquitous Haptic Device. In: Proc. IEEE World Haptics 2005, pp. 257–258 (2005)
2. Williamson, J., Murray-Smith, R., Hughes, S.: Shoogle: excitatory multimodal interaction on mobile devices. In: Proc. CHI 2007, pp. 121–124 (2007)
3. Hirota, K., Sasaki, S., Sekiguchi, Y.: Presentation of force-motion relationship by inertial force display. In: Ferre, M. (ed.) EuroHaptics 2008. LNCS, vol. 5024, pp. 567–572. Springer, Heidelberg (2008)
4. Hirose, M., Hirota, K., Ogi, T., Yano, H., Kakehi, N., Saito, M., Nakashige, M.: HapticGEAR: the development of a wearable force display system for immersive projection displays. In: Proc. IEEE Virtual Reality, pp. 123–129 (2001)
5. Yano, H., Yoshie, M., Iwata, H.: Development of a Non-Grounded Haptic Interface Using the Gyro Effect. In: Proc. Haptic Symposium 2003, pp. 32–39 (2003)
6. Amemiya, T., Ando, H., Maeda, T.: Directed Force Perception When Holding a Nongrounding Force Display in the Air. In: Proc. EuroHaptics 2006, pp. 317–324 (2006)
7. Yao, H.Y., Hayward, V.: An Experiment on Length Perception with a Virtual Rolling Stone. In: Proc. EuroHaptics 2006, pp. 325–330 (2006)

Perception of Stiffness during Interaction with Delay-Like Nonlinear Force Field

Raz Leib, Ilana Nisky, and Amir Karniel

Biomedical Engineering, Ben Gurion University of the Negev, Beer-Sheva 84105, Israel
{leibra,nisky,akarniel}@bgu.ac.il

Abstract. The perception of linear stiffness, as well as delayed linear stiffness, was studied extensively during the last decades. In this study we set to explore the effects of non linear relation between force and position on perception of stiffness. We designed a state dependent non-linear force field, similar to the previously explored delayed force field, which is essentially a piecewise linear force field depending only on the position and the direction of movement and not on time. We show that the stiffness of this force field is overestimated. We suggest a model based on the inverse of the slope of a regression of position over force in order to explain these behavioral results, which indirectly implies that force control is used during this exploratory probing.

Keywords: Stiffness, perception, force control.

1 Introduction

Interaction with the external world is daily, automatic series of actions in which we use perceptual analysis of mechanical properties of the environment. A prominent and extensively studied mechanical property is stiffness [1-9]. Nevertheless, it is unclear exactly how, and which components of the information stream do the perceptual centers use in order to perceive stiffness. Since there are no peripheral sensors of stiffness, the kinesthetic system must integrate cues of muscles position, movement, and forces in order to estimate the stiffness of the environment [5] as well as cutaneous cues [10].

Recently, the effect of delay on perception of linear stiffness was studied [1, 8, 11-12]. It was found that delay changes perception of stiffness, and that the effect is modulated by probing strategy and the joint that is dominant in probing movements.

A delay between force and position in linear elastic force field can be modeled as time independent nonlinear relation between force and position. In the current study we explore a similar type of nonlinearity in the relation between force and position: we explore the perception of the stiffness of a time independent delay-like piecewise linear elastic force field. The state dependent force field is similar to delay in the fact that the force experienced is different on the way out from the way in, however it is not identical since it is a piecewise linear approximation and it has similar nature in various velocities.

A.M.L. Kappers et al. (Eds.): EuroHaptics 2010, Part I, LNCS 6191, pp. 87–92, 2010.
© Springer-Verlag Berlin Heidelberg 2010

2 Methods

Five right handed participants aged 21-29 (3 males, 2 female) were tested. A seated subject held with his dominant hand the handle of PHANTOM® Desktop haptic device which rendered a virtual force field. The arm of the subject rested on an arm support with continuous air flow reducing friction with the table. The subject looked at a projection glass that displayed an image from LCD screen placed horizontally above it. The virtual environment consisted of an area where there were no force applied on the subject and an area where force was applied on his hand. The force field area was colored with red or blue background. An opaque screen was fixed under the glass and around it to prevent visual information about hand position. The location of the hand was displayed by a line perpendicular to the boundary of the force field. This provided subjects with the lateral position of the hand without revealing the degree of penetration inside the virtual object. Hand position and forces applied on it were sampled at 100 Hz, and this information was used online to calculate the force feedback, which was interpolated and rendered at 1 kHz.

We used a forced choice paradigm: in each trial we presented two force fields to the subject. One field - the *standard stimulus* force field - was either linear (L) or nonlinear (N) force field, and the second field - the *comparison stimulus* force field - was always linear elastic force field with stiffness that was chosen out of ten equally distributed stiffness levels between 55 N/m and 145 N/m with jumps of 10 N/m between them. The experiment included 30 practice trials to allow subjects to become acquainted with the system, followed by 10 trials for each value of the comparison stimulus with standard linear stimulus and 5 trials for each value with standard non-linear stimulus, summing to 150 trails. Subjects were asked to probe each of the force fields as long as they wished and answer "which one was stiffer?" To avoid force saturation, subjects were asked to generate only short movements into the field, and an intentionally annoying auditory cue was sounded at the maximum allowed level of penetration (4 cm). During training trials, subjects learned to make short movements to avoid the auditory cue in most of the trials. We implemented non-linear function between position and force in order to create time independent delay-like force field (see Fig. 1a): two-branched nonlinear function, each branch for a different direction of movement. Each branch was a piecewise linear function, i.e. it was constructed from 6 linear segments, $F = K_i \cdot x + F_i^0$, which differed in slope (stiffness) and interception point as specified in Table 1. We have selected low

Table 1. Stiffness and F-intersection value that we used for creating the non linear force field. The force field created using two piecewise linear branches, one for movement into the force field and the other for movement out of the force field.

Position [m]	Force- Way in branch [N]	Force- Way out branch [N]
0<x<0.006	-150·x	280·x
0.006<x<0.012	-0.9	140·x+0.84
0.012<x<0.018	50·x-1.5	80·x+1.56
0.018<x<0.024	90·x-2.22	60·x+1.92
0.024<x<0.03	180·x-4.38	40·x+2.4
0.03<x<0.036	430·x-11.88	3.6
0.036<x	100·x	100·x

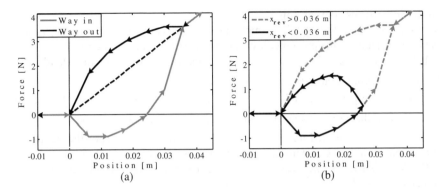

Fig. 1. (a) Force-position trajectory of a probing movement within a non linear delay-like elastic force field - N field. Subjects were instructed to perform back and forth movements in order to interact with this force field. They were allowed to cross the boundary of the field as many times as they wished. (b) An example of transition prior reaching the merging point dashed gray line- trajectory as preplanned and black line- the recalculated branch.

stiffness values as experienced in telesurgery applications such as operating on soft biological tissues [13], and in our previous studies on perception of delayed stiffness [1, 12]. The branches merge at x=3.6 cm. From the merging point and further into the force field the force is calculated according to $F = 100 \cdot x$. The "base value" (BV) of the force field was set to 100 N/m, which is the mean stiffness values, meaning that the 'way in branch' force values were smaller than force values of a linear function $F = 100 \cdot x$ while the 'way out branch' force values were larger than the same linear function. Branch-to-branch transitions occur at movement direction reversals, namely velocity zero crossings. The penetration distance was not constrained resulting in variable values of transition points, some of which before the point of merging of the two branches, i.e. in the range of 0<x<3.6 cm. In such case the transition points between the linear segments were recalculated (Fig. 1b): the position segments were all shrunk in their length by the same factor and two piecewise linear function segments $F = -150 \cdot x + F_1^0$ and $F = -100 \cdot x + F_2^0$ were added in order to create moderate increase or decrease of the force. The length of the two segments was equal and the parameters F_1^0 and F_2^0 were fitted to meet the transition point from one branch at the time of reversal and then to meet the other branch after eight millimeters.

Data Analysis
We used the method of constant stimuli in order to extract the probability of a subject to answer "standard stimulus force field is stiffer" as a function of difference between the levels of stiffness of standard stimulus and comparison stimulus force fields. We have fitted logistic psychometric curves to the answers of each subject and extracted the point of subjective equality (PSE) as described in detail in [1]. Then we calculated the perceived constant stiffness of the force field for each subject according to:

$$\hat{K}_{per} = 100 - PSE \qquad (1)$$

Models of stiffness perception

We assessed the ability of four computational models to predict the answers of subjects. We calculated the presumed estimation of stiffness according to:

I. FOP: The parameters of $F = bx$ were fitted to the force-position data, and then the slope was used as an estimate of stiffness $\hat{K}_{FOP} = b$.

II. POF: The parameters of $x = bF$ were fitted to the force-position data, and then the inverse of the slope was used as an estimate of stiffness $\hat{K}_{POF} = 1/b$.

III. Peak force: peak force divided by the length traveled from the beginning of force application to the maximum applied force point, as suggested in [8].

IV. Mean stiffness: the mean value of local stiffness values throughout the entire movement.

We evaluated the ability of each model to predict the answers of subjects by generating answers according to the sign of the difference between estimations generated from hand movement trajectory in standard stimulus and comparison stimulus force fields. We used two methods for this evaluation –prediction score and PSE difference. Prediction score measures the agreement between answers of the model and answers of the subject trial by trial regardless of the actual stiffness difference of the two fields. This score was calculated as the sum of matching answers between the subject and the model divided by sum of all trials. Clearly, the perfect model yields prediction score of 1. PSE difference is the mean absolute difference between PSEs extracted from the answers of the subjects and the model. The ideal model will have PSE difference close to zero.

3   Results

We found that all subjects overestimated the stiffness of non linear force fields while the linear force fields were perceived accurately (Fig. 2). The mean level of perceived

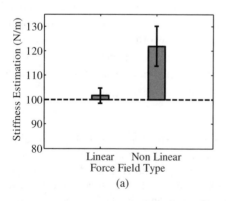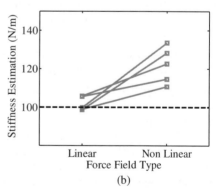

Fig. 2. (a) Linear force field with stiffness of 100 N/m was estimated accurately by subjects. On the other hand, the non linear force field with base stiffness of 100 N/m was overestimated. Bars are mean estimated level of stiffness across subjects; errorbars are 95% confidence intervals. (b) Individual subjects' estimations of stiffness level.

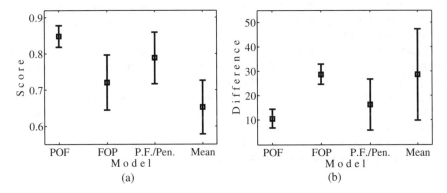

Fig. 3. Ranking of models (a) Models' prediction score. (b) Models' PSE difference. Symbols represent the mean, and error bars represent 95% confidence intervals for the mean, estimated using a t-distribution. Both tests indicate the POF model is best at predicting the answers of subjects.

stiffness of non linear force field across subjects was statistically significantly different from the base value (paired t-test t_4=5.22, p<0.01) unlike the mean level of perceived stiffness of the linear force field (paired t-test t_4=1.07, p=0.17). The POF model is more successful than other three models that we tested – FOP, maximum force divided by maximum penetration and mean stiffness – according to both measures – prediction score and PSE difference (Fig. 3).

4 Discussion

In this study we explored the effect of nonlinearity in the relation between force and position on subjective stiffness perception. This non linear force field was a piecewise linear elastic force field. We suggest that the overestimation that we observed can be explained by stiffness estimation according to the inverse of the slope of regression of position over force (see Fig 3 for comparison with other models). This result is consistent with the results observed in [14] and [1, 12] where it was suggested that estimation policy might be related to control policy. If indeed it is the case here estimation according to regression of position over force might be a result of force control. It was suggested that while moving inside an elastic field the appropriate control causality is implemented by a state controller that attempts to enforce a trajectory of the hand. On the other hand while switching between moving without encountering force and moving inside an elastic field, i.e. crossing a boundary the appropriate control causality is implemented by a force controller that attempts to regulate the interface force. Here we did not force subjects to probe entirely inside the force field or to cross the boundary repeatedly. However, subjects repeatedly encountered increase in the level of stiffness when they crossed boundaries between different regions ("pieces") of the piecewise linear elastic force field. Thus, these internal boundary crossings might have caused the subjects to maintain force control regardless to the external boundary crossing. Nevertheless, our results are limited to the range of stiffness tested, and one should note that there are other factors such as cutaneous cues which are not considered in our experimental setup. Further studies are required in order to consider these aspects of nonlinear stiffness perception.

Various developing fields, such as telerobotics and telesurgery can benefit from further exploring the effect of different nonlinearities of the relation between force and position in stiffness perception. In this experiment we explored the effect of time independent force field with typical trajectory of delayed force field; further studies with additional forms of nonlinearity required in order to further unveil the underlying processes in forming perception of mechanical properties of an object. Understanding these processes will improve haptic interaction between man and computer and help to develop the future generation of haptic applications.

References

1. Nisky, I., Mussa-Ivaldi, F.A., Karniel, A.: A Regression and Boundary-Crossing-Based Model for the Perception of Delayed Stiffness. IEEE Transactions on Haptics 1, 73–82 (2008)
2. Drewing, K., Ramisch, A., Bayer, F.: Haptic, visual and visuo-haptic softness judgments for objects with deformable surfaces. In: Third Joint Eurohaptics Conference and Symposium on Haptic Interfaces for Virtual Environment and Teleoperator Systems, Salt Lake City, UT, USA (2009)
3. Jones, L.A., Hunter, I.W.: A perceptual analysis of stiffness. Experimental Brain Research 79, 150–156 (1990)
4. Wu, W.C., Basdogan, C., Srinivasan, M.A.: Visual, haptic, and bimodal perception of size and stiffness in virtual environments. ASME dynamic systems and control division 67, 19–26 (1999)
5. Jones, L.A.: Kinesthetic Sensing. Human and Machine Haptics. MIT Press, Cambridge (2000)
6. LaMotte, R.H.: Softness Discrimination With a Tool. Journal of Neurophysiology 83, 1777–1786 (2000)
7. Srinivasan, M.A., Lamotte, R.H.: Tactual Discrimination of Softness. Journal of Neurophysiology 73, 88–101 (1995)
8. Pressman, A., Welty, L.H., Karniel, A., Mussa-Ivaldi, F.A.: Perception of delayed stiffness. The International Journal of Robotics Research 26, 1191–1203 (2007)
9. Lawrence, D.A., Pao, L.Y., Dougherty, A.M., Salada, M.A., Pavlou, Y.: Rate-Hardness: A New Performance Metric for Haptic Interfaces. IEEE Transactions On Robotics And Automation 16, 357–371 (2000)
10. Scilingo, E.P., Bianchi, M., Grioli, G., Bicchi, A.: Rendering Softness: Integration of Kinaesthetic and Cutaneous Information in a Haptic Device. IEEE computer Society Digital Library, Los Alamitos (2010)
11. Pressman, A., Nisky, I., Karniel, A., Mussa-Ivaldi, F.A.: Probing Virtual Boundaries and the Perception of Delayed Stiffness. Advanced Robotics 22, 119–140 (2008)
12. Nisky, I., Baraduc, P., Karniel, A.: Proximodistal gradient in the perception of delayed stiffness. Journal of Neurophysiology (in press)
13. Okamura, A.M., Simone, C., O'Leary, M.D.: Force Modeling for Needle Insertion Into Soft Tissue. IEEE Transactions on Biomedical Engineering 51, 1707–1716 (2004)
14. Han, G., Jeon, S., Choi, S.: Improving perceived hardness of haptic rendering via stiffness shifting: an initial study. In: Proceedings of the 16th ACM Symposium on Virtual Reality Software and Technology, pp. 87–90. ACM, Kyoto (2009)

Improving the Prediction of Haptic Impression User Ratings Using Perception-Based Weighting Methods: Experimental Evaluation

Christian Hatzfeld*, Thorsten A. Kern, and Roland Werthschützky

Technische Universität Darmstadt, Institute for Electromechanical Design
Merckstr. 25, DE-64283 Darmstadt
Tel.: +49 6151-16-2596; Fax: +49 6151-16-4096
{c.hatzfeld,t.kern,werthschuetzky}@emk.tu-darmstadt.de

Abstract. The prediction of haptic impressions of objects is an interesting topic for system designers. Valid prediction schemes would help to evaluate systems in an early stage of development. This paper investigates the approach of weighting mechanical measurements with three perception-inspired weighting procedures to obtain more accurate predictions of user ratings. Experiments are conducted using a set of five light switches as common examples for passive haptic control elements. The results imply that user ratings are mainly based on tactile information in the range of 10 to 1000 Hz, which is not covered completely by current industrial measurement procedures.

Keywords: FIP, haptic impression, user rating, system design.

1 Introduction

Passive haptic elements like switches and levers have been objects of investigation for quite a time. Studies like the *Haptic Camera* by *MacLean* [1] or works by *Colton and Hollerbach* [2] concentrate on recording and playing back haptic properties of such elements. Recent works concentrate on the relation between measurement data and haptic impression of such elements. In characterizing rotary switches, *Reisinger et al.* find energy more significant for user ratings than the absolute torque value of the switch [3]. Several works try to find integrated assessments of haptic and acoustic properties to find comparable values of the look-and-feel for automotive purposes [4], [5].

Studies like these are based on different subjective user ratings of certain impressions like "'hardness'" of real elements with different haptic and acoustic properties. These ratings are analyzed using factorial analysis to find independent rating dimensions. Correlation analysis is performed on these dimensions of rating and measurements of haptic and acoustic properties of the considered control elements. Using this approach, *Anguelov* proposes an impression index for automotive controls based on haptic and acoustic properties [4].

---

* Corresponding author.

A.M.L. Kappers et al. (Eds.): EuroHaptics 2010, Part I, LNCS 6191, pp. 93–98, 2010.

1.1 Intention of This Study

Most studies investigating user ratings of passive haptic elements use real examples of these controls with different haptic properties. Since it is desirable to predict user ratings without a real element at hand (for example by using CAD modeling), this study investigates the effect of weighting measured data on the quality of user rating prediction.

Methods of perception-based weighting are not uncommon in other sensual dimensions. Measurements of air pressure can be converted to perceived acoustic loudness using the weighted phon- and sone-curves [6]. The impression of arbitrary light waves on the human eye can be calculated using the $v(\lambda)$-curve of equal brightness. This leads to the assumption that weighting measurement data could improve the prediction of haptic user ratings.

The main hypothesis of this study is that variables derived from measurements weighted with perception-based methods will perform better in predicting user ratings of passive haptic control elements than non-weighted variables.

2 Experiment

The experiment to investigate the hypothesis is based on five European household light switches. Test persons were asked to rate their impressions on nine different scales (see sec. 2.2). In parallel, force-displacement-curves were recorded and weighted. For each switch, three parameter were extracted from the data (see sec. 2.1) that served as variables in predicting the user ratings for the five switches on each scale (see sec. 2.3).

Fig. 1. a) Switches as presented in the lab, b) test person pressing a switch

The switches used have a switching pad size of about $45 \cdot 45$ mm^2 and a push-button-characteristic. Switches were modified by replacing the internal springs resulting in five different force-displacement-characteristics. To ensure similar impressions, a $20 \cdot 20$ mm^2 touching area was marked. Figure 1 shows the switches.

2.1 Measurement of Force-Displacement-Curves

The force-displacement-curves of the switches shown in figure 2 were measured using a setup described in [9]. Using a stiff peg with a hemispherical contact area, the switches were pressed with a trapezoid-shaped deflection over time with a duration of 3 s (1 s linear rise, 1 s hold, 1 s linear fall). Force measurements were made using an ATI nano17 force sensor, displacement was recorded using a laser triangulation system. The obtained measurement data was weighted with the following methods:

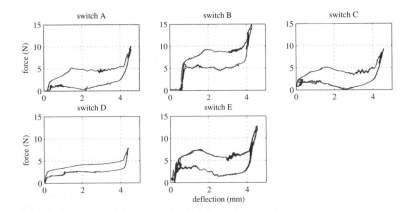

Fig. 2. Force-displacement-curves of the investigated switches, normal travel clockwise

- *Low-Frequency-Weighting* This weighting method uses a low-pass filter with a cutoff-frequency of 50 Hz. It is based on industrial testing instructions.
- *Perception-Bandwidth-Weighting* This method uses a band-pass filter on the measurement data. The cutoff-frequencies were set at 10 Hz and 1 kHz to address only the tactile sensory system. Compared to several other studies the upper cutoff-frequency was chosen higher, based on results of *Kuchenbecker et. al.* [7] who find also higher frequencies relevant for perception and identification of different materials.
- *Force-Impression-Weighting (FIP)* The method of Force-Impression was developed by the authors [8]. It is based on method 2 mentioned before, but performs an additional weighting of the haptic data based on the frequency-dependent haptic perception.

From each weighted curve the following parameters were derived as variables for predicting user ratings.

- *Switch Force* The absolute value of the force needed to generate a switching event while pressing the switch (upper part of the force-displacement-curve).
- *Switch Force Difference* The difference between the switch force and the lowest force following after the switching point while pressing the switch further. For prediction models with a high-pass-characteristic, the values of switch force and switch force difference show similar values for each model.
- *Click-Ratio* Quotient of the switch force difference to the switch force, a very common industrial quality control parameter.

2.2 User Rating Tests

To obtain user ratings, 15 test persons (6f, 9m, average age 24 years, std. dev. 2.25 years) were asked to rate the switches on nine Semantic Differential scales. Nine value pairs were taken from [5], where the same scales were used. The scales provided six rating alternatives ranging from -3 to +3 without a neutral value (zero) so that test persons were forced to make a judgment for each switch. Value pairs were

1. soft - hard
2. crisp - worn out
3. weak - strong
4. smooth-running - rough-running
5. sedate - sporty

6. gentle - bumpy
7. reliable - unreliable
8. fragile - robust
9. pleasing - displeasing

Test persons were given the scales in random order. They were required to press each switch at least one time before rating and were allowed to press as often as they wanted. Each rating session took about 10 to 15 minutes. Test persons wore ear plugs and headphones delivering white noise to block audio cues.

The user ratings were normalized to a (-1 ... +1) range and a two-way ANOVA (user and switch as independent variables) was conducted to verify that the user ratings were significantly different for each switch. This proved to be true for almost all ratings except of value pair no. 5 "sedate - sporty" (F=3.29, p=0.17), which was not considered further. No significant correlation to any user was found for the ratings. This was expected since all value pairs were reported as independent scales in [5]. Almost all ratings of each switch proved to be normally distributed.

2.3   Combination of Parameter and User Ratings

To assert a relation between the measured and weighted variables (see sec. 2.1) and user ratings (see sec. 2.2), linear regression analysis was done for each of the nine variables and the means of the eight ratings left. The assumption of a linear relation was made, since a better suited weighting method should perform better - even with a suboptimal model - than a worse weighting method.

As a performance measure for the linear fit, the probability that the given data would originate without a linear relation (p-value) was used. Table 1 shows the p-values of the investigated value pairs and variables. p-values less than 0.05, corresponding to a 95 % confidence interval, are highlighted. To test the accuracy of the linear models, the coefficient of determination R^2 is taken into account. Table 2 shows the values of this calculation. A good prediction is denoted by a low p-value (high probability that a linear relation exists) and a high R^2-value (little error of the linear fit).

2.4   Results

Comparing the results, the weighting-method considering the perception bandwidth performs best in terms of establishing a linear relation between user ratings and measured values. In general, the quality of the linear fits incorporating higher bandwidths (i.e. perception-bandwidth and FIP methods) is better than the quality of linear fits using the first weighting method.

The FIP-method shows some interesting performance in predicting the user ratings of value pair no. 6 "gentle - bumpy". While for most value pairs that imply a linear relation, the perception-bandwidth method shows better performance, the FIP-weighting shows a very good fit ($p < 0.0022$, $R^2 = 0.97$) for this value pair, while perception-bandwidth-weighting does not even confirm a linear relation ($p < 0.1025$). When using a weighting

Table 1. p-values of the linear regression of variables (columns) and ratings (rows)

p	low-frequency			perception-bandwidth			FIP		
value pair	switch force	force difference	click ratio	switch force	force difference	click ratio	switch force	force difference	click ratio
1	0.152	**0.049**	0.214	**0.005**	**0.025**	0.114	**0.035**	**0.035**	0.979
2	**0.046**	0.192	0.506	**0.002**	**0.005**	0.254	0.149	0.150	0.998
3	0.125	0.140	0.385	**0.001**	**0.001**	0.330	0.089	0.089	0.784
4	0.235	**0.028**	0.152	**0.008**	**0.023**	0.167	**0.017**	**0.017**	0.840
6	0.527	**0.011**	**0.027**	0.103	0.161	0.124	**0.002**	**0.002**	0.779
7	**0.024**	0.204	0.544	**0.008**	**0.018**	0.199	0.185	0.186	0.845
8	**0.029**	0.247	0.578	**0.008**	**0.014**	0.239	0.183	0.184	0.948
9	0.735	0.140	0.069	0.612	0.649	0.659	0.260	0.260	0.660

Table 2. R^2 of the linear regression of variables (columns) and ratings (rows)

R^2	low-frequency			perception-bandwidth			FIP		
value pair	switch force	force difference	click ratio	switch force	force difference	click ratio	switch force	force difference	click ratio
1	0.549	**0.775**	0.451	**0.947**	**0.855**	0.620	**0.819**	**0.817**	0.000
2	**0.785**	0.484	0.159	**0.970**	**0.949**	0.398	0.554	0.553	0.000
3	0.597	0.570	0.255	**0.987**	**0.995**	0.309	0.672	0.673	0.029
4	0.422	**0.842**	0.549	**0.930**	**0.858**	0.523	**0.888**	**0.887**	0.016
6	0.146	**0.915**	**0.847**	0.643	0.534	0.601	**0.970**	**0.968**	0.031
7	**0.856**	0.467	0.134	**0.930**	**0.882**	0.474	0.494	0.493	0.015
8	**0.838**	0.407	0.114	**0.930**	**0.900**	0.417	0.498	0.497	0.002
9	0.044	0.570	0.720	0.096	0.078	0.074	0.390	0.391	0.073

method with high-pass characteristic, the comparison of the p- and R^2-values implies that force-difference is a slightly worse indicator than the absolute switching force for user ratings.

The main hypothesis of this study could be verified considering the value pairs used. Helpful hints for development of testing methods could be extracted from the results. Detailed comparisons of these results to the results of similar studies ([4], [5]) could not be made, since measurement bandwidths were not given in those references.

3   Conclusions and Further Work

The results show that predictions of user ratings of passive haptic elements can be improved by incorporating knowledge of haptic perception. Weighting methods considering the whole range of tactile perception show better performance, indicating that user ratings are mainly based on information arising in the tactile range of haptic perception. Slowly changing haptic impressions seem to have less influence. Further analysis should determine the frequency range needed to get meaningful variables for user rating prediction. With the results from this study, this frequency range can only be limited to the range of 50 Hz to 1 kHz. Further investigation is also needed to prove the results valid for older test persons.

Another result is the inapt use of the parameter *click ratio* for predicting user ratings. Since it is part of industrial testing regulations, the need and benefit of other testing methods should be evaluated for applications like quality control and harmony judgments.

Regarding the method of force-impression (FIP), further investigations whether this method could improve the assessment of haptic systems working in a wide frequency range should be made. Recent studies by *Cholewiak et al.* [10] show a direct relation of the recognition of gratings to the absolute perception threshold, which is also predicted by this weighting method.

Acknowledgments. This work was partly funded by DFG grant WE2308/7-1.

References

1. MacLean, K.: The Haptic Camera: A Technique for Characterizing and Playing back Haptic Properties of real Environments. In: IMECE (1996)
2. Colton, M.B., Hollerbach, J.M.: Reality-Based Haptic Force Models of Buttons and Switches. In: IEEE Int. Conf. on Robotics and Automation (2007)
3. Reisinger, J., Wild, J., Mauter, G., Bubb, H.: Haptical feeling of rotary switches. In: Proc. of the Eurohaptics Conf. (2006)
4. Anguelov, N.: Haptische und akustische Kenngrößen zur Objektivierung und Optimierung der Wertanmutung von Schaltern und Bedienfeldern für den KFZ-Innenraum. PhD thesis, TU Dresden, Fakultät Maschinenwesen (2009)
5. Rösler, F., Schüttler, F., Battenberg, G.: Subjective perceptions and objective characterisrtics of control elements. ATZ- Autotechnology (2009)
6. Zwicker, E., Fastl, H.: Psychoacoustics. Springer, Heidelberg (1999)
7. Kuchenbecker, K.J., Fiene, J., Niemeyer, G.: Improving Contact Realism Through Event-Based Haptic Feedback. IEEE Trans. on Visualization and Computer Graphics (2006)
8. Kern, T.A., Schaeffer, A., Werthschützky, R.: An Interaction Model for the Quantification of Haptic Impressions. In: Ferre, M. (ed.) EuroHaptics 2008. LNCS, vol. 5024, pp. 139–145. Springer, Heidelberg (2008)
9. Hatzfeld, C., Kern, T.A., Werthschützky, R.: Design and Evaluation of a Measuring System for Human Force Perception Parameters. Sensors And Actuators A: Physical (2010) (in press) doi:10.1016/j.sna.2010.01.026
10. Cholewiak, S., Kim, K., Tan, H., Adelstein, B.: A Frequency-Domain Analysis of Haptic Gratings. IEEE Trans. on Haptics (2009) (to be published)

Vibrotactile Force Perception
Thresholds at the Fingertip

Christian Hatzfeld and Roland Werthschützky

Technische Universität Darmstadt, Institute for Electromechanical Design
Merckstr. 25, DE-64283 Darmstadt,
Tel.: +49 6151-16-2596; Fax: +49 6151-16-4096
{c.hatzfeld,werthschuetzky}@emk.tu-darmstadt.de

Abstract. In this paper, the first measurements of human vibrotactile force perception at the fingertip are presented. Eight stimuli in the frequency range of 5
to 700 Hz were delivered by a circular contactor with an area of 2.9 cm, finding lowest thresholds of 6.9 dB resp. 1 mN for a frequency of 250 Hz. Highest
thresholds were determined to about 25 dB for frequencies higher than 500 Hz.
A force prediction and measurement model is presented to obtain highly accurate
force measurements independent of the mechanical impedance of the user.

Keywords: force perception, perception threshold, vibrotactile stimuli.

1 Introduction

Determination of perception thresholds is one of the basic tasks of psychophysical experiments. In the area of haptics, this has been done in several studies investigating
vibrotactile haptic stimuli that are defined by the mechanical dimension of deflection
(or velocity or acceleration). *Gescheider et al.* have been investigating the tactile sensory system for several decades and are able to assert thresholds and their dependence
on age, temperature and contact area [1]. Their findings are based on stimuli that are
presented perpendicular to the skin. *Brisben et al.* investigate detection thresholds for
tangential stimuli [2] and *Israr et al.* measure detection thresholds using a stylus for
presenting stimuli [3]. In general, the majority of studies show a relevant bandwidth
of vibrotactile perception of up to 1000 Hz with a minimum threshold at about 250 -
300 Hz.

Few studies can be found that define vibrotactile stimuli by the amplitude and bandwidth of forces coupled into the human skin. For forces with frequencies less than 1 Hz,
Abbink et al. provide psychometric functions and Just Noticeable Differences (JND)
[4]. *Israr et al.* measure force perception thresholds while presenting deflection-based
stimuli and hypothesize mechanical impedance as a coupling factor not only for the
mechanical properties but also for vibrotactile perception [3].

1.1 Applications for Force Perception Data

The authors agree that measurement and perception of deflection-defined and force-
defined vibrotactile stimuli are very closely related. The most known studies based on

A.M.L. Kappers et al. (Eds.): EuroHaptics 2010, Part I, LNCS 6191, pp. 99–104, 2010.
© Springer-Verlag Berlin Heidelberg 2010

deflection-defined stimuli give valuable details for the design of haptic systems. However, certain applications, theories and controlling strategies actually could be improved by using force perception data:

- A common controlling strategy of haptic devices is an open loop impedance-control scheme. In this case, deflections of a haptic display are measured and a force depending on the underlying model is presented to the user. To evaluate this force output of an impedance-controlled device, force perception data could be useful.
- *Hinterseer et al.* present a compression algorithm to reduce packet rate on data transmission lines for haptic interfaces based on the JND of the human force perception [7]. Lacking data they use experimental data to verify their results.
- Several evaluation algorithms such as proposed by *Kern et al.* [5] or incorporated in industrial quality control measurements [6] depend on valid force perception data for experimental validation. Such algorithms may be part of measurement systems to quantify haptic qualities of surfaces, fabrics or active devices and try to assess the impression of the user based on measurement data rather than on user tests.

2   Experimental Setup

2.1   Procedure

Five test persons (1 female, 4 male, aged 21-32 years (average 24 years old), all right-handed by self report) participated in the study. None of them was an experienced user of haptic devices. Test persons were monetarily compensated for participating in the study.

Thresholds were determined for eight different frequencies (5, 10, 50, 150, 250, 320, 500, and 700 Hertz). The order of the frequencies was randomized but the same order for each participant. The duration of the stimulus was fixed at 1 second with a 100 ms linear rise and fall to reduce transient effects. Two measurements were conducted for each frequency.

To obtain thresholds, an adaptive staircase method was used. This method changes the intensity of the stimulus of each trial depending on the performance of the subject. A one-up three-down paradigm was used. According to *Levitt*, this paradigm aims at the 79.4 percentile point of the psychometric function [9]. Step-sizes were set to 5 dB (for faster convergence) and to 1 dB after the first three reversals (for higher resolution). The initial value of the stimulus was chosen to be well above the detection threshold. Measurement ended after 12 reversals at the 1 dB level.

To avoid changing decision criteria, answers were obtained using a three-interval forced-choice scheme. On each trial, three 1.5 second long intervals were presented to the subjects. One randomly chosen interval contained the above described stimulus. The subject's task was to indicate which interval contained the stimulus. The duration of the intervals was denoted by visual cues. After the end of the third interval, participants were required to enter a response via three push-buttons, one assigned to each interval. Test persons wore earplugs and headphones delivering white noise to block audio cues of the setup.

Each measurement lasted about 6-8 minutes; participants were required to take a minimum-1-minute break between measurements. The entire experiment took about 90 minutes.

2.2 Apparatus

The apparatus used consists of an electrodynamic force source based on the magnetic system of a commercial loudspeaker (Visaton TIW-300). Forces were measured by an ATI nano17 force sensor that was equipped with custom-made secondary electronics to reduce latency and to provide an external offset correction of the force signal (see next section). To ensure high accuracy and to adapt the system to different loads, an analog PID-controller was used to establish a closed-loop force control.

Displacement and velocity were recorded using a laser triangulation system (Keyence LK-G32) and a custom-made voice-coil assembly. The force source was driven by a high-bandwidth linear amplifier (Spitzenberger + Spies GV250/40). The measurement system was controlled by a data acquisition board (National Instruments PCI-7833R). Force, velocity and displacement data were recorded with 16-bit resolution at a sampling rate of 10 kHz. Additional information about the measurement system can be found in [8].

Stimuli were delivered through a circular contactor with a contact area of 2.9 cm^2. The contactor was surrounded by a rigid surface with a 1 mm intermediate gap. A concave cut-out was made to provide better contact with the fingertip. This setup was chosen to make certain measurements comparable to the results reported in [1] where an almost identical setup was used. The test person's left index finger was placed on the contactor as shown in figure 1.

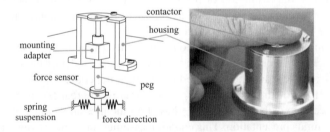

Fig. 1. Schematic view of contactor and structure of major functional parts (left), participants hand during the test (right)

The contactor was placed about 1 mm higher than the rigid surrounding. Placing a finger as pictured in figure 1 would bring contactor and surrounding to a equal level, leading to a contact force of 1 N originating in the spring suspension of the peg and preventing a lift-off during the test.

2.3 Force Prediction and Measurement Model

The force sensor could not be placed directly at the contactor, due to the fact that the setup was designed to be used with other grip configurations. Therefore, an analytical

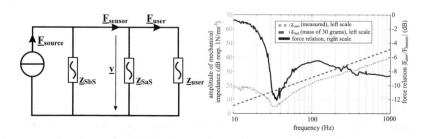

Fig. 2. Force measurement model. Network parameters (left), typical values (right).

model of the setup was developed to evaluate the influence of the mechanical components placed between force sensor and contactor. The model is shown in figure 2. It is based on concentrated network elements and characterizes the influence of the mechanical components as a complex[1] complex mechanical impedance. The figure shows two relevant impedances, the user impedance $\underline{z}_{user}$ and the mechanical impedance $\underline{z}_{SaS}$ of the mechanical parts of the setup located between force sensor and user. $\underline{z}_{SbS}$ stands for the mechanical parts of the setup before the sensor and doesn't have to be considered for the prediction model. The force $\underline{F}_{sensor}$ is measured by the sensor, while the force $\underline{F}_{user}$ is the force actually coupled into the test person's skin.

The right part of figure 2 shows $\underline{z}_{user}$ (dotted), $\underline{z}_{SaS}$ (dashed) and the relation $|\underline{F}_{user}/\underline{F}_{sensor}|$ (solid). Depending on frequency, the force actually presented to the user is 1 to 12 dB smaller than the force measured at the sensor. Therefore this prediction method improves the resolution of the force sensing setup up to a factor of 4. With a force sensor resolution of 1/1280 N as reported by the manufacturer, a theoretical accuarcy of less than 1 mN can be assumed.

From the model, two relevant equations can be determined. Eq. 1 denotes the value of the commanded force depending on the frequency, a model of the user impedance $\underline{z}_{user}$ (taken from [10]) and the measured mechanical impedance $\underline{z}_{SaS}$ of the system. To compensate errors of the model for $\underline{z}_{user}$ compared to the real test user, eq. 2 allows for a more accurate calculation of $\underline{F}_{user}$ based on the measured value of velocity $\underline{v}$ in the actual stimulus presentation. This equation assumes an identical velocity drop over $\underline{z}_{user}$ and $\underline{z}_{SaS}$, which is reasonable since the peg of the force source has a considerable higher stiffness than the user.

$$\underline{F}_{sensor} = \underline{F}_{user} \cdot \frac{\underline{z}_{user} + \underline{z}_{SaS}}{\underline{z}_{user}} \qquad (1)$$

$$\underline{F}_{user} = \underline{F}_{sensor} - \underline{z}_{SaS} \cdot \underline{v} \qquad (2)$$

When presenting a force, first eq. (1) is calculated for the given frequency. Just prior to measurement, the offset force measured by the force sensor is compensated by an external offset voltage to the force signal. This is a crucial step in the procedure, since even small movements of the test person's finger will generate an offset force and have an influence

---

[1] In the following, underlined letters stand for complex variables, for example a force with given amplitude and phase in respect to other variables in the described system.

on the force control loop. Just after presenting a stimulus, the actual force presented to the user is calculated with the measured values of $\underline{F}_{sensor}$ and $\underline{v}$ using eq. (2).

3   Results and Conclusions

For each series, the values of the last eight peaks (four peaks and four valleys) at 1 dB were used to calculate the threshold as the mean of these values for each frequency and each participant. For each frequency, the frequency average and experimental standard deviation was calculated over the participant means.

Figure 3 shows the obtained thresholds. A two-way ANOVA with frequency and participants as independent variables showed a significant influence of the frequency ($F = 3.63$, $p < 0.0066$) but no significant influence of the participant ($F = 1.58$, $p < 0.2061$) on the measured averages.

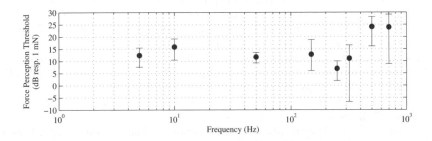

Fig. 3. Force perception thresholds, frequency average and experimental standard deviation

The force perception curve seems to be lowest in the frequency range from 150 - 320 Hz. This is in accordance with many studies dealing with vibrotactile perception. In general, measured thresholds are about 20 dB higher than the force perception thresholds measured in [3]. This is probably due to the different grip situation in the two studies (normal indention of the fingertip vs. pen-hold posture with a larger contact area). The difference between the highest and the lowest threshold is only about 20 dB compared to about 50 dB in [3]. Possible reasons could be large differences in the mechanical impedance of the user or lower thresholds for lower and higher frequencies at the fingertip.

Due to the small number of test persons, experimental standard deviations are very large for most frequencies. In addition, changes in the mechanical properties of the skin due to, for example, small movements of the test persons have an influence on the accuarcy of the measurement values. This has to be evaluated further by conducting studies with more test persons and adjustments of the psychophysical methods used, for example by increasing the number of reversals before ending a trial or using interleaved staircases.

Further studies are planned to investigate the force perception threshold for pen-hold postures and power grips. Also just noticeable force differences over the tactile frequency range shall be investigated. Results are intended to provide fundamentals for developing and testing new haptic devices. Also the hypothesis of the mechanical user impedance as a coupling factor not only for mechanical properties but also for perception made by *Israr et al.* [3] should be verified by force-defined vibrotactile stimuli. If this hypothesis could be verified, many already existing results regarding human vibrotactile perception could be used for applications stated in section 1.1.

Acknowledgements. This work was funded by DFG grant WE2308/7-1.

References

1. Gescheider, G.A., Wright, J.H., Verillo, R.T.: Information-Processing Channels in the Tactile Sensory System. Psychology Press, San Diego (2009)
2. Brisben, A., Hsiao, S., Johnson, K.: Detection of Vibration Transmitted through an Object grasped in the Hand. J. Neurophysiol. (81) (1999)
3. Israr, A., Choi, S., Tan, H.Z.: Mechanical Impedance of the Hand Holding a Spherical Tool at Threshold and Superthreshold Stimulation Levels. In: Proc. Eurohaptics (2007)
4. Abbink, D.A., van der Helm, F.C.: Force Perception Measurements at the Foot. In: IEEE Conf. on Systems, Man and Cybernetics (2004)
5. Kern, T.A., Schaeffer, A., Werthschützky, R.: An Interaction Model for the Quantification of Haptic Impressions. In: Ferre, M. (ed.) EuroHaptics 2008. LNCS, vol. 5024, pp. 139–145. Springer, Heidelberg (2008)
6. Battenberg Robotics, `http://www.battenberg.biz/content/EN/produkts.html`, status (January 27, 2010)
7. Hinterseer, P., et al.: Perception-Based Data Reduction and Transmission of Haptic Data in Telepresence and Teleaction Systems. IEEE Trans. Signal Process (2008)
8. Hatzfeld, C., Kern, T.A., Werthschützky, R.: Design and Evaluation of a Measuring System for Human Force Perception Parameters. Sensors And Actuators A: Physical (2010) (in press), doi:10.1016/j.sna.2010.01.026
9. Levitt, H.: Transformed Up-Down Methods in Psychoacoustics. JASA (49) (1971)
10. Kern, T.A., Werthschützky, R.: Studies of the Mechanical Impedance of the Index finger in Multiple Dimensions. In: Ferre, M. (ed.) EuroHaptics 2008. LNCS, vol. 5024, pp. 175–180. Springer, Heidelberg (2008)

Optimum Design of 6R Passive Haptic Robotic Arm
for Implant Surgery

Serter Yilmaz[1], E. Ilhan Konukseven[1], and Hakan Gurocak[2]

[1] Middle East Technical Uni., Dep. of Mechanical Engineering, 06531, Ankara / Turkey
[2] School of Engineering and Computer Science Washington State University Vancouver
serteryilmaz@gmail.com, konuk@metu.edu.tr,
hgurocak@vancouver.wsu.edu

Abstract. The aim of this research was to design an optimum 6R passive haptic robotic arm (PHRA) to work in a limited workspace during dental implant surgery. Misplacement of an implant during dental surgery causes longer recuperation periods and functional disorders. In this study, a passive guidance robot arm was designed as a surgical aid tool for a dentist during the operation to reduce the surgical complications. Optimum design of a 6R robot is a complex issue since minimum energy has to be consumed while maximum workspace is to be achieved using optimized link lengths. The methodology used deals not only with link lengths of manipulator but also mass and inertia of the links along with the location of the tool path. Another feature of the methodology is to maximize haptic device transparency using an objective function that includes end-effector torques/forces with workspace limits taken as constraints. The objective function was obtained from dynamic equations and the constraints were defined using kinematic equations. The constrained nonlinear optimization problem was solved using Sequential Quadratic Programming (SQP) and Genetic Algorithms (GA). Main contribution of this paper is an optimization algorithm that considers spatial dynamics to reduce parasitic torques leading to an optimal 6R robot design. Details of the methodology, solutions, and performance of the optimization techniques are presented.

Keywords: Passive guidance, multivariable optimization, dental implant surgery, haptic feedback, haptic transparency.

1 Introduction

In recent years, dental implants are widely used to replace missing teeth in prosthetic dentistry [1]. The implant operation has two critical problems: The proper placement of the implant and avoiding drilling the inferior alveolar nerve (IAN). Misplacement of the implant causes longer recuperation periods and function disorders. To prevent the complications drill guides and image guidance are widely used [1]. The widespread usage of the image guidance systems in dentistry and the accuracy of these operations have been discussed in [2]. The implant hole should be at least 2 mm away from the the IAN and the jaw bone. The misalignment between the desired and the actual hole has to be less than 0.3mm. The desired system must have an accuracy of at

A.M.L. Kappers et al. (Eds.): EuroHaptics 2010, Part I, LNCS 6191, pp. 105–110, 2010.
© Springer-Verlag Berlin Heidelberg 2010

least 0.5mm. On average the image guided systems provide 0.9mm [2]. Theodossy et. al. [3] used a coordinate measuring machine (CMM) as a passive robot arm to "assess the degree of accuracy" and to compare it with that of traditional surgery. Their results showed that usage of CMM yields more accurate results.

The main goal of our research team is to develop a PHRA as part of a dental surgical aid system. Haptic feedback to the surgeon in real time can decrease the dependence on the surgeon's skills and experience for accurate implant positioning and increase the overall safety of the procedure. The system would track the surgeon's hand-piece and the patient to provide graphical user interface and haptic feedback to the surgeon in real time to guide him during the operation. The research explores use of a passive haptic interface by employing magnetorheological fluid (MR) brakes as actuators in the robot. The MR brakes are inherently safe and have excellent characteristics in providing rigid interaction forces to the user [4]. In active feedback, the actuators can easily move the tip point to the desired position. In passive feedback, the user gives motion to the manipulator. When the user gets closer to the target position, the brakes start to apply torque to prevent the user from moving away the desired position. In this paper, we present a methodology used to optimize the kinematic parameters of the PHRA.

The optimization of the robot arm is done to obtain a lightweight mechanism with maximum transparency while consuming minimum energy. The transparency of a PHRA is how purely one feels the virtual environment using the robotic arm. The transparency of the haptic device is also important which is associated with the end–effector "parasitic torques/forces during its motion, e.g., mass/inertia, gravity forces, and friction" [5]. Various optimization techniques are applied to design of manipulators. The inertial and acceleration characteristics of the manipulators have been investigated [6]. Ceccarelli formulated the optimization problem through workspace volume, Jacobian matrices, and the compliant displacements as the objective functions and workspace limits as the constraints, respectively [7]. Numerical examples on both parallel and serial manipulators were reported.

This paper presents a methodology to optimize the link lengths and other parameters associated with link lengths including mass and inertia elements. As an application of the method, a low cost 6R PHRA has been designed for dental implant surgery. The objective function used to maximize transparency includes mass and inertia elements as seen by the user along the motion path. The methodology allows identification of the optimum link lengths together with the tool path. The optimization problem was solved by using Sequential Quadratic Programming (SQP) and Genetic Algorithms (GA).

2   Kinematics of the Robotic Arm

To maximize the transparency, an objective function based on dynamic equations was used. Necessary constraints to solve the optimization problem were obtained by using kinematic equations derived from the D-H convention.

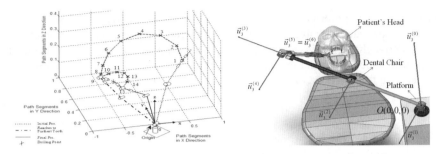

Fig. 1. The given path and CAD model ("Reaches to the Furthest Tooth" position same as in CAD model

Figure 1 shows the generated path and robotic arm in three different positions and a CAD model including the dentist chair and patient skull model. The D-H parameters for the arm are given in Figure 2 where α_i, θ_i, d_i, a_i represent the twist angles, the joint variables, the link offsets, and the effective link lengths, respectively. Using forward kinematics, orientation and position of the end-effector's tip point used in the constraints can be defined with respect to the base frame.

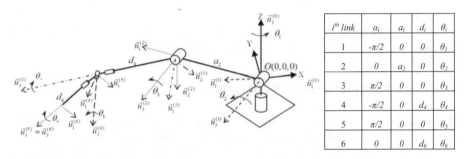

i^{th} link	α_i	a_i	d_i	θ_i
1	$-\pi/2$	0	0	θ_1
2	0	a_2	0	θ_2
3	$\pi/2$	0	0	θ_3
4	$-\pi/2$	0	d_4	θ_4
5	$\pi/2$	0	0	θ_5
6	0	0	d_6	θ_6

Fig. 2. 6R robotic arm with kinematic model and kinematic parameters

The CAD model was built based on the typical dimensions of a dentist chair. Using this model, the robot arm was extended to the furthest tooth to acquire the orientation and position of the end-effector's tip point. Inverse kinematics solutions for the arm provided the necessary joint variables. An appropriate configuration that satisfied the constraints was chosen from 8 different configurations of the arm. Using joint variables obtained from the solution, a path can be generated from the base point to the furthest tooth. The generated path in Figure 1 shows that the manipulator's wrist point starts from the initial position, reaches to the furthest tooth, then starts the drilling operation and stops at the final position. This path is a sample path that is obtained from the ideas of dentists and can be applicable to different patients.

3 Objective Function for Maximum Transparency

In this study, the main goal is to improve transparency of the PHRA while minimizing energy consumption. To achieve this, we explored minimizing the parasitic torques.

Therefore, first joint torques of the robotic arm need to be derived based on the end-effector's kinematic variables. In this study the recursive Newton-Euler method was used to derive the dynamics equations. The operation path is divided into 15 segments to obtain a smooth path and more accurate optimization results. In each path segment, the recursive formulation computes joint torques in joint state space:

$$\tau' = \mathbf{m}(\theta)\ddot{\theta} + \mathbf{v}(\theta,\dot{\theta}) + \mathbf{g}(\theta) \tag{1}$$

Here "$\mathbf{m}$" denotes the 6-by-6 mass matrix, "$\ddot{\theta}$" denotes angular acceleration vector, "$\mathbf{v}$" is the nonlinear velocity matrix, and "$\mathbf{g}$" is the gravity torque matrix. First, the joint torque values were calculated in the joint space. Then, they were transformed into the Cartesian space using the Jacobian. The Jacobian matrix used for transformation is derived similarly to the dynamic equations using the recursive method.

After obtaining torque values in the Cartesian space, the objective function is calculated in each path segment as the manipulator moves along the operation path. Since the path was divided into fifteen segments, the overall objective function was built by a weighted sum of the norm computed in each segment [5]:

$$f_{TOT} = \sum_{i=1}^{j} w_i Norm(\mathbf{M} \cdot \mathbf{a} + \mathbf{V} + \mathbf{G}) \tag{2}$$

In Eqn. (2) "$\mathbf{M}$" is the mass matrix, "$\mathbf{a}$" is the linear acceleration vector, "$\mathbf{V}$" is the nonlinear velocity matrix, and "$\mathbf{G}$" is the vector of gravity terms.

4 Design Parameters and Constraints

The objective function defined in Eqn. (2) includes the design parameters of an optimum 6R PHRA. The methodology that is used in the optimization problem deals with the size and shape of the manipulator's links and the location of the operation path with respect to the base location. Since the shape of operation path in addition to the velocity and acceleration of the tip point along the path can vary with characteristics of the dental operations, they are taken into consideration [5].

Mass matrix includes elements which are functions of link masses, link lengths, and link moments of inertia. Link masses and link moments of inertia can be parameterized as functions of link lengths. Both nonlinear velocity and the gravity terms are the functions of link lengths. If the link lengths are selected as design parameters, then minimization of the torque values at the joints optimizes the link lengths.

Location of the operation path with respect to base frame of the robotic arm is an important parameter for the optimization problem since the size of the manipulator depends on this path. Therefore, the link lengths (a_2, d_4, d_6) and the coordinates of the base frame (X, Y, Z) are taken as optimization parameters.

Another important point of the optimization process is the determination of constraints. The PHRA is planned to be placed in the operation room. The face, lips, and cheeks of the patient restrict the movement of the dentist's arm. Another factor is to avoid singularities of the arm which causes loss of control. Therefore, the longest path from the base position to the furthest tooth is taken so that the dentist can move the tip of the manipulator freely within the workspace.

As inequality constraints, wrist points of the robotic arm have to be in an allowable workspace. Eqn (3) describes necessary constraints for the entire operation path:

$$(a_2 - d_4) \leq \sqrt{x_i^2 + y_i^2 + z_i^2} \leq (a_2 + d_4) \tag{3}$$

where x_i, y_i, z_i are the coordinates of the wrist point calculated at each operation path segments. Also the joint variables, θ_i's, are bounded to avoid singularities. To let the robotic arm move freely in the defined workspace, different lower and upper bounds are defined for each joint variable. On a haptic robotic arm these limits are assumed to be realized by means of hard-limits. Though defining these boundaries, the singularities are avoided.

The objective function in Eqn. 2 along with the constraints in Eqn. 3 represent a constrained nonlinear optimization problem.

5 Optimization and Results

The nonlinear optimization problem has been solved using two optimization techniques: (1) Sequential Quadratic Programming (SQP) and, (2) Genetic Algorithms (GA). The MATLAB® Optimization Toolbox was used.

In MATLAB, dynamic and kinematic equations are embedded into the objective function and the constraints are defined. Table 1 lists the initial guesses for the link sizes and base frame location along with the joint variable bounds. The optimization results shown satisfy all constraints.

Table 1. Initial configuration, lower and upper parameter bounds and optimization results

Parameter	a_2 (mm)	d_4 (mm)	d_6 (mm)	X (mm)	Y (mm)	Z (mm)
Initial Configuration	400.00	400.00	264.14	0.00	0.00	0.00
Lower Bound	100	100	10	-150	-150	-500
Upper Bound	600	600	250	150	100	500
SQP	599.85	599.85	13.68	-14.25	58.73	-394.29
GA	599.15	597.96	11.64	-115.62	99.92	-319.34

The optimized base coordinates for the robot require moving the base (X, Y, and Z in Table 1). But the newly found coordinates still remain on the platform attached to the arm of the dentist chair. This was achieved through the constraints used in the optimization. Lower and upper bounds can be increased to get lower objective function values but this causes the base of the robot to move out of the platform.

Norm of the parasitic torques and forces for the initial configuration and optimization results along the operation path are shown in Figure 3. Initial configuration has very high parasitic torques at some segments of the path which causes from getting closer to singularity at the given path. By using the optimization we also wanted to get the manipulator away from the singularity which was achieved. After optimization, parasitic torques are minimized as well as shown in Figure 3. GA results are slightly lower than the SQP results.

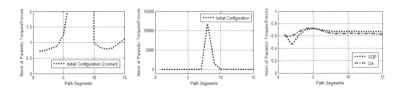

Fig. 3. Inital Configuration with Zoomed Part and Optimization Results

GA gives a little lower value for the objective function than SQP. Link lengths are nearly the same in both optimization techniques. The coordinates of the operation path with respect to the base is slightly different. Since the results from both algorithms are very close, we concluded that a global solution was found in the constrained search space. The computational time consumed by the GA is nearly 10 times longer than that of SQP on same computer.

6 Conclusions

In this paper, optimum design of a spatial 6R PHRA was achieved. The methodology developed by Vlachos et. al. was applied to maximize the transparency of the spatial 6R haptic robotic. The objective function was derived from the dynamic equations of 6R robotic arm. The kinematic equations were used to define the constraints. Link lengths and other parameters associated with link lengths including mass and inertia elements together with the location of the operation path with respect to the base position are optimized. The optimization results showed that the parasitic torques, hence the transparency of the arm, could be minimized. The results from both GA and SQP optimization techniques led to very close solutions. Hence, a global solution was believed to be found in the search space.

References

[1] Casap, N., Wexler, A., Lustmann, J.: Image-Guided Navigation System for Placing Dental Implants. Technology in Practice 25(10), 783–788 (2004)
[2] Brief, J., Edinger, D., Hassfeld, S., Eggers, G.: Accuracy of image-guided implantology. Clin. Oral Impl. Res. 16, 495–501 (2005)
[3] Theodossy, T., Bamber, M.A.: Model surgery with a passive robot arm for orthognathic surgery planning. Jour. of Oral and Max. Surgery 61(11), 1310–1317 (2003)
[4] Senkal, D., Gurocak, H., Konukseven, I.: Passive Haptic Interface with MR-Brakes for Dental Implant Surgery, Presence. MIT Press, Cambridge (2010) (in review)
[5] Vlachos, K., Papadopoulos, E.: Transparency Maximization Methodology for Haptic Devices. IEEE/ASME Transactions on Mechatronics 11(3), 249–255 (2006)
[6] Khatib, O., Bowling, A.: Optimization of the inertial and acceleration characteristics of manipulators. In: Proc. IEEE ICRA, vol. 4, pp. 2883–2889 (1996)
[7] Carbone, G., Ceccarelli, M.: An optimum design procedure for both serial and parallel manipulators. In: Proc. I. Mech. E., J. Mech. Eng. Sci., Part C, vol. 221, pp. 829–843

Creating Virtual Stiffness by Modifying Force Profile of Base Object

Atsutoshi Ikeda[1], Yuichi Kurita[1], Takeshi Tamaki[1],
Kazuyuki Nagata[2], and Tsukasa Ogasawara[1]

[1] Graduate School of Information Science,
Nara Institute of Science and Technology, Japan
{atsutoshi-i,kurita,takeshi-t,ogasawar}@is.naist.jp
[2] Intelligent Systems Research Institute,
National Institute of Advanced Industrial Science and Technology, Japan
k-nagata@aist.go.jp

Abstract. This paper presents a haptic augmented reality (AR) system that consists of a real object and a haptic device. The desired force response is achieved by the combination of the real force response of a base object and the virtual force exerted by a haptic device. The proposed haptic AR system can easily generate the force response of an object with a cheap haptic device and a base object. In the haptic AR method, how we select the base object is very important because virtual stiffness provided to users is created by modifying the reaction force profile of the base object. We compare the three method: VR method , AR method with a soft object and AR method with a hard object in the questionnaire experiment. These results show that the AR method with a soft object has better performance than the other methods.

Keywords: haptic interface, augmented reality.

1   Introduction

Haptic devices are one of promising interfaces as a human-computer interaction tool that provides users further information in virtual reality environment. Recently, haptic devices are used for a surgery simulator which is required to exert a complicated reaction force [1] [2]. On the other hand, many modeling method which calculates feedback force and deformation of a viscoelastic object are proposed [3] [4] [5]. However, in order to enhance these feedback force, the actuators and sensors have to be improved and it comes with a high cost.

Nagata et al. have developed a haptic recorder system. It can 1) visualize a human skill, 2) measure, record and display the physical parameters between the tool and an environment, and 3) present an augmented reality of haptics [6,7]. Jeon et al. have proposed basic algorithm of the haptic AR that can alter the stiffness of a real object perceived by a user via a force feedback haptic interface [8]. We have presented a haptic augmented reality (AR) system that can easily generate force response of a viscoelastic object with a haptic device and a base object [9]. Fig. 1 shows the concept of the proposed method. It is difficult to exert the non-linear force of viscoelastic object using the

A.M.L. Kappers et al. (Eds.): EuroHaptics 2010, Part I, LNCS 6191, pp. 111–116, 2010.

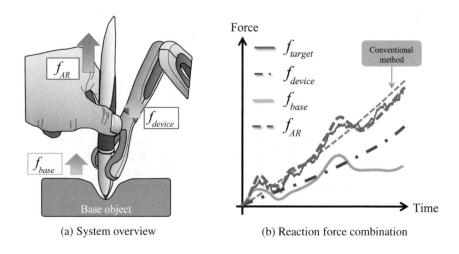

(a) System overview   (b) Reaction force combination

Fig. 1. Concept of the haptic augmented reality method

haptic device only (fig. 1 (b) thin dashed line). The haptic AR interface has potential to easily generate the non-linear force of viscoelastic objects by using a base object that has similar property to the target object (fig. 1 (b) heavy dashed line). The desired force f_{target} is generated as f_{AR} by the combination of the real force of a base object f_{base} and the virtual force exerted by a haptic device f_{device}:

$$f_{AR} = f_{base} + f_{device}. \tag{1}$$

The long term goal of our study is to propose a haptic system that operate viscoelastic objects like a medical simulator using the haptic AR method.

In the haptic AR method, how we select the base object is very important because virtual stiffness provided to users is created by modifying the reaction force profile of the base object. The haptic force presented to users can be altered in weakening and strengthening manners. Additional positive force on the reaction force of the base object creates a virtual softer object; negative force creates a harder objects. In this paper, we try the weakening and strengthening manners on the elastic gels and evaluate the performance through the experiment and questionnaire survey. The haptic AR system and the object models that are used in this paper are explained. The questionnaire survey results by 10 subjects are shown. These results show that the AR strengthening method with a soft object has better performance than the other methods.

2   Experimental System

Fig. 2 shows the overview of the experiment system. The haptic device (SensAble Technologies: PHANTOM Omni) with a force sensor (BL AUTOTEC: Nano25). The haptic device is activated by a linear slider robot (YAMAHA Motor: F10) when a reaction force is measured. The reaction force of the object is recorded in a computer via an

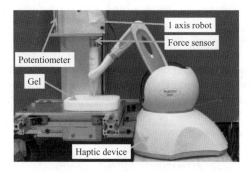

Fig. 2. Overview of the experimental system

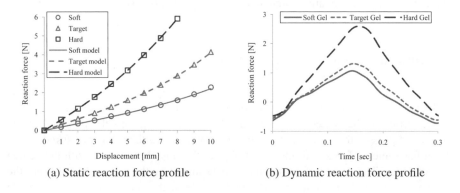

(a) Static reaction force profile   (b) Dynamic reaction force profile

Fig. 3. Reaction force profile of the objects

A/D board with the sampling rate of 1 [kHz] from the force sensor. The haptic device controlled by a computer using a force sensor and a potentiometer (COPAL: JCL300B) to exert a accurate force.

Before the experiment, the reaction force of three objects (Target gel, Soft gel, hard gel) that have different stiffness were measured. These objects are made of an elastic gel (EXSEAL: Hitohada gel). Based on the force profiles of the objects, the desired force profiles f_{target}, f_{soft} and f_{hard} are modeled by the third order polynomial functions:

$$f_{target} = 1.8 \times 10^{-3}x^3 - 7.9 \times 10^{-3}x^2 + 3.1 \times 10^{-1}x \tag{2}$$

$$f_{soft} = 7.1 \times 10^{-4}x^3 - 0.3 \times 10^{-3}x^2 + 1.8 \times 10^{-1}x \tag{3}$$

$$f_{hard} = 2.2 \times 10^{-3}x^3 + 6.1 \times 10^{-3}x^2 + 5.5 \times 10^{-1}x \tag{4}$$

where x is the displacement. Fig. 3 (a) shows the model force profiles and the static reaction force profiles. Fig. 3 (b) shows the reaction force profiles when the linear slider robot pushed and popped the object with 4.0 [mm] stroke at 30.0 [mm/sec]. The robot motion is imitated human active sensing motion of an object stiffness. Each object has a different reaction force profile.

In the VR method, the force generated from the haptic device is determined by the desired force profile only:

$$f_{deviceVR} = f_{target}.$$ (5)

In the AR method, the device force $f_{deviceARsoft}$ and $f_{deviceARhard}$ are given by subtracting the force response of the base objects f_{soft} and f_{hard} from the desired force profile f_{target}:

$$f_{deviceARsoft} = f_{target} - f_{soft}$$ (6)

$$f_{deviceARhard} = f_{target} - f_{hard}$$ (7)

where $f_{deviceARsoft}$ is negative force and $f_{deviceARhard}$ is positive force because $f_{soft} < f_{target} < f_{hard}$.

3 Subjective Assessment Experiment

In this experiment, the subjective assessment of the haptic sensation was conducted by 10 male subjects aged $22 \sim 31$. Prior to beginning the experiment, the informed consent from all the subjects were obtained. The subject grasps the pen tool of the device and presses the tip onto the virtual/real object, and then they are asked which object has same stiffness with the target object. The answer is scored with his degree of confidence. The degree of confidence is determined by the subject himself, but the summation of the degree must be 10. For example, if the subject hesitates to decide between soft and medium, he can answer "soft with 3 degree; medium with 7 degree". In the experiment, 12 experimental setups were performed. The setups consist of 3 object types (Soft gel, Target gel, Hard gel) and 4 patterns of the force generation (Real, VR, AR(strengthening), AR(weakening)). The haptic device exert vertical force only.

It is well known that the visual information largely affects the subjective assessment of the haptic sensation [10]. In order to eliminate the influence of the visual information, the system was covered with a box and consequently subjects can not see that the haptic feedback is generated by the real force response of the base object, the VR method, or the AR method.

Fig. 4 shows questionnaire results. The scores in the figure are the average of the degree of confidence. This result shows that the subjects can find the correct object when participants touch the real objects. When the reaction force is generated by the VR method, few subjects feel the desired stiffness. When the reaction force is generated by the AR method using a hard base object, i.e. weakening case, subjects feel harder stiffness than the desired stiffness. On the other hand, when the reaction force is generated by the AR method using a soft base object, i.e. strengthening case, relatively better performance is observed than the other method. The t-test result shows the statistically significant difference between the VR and AR methods using a soft base object.

Fig. 5 shows the reaction force profiles produced by each method when the robot pushed and popped the object with 4.0 [mm] at 30.0 [mm/sec]. The force profile produced by the VR method is relatively weak; force produced by the AR method using a

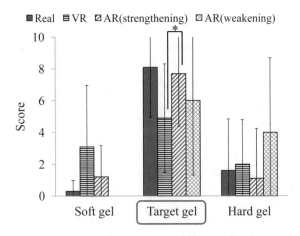

Fig. 4. Score distribution of subjective assessment (*: $p \leq 0.05$)

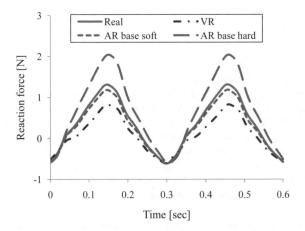

Fig. 5. Reaction force profile of each method

hard base object is strong. On the other hand, the AR method using a soft base object presented good force profile. A possible reason why such a difference is observed is the limitation of the response capability of the haptic device we use. The haptic device we use in the experiment does not have the response capability good enough to follow the desired force response. Although a well-selected base object counteracts force response that is hard to follow for the cheap haptic device, modifying the stiffness of hard objects requires high response capability for a haptic device because the force response of hard objects is high. If the haptic device has performance good enough, both strengthening and weakening manners could be adopted. However, if not, strengthening the force would be relatively easy to create the virtual stiffness illusion.

4   Conclusion

This paper presented the haptic augmented reality (AR) that consists of a real object and a haptic device. The proposed haptic AR system can easily generate the force response of an object with a cheap haptic device and a base object. In the questionnaire experiments, we compare the three method: VR method , AR method using soft base object and AR method using hard base object. Experimental results show that the better performance of the AR method than the VR method.

Promising applications of the proposed haptic AR are the manipulation of the objects that have a complex force response and are not easy to be obtained. A training simulator of cleaning rare fishes and cutting expensive meat, and a medical simulator that represents the haptic forces of the body organs and tissues are good examples of potential applications.

Future work includes improving the model and control method of the AR interface. We plan to utilize the haptic recorder system to construct the force feedback model of the AR interface. We also plan to examine the effect not only vertical force but also another direction forces.

References

1. (Lap mentor), http://www.simbionix.com/LAP_Mentor.html
2. (Mentice mist), http://www.mentice.com/
3. Wu, W., Heng, P.A.: An improved scheme of an interactive finite element model for 3d soft-tissue cutting and deformation. The Visual Computer 21(8-10), 707–716 (2005)
4. Ghoi, C., Kim, J., Han, H., Ahn, B., Kim, J.: Graphic and haptic modeling of the oesophagus for vr-based medical simulation. International Journal of Medical Robotics and Computer Assisted Surgery 5(3), 257–266 (2009)
5. Lim, Y.J., Deo, D., Singh, T.P., Jones, D.B., De, S.: In situ measurement and modeling of biomechanical response of human cadaveric soft tissues for physics-based surgical simulation. International Journal of Medical Robotics and Computer Assisted Surgery 23(6), 1298–1307 (2009)
6. Nagata, K., Tada, M., Iwasaki, H., Kida, Y.: Development of haptic recorder 1st report: Development of basic system. In: Proc. of the SICE System Integration Symposium, pp. 484–485 (2006) (in Japanese)
7. Nagata, K., Tada, M., Iwasaki, H., Kida, Y.: Development of haptic recorder 2nd report: Constructing a virtual object model based on actual measurment. In: Proc. of the SICE System Integration Symposium, pp. 11–12 (2007) (in Japanese)
8. Jeon, S., Choi, S.: Modulating real object stiffness for haptic augmented reality. In: Ferre, M. (ed.) EuroHaptics 2008. LNCS, vol. 5024, pp. 609–618. Springer, Heidelberg (2008)
9. Kurita, Y., Ikeda, A., Tamaki, T., Nagata, K., Ogasawara, T.: Haptic augmented reality interface using the real force response of an object. In: The 16th ACM Symposium on Virtual Reality Software and Technology, pp. 83–86 (2009)
10. Hayashi, D., Ohnishi, H., Nakamura, N.: Understand the effect of visual information and delay on a haptic display. IEICE technical report. Education technology 106(437), 7–10 (2006)

Extended Rate-Hardness: A Measure for Perceived Hardness

Gabjong Han and Seungmoon Choi

Haptics and Virtual Reality Laboratory
Department of Computer Science and Engineering
Pohang University of Science and Technology (POSTECH)
{hkj84,choism}@postech.ac.kr

Abstract. This paper presents a measure for assessing the perceived hardness of a haptic surface based on associated physical variables. This metric, named extended rate-hardness (ERH), is extended from rate-hardness originally proposed by Lawrence et al. in order to cover a larger class of rendering algorithms and applications. We also performed a psychophysical evaluation using absolute magnitude estimation to quantify the extent to which the ERH can account for perceived hardness. The findings have implications to developing haptic interfaces and rendering algorithms with improved perceptual hardness.

Keywords: Hardness perception, stiffness perception, rate-hardness, extended rate-hardness.

1 Introduction

Since Harper and Stevens showed that stiffness is related to perceived hardness through the power law [6], a number of studies on the perception of hardness have followed, with more emphasis on bare-hand perception (for example, see [15,3,1]). Studies relevant to tool-mediated interaction have been relatively scarce, except [9,10], despite its prevalence in current force-reflecting haptic interfaces. Elucidating the physical cues that determine hardness perception in tool-mediated perception is of fundamental significance for the design of haptic interfaces and rendering algorithms.

A virtual wall has long been used as a benchmark for perceived hardness that a haptic system can provide [14]. In the past, a great number of studies have attempted to increase the range of apparent impedance that can be stably rendered by presenting suitable kinesthetic cues (see [2] for a classic study). The persistent research efforts have brought significant improvements in both device designs and stable control algorithms, but the range of perceptual hardness achievable with this approach is still quite limited.

More recently, related research has turned eyes to the contact transients that occur at a contact between an object surface and a tool held in the hand. Such transient vibrations resulted from real objects have frequency components from tens to hundreds Hz [8]. There has been increasing evidence that creating tactile contact transients at a contact greatly improves the hardness and realism of virtual object rendering [11,8,5]. At present, however, our understandings on the extent of improvements with this new approach are immature, especially for the range of perceived hardness (although see a

A.M.L. Kappers et al. (Eds.): EuroHaptics 2010, Part I, LNCS 6191, pp. 117–124, 2010.

case study in [5]). This is in part due to the lack of appropriate physical measures that can be directly linked to perceived hardness.

In this paper, we report the results of an investigation regarding the feasibility of rate-hardness, proposed by Lawrence et al. [10], being an adequate metric for assessing the perceived hardness resulted from contact tactile transients in tool-mediated haptic perception. We slightly extended the original definition of rate-hardness in order to cover a larger class of rendering algorithms and applications. To assess its applicability, we performed a psychophysical evaluation using absolute magnitude estimation for a large number of sample surfaces. Evaluation results demonstrated the adequacy of extended rate-hardness for a measure of perceived hardness in tool-mediated exploration. Compared to the pairwise discrimination approach used in [10], the present evaluation has more direct implications to haptic virtual surface rendering.

2   Extended Rate-Hardness

The original rate-hardness (ORH) is defined as

$$\text{ORH} = \frac{\text{Initial rate of change of force (N/s)}}{\text{Initial penetration velocity (m/s)}}. \tag{1}$$

The ORH was shown to be a more relevant metric than stiffness for predicting the perceived hardness of a virtual surface with physical variables [10].

Since the proposal of rate-hardness, new haptic rendering algorithms and applications which call for an extension have emerged. Some of them include a time difference between an initial contact and an abrupt rise of force response after the contact. The time gap can result from various sources, e.g., communication delays between sensing and actuation [12] and special rendering techniques that produce additional contact transients to improve surface hardness [5]. As the ORH does not consider such cases, a more general form of rate-hardness is desired (e.g., see Fig. 4 in [5]). Therefore, we define an extended form of rate-hardness, such that

$$\text{ERH} = \frac{\text{Maximum rate of change of force (N/s)}}{\text{Initial penetration velocity (m/s)}}. \tag{2}$$

The extended rate-hardness (ERH) shares the same idea with the ORH, but also takes into account the steepest force change that can occur within a short time interval after a contact. Note that the denominator in (2) is the same as that of the ORH. Correlation between initial and maximum penetration velocities is very high. Penetration velocity inside a surface is usually lower than initial penetration velocity due to the resistance force, but sampling and sensor noises can make maximum velocity be observed a few milliseconds later. Thus, either term can be used, but we have preferred to keep the original definition.

3   Evaluation Methods

Participants. Ten paid participants (9 males and 1 female; 19–24 years old with an average of 21.6) participated in the experiment. All participants were inexperienced users of a force-feedback device, and right-handed by self-report.

Apparatus. A PHANToM 1.5 high force model (SensAble Technology; maximum force 37.5 N) was used to render virtual surfaces. A 6D force/torque sensor (ATI Industrial Automation; model Nano 17) was attached between the last link of the PHANToM and its stylus with a custom-made adapter to measure forces delivered to the participant's hand. The PHANToM was controlled at 1 kHz using the GHOST library. The force sensor output was sampled at 2 kHz using a data acquisition card (National Instrument; model 6351), and each two consecutive samples were averaged for noise reduction.

Experimental Conditions. We used two methods to render virtual surfaces. The first method made use of the traditional linear impedance model with a stiffness coefficient K only. The other was a stiffness shifting algorithm that increments rendering stiffness from initial stiffness K_i to K when a short time interval ΔT elapses after a contact [5]. This algorithm creates tactile contact transients that greatly improve perceived hardness (up to 2.5 times; see [5]) in an efficient manner. We set $K_i = 0.1$ N/mm and $\Delta T = 30$ ms. These values did not incur any unrealistic sensation, including the instability problem, for the PHANToM 1.5 high force model. Note that the two rendering methods were identical when $K = 0.1$ N/mm. The virtual surfaces were horizontal, and the participant tapped the surfaces vertically. For rendering stiffness K, we used four values: 0.1 and 0.4 N/mm representing soft surfaces, and 0.7 and 1.0 N/mm representing relatively stiff surfaces. Higher stiffness led to unstable rendering. As a result, a total of eight experimental conditions were defined by combining two rendering methods and four stiffness values.

To obtain data in a large range of contact velocities, we selected the 15 target velocities that were evenly spaced between 0.05 and 0.75 m/s. Human tapping velocity for stiffness perception usually falls in 0.05–1.00 m/s [7]. Target velocities higher than 0.75 m/s were not used due to the PHANToM safety feature that quits rendering for tip movements faster than 1 m/s. Including each target tapping velocity, the total number of trials was 120 in each session.

Procedures. The perceived hardness of a virtual surface was assessed via absolute magnitude estimation [4]. In each trial, the participant was asked to tap a virtual surface once, while maintaining target contact velocity. The participant then reported the absolute hardness of the surface in a positive real number. After the response, feedback for measured tapping velocity was given on a monitor screen. The participant was encouraged to match target tapping velocity based on the feedback. Since our purpose was to obtain data in a large velocity range, we did not enforce more strict tapping velocity control. No other visual information was provided. Auditory cues were also blocked by the white noise played through headphones worn by the participant.

The experiment consisted of four sessions (one training and three main). In each session, the participant finished all of the 120 trials. An order of trials was randomized for each participant and session. The first session was for training; the participant practiced tapping a virtual surface with target tapping velocity, and stabilized an absolute scale for perceived hardness. The data of this training session was discarded, and was not used for data analysis. Each session took about 10–15 minutes, and the whole experiment took about one and half hours. The participant was given a break between the sessions.

Data Analysis. Relevant physical variables were processed as follows. Position and force measurements in the height direction, thus perpendicular to the virtual surfaces used in the experiment, were taken. Tapping velocities were estimated by applying the backward difference on the position data. They were then filtered by a 1-pole Butterworth low-pass filter with a cutoff frequency of 20 Hz, preserving information on human voluntary movements (the bandwidth is less than 10 Hz). To obtain the actual stiffness provided to the user, the raw penetration depth and force data were filtered by the same low-pass filter, and their ratios were computed. These values were averaged for the stiffness of each trial. The instantaneous rate of force change was estimated by applying the backward difference to the raw force data (not filtered) and then a 4-pole Butterworth low-pass filter with a cutoff frequency of 500 Hz to these force rate data for smoothing, which allowed to preserve information on the contact transients [8]. To compute the ERH, force change rates in a 100-ms time window after a contact were examined to find a maximum change rate. In addition, to compare the peak force rate considered in a previous study [3] with our ERH, the maximum force and its time from the contact were found from the raw data.

The estimates of perceived hardness were normalized following the standard procedures to adjust for intersubject differences in the ranges of numeric responses. All the data were transformed into a logarithmic scale of base 10, and each raw score was subtracted from the difference between the grand mean and the mean of the participant. The normalized logarithmic score was then transformed back. This normalization process eliminates between-subject differences without affecting within-subject differences.

4   Evaluation Results

We first examined the relevance of many physical variables obtained in the experiment to the hardness perception of virtual surface. The variables considered were rendering method, measured stiffness, contact velocity, ORH, ERH, peak force, and peak force rate. The correlations between the physical variables and perceived hardness are shown in Table 2. The table suggests that the ERH has the greatest relevance to hardness perception. It was the only variable that exhibited high correlation with perceived hardness (0.610). On the other hand, the ORH showed negligible correlation (-0.027), since the ORH cannot capture the steepest force change present in the stiffness shifting algorithm [5]. The other five variables showed very low or little correlation with perceived hardness (all less than 0.378). In particular, hardness perception was independent from tapping velocity (correlation -0.004), consistently with a previous observation in [9]. The low correlations of peak force and peak force rate with perceived hardness (0.378 and 0.308, respectively) were also in agreement with [3]. Note that the correlations of tapping velocity with all of the other variables were also very low, except peak force and peak force rate.

Next, we applied stepwise linear regression using the seven variables to select the best candidates for further analysis. Results are presented in Table 1 where only three

Table 1. Correlation matrix of physical variables and perceived hardness

Variable	(1)	(2)	(3)	(4)	(5)	(6)	(7)	(8)
(1) Rendering Method	1.000							
(2) Peak Force	0.183	1.000						
(3) Peak Force Rate	0.041	-0.746	1.000					
(4) Measured Velocity	0.001	0.269	0.263	1.000				
(5) Measured Stiffness	-0.226	0.286	0.306	-0.104	1.000			
(6) Original Rate-Hardness	-0.578	0.146	0.219	-0.037	0.588	1.000		
(7) Extended Rate-Hardness	0.435	0.638	0.486	-0.008	0.371	0.014	1.000	
(8) Perceived Hardness	0.323	0.378	0.308	-0.004	0.242	-0.027	**0.610**	1.000

Table 2. Results of stepwise linear regression performed for variable selection

Step	Variable	Partial R^2	F	p
1	Extended Rate-Hardness	0.3717	2128.23	<.0001
2	Rendering Method	0.0041	23.67	<.0001
3	Measured Stiffness	0.0028	16.14	<.0001

statistically significant variables are listed in the order of importance. The ERH was the most important variable for perceived hardness with the highest coefficient of determination ($R^2 = 0.3717$). The other two significant variables were rendering method and measured stiffness, but their R^2 values were considerably smaller (0.0041 and 0.0028, respectively). As a result, the variability of perceived hardness explained by the ERH was as high as 98% in the model. Note that the total R^2 was relatively small, presumably because of nonlinear relationships between the three variables and perceived hardness and the inevitably noisy nature of measured variables.

To present summarized results, we averaged the values of measured stiffness, ORH, and ERH across target velocities for the eight virtual surfaces used in the experiment. Recall that the measured stiffness, ORH, and ERH were independent from tapping velocity in Table 2. The results are shown in Fig. 1 where surfaces 1 – 4 and 5 – 8 represent those rendered using the linear spring model and the stiffness shifting algorithm, respectively. The surfaces in each group had stiffness commands in $K = 0.1 - 1.0$ N/mm in an increasing order with 0.3 N/mm step. For surfaces 1 – 4, all of the measured stiffness, ORH, and ERH were highly correlated to the perceived hardness. This was due to the use of a linear impedance model with no damping. In contrast, for surfaces 5 – 8 where contact transients were added by the stiffness shifting algorithm, the stiffness and ORH ceased to be good measures. The perceived hardness was significantly increased compared to that of a virtual surface rendered using the linear spring model with the same stiffness command (recall that surfaces 1 and 5 were the same when $K = 0.1$ N/mm). However, the measured stiffness dropped off because of the use of lower initial stiffness in the stiffness shifting algorithm. The ORH values were almost constant for surfaces 5 – 8, since the ORH only considers an initial response force change. The values of ERH for surfaces 5 – 8 were significantly higher than the corresponding values for surfaces 1 – 4, faithfully reflecting the perceived hardness increases.

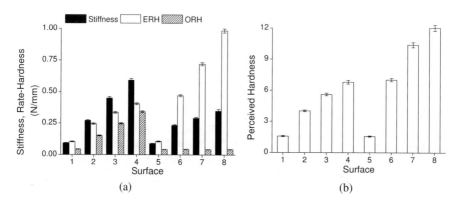

Fig. 1. Summarized results of (a) measured stiffness, ORH, and ERH, and (b) perceived hardness on eight virtual surfaces. The error bars represent standard errors.

In summary, all of the analysis results support that the ERH can be a robust measure for predicting the perceived hardness of a virtual surface perceived via a tool held in the hand, at least under the conditions used in the experiment.

5   Discussion

Peak force and peak force rate were once believed to be important cues for hardness perception [9], but a recent study showed that both measurements were irrelevant to hardness perception via a rigid tool [3]. Our results in Table 2 were also in agreement with this finding. However, the concepts behind peak force, peak force rate, and ERH (or ORH) may appear similar, so this issue deserves further discussion.

Owing to the momentum conservation, tapping velocity must be highly correlated to peak force and peak force rate. On the contrary, their correlations were shown relatively low, 0.269 and 0.263, respectively, in Table 2. Thus, we graphically inspected their relations as shown in Fig. 2a. The figure indicates high correlations when tapping velocities were lower than 0.9 m/s, along with an outlier pattern for velocities larger than 0.9 m/s. As a very small number of data were included in the outlier interval and the velocity limit allowed by the PHANToM is about 1.0 m/s, we questioned the reliability of measurements in the interval, and recomputed the correlations after excluding the high velocity outliers. Then the correlations were significantly increased to 0.538 and 0.502, confirming the expectation based on mechanics.

Peak force and peak force rate averaged across tapping velocities for the eight virtual surfaces indeed looked well correlated with perceived hardness, as shown in Fig. 2b. However, their actual correlations to perceived hardness, when all individual data were included, were fairly low, 0.378 and 0.308, as in Table 2. In contrast, maximum instantaneous force change rate (often correlated with peak force and peak force rate) normalized by tapping velocity, i.e., the ERH, exhibited much higher correlation (0.610). This comparison indicates that the ERH is a more accurate and robust measure for hardness perception through a rigid link. It can also be evidence for human ability to compensate afferent information on dynamic stimuli using efferent information on motor intents.

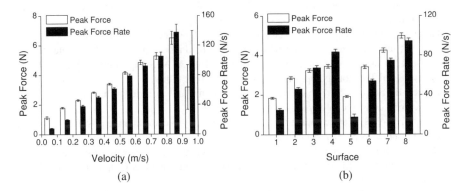

Fig. 2. Peak force and peak force rate for (a) different velocity bands and (b) the eight virtual surfaces. The error bars represent standard errors.

We also plan to expand investigations for ERH by including other contact transient rendering algorithms (e.g., adding a pulse [13] or an exponentially decaying sinusoidal signal [8] at contact) and more general impedance models with a damping term or communication delays. Such efforts would eventually determine the general applicability of ERH. If the ERH is indeed shown as a faithful measure for hardness perception, then we can use the ERH as a measure for contact tactile transients and the stiffness as a measure for kinesthetic cues, which may lead to further studies finding the relative contributions of tactile and kinesthetic cues for tool-mediated hardness perception. Such knowledge would have fundamental significance for research directions toward hard wall rendering.

6   Conclusions

In this paper, an extended form of rate-hardness is presented which can be applied to a larger class of rendering algorithms and applications than its original definition. A psychophysical experiment verified that the ERH can be a powerful measure for explaining perceptual hardness with the values of associated proximal stimuli at supra-threshold levels. The results have direct implications for improving the perceived hardness of virtual wall rendering.

Acknowledgments. This work was supported in parts by an NRL program R0A-2008-000-20087-0 from NRF and by an ITRC program NIPA-2010-C1090-1031-0006 from NIPA, both funded by the Korean government.

References

1. Bergmann Tiest, W.M., Kappers, A.M.L.: Cues for haptic perception of compliance. IEEE Transactions on Haptics 2, 189–199 (2009)
2. Colgate, J., Brown, J.: Factors affecting the z-width of a haptic display. In: Proc. of IEEE International Conference on Robotics and Automation, pp. 3205–3210 (1994)

3. Friedman, R., Hester, K., Green, B., LaMotte, R.: Magnitude estimation of softness. Experimental Brain Research 191(2), 133–142 (2008)
4. Gescheider, G.: Psychophysics: The Fundamentals. Lawrence Erlbaum, Mahwah (1997)
5. Han, G., Jeon, S., Choi, S.: Improving perceived hardness of haptic rendering via stiffness shifting: An initial study. In: Proceedings of the 16th ACM Symposium on Virtual Reality Software and Technology, pp. 87–90. ACM, New York (2009)
6. Harper, R., Stevens, S.: Subjective hardness of compliant materials. The Quarterly Journal of Experimental Psychology 16(3), 204–215 (1964)
7. Jeon, S., Choi, S.: Haptic augmented reality: Taxonomy and an example of stiffness modulation. Presence 18(5), 387–408 (2009)
8. Kuchenbecker, K., Fiene, J., Niemeyer, G.: Improving contact realism through event-based haptic feedback. IEEE Transactions on Visualization and Computer Graphics 12(2), 219–230 (2006)
9. LaMotte, R.: Softness discrimination with a tool. Journal of Neurophysiology 83(4), 1777–1786 (2000)
10. Lawrence, D., Pao, L., Dougherty, A., Salada, M., Pavlou, Y.: Rate-hardness: A new performance metric for haptic interfaces. IEEE Transactions on Robotics and Automation 16(4), 357–371 (2000)
11. Okamura, A., Cutkosky, M., Dennerlein, J.: Reality-based models for vibration feedback in virtual environments. IEEE/ASME Transactions on Mechatronics 6(3), 245–252 (2001)
12. Pressman, A., Welty, L., Karniel, A., Mussa-Ivaldi, F.: Perception of delayed stiffness. The International Journal of Robotics Research 26(11-12), 1191–1204 (2007)
13. Salcudean, S., Vlaar, T.: On the emulation of stiff walls and static friction with a magnetically levitated input/output device. Journal of Dynamic Systems, Measurement, and Control 119(1), 127–132 (1997)
14. Salisbury, K., Brock, D., Massie, T., Swarup, N., Zilles, C.: Haptic rendering: Programming touch interaction with virtual objects. In: Proc. of the ACM Symposium on Interactive 3D Graphics, pp. 123–130 (1995)
15. Srinivasan, M., LaMotte, R.: Tactual discrimination of softness. Journal of Neurophysiology 73(1), 88–101 (1995)

Using a Fingertip Tactile Device to Substitute Kinesthetic Feedback in Haptic Interaction

Domenico Prattichizzo, Claudio Pacchierotti, Stefano Cenci,
Kouta Minamizawa, and Giulio Rosati

[1]Dept. of Information Engineering, University of Siena, Italy
[2]Italian Institute of Technology, Genova, Italy
[3]Dept. of Innovation in Mechanics and Management, University of Padua, Italy
[4]Graduate School of Media Design, University of Keio, Japan
prattichizzo@ing.unisi.it, pacchierott4@student.unisi.it,
stefano.cenci@mechatronics.it, Kouta_Minamizawa@ipc.i.u-tokyo.ac.jp,
giulio.rosati@unipd.it

Abstract. A prototype of a joystick where the kinesthetic feedback is substituted by tactile feedback is proposed. Tactile feedback is provided by a wearable device able to apply vertical stress to the fingertip in contact with the joystick. To test the device, rigid wall rendering is considered. Preliminary experiments show that the sensation of touching a virtual wall using the force feedback provided by the electric motor of the joystick is nearly indistinguishable from the sensation felt by the user using the tactile display only. The proposed device does not suffer from typical stability issues of teleoperation systems and is intrinsically safe.

Keywords: tactile display, force rendering, stability.

1   Introduction

Haptic feedback is fundamental for the human operator to perform complex tasks safely. For instance, studies on manual minimally invasive surgery (MIS) have linked the lack of significant haptic feedback in MIS to increased intraoperative injury [1]. To obtain a realistic representation of the remote environment, haptic interfaces, of the impedance type, available today use active input devices as motors to generate forces on the operator's hand. However, stability and transparency of such systems can be significantly affected by communication latency, reducing their applicability and effectiveness in case of stiff remote environments [2,3]. This limitation can be alleviated by implementing proper control systems [4,3], or by substituting master actuation with passive components such as brakes [5]. However, passive input devices have rendering limitations and may lead to large steady-state errors in teleoperation tasks. A more recent approach consists of using motors and brakes together, with the aim of obtaining a safer teleoperation while preserving system transparency [6]. Another interesting way of achieving stability is sensory substitution, which consists of replacing kinesthetic feedback with other forms of feedback such as auditory and/or visual feedback [7,8] or vibrotactile feedback [9]. Passive devices and sensory substitution approaches are particularly interesting, as the risk of producing motion of the master device due to active actuation is dramatically reduced.

A.M.L. Kappers et al. (Eds.): EuroHaptics 2010, Part I, LNCS 6191, pp. 125–130, 2010.

We propose here a novel approach in which a non-actuated master handle is used in combination with a wearable tactile feedback device. In this system, the slave device can track the position of the human hand, as in conventional teleoperation systems, while the contact force between the hand and the handle is substituted by a normal force produced at fingertips by a tactile device. It is worth noting that, differently from other examples of sensory substitution as in [9], where a vibrotactile force is produced on the bottom surface of the foot, in our system the tactile force, fed back to the user, is similar, in terms of application area and intensity, to the one perceived by interacting with an active handle. It will be shown in the experiment section that the absence of active actuation of the handle makes the system very safe to operate, even in the presence of large transmission delays.

2   The Tactile Device Substituting Kinesthetic Feedback

Inspired by the recent work on tactile feedback developed in [10,11], we propose an innovative combination of tactile force feedback and a handle able to track the position of the human hand. The prototype is shown in Fig. 1 where a joystick is held by the subject hand wearing a tactile device applying normal forces at the index fingertip. The joystick is thought of as a device with no actuation: the only force feedback at the user's hand is provided by the tactile device. Indeed, in Sec. 3 joystick motors will be used to compare results with conventional haptic rendering techniques. The joystick employed in this study was first used for testing a teleoperation scheme to enhance stability of heavy duty machines [12].

The idea behind tactile substitution is that the role of kinesthetic force feedback generated with proper actuation of the joystick can be partially replaced by a local tactile action: a normal stress at the fingertip generated by a simple mechanism consisting of two motors and a belt wrapping the fingertip as in Fig. 1. Note that this device has been designed to generate also tangential stress [11] but here only vertical stress is taken into account.

It will be shown in the experiment that there is no relevant degradation of performances in haptic interaction tasks, like touching virtual walls, when using the vertical stress instead of the kinesthetic force feedback. The substitution idea is supported also by recent findings in [10] where the authors use a single point kinesthesia model to simulate complex contact interaction with objects through multiple points.

3   Experiments

Preliminary experiments have been performed. The experimental setup consists of the device shown in Fig. 1, simulating a haptic interaction along 1–Dof. The simulator for the virtual environment was developed in Matlab. Communication between simulator, joystick and tactile display was realized using the UDP protocol over a local network. Control update rate was set to 1000 Hz.

Regarding haptic rendering, the joystick position is linked to a point (x_h) moving in a 1-DoF virtual environment, with a virtual wall in $x_{wall} = 52$mm. A spring $(K = 3$N/mm$)$ is used to model the contact force F according to the god-object model [13]. Note that

 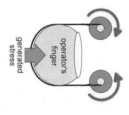

Fig. 1. Shot of the prototype, including the joystick and the tactile device (left). Scheme of the tactile device: two motors allow to generate a stress normal to fingertip (right).

the measured variable is joystick angle θ, while the linear displacement is computed as $x_h = L\theta$ with $L = 1.5$mm/deg.

Five participants (5 males, age range 23–30 years) took part in the trials, all of them were right-handed. Two of them had previous experience with haptic interfaces and perception experiments. None of the participants reported any deficiencies in perception abilities. We asked the subjects to control the joystick with their right hand using the thumb and the index fingers only (Fig. 1), and to stop when they touched the virtual wall (starting point: $x_h = 0$ for all trials).

3.1 Experiment 1: Comparison of the Feedback Modalities

Kinesthetic and tactile feedback were considered alternatively. Force feedback was either applied by the motor of the joystick (in the case of kinesthetic feedback) or it was produced by the motors of the tactile display, rolling up the belt to provide a normal stress at the fingertip of the index finger (in the case of tactile feedback)[1]. Visual feedback, which consisted in showing a moving box and a wall on a computer screen, was either used or switched off.

Each participant made four different tests, whose order was randomly generated for each subject:

- kinesthetic feedback w/ visual feedback, no tactile feedback (task A)
- kinesthetic feedback w/o visual feedback, no tactile feedback (task B)
- tactile feedback w/ visual feedback, no kinesthetic feedback (task C)
- tactile feedback w/o visual feedback, no kinesthetic feedback (task D)

The mean and the maximum values of contact force were estimated from penetration depth $F = K(x_h - x_{\text{wall}})$, for each subject and for each trial. Fig. 2 shows the means and standard deviations of measured mean (left) and maximum (right) contact forces. Comparison between tasks suggests that kinesthetic feedback (A-B) exhibits better performances than tactile feedback (C-D) with or without visual feedback in terms of both maximum and mean contact forces. Note that larger contact forces correspond to larger penetration depth of the virtual wall according to the elastic coefficient K. Nonetheless,

---

[1] Due to the specific tactile device used, the normal stress was discretized into 4 levels.

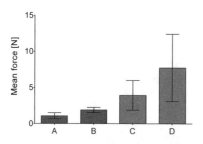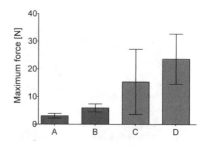

Fig. 2. Mean (left) and maximum (right) contact forces, expressed in [N], during tasks A, B, C ad D. Each bar represents the average of all participants for a single task. Red bars indicate kinesthetic feedback, green bars indicate tactile feedback.

the results observed in tasks C and D suggest that all subjects were able to perceive the presence of the wall and to reach a stable contact position within the wall thanks to tactile feedback only. It is worth noting that the larger contact forces observed when tactile feedback was used may be partly due to the delay of the tactile actuators and in particular to the dynamics of the belt [10,11].

3.2   Experiment 2: Stability with Time Delay

As already pointed out, the main advantage of tactile feedback is not that it is more realistic than kinesthetic feedback, but that it makes the haptic loop intrinsically safe, showing no instability behaviors neither in presence of delays. In Fig. 3, we report probe position $x_h(t)$ versus time for two representative runs in presence of transmission delays. We asked the subject to touch the wall three times. The experiment was performed with kinesthetic feedback (left) and with tactile feedback (right), with no visual feedback. In both cases, a delay of 100ms was introduced in the haptic loop[2]. Fig. 3 clearly shows

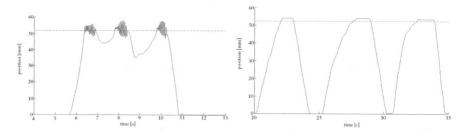

Fig. 3. Joystick probe position $x_h(t)$ expressed in [mm] using kinesthetic feedback (left) and tactile feedback (right), with a network delay of 0.1s in the haptic loop. Dotted red lines represent the position of the virtual wall.

---

[2] Instability of haptic feedback in the presence of time delay can be fixed with wave variable transformation [14]. Nonetheless, with the aim of emphasizing the intrinsic stability of tactile feedback, this method was not used in the trials.

that kinesthetic feedback can bring the haptic loop near to instability, as significant oscillations of the probe x_h position occurred, whereas tactile feedback allows for stable contact with the wall despite the presence of transmission delays.

4 Conclusion

Preliminary experiments with a joystick have shown that tactile feedback at the fingertips may be effectively used to substitute kinesthesia in haptic displays.

The main advantage of using fingertip tactile displays instead of kinesthetic feedback given by the joystick is that the stability of the haptic loop is intrinsically guaranteed. This can be very convenient for critical applications like robotic surgery or hazardous environment robotics. Note also that actuation for tactile displays usually requires less power and is less bulky than that required to generate kinesthetic feedback, with a direct effect on simplifying mechanical design and cost reduction.

The main drawback is that, in spite of a practically indistinguishable sensation of touching a virtual wall, the realism of the interaction certainly improves with kinesthetic feedback. Moreover, it is worth underlying that, to exploit this idea in medical applications like robotic surgery, we need to prove that applying tactile feedback to the fingertips of the operator would not distract him/her from the surgical task. On the other hand, it must be noticed that the fingertip, and the hand in general, is exactly the place where kinesthetic feedback is expected.

Another possible drawback with the tactile feedback option, as proposed in the paper, is that it could put higher stresses on tissues with respect to traditional haptic interaction, unless the tactile device is properly tuned.

While preliminary experiments validate the approach, further analysis is required for a complete evaluation of the proposed concept. We are building new tactile displays with better dynamic performances in order to design and conduct additional psychophysical experiments to assess other relevant parameters, like for instance the JND for stiffness perception.

Acknowledgments

This work has been partially supported by the EC with the Collaborative Project FP7-ICT-2007-215190 "ROBOCAST" and by the Ministero dell'Università e della Ricerca with the PRIN 2008 project "Attuatori innovativi per sistemi avanzati di manipolazione e di interazione aptica".

References

1. Okamura, A.M.: Haptic feedback in robot-assisted minimally invasive surgery. Current Opinion in Urology 18, 1–6 (2008)
2. Colgate, J.E., Stanley, M., Brown, J.: Issues in the haptic display of tool use. In: Proceedings of 1995 IEEE/RSJ International Conference on Intelligent Robots and Systems 1995. Human Robot Interaction and Cooperative Robots, Pittsburgh, PA, vol. 3, pp. 140–145 (1995)

3. Aziminejad, A., Tavakoli, M., Patel, R.V., Moallem, M.: Stability and performance in delayed bilateral teleoperation: Theory and experiments. Control Engineering Practice 16, 1329–1343 (2008)
4. Hashtrudi-Zaad, K., Salcudean, S.: Transparency in time-delayed systems and the effect of local force feedback for transparent teleoperation. IEEE Transactions on Robotics and Automation 18(1), 108–114 (2002)
5. Black, B., Book, W.: Dynamic compensating controller for passive haptic manipulators in teleoperation. In: Proc. of the IEEE International Conference on Robotics and Automation, Kobe, Japan, pp. 1485–1491 (2009)
6. Conti, F., Khatib, O.: A new actuation approach for haptic interface design. The International Journal of Robotics Research 28, 834–848 (2009)
7. Tavakoli, M., Patel, R.V., Moallem, M.: Haptic feedback and sensory substitution during telemanipulated suturing. In: Proceedings of the First Joint Eurohaptics Conference and Symposium on Haptic Interfaces for Virtual Environment and Teleoperator Systems, Pisa, Italy (2005)
8. Kitagawa, M., Dokko, D., Okamura, A.M., Yuh, D.D.: Effect of sensory substitution on suture manipulation forces for robotic surgical systems. Journal of Thoracic and Cardiovascular Surgery 129, 151–158 (2005)
9. Schoonmaker, R.E., Cao, C.G.L.: Vibrotactile force feedback system for minimally invasive surgical procedures. In: Proceedings of the 2006 IEEE International Conference on Systems, Man, and Cybernetics, Taipei, Taiwan (2006)
10. Minamizawa, K., Prattichizzo, D., Tachi, T.: Simplified design of haptic display by extending one-point kinesthetic feedback to multipoint tactile feedback. In: IEEE Haptic Symposium, Waltham, Massachusetts, USA (2010)
11. Minamizawa, K., Fukamachi, S., Kajimoto, H., Kawakami, N., Tachi, S.: Gravity grabber: wearable haptic display to present virtual mass sensation. In: SIGGRAPH 2007: ACM SIGGRAPH 2007 emerging technologies, p. 8. ACM, New York (2007)
12. Rosati, G., Biondi, A., Cenci, S., Boschetti, G., Rossi, A.: A haptic system to enhance stability of heavy duty machines. In: Proc. of the ASME International Mechanical Engineering Congress Exposition, Boston, Massachusetts (2008)
13. Zilles, C., Salisbury, J.: A constraint-based god-object method for haptic display. In: Proceedings of 1995 IEEE/RSJ International Conference on Intelligent Robots and Systems. Human Robot Interaction and Cooperative Robots, vol. 3 (1995)
14. Lam, T.M., Mulder, M., Van Paassen, M.M.: Haptic feedback in UAV tele-operation with time delay. Journal of Guidance, Control & Dynamics 31(6), 1728–1739 (2008)

The Effect of Bimanual Lifting on Grip Force and Weight Perception

Christos Giachritsis and Alan Wing

Behavioural and Brain Sciences Centre, School of Psychology, The University of Birmingham, Edgbaston, Birmingham, B15 2TT, UK
C.Giachritsis@gmail.com, A.M.Wing@bham.ac.uk

Abstract. Previous studies have shown that lifting a weight with two hands feels lighter than lifting the same weight with one hand. One explanation for this effect could be that increasing the number of digits decreases the total grip force required to lift and hold the object therefore, resulting in a 'lighter' percept. Here, we carried out a pilot study on the effect of bimanual lifting on weight perception and total grip force. Preliminary results indicate that bimanually lifted weights feel lighter than unimanually lifted weights and that the total bimanual grip force is not significantly different than the unimanual grip force. Alternative explanations for the illusion of the bimanual 'lighter' weight percept are discussed.

Keywords: Weight Perception, Bimanual Manipulation, Grip Force.

1 Introduction

In everyday life, we may choose to manipulate large or heavy objects with both hands rather than a single hand. Bimanual handling could enable us to secure an object during displacement by effectively doubling the number of digits, as well as sharing its weight between the two hands. Either of these two benefits of bimanual handling could potentially have an effect on weight perception. For example, previous research has shown that weights lifted with both hands feel 'lighter than' similar weights lifted with one hand [1]. There could be at least two possible explanations for this effect. First, increasing the number of digits could decrease the total grip force required to lift and hold the object [2, 3] resulting in a 'lighter' percept [4]. Second, sharing the weight between the two hands could also result in a 'lighter' percept given that some contralaterally accessible sensorimotor weight information could be lost due to lateralisation [5]. Here, we carried out a pilot study to investigate whether the bimanual 'lighter' weight judgments are based on a reduced bimanual grip force due to doubling the digits involved in the grip.

2 Methods

2.1 Participants

Six undergraduates (3 female and 3 male) students from the University of Birmingham, aged between 20 and 22, volunteered to take part in the study. All participants were right-handed and were paid for their participation.

A.M.L. Kappers et al. (Eds.): EuroHaptics 2010, Part I, LNCS 6191, pp. 131–135, 2010.
© Springer-Verlag Berlin Heidelberg 2010

2.2 Stimulus and Apparatus

Three weights were loaded on a box attached to a Novatech 200N force transducer which measured forces normal to the surface where the grip was applied (Figure 1). The total weight of the apparatus was 200, 232 and 264 g. The width of the grip was 55 mm and its sides were covered with a fine (320 grade) sand paper to provide a firm and comfortable grip. The grip forces were recorded using National Instruments LabVIEW software.

Fig. 1. The apparatus used in the experiments consisted of a force transducer attached to the top of a box in which different weights were loaded

2.3 Procedure

The participants used their precision grip to lift a single weight (200, 232, or 264 g) consequently with one hand (RH/LH) and both hands (BH) and then they reported which weight felt heavier. Before the start of the session, they had been told that they would be lifting two different weights. The weight was lifted for about 100 mm and then was returned to its resting position immediately. Each weight was tested 12 times, the presentation order was balanced and the trials were randomised.

3   Results

The unimanual (RH/LH) and bimanual grip forces were recorded while their peak forces were averaged across weights and compared. Figure 2 shows an example of recorded grip forces and their peaks during a single trial.

Figure 3 shows that there was no clear indication that the total unimanual grip force was higher than the bimanual grip force. A two-way (weight x grip mode) repeated measures ANOVA was carried out for each hand. No statistically significant effect of grip mode on peak grip force was found in either LH-BH or RH-BH conditions. As it would be expected, there was a significant main effect of weight on grip

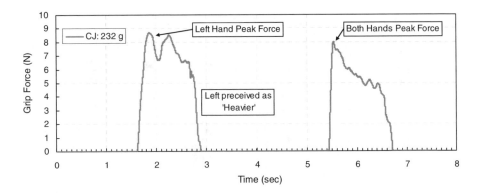

Fig. 2. Example of recorded grip forces when lifting the same weight (232 g) with the left hand and then with both hands (participant CJ)

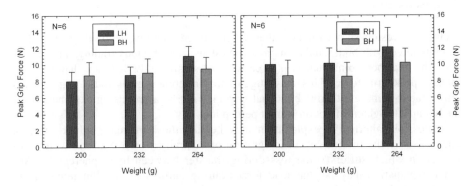

Fig. 3. Mean peak grip force during unimanual (LH/RH) and bimanual (BH) lifting. Error bars represent standard error.

force in both LH-BH (Greenhouse-Geisser correction for sphericity showed $F_{(1.122)}=8.772$, $p=0.26$) and RH-BH ($F_{(2)}=7.804$, $p=0.12$) conditions, indicating that grip force increased with weight. There was also an interaction in the LH-BH condition between weight and grip force ($F_{(2)}=6.529$, $p=0.15$). A linear regression showed that the rate of increase of LH peak grip force (0.0473 Ng^{-1}) with weight was nearly four times higher than the increase of BH peak grip forces (0.0119 Ng^{-1}).

In addition, the proportion of trials in which the unimanually (LH/RH) and the bimanually (BH) lifted weights were perceived as 'heavier' were averaged and compared. Figure 4 shows that weights lifted with the LH or RH felt heavier than weights lifted with BH. A two-way repeated measures ANOVA showed statistically significant effect of grip mode on weigh perception in both LH-BH ($F_{(1)} = 13.466$, $p=0.14$) and RH-BH ($F_{(1)} =7.848$, $p=0.38$) conditions.

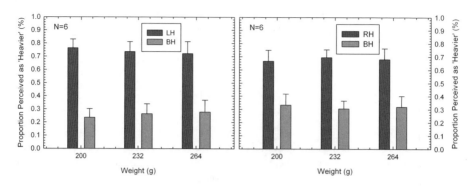

Fig. 4. Mean proportion of trial where unimanually (LH/RH) and bimanually (BH)   lifted weights perceived as heavier. Error bars represent constant error

4   Discussion

Preliminary results showed mainly that weights lifted with one hand felt heavier than weights lifted with both hands which is consistent with previous findings [1]. However, the total peak bimanual grip force was not significantly different than the unimanual peak grip force. This may suggest that afferent signals indicating reduced effort due to a more effective bimanual grip may not be a promising explanation for the bimanual 'lighter' effect on weight perception.

A possible alternative explanation may be that the bimanual 'lighter' percept could also be the product of an integration of centrally stored bilateral weight information which suffers some loss during transfer between hemispheres [5]. Another explanation may be that load forces during unimanual and bimanual lifting could depend both on internal motor commands as well as peripheral signals. For example, we know from experience that we use both hands to manipulate heavy or large objects. This may have formed internal expectations about the physical weight of an object which is handled bimanually: that is, expectation of a heavy weight when employing both hands. This in turn may result in a bimanual motor command that employs a stronger grip and/or faster lifting to overcome the gravitational forces acting on the 'expected' greater mass. Currently, we conduct further research to test these alternative explanations.

Acknowledgments. This work was funded by the European Commission under the IMMERSENCE Integrated Project of the Sixth Frame Program (IST-4-027141-IP).

References

1. Giachritsis, C.D., Wing, A.M.: Unimanual and bimanual weight discrimination in a desktop setup. In: Ferre, M. (ed.) EuroHaptics 2008. LNCS, vol. 5024, pp. 378–382. Springer, Heidelberg (2008)
2. Kinoshita, H., Kawai, S., Ikuta, K.: Contributions and co-ordination of individual fingers in multiple finger prehension. Ergon. 38(6), 1212–1230 (1995)

3. Kinoshita, H., Murade, T., Bandu, T.: Grip posture and forces during holding cylindrical objects with circular grips. Ergon. 39(9), 1163–1176 (1996)
4. Flanagan, J.R., Bandomir, C.A.: Coming to grips with weight perception: Effects of grasp configuration on weight heaviness. Percept. Psychophys. 62(6), 1204–1219 (2000)
5. Gordon, A., Forssberg, H., Iwasaki, N.: Formation and lateralization of internal representations underlying motor commands during precision grip. Neuropsychologia 32, 555–568 (1994)

How to Build an Inexpensive 5-DOF Haptic Device Using Two Novint Falcons

Aman V. Shah, Scott Teuscher, Eric W. McClain, and Jake J. Abbott

Department of Mechanical Engineering, University of Utah
Salt Lake City, UT, 84112, USA
{aman.shah,scott.teuscher,eric.mcclain,jake.abbott}@utah.edu

Abstract. We demonstrate how two Novint Falcons, inexpensive commercially available haptic devices, can be modified to a create a reconfigurable five-degree-of-freedom (5-DOF) haptic device for less than $500 (including the two Falcons). The device is intended as an educational tool to allow a broader range of students to experience force and torque feedback, rather than the 3-DOF force feedback typical of inexpensive devices. We also explain how to implement a 5-DOF force/torque control system with gravity compensation.

Keywords: Falcon, Torque Feedback, Gravity Compensation, Education.

1   Introduction

A number of commercially available haptic devices are available on the market. Inexpensive devices are limited to three degree-of-freedom (3-DOF) of force feedback, limiting users to point-like interactions, which places limits on the realism of haptic virtual environments. Haptic devices with 5- or 6-DOF of actuation exist—enabling both force and torque feedback—but cost many tens of thousands of dollars. One solution to this problem is to construct a 5-DOF haptic device by connecting two 3-DOF devices [1]. In this paper we demonstrate how two Novint Falcons—commercially available devices that costs less than $200 each [2]—can be nondestructively modified to a create a reconfigurable 5-DOF device for less than an additional $100. We explain how to implement gravity compensation on Falcons, and we show how to modify the two Falcon control systems to display a single 5-DOF force/torque. The complete instructions, mechanical drawings, and parts list to build the device shown in Fig. 1 can be found on the Utah Telerobotics Lab web page [3]. In addition, we have posted sample code implementing a 5-DOF controller with gravity compensation and a simple virtual environment using the open-source CHAI 3D software [4].

2   Hardware

Our modified 5-DOF device is shown in Fig. 1. The stylus is a simple rod with ball joints attached on each end. The concept behind the our device is to allow the same hardware to be reconfigured such that the stylus of the device can be either vertical or horizontal when the Falcons are in their respective zero positions, which roughly

A.M.L. Kappers et al. (Eds.): EuroHaptics 2010, Part I, LNCS 6191, pp. 136–143, 2010.

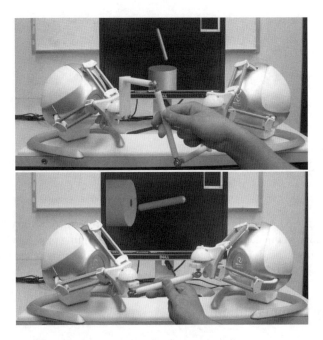

Fig. 1. Two Novint Falcon haptic devices modified for 5-DOF. The same hardware can be used in both a vertical (top) and horizontal (bottom) stylus configuration. The right-handed vertical configuration is shown; we find that a conflict between the user's hand and the device occurs between the hand and the upper extension piece. The device can be reversed for left-handed use.

correspond to the centers of their respective workspaces. Being able to reconfigure the stylus is desirable because of the limited workspace of the Falcons, which leads to limited angular movement of the stylus. The Falcons each apply a 3-DOF force to their respective ball joint, resulting in a total 3-DOF force, 2-DOF torque applied to the stylus. The stylus can rotate freely about its axis. The Falcons are mounted on a common baseplate, which is not strictly necessary, but is desirable because it keeps the Falcons properly aligned and provides some additional ballast. The Falcons are each rotated inward by 45°, such that they are perpendicular to one another. This rotation has the effect of (1) letting the stylus hang over the edge of the table to take advantage of the total workspace, (2) allowing the stylus to be a comfortable length while still allowing relatively large rotations of the stylus, (3) enabling simple outward extension pieces for the vertical-stylus configuration, and (4) keeping the overall width of combined 5-DOF device small. The length and diameter of the stylus, as well as the separation distance of the Falcons, were iteratively chosen based on comfort and range of motion. Collisions of the stylus with other components occur slightly beyond the workspace limits of the Falcons. Components were designed to be fabricated from common stock, which keeps the cost of the hardware low.

A Falcon will not function if the grip is removed, so any simple modification of a Falcon requires that the grip stay in place. Fortunately, the design of the grip facilitates simple modifications. After peeling away a thin backing, the lower hemisphere of the

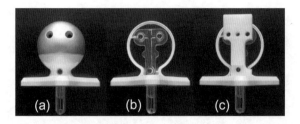

Fig. 2. Modification of the Falcon grip. (a) The original grip, shown from below. (b) Removing the lower hemisphere reveals a mounting plate. (c) A modified component can utilize the existing mounting plate.

grip can be removed, revealing a mounting plate that holds the circuitry for the grip's buttons, as shown in Fig. 2(b). The screw holes in this mounting plate can be utilized for mounting additional hardware. The component added in Fig. 2(c) is designed to allow the stylus to be attached in both the vertical and horizontal configurations shown in Fig. 1.

3   Gravity Compensation

After adding more mass to the already-heavy Falcon grip, it is desirable to implement gravity compensation, such that the Falcons will remain in any configuration in which they are placed, rather than falling under their own weight. We find that the fidelity of even a standard Falcon is noticeably improved when gravity compensation is implemented.

The kinematics of the Falcon are similar to the popular Delta mechanism, but are actually that of a modified mechanism designed at the University of Maryland [5]. A labeled photo of a Falcon along with a matching schematic of the kinematics is shown in Fig. 3. As described in [5], two Jacobian matrices relate velocities of the joints and the grip:

$$J_I \dot{\theta} = J_F \dot{p} \tag{1}$$

$$\dot{\theta} = \begin{bmatrix} \dot{\theta}_{11} \\ \dot{\theta}_{12} \\ \dot{\theta}_{13} \end{bmatrix}, \ \dot{p} = \begin{bmatrix} V_{p,x} \\ V_{p,y} \\ V_{p,z} \end{bmatrix}, \ J_F = \begin{bmatrix} J_{F_{11}} & J_{F_{12}} & J_{F_{13}} \\ J_{F_{21}} & J_{F_{22}} & J_{F_{23}} \\ J_{F_{31}} & J_{F_{32}} & J_{F_{33}} \end{bmatrix}, \ J_I = \begin{bmatrix} J_{I_1} & 0 & 0 \\ 0 & J_{I_2} & 0 \\ 0 & 0 & J_{I_3} \end{bmatrix} \tag{2}$$

θ_{ji} is angular displacement of joint j on chain i (joint 1 is actuated), $V_{p,x}$ is the velocity of the point p in the center of the moving platform in direction x of the Falcon's coordinate system (y is right, z is up, and x is toward the user), and

$$J_{F_{i1}} = \cos(\theta_{2i}) \sin(\theta_{3i}) \cos(\phi_i) - \cos(\theta_{3i}) \sin(\phi_i) \tag{3}$$

$$J_{F_{i2}} = \cos(\theta_{3i}) \cos(\phi_i) + \cos(\theta_{2i}) \sin(\theta_{3i}) \sin(\phi_i) \tag{4}$$

$$J_{F_{i3}} = \sin(\theta_{2i}) \sin(\theta_{3i}) \tag{5}$$

$$J_{I_i} = a \sin(\theta_{2i} - \theta_{1i}) \sin(\theta_{3i}) \tag{6}$$

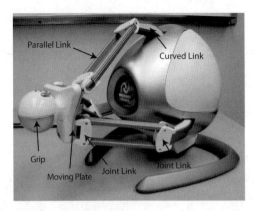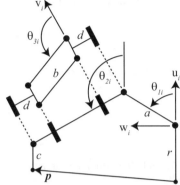

Fig. 3. Falcon kinematics based on [5]. Links a and b represent the curved and parallel links, respectively. The location of the center of the moving plate with respect to the origin is given by p. The distance from the origin to each actuated joint axis is r. The distance from the center of the moving plate to each of its joint axes is c. Links labeled d represent the joint links, which are not present in a Delta mechanism.

The manipulator Jacobian for this closed-chain robot is computed as

$$J = J_I^{-1} J_F \tag{7}$$

The above calculation assumes knowledge of the joint angles, but this might not be available directly. For example, the CHAI 3D package only provides the position of a Falcon end-effector. Here we present a simplified version of the inverse kinematics of the general Maryland manipulator [5] as applied to the Falcon. The Falcon returns its coordinates as $[f_x \quad f_y \quad f_z]^T$, and these coordinates must be converted to the base frame as $p_x = f_y$, $p_y = f_z$ and $p_z = f_x + p_{z,0}$. $p_{z,0}$ and $p_{v,0}$ are offset distances from the base plate to the center of the moving plate of the Falcon end-effector when the Falcon returns $f_x = f_y = f_z = 0$. We convert the position of point p to the local uvw coordinate frame of each leg i, centered at its actuated joint (see Fig. 3) as:

$$\begin{bmatrix} p_{ui} \\ p_{vi} \\ p_{wi} \end{bmatrix} = \begin{bmatrix} \cos(\phi_i) & \sin(\phi_i) & 0 \\ -\sin(\phi_i) & \cos(\phi_i) & 0 \\ 0 & 0 & 1 \end{bmatrix} \begin{bmatrix} p_x \\ p_y \\ p_z \end{bmatrix} + \begin{bmatrix} -r \\ p_{v,0} \\ 0 \end{bmatrix} \tag{8}$$

The expressions for p_{ui}, p_{vi}, and p_{wi} are given by:

$$p_{ui} = a\cos(\theta_{1i}) - c + (2d + b\sin(\theta_{3i}))\cos(\theta_{2i}) \tag{9}$$

$$p_{vi} = b\cos(\theta_{3i}) + s \tag{10}$$

$$p_{wi} = a\sin(\theta_{1i}) + (2d + b\sin(\theta_{3i}))\sin(\theta_{2i}) \tag{11}$$

s is the offset distance of each arm measured along the actuated-joint axis, which is not present in the Maryland manipulator. Solving (10) gives two values for θ_{3i}, but the

Falcon uses only the positive value (θ_{3i} near $90°$):

$$\theta_{3i} = \cos^{-1}\left(\frac{p_{vi} - s}{b}\right) \tag{12}$$

Squaring and adding (9) and (11) gives

$$(p_{ui} + c)^2 + p_{wi}^2 + a^2 - 2a(p_{ui} + c)\cos(\theta_{li}) - 2ap_{wi}\sin(\theta_{li})$$

$$= 4d^2 + 4db\sin(\theta_{3i}) + b^2\sin(\theta_{3i})^2 \tag{13}$$

Define a half-angle tangent as:

$$t_{1i} = \tan\left(\frac{\theta_{1i}}{2}\right) \quad \Rightarrow \quad \sin(\theta_{1i}) = \frac{2t_{1i}}{1 + t_{1i}^2}, \quad \cos(\theta_{1i}) = \frac{1 - t_{1i}^2}{1 + t_{1i}^2} \tag{14}$$

Substitution into (13) gives

$$l_{2i}t_{1i}^2 + l_{1i}t_{1i} + l_{0i} = 0 \tag{15}$$

$$l_{0i} = p_{wi}^2 + p_{ui}^2 + 2cp_{ui} - 4d^2 - b^2\sin^2(\theta_{3i}) - 4bd\sin(\theta_{3i}) - 2ap_{ui} + (a - c)^2 \tag{16}$$

$$l_{1i} = -4ap_{wi} \tag{17}$$

$$l_{2i} = p_{wi}^2 + p_{ui}^2 + 2cp_{ui} - 4d^2 - b^2\sin^2(\theta_{3i}) - 4bd\sin(\theta_{3i}) + 2ap_{ui} + (a + c)^2 \tag{18}$$

Only one solution of (15) is applicable to the Falcon (due to the limited range of θ_{1i}), which is used with (14) to solve for θ_{1i}:

$$t_{1i} = \frac{-l_{1i} - \sqrt{l_{1i}^2 - 4l_{2i}l_{0i}}}{2l_{2i}} \quad \Rightarrow \quad \theta_{1i} = 2\tan^{-1}(t_{1i}) \tag{19}$$

Finally, combining (9) and (11) gives:

$$\theta_{2i} = \tan^{-1}\left(\frac{p_{wi} - a\sin(\theta_{1i})}{p_{ui} - a\cos(\theta_{1i}) + c}\right) \tag{20}$$

Once we are equipped with a manipulator Jacobian and inverse kinematics, we are ready to implement gravity compensation. The joint torques $\tau_g = [\tau_1 \quad \tau_2 \quad \tau_3]^T$ for gravity compensation are

$$\tau_g = gm_aq\begin{bmatrix} \sin(100° - \theta_{11})\sin(\phi_1) \\ \sin(100° - \theta_{12})\sin(\phi_2) \\ \sin(100° - \theta_{13})\sin(\phi_3) \end{bmatrix} - g(m_b + m_d)a\begin{bmatrix} \sin(\theta_{11})\sin(\phi_1) \\ \sin(\theta_{12})\sin(\phi_2) \\ \sin(\theta_{13})\sin(\phi_3) \end{bmatrix}$$
$$+ g(3(m_b + m_d) + m_c + m_e)J^{-T}[0 \quad 1 \quad 0]^T \tag{21}$$

where the mass labeling corresponds to Fig. 3, $g = 9.81$ is the acceleration of gravity, and m_e is the mass of the end-effector. In the case of a standard Falcon, m_e is the mass of the detachable grip. In the case of of our 5-DOF device, m_e includes the mass of the modified grip of Fig. 2(c), as well as 50% of the mass of the additional added hardware (the two Falcons equally share the load of the new hardware). When using a Falcon, the user does not command motor torques, but rather, commands forces to the grip. The equivalent gravity-compensation force is computed as $f_g = J^T \tau_g$. In Table 1 we report important mass and length parameters, which we measured from a disassembled Falcon. Additional Falcon characterization can be found in [6].

Gravity compensation for the Maryland manipulator is given in [5], so we followed that derivation here, making two key modification for use with a Falcon. First, the Falcon sits on its side, making gravity loads unequal on each of the three motors, as opposed to the vertical Maryland manipulation. This leads to the terms that include the ϕ's in (21). The Falcon's three actuated joints lie in a vertical back plane. We experimentally measured these axes to be described by $\phi_1 = 105°$, $\phi_2 = -15°$, and $\phi_3 = -135°$, measured about z from y in the base frame such that $\phi = 0$ corresponds to aligned uvw and xyz frames. Second, the mass distribution in the first link of the Falcon is significantly different than that of the Maryland robot

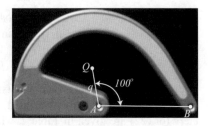

Fig. 4. Curved first link of the Falcon. The center of mass was experimentally determined to be at the point Q, with $q = 22$ mm.

[5], where the center of mass of the first link is at the midpoint between the two joints A and B. As shown in Fig. 4, we experimentally found the center of mass of the Falcon's first link to be far from that midpoint, leading to the q and $100°$ terms in (21).

Table 1. Measured mass and length parameters

Part Name	Mass (kg)	Length (m)
Curved Link	$m_a = 0.089$	$a = 0.060$
Parallel Link	$m_b = 0.008$	$b = 0.103$
Moving Plate	$m_c = 0.033$	$c = 0.016$
Joint Link	$m_d = 0.010$	$d = 0.011$
Back Plate Radius	—	$r = 0.037$
Back Plate Actuator Offset	—	$s = 0.025$
Zero-Configuration z-Offset	—	$p_{z,0} = 0.134$
Zero-Configuration v-Offset	—	$p_{v,0} = 0.022$
Standard Falcon Grip (Fig. 2(a))	$m_e = 0.052$	—
Stylus, From Centers of Ball Joints	—	$l_S = 0.166$
50% Vertical Stylus Assembly (Fig. 1(a))	$m_e = 0.128$	—
50% Horizontal Stylus Assembly (Fig. 1(b))	$m_e = 0.083$	—

4   The 5-DOF Controller

The final step is to coordinate the individual 3-DOF forces of the Falcons such that the user experiences a single 5-DOF device. We define a world coordinate system such that when both Falcons are at their respective zero positions, the stylus is at its zero position in the world coordinate frame. The world frame is such that stylus movements in the y direction are to the right, z is up, and x is toward the user. The positions of interest kinematically are those of the two ball joints on the ends of the stylus, so when we refer to the position of, say, the left Falcon, we are referring to the position of the center of its ball joint. The homogeneous transformation that relates the position p_i of Falcon i in its own frame to the world frame is

$$\begin{bmatrix} {}^w p_i \\ 1 \end{bmatrix} = \begin{bmatrix} \cos(\alpha) & -\sin(\alpha) & 0 & 0 \\ \sin(\alpha) & \cos(\alpha) & 0 & \beta \\ 0 & 0 & 1 & \gamma \\ 0 & 0 & 0 & 1 \end{bmatrix} \begin{bmatrix} {}^i p_i \\ 1 \end{bmatrix} \tag{22}$$

There are three different arrangements of stylus, two of which are shown in Fig. 1: vertical right-handed, vertical left-handed, and horizontal. The arrangement-specific parameters for (22) are given in Table 2, where l_S is the length of the stylus measured from the centers of the ball joints.

Our goal is to display an effective force and torque at a single point p_S somewhere along the length of the stylus. We first define a vector Δ from the left Falcon position (ball joint) to the right Falcon position:

$$\Delta = p_R - p_L \tag{23}$$

Then we define p_S relative to p_L:

$$p_S = p_L + \delta\Delta \tag{24}$$

Choosing $\delta = 0$ sets $p_S = p_L$, $\delta = 1$ sets $p_S = p_R$, and $\delta = 0.5$ sets p_S at the center of the stylus. By choosing $\delta < 0$ or $\delta > 1$, we can place the effective stylus point outside of the physical stylus.

To display a pure force f_S at the stylus point p_S, we decompose the force into individual right and left Falcon forces as

$$f_{Rf} = \delta f_S, \quad f_{Lf} = (1 - \delta) f_S \tag{25}$$

Table 2. Coordinate-frame parameters for different arrangement of the stylus

Parameters	Left Falcon	Right Falcon
α	45°	-45°
β - Horizontal Stylus	$-l_S/2$	$l_S/2$
γ - Horizontal Stylus	0	0
β - Vertical Right-Handed Stylus	0	0
γ - Vertical Right-Handed Stylus	$l_S/2$	$-l_S/2$
β - Vertical Left-Handed Stylus	0	0
γ - Vertical Left-Handed Stylus	$-l_S/2$	$l_S/2$

To display a pure torque τ_S at the stylus point p_S, we apply individual Falcon forces as

$$f_{R\tau} = \frac{1}{l_S^2} \left(\tau_S \times \Delta \right), \quad f_{L\tau} = -f_{R\tau} \tag{26}$$

To display an arbitrary force/torque, the pure force and pure torque simply sum before being commanded to the Falcons:

$$f_R = f_{Rf} + f_{R\tau}, \quad f_L = f_{Lf} + f_{L\tau} \tag{27}$$

The above equations assume all forces and torques are described with respect to the world frame. The left and right Falcon forces must be transformed into their respective frames, which is accomplished using the inverse of the transformation matrix in (22). The final step is to sum the forces from this 5-DOF controller with the gravity-compensation forces of Section 3 such that a single force vector can be commanded to each of the Falcons.

5   Conclusion

Many students who are exposed to haptics only get to experience inexpensive 3-DOF devices. Using the steps outlined in this paper, a student can build a 5-DOF device by nondestructively modifying two Novint Falcons for less than an additional $100. This 5-DOF device will allow more students to get to experience realistic force/torque interactions with virtual environments. In this paper, we designed a simple 5-DOF modification mechanism, we summarized the manipulator Jacobian and inverse kinematics for a Novint Falcon, we derived a gravity compensation algorithm that applies to both a standard Falcon as well as the 5-DOF system presented here, and we provided a number of useful length and mass parameters obtained empirically by destructively disassembling a Falcon. Additional details can be found on the Utah Telerobotics Lab web page [3].

References

1. Martín, J., Savall, J.: Mechanisms for haptic torque feedback. In: Proc. Joint Eurohaptics Conf. and Symp. Haptic Interfaces for Virtual Environment and Teleoperator Systems, pp. 611–614 (2005)
2. Novint Falcon, http://home.novint.com/products/novint_falcon.php
3. The Univerisity of Utah Telerobotics Lab, http://www.telerobotics.utah.edu
4. CHAI 3D: The open source haptics project, http://www.chai3d.org/
5. Stamper, R.E.: A Three Degree of Freedom Parallel Manipulator with Only Translational Degrees of Freedom. PhD thesis, Department of Mechanical Engineering, The University of Maryland (1997)
6. Martin, S., Hillier, N.: Characterisation of the Novint Falcon haptic device for application as a robot manipulator. In: Proc. Australasian Conf. Robotics and Automation (2009)

Revisiting the Effect of Velocity on Human Force Control

Manikantan Nambi, William R. Provancher, and Jake J. Abbott

Department of Mechanical Engineering, University of Utah
Salt Lake City UT 84112, USA
m.nambi@utah.edu, wil@mech.utah.edu, jake.abbott@utah.edu

Abstract. Human-robot collaborative systems (HRCS) have the potential to dramatically change many aspects of surgery, manufacturing, hazardous-material handling, and other dextrous tasks. We are particularly interested in precise manipulation tasks, which are typically performed under an admittance-control regime, where the controlled velocity is proportional to the user-applied force. During precise fast movements, there is a noticeable degradation in control precision, and prior results have indicated that system velocity, and not system admittance, is the factor that is correlated with force-control precision. In this paper, we report evidence that system admittance is more important than velocity in determining the user's ability to control force, and we provide an explanation as to why prior results might have indicated otherwise.

Keywords: Human force control, admittance control.

1 Introduction

Human-robot collaborative systems (HRCS) can take the form of teleoperation systems, where movement of a master manipulandum is coupled to movements of a remote slave manipulator, or they can take the form of cooperative systems, where the human directly interacts with a robotic manipulator. For tasks requiring the greatest degree of precision, admittance-type robots are used, which contain a great deal of gearing and inertia such that they appear nonbackdrivable to a human. Such a system is controlled using admittance control: a human interacts directly with a force sensor mounted to the robot, and the robot is computer controlled to move in response to the applied force. The most common and simplest type of admittance control is proportional-velocity control, where the admittance of the system reduces to a simple gain k, making the velocity of the robot V linearly proportional to the applied force F:

$$V = kF \tag{1}$$

Examples of such systems include the Johns Hopkins University Steady-Hand Robot [1] and the University of Utah Active Handrest [2]. The control law (1) behaves similarly to a "programmable damper" implemented on an impedance-type haptic device (i.e., backdrivable, low inertia), however, it is possible to stably implement much higher levels of damping with an admittance-type device.

A.M.L. Kappers et al. (Eds.): EuroHaptics 2010, Part I, LNCS 6191, pp. 144–151, 2010.
© Springer-Verlag Berlin Heidelberg 2010

Precise tasks are typically performed at low velocities, but we would like the user to be able to move as fast as possible and still maintain maximum precision. Thus, a better understanding of human force control during admittance control would help us design systems for precise and efficient manipulation. The purpose of this research is to quantify the effects of velocity (V) and admittance gain (k) on human force control precision with visual and haptic feedback.

An 11–15% mean absolute error was found by Srinivasan and Chen [3] when applying a constant force on a stationary target in the range of 0.25 N to 1.25 N with no visual feedback. In the same experiment they found that the error reduced significantly and remained approximately constant at 0.039 N when visual feedback was provided. Allin et al. [4] found the just noticeable difference (JND) for force with visual feedback to be 10% for the index finger for a base force of 2.25 N. Lederman et al. [5] studied the force variability with the subject moving their hand at different velocities and under different force levels. They found the end effector, force level, and velocity of the device to have a statistically significant effect on the mean force values.

In the most related prior work, Wu et al. [6] (prior work of one author) studied the effect of velocity and admittance gain on subjects applying force on a moving robotic device. In two separate experiments, the device was controlled under proportional-velocity control and under velocity control (i.e. independent of the applied force), respectively. They determined that the velocity (V), and not admittance gain (k), directly affects force-control precision. However, the conclusion of [6] runs counter to more recent anecdotal experiences in the authors' labs, motivating a reconsideration of the findings. In this paper, we report evidence that, at least for the range of velocities and admittance gains considered here, the conclusion of [6] does not appear to be correct for systems running under proportional-velocity control, and that the admittance gain (k) is in fact the dominant factor in human force control precision. A number of choices made during the design of the experiment in [6] could have contributed to the conclusion. First, 50% of the data obtained were under velocity control, which may not be representative of performance under proportional-velocity control. Second, in the experiments the controllers were turned on after the human subject reached a desired target force, creating large accelerations at the beginning of each trial that may have affected the results. With real proportional-velocity systems, the velocity naturally ramps up from rest as the human applies force. In addition, the experiments in [6] were conducted with only haptic feedback, requiring the subject to remember a target force value. It is not clear if the discrete event of turning the controller on affected the subjects' ability to remember the target force. In real-life systems, some method of visual feedback conveys information about the amount of applied force. Research by Jones [7] indicates the coefficient of variance for finger and elbow forces to be much lower with both visual and haptic feedback (4%) than when only haptic feedback (12%) is provided.

2   Methods

2.1   Hardware

A one degree-of-freedom (1-DOF) robotic device is used to perform the experiment (Fig. 1-a). It consists of a lead-screw-driven linear stage (Servo Systems Co.

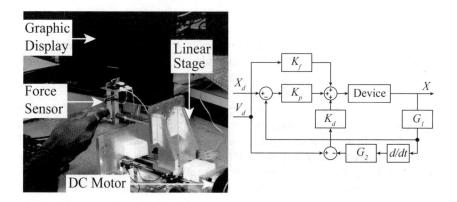

Fig. 1. (a) Experimental apparatus. (b) Control System

MLPS-4-10) with a DC motor (Servo Systems Co. 23SMDC-LCSS). Position feedback is given by an optical encoder mounted on the motor shaft. The lead screw has a pitch of 12.7 mm and the encoder resolution is 4000 counts/rev after quadrature, which translates to a linear resolution of 3 μm for the device. A cantilever-type force sensor was developed for the device. The force sensor has a resolution of 0.7 mN (noise < 0.01 N) and is mounted on the linear stage using a rigid rod. A Sensoray 626 DAQ card is used for data acquisition. It has a 16-bit ADC that is used to read force data and a 14-bit DAC which is used to command voltages to the current amplifier (Advanced Motion Control 12A8), which is powered by a 24-V linear power supply, and which is used to drive the motor. The software for the device was developed in C++ using the CHAI 3D library. Visual feedback is provided to the subject on the computer screen. The force readings are sampled at 1 kHz and graphics are displayed at 33 Hz.

2.2 Control Systems

A PD-plus-feedforward controller has been implemented for the device (Fig. 1-b). Unit-DC-gain digital low-pass filters G_1 and G_2 with time constants $\tau_1 = 0.001$ s and $\tau_2 = 0.0005$ are used to reduce quantization error and differentiation noise. The proportional gain K_p is set at 30 V/mm and derivative gain K_d is set at 0.1 V·s/mm. The feedforward model for the device was experimentally derived and is given by $K_f = 0.06V_d + 2.2(1 - e^{(-3.3V_d)})$ V·s/mm, where V_d is the desired velocity. This feedforward model is a smooth function that approximates Coulomb-plus-viscous friction. The inputs for the system are calculated as:

$$V_d(n) = kF(n), \quad X_d(n) = X_d(n-1) + V_d(n)\Delta t \qquad (2)$$

The controlled device is capable of faithfully tracking signals at frequencies below 7 Hz (44 rad/s), which is sufficient for signals of interest here (Fig. 2).

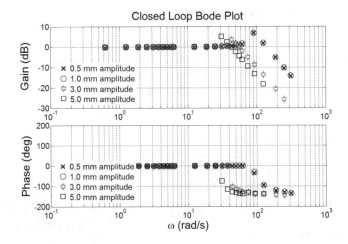

Fig. 2. Closed-loop Bode plot for the system for sinusoidal trajectories in X_d

2.3 Pilot Testing

Using our device and a single subject, we recreated the experiment performed in Wu et al. [6]. The subject had to apply force on a 1-DOF force sensor (Fig. 1) similar to the one used in [6]. Two experiments, one balanced in force (F) and admittance gain (k) and the other balanced in force (F) and velocity (V) were performed. Our analysis of variance (ANOVA) showed that both k and F have an effect on the metric (standard deviation of force for the second half of the trial when the device is moving, divided by the standard deviation of force for the first half of the trial when the device is stationary) in the experiment balanced in k and F. For the experiment balanced in V and F, only V has an effect on the metric. These results are consistent with those obtained in [6], indicating that it is unlikely that the data collection or analysis in [6] were problematic. Rather, the reasons outlined in Section 1 are the likely causes for their conclusions.

2.4 Experimental Design

Our goal is to conduct an experiment that gives information specifically about human force-control precision under the control law (1), rather than about human force control on moving objects in general. An experiment balanced in velocity (V) and admittance gain (k) was designed to test the effect of each factor on human force control precision. Specifically, we are interested in determining when force-control ability is affected by the movement of the device, as compared to force control on a stationary device. The experiment was performed by ten right-handed subjects using their right index fingers. The subjects were all male, with ages ranging from 22 to 37. Only one of the subjects had prior experience with haptic interfaces. The experiment has institutional-review-board approval. Results from pilot studies showed that V and k at which human force control precision is similar to the stationary case occurs for very slow moving systems. Also, limitations in the force sensor restrict the range of values of V and k that can be used. Therefore, subjects are tested for values of $V = 0.5, 0.9, 1.6, 2.8, 5.0$ mm/s and admittance gains of $k = 0.5, 0.9, 1.6, 2.8, 5.0$ mm/(N·s). The target force value to be applied by the subject was calculated using (1). Table 1 shows the target force level for each of the commanded admittance gains to achieve the desired velocity values.

It can bee seen from Table 1 that each combination of V and k has a different target force value associated with it. For each different force value, trials with $k = 0$ are also conducted. These values are shuffled to generate a random sequence called a block. Eight such blocks with randomly distributed combinations of V and k are generated for each subject, so we have eight repetitions of each combination. Values of target force and admittance gains in a trial are selected according to these randomly generated blocks for each subject.

Table 1. Force (N) values for different values of V (mm/s) and k (mm/(N·s))

$V \backslash k$	0.5	0.9	1.6	2.8	5.0
0.5	1	0.55	0.31	0.18	0.1
0.9	1.8	1	0.56	0.32	0.18
1.6	.32	1.78	1	0.57	0.32
2.8	5.6	3.11	1.75	1	0.56
5.0	10	5.56	3.12	1.79	1

During the experiment, subjects are instructed to apply force on the force sensor using their index finger. Their arm is placed perpendicular to the direction of motion of the device with their elbow supported on the table. Subjects had to apply force away from the device (i.e. to their left). Visual feedback is provided on a computer screen in the form of a vertical grey line at the center of the screen indicating the target force to be achieved by the subject. This grey line is surrounded by a green box whose width is set at $\pm 5\%$ of the target force value. The width of the green box is 15 mm, and the screen is 70 cm from the subject. The force applied by the subject is displayed by a white vertical line that moves from right to left when force is applied. The force display is scaled such that the center of the screen corresponds to the target force, the right edge corresponds to no force, and the left edge corresponds to twice the target force. Because the target force is always located at the center of the screen, a subject has no indication at the beginning of a trial as to what the target force is, and must use the movement of the white vertical line accompanying their applied force in order to determine the correct force. Subjects are instructed to hit the target force and keep the applied force within the green box to the best of their ability. Each trial lasts for 4 s. The device begins moving at the instant the subject begins to apply force, based on (1). Only the last 2 s of data are analyzed to remove the effects of the rise time required to achieve the target force (Fig. 3). White noise is played through headphones during the experiment to remove auditory cues. The device is hidden from the subjects by a curtain. Subjects could pause the experiment to rest at any time. Before the experiment, each subject was allowed to interact with the device and experience different force levels and admittance gains.

3   Results

We have used two metrics to measure force control precision.

$$M_n = \frac{M}{M_0}, \quad S_n^2 = \frac{S^2}{S_0^2} \tag{3}$$

The first is the normalized mean value of force M_n, where M is the mean force value for a trial and M_0 is the mean force value for the static case ($k = 0$) at the same force level in the corresponding block. This metric measures the user's mean force control ability compared to pushing on a stationary sensor. The second metric is the normalized variance in force S_n^2, where S^2 is the variance for a trial and S_0^2 is the variance for the static case ($k = 0$) at the same force level in the corresponding block. This metric is a measure of the user's tremor, compared to pushing on a stationary sensor. These metrics were specifically chosen to mitigate the effect of force levels, by normalizing all values at a given force level with respect to the static case at that same force level. Using the response of the static case within a given block mitigates bias due to time (fatigue or learning). Because of the design of the metrics, a value of both metrics equal to 1 would mean that the user has a precision similar to that of applying force when the device is stationary, leading to a conclusion that the user's force control is unaffected by the movement of the device.

A fixed-effect ANOVA model is used to test for main effects of V and k on the metrics. The ANOVA shows that both V and k have a main effect on both S_n^2 and M_n (p < 0.01). The partial effect sizes are given by $\omega_k^2 = 0.111$ and $\omega_V^2 = 0.009$ for the metric M_n, and the partial effect sizes for metric S_n^2 are $\omega_k^2 = 0.008$ and $\omega_V^2 = 0.015$. The results for the metric M_n (Fig. 4) show that force control precision degrades rapidly as k increases. We see that the effect of any device motion is that the user's mean force level is reduced (see Fig. 3). It also appears that, at high values of k, increasing the velocity has the effect of improving performance (i.e. bringing M_n closer to 1). Fig. 5 shows that

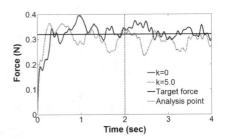

Fig. 3. Typical force-versus-time data for stationary and moving systems. Here, a 0.32-N force is applied by a subject with k=0 and k=5.0. Only the final two seconds of data are used during analysis.

the metric S_n^2 at high velocities and high admittance gains is noticeably different than at lower velocities and admittance gains. The variance in force is noticeably higher than the static case (i.e. not equal to 1) even at the lowest velocities and admittance gains used.

4   Discussion and Conclusion

From our statistical analysis it can be seen that both admittance gain (k) and velocity (V) have an effect on force control precision. From Fig. 4, it appears that force control precision degrades rapidly as we increase k for the general population. Wu et al. [6] concluded that only velocity determines human force control precision during admittance control. In this paper we have provided compelling evidence that, at least in the velocity range considered here, both velocity and admittance gain have an effect on force control precision, and that admittance gain has the most pronounced effect. Not all of the tests for force control performed in [6] were conducted using the proportional-velocity control law (1). This could explain the difference in results between the two studies.

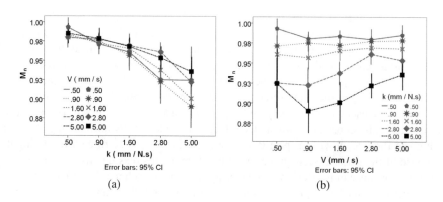

Fig. 4. Experimental results for metric M_n for all 10 subjects combined

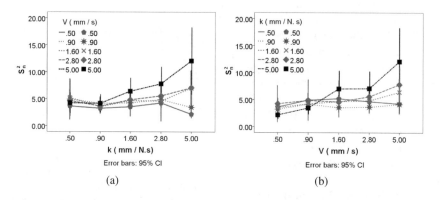

Fig. 5. Experimental results for metric S_n^2 for all 10 subjects combined

Only for the single data set {k=0.5 mm/s, V=0.5 mm/s} did the data interval for the metrics in our experiment include the value 1. This implies that even at the lowest velocities and admittance gains used here, the subjects' force control precision is different than the static case. In other words, their force control precision is affected by the movement of the device. Also, from the partial effect sizes we can infer that 11 % of the total variance in metric M_n can be explained by k, while only 1 % of the total variance is explained by V. Thus, the admittance gain k had a predominant effect on human force control precision.

Based on the control law (1), we could also conclude that poor force control at high k and low V is actually a measurement of poor force control at low values of applied force F. Although we normalized the metrics by the static case at each force value, in an attempt to control for the effect of changing the applied force level, it may be the case that when the subject is pushing harder and has a stiffer finger, the subject is more robust to movement of the system.

In the future, we will attempt to quantify the effect of admittance gain, velocity, and force level on force control precision. We will attempt to find the conditions under which the human user is controlling force with a level of precision equivalent to the isometric (stationary) case. In addition, research indicates that the end effector and gripping configuration has an effect on mean force value while applying force on a stationary target [5]. We intend to study the effect of different gripping configurations on force control precision under different V and k. Such a study will help us compare the trends observed in force control presented in this paper with similar results obtained under different common gripping configurations. This would also make the research more applicable to real-life systems where different gripping configurations may be used.

References

1. Taylor, R., Jensen, P., Whitcomb, L., Barnes, A., Kumar, R., Stoianovici, D., Gupta, P., Wang, Z., de Juan, E., Kavoussi, L.: Steady-hand robotic system for microsurgical augmentation. Int. J. Robotics Research 18(12), 1201–1210 (1999)
2. Fehlberg, M.A., Gleeson, B.T., Leishman, L.C., Provancher, W.R.: Active handrest for precision manipulation and ergonomic support. In: Proc. Symp. Haptic Interfaces for Virtual Environments and Teleoperator Systems, pp. 489–496 (2010)
3. Srinivasan, M.A., Chen, J.S.: Human performance in controlling normal forces of contact with rigid objects. In: Proc. ASME Dynamic Systems and Control Division: Advances in Robotics, Mechatronics, and Haptic Interfaces, pp. 119–125 (1993)
4. Allin, S., Matsuoka, Y., Klatzky, R.: Measuring just noticeable differences for haptic force feedback: Implications for rehabilitation. In: Proc. Symp. Haptic Interfaces for Virtual Environments and Teleoperator Systems, pp. 299–302 (2002)
5. Lederman, S.J., Howe, R.D., Klatzky, R.L., Hamilton, C.: Force variablitiy during surface contact with bare finger or rigid probe. In: Proc. Symp. Haptic Interfaces for Virtual Environments and Teleoperator Systems, pp. 154–160 (2004)
6. Wu, M., Abbott, J.J., Okamura, A.M.: Effect of velocity on human force control. In: Proc. Joint Eurohaptics Conf. and Symp. Haptic Interfaces for Virtual Environment and Teleoperator Systems, pp. 73–79 (2005)
7. Jones, L.A.: Visual and haptic feedback in the control of force. Experimental Brain Research 130, 269–272 (2000)

PART II
Teleoperation

A Coordinating Controller for Improved Task Performance in Multi-user Teleoperation

Hiroyuki Tanaka[1], Thomas Schauß[2], Kouhei Ohnishi[1],
Angelika Peer[2], and Martin Buss[2]

[1] Department of System Design Engineering, Keio University, Japan
tanahiro@sum.sd.keio.ac.jp, ohnishi@sd.keio.ac.jp
[2] Institute of Automatic Control Engineering, Technische Universität München
Theresienstrasse 90, 80333 München, Germany
{schauss,angelika.peer,mb}@tum.de
http://www.lsr.ei.tum.de

Abstract. A teleoperation system extends cognitive and manipulatory skills of a human to a remote site. Here, a multi-user teleoperation system consisting of two haptic interfaces and two teleoperator arms is considered. In addition to a position-based admittance control scheme between corresponding master and slave systems, we introduce a virtual coupling as coordinating controller between the two master and slave systems. Using a robust stability analysis we determine enlarged stability regions in the parameter space compared to the case without coordinating controller. As shown in a complementary paper, an evaluation of the proposed approach moreover yields significant improvements in performance and efficiency.

Keywords: teleoperation, telepresence, collaboration, multi-user, coordinating controller, robust stability, stability analysis, parameter-space approach.

1 Introduction

Teleoperation has been a topic of ongoing research for many years. Hereby, haptic interaction over teleoperation systems is especially interesting and challenging due to the bilateral energy exchange involved in the process. Please refer to [1] for an overview of research conducted in this field.

So far, however, only little work considered multi-user teleoperation systems like the one illustrated in Fig. 1. An extension of controllers developed for autonomous multi-robot systems ([2,3,4]) to teleoperation was pursued in [5]. Hereby, interaction with an object is controlled using an internal force controller. The object dynamics of the environment is canceled and replaced by that of a virtual object using an adaptive-control approach [6]. Thus, dynamic properties of the environment are not observable by the operators, and forces applied to the object are predefined by the desired internal force. In teleoperation this is undesirable, as object properties should be transparently perceivable by the operators, and forces applied to the environment must be directly controllable, e.g. in cases where sensitive objects are manipulated.

In previous work, a multi-modal multi-user teleoperation system has been developed [7] and a complex application scenario illustrating the range of tasks addressable with

A.M.L. Kappers et al. (Eds.): EuroHaptics 2010, Part I, LNCS 6191, pp. 155–160, 2010.

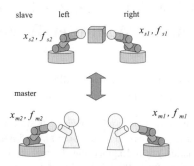

slave   left   right

x_{s2}, f_{s2} x_{s1}, f_{s1}

master

x_{m2}, f_{m2} x_{m1}, f_{m1}

Fig. 1. Schematics of the multi-user teleoperation system considered in this work

such a system has been presented. Position-based admittance-controllers bilaterally exchanging forces between corresponding systems (FaFa-architecture) were used for the haptic subsystem. Therefore, the haptic subsystem consisted of two single-user systems that interacted over a common object, see also Fig. 1.

In this work, we investigate properties of coordinating controllers inserted between the two single-user systems. The controllers implement a virtual coupling, which enhances coordination of the two systems. In section 2 we introduce the new controller before performing a robust stability analysis in section 3. Finally, conclusions are drawn taking into account results of a performance evaluation described in detail in [8], and an outlook on future work is given.

2   Coordinating Controller

Local position-based admittance controllers are used to control haptic interfaces and teleoperator arms. The control structure is well suited for admittance-type devices with non-negligible dynamics, e.g. high mass and friction [9]. Here, we use a control architecture which couples two position-based admittance controllers by implementing a bilateral force-force exchange (FaFa), see Fig. 2. This control structure offers a high performance while also allowing easy parametrization due to the small number of tunable parameters [10].

The measured forces f_{m1} and f_{s1} are summed up and used as input for admittance filters of master 1 and slave 1, whereas f_{m2} and f_{s2} are summed up and used as input for admittance filters of master 2 and slave 2. The admittance filters Y_v are given by

$$Y_v = \frac{1}{m_d s^2 + b_d s},\tag{1}$$

where m_d represents the virtual mass and b_d the virtual damping. Inner position control loops are used to drive the devices to desired positions which are obtained as outputs of the admittance filters.

The coordinating controllers in Fig. 2 are marked by dashed lines. They are added to enhance task performance and improve stability of the overall multi-user system by

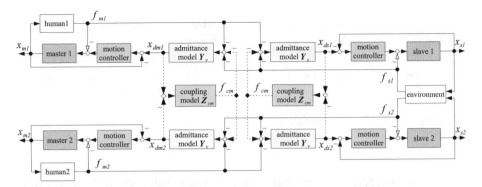

Fig. 2. Control architecture of the multi-user teleoperation system. As coordinating controller a virtual coupling via the impedance Z_{cm} is introduced.

influencing the relative motion between the two master and slave systems. More specifically, the controllers are introduced to prevent undesired asynchronous movements of the two operators, as only synchronized movements lead to a successful task completion in a joint manipulation task. Therefore, movement of one operator is indicated to the other operator by a force in the appropriate direction.

The controllers are implemented as impedance filters Z_{cm}, i.e. as virtual spring-damper coupling

$$Z_{cm} = b_{cm}s + c_{cm} \tag{2}$$

between the two single-user systems, where b_{cm} and c_{cm} represent damping and stiffness respectively. In the following we consider a damper only, i.e. $c_{cm} = 0$. In this case, the virtual coupling only generates a force if there is a difference in the velocities of the two systems. Thus, a variable relative position of the end-effectors is possible[1].

3   Stability Analysis

Several plant parameters of a teleoperation system, specifically parameters related to the operators and environment are not fixed but can instead vary greatly. Therefore, a robust stability analysis is performed to determine stability boundaries for the given system with and without coordinating controller. To this end, the parameter space approach, described in detail in [11] and applied to a teleoperation system in [10], is used. The parameter space approach is based on the boundary crossing theorem of polynomials. Boundaries in the s-plane are mapped into the desired parameter space. Thereby, the parameter space is partitioned into several subspaces. By performing a stability test for one parameter set within such a subspace stability of the complete subspace can be determined. In the following the models used for the different subsystems are given, and results of the stability analysis are shown.

---

[1] If a spring were used in addition to or instead of the damper there would be a fixed relative equilibrium point of the two end-effectors.

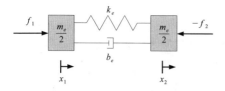

Fig. 3. Model of environment

Table 1. Parameters used for the stability analysis

K_p	7500 N/m	m_h	5 kg
K_d	$2\sqrt{7500}$ N s/m	b_h	6 N s/m
b_{cm}	100 N s/m	k_h	40 N/m
T_s	0.0015 s		
T_m	0.0003 s		

To be able to apply the stability analysis to a system with multiple degrees of freedom, dissimilar kinematics, and different dynamics on master and slave side, we assume and implement well tuned computed torque controllers with gravity compensation for the teleoperator arms and haptic interfaces. Therefore, these devices are modeled as masses of 1 kg only. A PD-controller with proportional gain K_p and derivative gain K_d is used to compensate for modeling errors.

As environment we use a mass-spring-damper system, where the mass is lumped on either side of the environment, see Fig. 3.

The interaction forces with the environment are given by

$$F_{s1} = (k_e + b_e s)(X_{s1} - X_{s2}) + \frac{m_e}{2}s^2 X_{s1}, \tag{3}$$

$$F_{s2} = (k_e + b_e s)(X_{s2} - X_{s1}) + \frac{m_e}{2}s^2 X_{s2}, \tag{4}$$

where m_e, b_e, and k_e are the mass, viscous damping, and stiffness of the environment. The interaction forces at the slave end-effectors are denoted $F_{s1/2}$ while the positions of the two slaves are $X_{s1/2}$.

The operators are modeled as passive impedance and additional exogenous force. Interaction forces $F_{m1/2}$ at the master end-effectors are determined as

$$F_{m1} = \alpha(k_h + b_h s + m_h s^2)X_{m1} + F_1^*, \tag{5}$$

$$F_{m2} = \alpha(k_h + b_h s + m_h s^2)X_{m2} + F_2^*, \tag{6}$$

where k_h, b_h, and m_h are stiffness, damper and mass of the human arm and F_1^* and F_2^* are the exogenous forces applied by the two operators. The factor α is varied in the stability analysis to account for the variability in the human-arm impedance. Here, the same value of α is used for both operators[2]. Sensor dynamics of the force-torque sensors and actuator dynamics are also taken into account. The dynamics are approximated by first-order low-pass filters with time constants T_s and T_m respectively. Table 1 shows the fixed parameters used in the stability analysis. The parameters for the human arm model were hereby taken from previous work [10] and the low-level controller parameters were tuned for good position tracking. The same controller parameters were also used in the evaluation which is described in detail in the complementary paper [8].

---

[2] The stability analysis was also performed with two independent values, but no qualitative difference was observed.

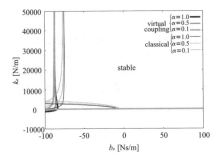

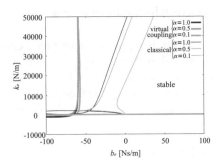

Fig. 4. Stability boundaries in the k_e-b_e plane for $m_e = 1$ kg ($m_d = 5$ kg, $b_d = 10$ Nsm^{-1})

Fig. 5. Stability boundaries in the k_e-b_e plane for $m_e = 1$ kg ($m_d = 0.5$ kg, $b_d = 1$ Nsm^{-1})

Using the models given above, a robust stability analysis was performed, and stable regions were determined in the parameter space. Fig. 4 and Fig. 5 depict the stability region in the k_e-b_e plane for different parameters of the virtual admittance. A variation of the operator impedance was taken into account by different values of α (0.1, 0.5, 1.0). To increase readability of the plots, the influence of m_e on the results is not shown[3].

In Fig. 4 the system is robustly stable (with respect to variations in human and environment) for all positive values of damping b_e, independently of the virtual coupling. However, a larger stability region, i.e. a more robustly stable system is achieved with virtual coupling activated. In Fig. 5, where smaller values are chosen for the parameters of the virtual admittance, this is even clearer. For a stiff environment (large k_e) some damping b_e of the environment is necessary in case no virtual coupling is provided.

4 Conclusion

In this paper, a new coordinating controller for a multi-user teleoperation system was proposed. The damping-based controller was inserted between two single-user teleoperation systems. A robust stability analysis showed enlarged stability regions for the resulting system. An experimental evaluation of the proposed approach was performed in [8]. There, a significantly higher task performance and efficiency could be determined if the coordinating controller was active.

Summarizing, it can be concluded that the proposed controller results in a more robustly stable system, while at the same time enhancing performance. Future work will focus on extending the proposed scheme to rotational degrees of freedom. Moreover, a more general impedance will be considered, and effects on transparency will be examined.

---

[3] No qualitative difference was observed when varying m_e between 0.1 kg and 10 kg.

Acknowledgements

This work is supported in part by a Grant-in-Aid for the Global Center of Excellence for High-Level Global Cooperation for Leading-Edge Platform on Access Spaces from the Ministry of Education, Culture, Sport, Science, and Technology in Japan. It is also supported in part by the German Research Foundation (DFG) within the collaborative research center SFB453 "High-Fidelity Telepresence and Teleaction".

References

1. Hokayem, F.P., Spong, W.M.: Bilateral teleoperation: An historical survey. Automatica 42(12), 2035–2057 (2006)
2. Uchiyama, M., Iwasawa, N., Hakomori, K.: Hybrid position/force control for coordination of a two-arm robot. In: Proc. of IEEE Int. Conf. on Robotics and Automation, pp. 1242–1247 (1987)
3. Yoshikawa, T., Zheng, X.: Coordinated dynamic hybrid position/force controlfor multiple robot manipulators handling one constrained object. In: IEEE Int. Conferecne on Robotics and Automation, vol. 2, pp. 1178–1183 (1990)
4. Williams, D., Khatib, O.: The virtual linkage: A model for internal forces in multi-grasp manipulation. In: Proc. of the IEEE Int. Conf. on Robotics and Automation, vol. 1, pp. 1025–1030 (1993)
5. Sirouspour, S., Setoode, P.: Adaptive nonlinear teleoperation control in multi-master/multi-slave environments. In: Proc. of the IEEE Conf. on Control Applications, Tronto, Canada, pp. 1263–1268 (2005)
6. Zhu, W.H., Salcudean, S.E.: Stability guaranteed teleoperation: an adaptive motion/force control approach. IEEE Transactions on Automatic Control 45(11), 1951–1969 (2000)
7. Buss, M., Peer, A., Schauss, T., Stefanov, N., Unterhinninghofen, U., Behrendt, S., Leupold, J., Durkovic, M., Sarkis, M.: Development of a Multi-modal Multi-user Telepresence and Teleaction System. The International Journal of Robotics Research (2009)
8. Schauß, T., Groten, R., Peer, A., Buss, M.: Evaluation of a Coordinating Controller for Improved Task Performance in Multi-User Teleoperation. In: Eurohaptics (2010)
9. Hashtrudi-Zaad, K., Salcudean, S.E.: Analysis of control architectures for teleoperation systems with impedance/admittance master and slave manipulators. The Int. Journal of Robotic Research 20(6), 419–445 (2001)
10. Peer, A., Buss, M.: Stability analysis of a bilateral teleoperation system using the parameter space approach. In: Proc. of the IEEE/RSJ Int. Conf. on Intelligent Robots and Systems, Nice, France, pp. 2350–2356 (2008)
11. Ackermann, J.: Robust Control, The Parameter Space Approach, 2nd edn. Springer, Heidelberg (2002)

Mechatronic Design Optimization of a Teleoperation System Based on Bounded Environment Passivity

Bert Willaert, Brecht Corteville, Herman Bruyninckx, Hendrik Van Brussel, and Emmanuel B. Vander Poorten

Dept. of Mechanical Engineering, K.U. Leuven, Belgium
{bert.willaert,brecht.corteville,herman.bruyninckx,
hendrik.vanbrussel,emmanuel.vanderpoorten}@mech.kuleuven.be

Abstract. This paper presents a mechatronic analysis of a teleoperation system that provides haptic feedback. The analysis, based on the Bounded Environment Passivity method, describes the combined effect of the teleoperation controller and the master and slave hardware, including the effect of structural flexibilities, which have often been neglected in the domain of teleoperation. This results in rules of thumb for the design of the hardware and the tuning of the controller. As two of these rules of thumb pose a trade-off in hardware design, an unprecedented conceptual design optimization is described in a second part of this paper. The objective is to demonstrate the need for a mechatronic approach to the design of teleoperation systems in order to obtain maximal system performance.

Keywords: Mechatronics, Teleoperation, Passivity.

1 Introduction

In literature, most stability analyses of teleoperation systems with a bilateral controller assume rigid body dynamics for both master and slave robot [1,2,3,4,5]. However, typical master and slave robots, especially the multi-d.o.f. systems, possess non-negligible flexibilities. Although the importance of structural flexibilities is well recognized in general [6], the effect of such flexibilities has received little attention in the domain of teleoperation. In [7], the *closed-loop stability* is analysed of teleoperation systems with a flexible slave. The generality of the obtained results, however, is restricted, as a fixed human operator is assumed and stability is quantified by time delay robustness. In [8], for teleoperation systems with a flexible slave, *absolute stability* is calculated based on Lewellyn's criteria. Here, the generality of the results is restricted by the assumption of a perfect position controller, i.e. $K_p \to \infty$.

This paper presents a mechatronic analysis of a teleoperation system with a flexible slave and a realistic position controller, based on *bounded environment passivity* [5]. Passivity theory is widely used to analyse the stability properties of teleoperation systems interacting with a wide range of human operators and environments. Here, the analysis is done for a Position-Force teleoperation controller. In the first part of this paper (section 2 and 3), the teleoperation system is described and its passivity properties are derived for both a rigid and a flexible slave robot. These properties result in rules of thumb for the design of the slave robot and the tuning of the controller.

A.M.L. Kappers et al. (Eds.): EuroHaptics 2010, Part I, LNCS 6191, pp. 161–168, 2010.

Such rules of thumb, however, can be conflicting. A classical example is the trade-off between the structural stiffness of a robot and the total mass of the robot. Consequently, these rules of thumb give rise to an optimization problem. Therefore, in the second part of this paper (section 4), a conceptual example of such a mechatronic optimization problem is addressed. This example clearly demonstrates the importance of a mechatronic approach to the design of teleoperation systems.

2   A Mechatronic System

A teleoperation system is a good example of a mechatronic system as it consists of two electronically controlled mechanical devices. The controller used here is the Position-Force controller (the **PD-F** scheme in [5]) shown in Fig. 2a. The following equations, describe the forces applied by the motors of the master and the slave:

$$\tau_m = -\lambda . F_e \tag{1}$$

$$\tau_s = (K_v s + K_p).(\mu.x_m - x_s). \tag{2}$$

The parameters μ and λ are the position and force scaling factors. Note that, at the master side, a low-impedance-type device is assumed and pure open-loop force control is used.

2.1   A Rigid Body Slave

The teleoperation system analyzed in subsection 3.1 consists of a 1-d.o.f rigid body master and slave. These rigid body models for master and slave obey the following equations of motion:

$$F_h + \tau_m = M_m \ddot{x}_m + B_m \dot{x}_m, \tag{3}$$

$$\tau_s - F_e = M_s \ddot{x}_s + B_s \dot{x}_s, \tag{4}$$

$$Z_m = M_m s + B_m, \quad Z_s = M_s s + B_s, \tag{5}$$

with Z_m and Z_s representing the rigid body impedances of the master and the slave robot. Remark that for a rigid body model the positions x_m and x_s (the positions of the motors) are equal to respectively x_h and x_e (the positions of the end-effectors).

2.2   A Flexible Slave

The teleoperation system analyzed in subsection 3.2 consists of a 1-d.o.f rigid body master and a fourth-order flexible slave. This fourth-order flexible slave obeys the following equation of motion:

$$\begin{bmatrix} \dot{x}_s \\ \dot{x}_e \end{bmatrix} = \begin{bmatrix} \dfrac{M_{s2}s^2 + B_{s2}s + K_s}{Denum(s)} & -\dfrac{(B_{s2}s + K_s)}{Denum(s)} \\ \dfrac{B_{s2}s + K_s}{Denum(s)} & -\dfrac{M_{s1}s^2 + (B_{s1} + B_{s2})s + K_s}{Denum(s)} \end{bmatrix} \cdot \begin{bmatrix} \tau_s \\ F_e \end{bmatrix} \tag{6}$$

with $Denum(s) = M_{s1}M_{s2}s^3 + (M_{s2}(B_{s1} + B_{s2}) + M_{s1}B_{s2})s^2 + ((M_{s1} + M_{s2})K_s + B_{s1}B_{s2})s + K_s B_{s1}$.

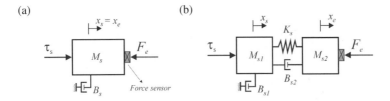

Fig. 1. A mechanical model for (a) a rigid body system and (b) a flexible system, represented by a fourth-order model

Both slave configurations are shown in Fig. 1. The rigid body parameters of the real 1-d.o.f. experimental master-slave setup described in [5], serve as a starting point for the calculations reported in this paper. The values of the parameters, based on a linear model identification of the master and slave and the implementation of the controller on this setup, are as follows: $M_m = 0.64$ kg, $M_s = 0.61$ kg, $B_m = 3.4$ Ns/m, $B_s = 11$ Ns/m, $K_p = 4000$ N/m, $K_v = 80$ Ns/m ($\zeta = 0.81$), and $\mu = \lambda = 1$.

3   A Mechatronic Analysis

This section describes a passivity analysis of the two teleoperation systems described above. The passivity analysis makes use of the *bounded environment passivity* method presented in [5]. This method is based on checking the positive realness of the admittance Y_{MS}, which represents the combined dynamics of the master, the slave, the controller and the environment. As can be seen in Fig. 2a, this is the admittance the human operator interacts with. Passivity of this admittance Y_{MS} is a sufficient condition for stable interaction between the teleoperation system and any (passive) human operator. The environment considered in this work is a pure spring (K_e), because in the case of the Position-Force controller, stability problems are being reported especially for stiff environments [1,2,5]. Moreover, the authors proved that a pure mass cannot make the admittance Y_{MS} active for a rigid body slave [9].

3.1   A Rigid Body Slave

For the teleoperation system described in subsection 2.1, having a rigid body slave, and assuming a pure stiffness as environment, the admittance $Y_{MS(K_e)}$ can be written as:

$$Y_{MS(K_e)} = \frac{v_h}{F_h} = \frac{s(M_s s^2 + (B_s + K_v)s + (K_p + K_e))}{(M_m s^2 + B_m s)(M_s s^2 + (B_s + K_v)s + (K_p + K_e)) + \mu\lambda K_e(K_v s + K_p)}, \quad (7)$$

(a)   (b)

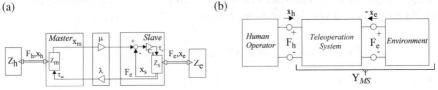

Fig. 2. (a) The controller representation and (b) the network representation of the analyzed teleoperation system

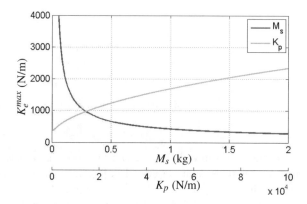

Fig. 3. The effect of the slave inertia M_s and the stiffness of the position controller K_p on the maximum environment stiffness K_e^{max}, based on Bounded Environment Passivity

by combining (1), (2), (3) and (4). In [5], it is shown that the positive-realness condition for this $Y_{MS(K_e)}$ results in a complex set of conditions, that can be summarized as an upper boundary on the product of the scaling factors, $\mu\lambda$. Here, this boundary is rewritten as an upper boundary on the environment stiffness:

$$K_e \leq \frac{B_m(B_s+K_v)}{\mu^2\lambda^2 M_s K_v^2} \left(\mu\lambda(K_v(B_s+K_v)-2M_sK_p)+2B_m(B_s+K_v)+2\sqrt{Root} \right) \qquad (8)$$

with $Root = (B_m^2+\mu\lambda B_m K_v)(K_v+B_s)^2 - \mu\lambda M_s K_p B_m(K_v+B_s)+\mu^2\lambda^2 M_s K_p(M_s K_p-B_s K_v)$.

Condition (8) specifies the maximum environment stiffness K_e^{max} for which the admittance $Y_{MS(K_e)}$ is passive as a function of all parameters of the system. Based on (8), Fig. 3 clearly shows the negative effect of the slave inertia M_s and the positive effect of the stiffness of the position controller K_p on the maximum environment stiffness K_e^{max}. Note that both relations M_s-K_e^{max} and K_p-K_e^{max} shown here, suppose a fixed damping ratio ζ for the slave, i.e. $K_v = 0.81 \cdot 2\sqrt{M_s K_p}$. Based on (8), one can calculate that, for the parameters mentioned above, the maximum environment stiffness for which $Y_{MS(K_e)}$ is passive is 580 N/m.

3.2   A Flexible Slave

For the teleoperation system described in subsection 2.2, i.e. with a flexible slave, the admittance $Y_{MS(K_e)}$ can be derived by combining (1), (2), (3) and (6):

$$Y_{MS(K_e)} = \frac{v_h}{F_h} = \frac{Num(s)}{(M_m s+B_m)(Num(s))+\mu\lambda K_e(B_{s2}s+K_s)(K_v s+K_p)} \qquad (9)$$

with $Num(s) = (M_{s1}s^2+(B_{s1}+B_{s2}+K_v)s+(K_s+K_p)).(M_{s2}s^2+B_{s2}s+(K_s+K_e))-(B_{s2}s+K_s)^2$.

The condition of positive realness for this admittance is too complex to be analyzed analytically. Therefore, the bounded environment passivity is analyzed numerically in

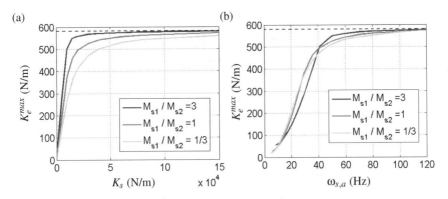

Fig. 4. The maximum environment stiffness for which $Y_{MS(K_e)}$ is passive as a function of (a) the structural stiffness K_s of the slave and (b) the structural anti-resonance frequency, $\omega_{s,a} = \sqrt{\frac{K_s}{M_{s2}}}$

Matlab®. For a set of fixed system parameters, K_e^{max} is found as follows: starting from $K_e = 0$, the condition $\Re(Y_{MS(K_e)}(j\omega)) \geq 0$ is verified for $\omega \in [0.1 - 10^9 rad/s]$ and for increasing values of K_e (increment: 1 N/m). When the condition $\Re(Y_{MS(K_e)}(j\omega)) \geq 0$ no longer holds, K_e^{max} is obtained.

First, the effect of the structural stiffness K_s of the slave on the maximum environment stiffness K_e^{max} is analyzed. This is done for the parameters given in section 2.2 ($B_{s1} = B_s$ and $B_{s2} = 2Ns/m$) and three different mass distributions, while the total mass of the slave is kept constant, i.e. $M_s = M_{s1} + M_{s2} = 0.61$ kg. Fig. 4a shows the maximum environment stiffness K_e^{max} as a function of the structural stiffness of the slave, while Fig. 4b shows the same information but as a function of the structural anti-resonance frequency of the slave, $\omega_{s,a}$. One can see that for high structural anti-resonance frequencies (> 50 Hz), the flexibility of the slave has little effect on the maximum environment stiffness, but for low structural anti-resonance frequencies (< 50 Hz), the effect is very clear. One can see that for a structural stiffness going to infinity, K_e^{max} tends to 580 N/m, which is exactly the value found in section 3.1 for a rigid body slave (blue dashed line).

Next, in analogy of subsection 3.1, the effect of the controller stiffness, K_p, and the total mass of the slave, M_s, is analyzed. Fig. 5a and Fig. 5b respectively show the maximum environment stiffness K_e^{max} as a function of the controller stiffness of the slave, K_p, and as a function of the total mass of the slave, M_s. The calculation is done for five different values of the structural stiffness K_s and the damping ratio for the slave is kept constant ($\zeta = 0.81$), i.e. K_v is set to $0.81 \cdot 2\sqrt{(M_{s1} + M_{s2})K_p}$. In both figures, the curve for a rigid slave, derived in section 3.1, is also shown (blue dashed line). Based on classical control theory, one can assume that there is an optimal relation between the first structural anti-resonance frequency $\omega_{s,a}$ of the slave and the bandwidth of the position controller ω_c. Fig. 5a confirms this assumption: it is clear that there is an optimal value for K_p depending on the value of K_s. Here, it turns out that the optimal value for K_p is $\pm \frac{1}{4}K_s$. Although the trend is general for the Position-Force controller, it is important to stress that this ratio is not, as it depends on all parameters of the system. Stated differently, one can say that for a maximal K_e^{max} the bandwidth of the position controller ω_c should be 'sufficiently smaller' than the first structural anti-resonance frequency $\omega_{s,a}$.

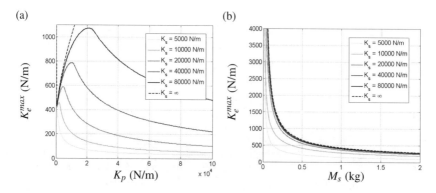

Fig. 5. The maximum environment stiffness for which $Y_{MS(K_e)}$ is passive as a function of (a) the controller stiffness K_p and (b) the total mass M_s of the slave

Note that the effect of K_p described here is a good example of the important fact that rules of thumb derived for a system with rigid body devices are not necessarily valid for a system with flexible devices.

4   A Mechatronic Optimization

The previous section describes a mechatronic analysis of a 1-d.o.f teleoperation system resulting in a few rules of thumb, specific for the Position-force controller:

1. the slave robot should be as lightweight as possible, for a rigid body slave as well as for a flexible slave,
2. the structural stiffness of the slave robot should be as high a possible,
3. the stiffness of the position controller has an optimal value depending on the first structural resonance of the slave.

The first and second rule of thumb pose a well-known and often appearing trade-off in hardware design. Furthermore, it can be shown that this trade-off depends on the relation between the structural resonance of the slave and the bandwidth of the position controller. The relevance of these considerations is demonstrated through the following conceptual mechatronic design optimization.

Assume a slave robot consisting of two masses ($m_1 = 0.3$ and $m_2 = 0.2$) connected through a link as shown in Fig. 6a. The geometry of the link (length: $l = 0.2$ m, rectangular section with thickness: $t = 0.01$ m) and the material (Aluminium with ρ: 2700 kg/m³ and E: 69 GPa) are fixed a priori, while the width of the rectangular section, w, is the parameter to be optimized. This conceptual design can be represented by a fourth-order model according to (6), with the following parameters:

$$M_{s1} = m_1 + \frac{m_{beam}}{2} \text{ and } M_{s2} = m_2 + \frac{m_{beam}}{2} \quad (m_{beam} = \rho \cdot l \cdot t \cdot w) \tag{10}$$

$$K_s = \frac{2EI}{l^3} \quad (I = \frac{t \cdot w^3}{12}) \quad \text{and} \quad B_{s2} = 2 \text{ Ns/m} \tag{11}$$

As such, for increasing values of w, both the structural stiffness, K_s, and the mass of the slave, M_s, increase. Consequently, an optimal value for w can be expected. Note

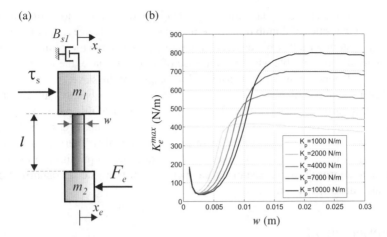

Fig. 6. (a) The conceptual design and (b) the maximum environment stiffness for which $Y_{MS(K_e)}$ is passive as a function of the geometrical parameter w

that all other parameters, i.e. for the master and the controller, are the same as given in section 2.2. Now, for this teleoperation system, the Bounded Environment Passivity can be analyzed in the same way as described in section 3.2. Fig. 6b shows the maximum environment stiffness K_e^{max} as a function of the geometrical parameter w, for five different values of the control parameter K_p. Again the damping ratio of the slave is kept constant ($\zeta = 0.81$). The following observations can be made:

- There is an optimal value for the geometrical parameter w. Initially, K_e^{max} increases for increasing values of w, which can be explained by the positive effect, shown in Fig. 4a, of increasing the structural stiffness. However, Fig. 4a also shows that once the structural stiffness has reached a certain level, the benefit of further increasing K_s is minimal. Therefore, w reaches an optimal value at the moment the negative effect of the increasing total inertia M_s becomes more dominant than the positive effect of the further increasing structural stiffness.
- The optimal value for the geometrical parameter w depends on the controller stiffness K_p. In correspondence with the trend shown in Fig. 5a, the optimal value for w, and thus the optimal structural stiffness, increases for increasing values of the controller stiffness K_p.

These observations underline the importance of a concurrent hardware and control design. How this should be done in practice for multi-d.o.f systems will be addressed in future research.

5 Conclusions

This paper presents a mechatronic analysis of the passivity of a 1-d.o.f. teleoperation system with a Position-force controller. Both a teleoperation system with a rigid body slave and with a flexible slave are analyzed. The analysis demonstrates the need for a lightweight, structurally stiff slave robot. Another important conclusion from this analysis is the fact that rules of thumb for a system with rigid body devices are not necessarily valid for a system with flexible devices: in case of a rigid slave the position controller has to be as stiff as possible while for the case of a flexible slave, there is a maximum value for K_p depending on the first structural resonance of the slave.

However, the above requirement for a lightweight, structurally stiff slave robot poses a trade-off in hardware design. Therefore, in a second part of this paper, a conceptual design optimization of a geometrical parameter of a robotic link is described. The objective of the optimization is to maximize the environment stiffness with which any passive human operator can stably interact. This conceptual optimization motivates a mechatronic approach to the design of teleoperation systems, i.e. a concurrent design of the hardware and the controller.

Acknowledgments

This work was supported by a PhD grant from the Institute for the Promotion of Innovation through Science and Technology in Flanders (I.W.T.-Vlaanderen), two I.W.T projects, IWT/OZM/080086 and /080003, and by an FP7-People Marie Curie Reintegration Grant, PIRG03-2008-231045.

References

1. Lawrence, D.A.: Stability and transparency in bilateral teleoperation. IEEE transactions on robotics and automation 9(5), 624–637 (1993)
2. Daniel, R.W., McAree, P.R.: Fundamental limits of performance for force reflecting teleoperation. The Int. J. of Robotics Research 17(8), 811–830 (1998)
3. Hashtrudi-Zaad, K., Salcudean, S.E.: Analysis of control architectures for teleoperation systems with impedance/admittance master and slave manipulators. The Int. J. of Robotics Research 20(6), 419–445 (2001)
4. Vander Poorten, E.B., Yokokohji, Y., Yoshikawa, T.: Stability analysis and robust control for fixed-scale teleoperation. Advanced Robotics 20, 681–706 (2006)
5. Willaert, B., Corteville, B., Reynaerts, D., Van Brussel, H., Vander Poorten, E.B.: Bounded environment passivity of the classical position-force teleoperation controller. In: Proceedings of the IEEE/RSJ Int. Conference on Intelligent Robots and Systems, St. Louis, MO, USA, October 2009, pp. 4622–4628 (2009)
6. Dwivedy, S.K., Eberhard, P.: Dynamic analysis of flexible manipulators, a literature review. Mechanism and Machine Theory 41, 749–777 (2006)
7. Christiansson, G.A.V., van der Helm, F.C.T.: The low-stiffness teleoperator slave - a trade-off between stability and performance. The Int. J.l of Robotics Research 26(3), 287–299 (2007)
8. Tavakoli, M., Howe, R.D.: Haptic effect of surgical teleoperator flexibility. The Int. J. of Robotics Research 28(10), 1289–1302 (2009)
9. Willaert, B., Corteville, B., Reynaerts, D., Van Brussel, H., Vander Poorten, E.B.: A mechatronic analysis of the classical position-force controller based on bounded environment passivity. Submitted to The Int. J. of Robotics Research

On the Impact of Haptic Data Reduction and Feedback Modality on Quality and Task Performance in a Telepresence and Teleaction System[*]

Verena Nitsch[1], Julius Kammerl[2], Berthold Faerber[3], and Eckehard Steinbach[4]

[1,3] Human Factors Institute,
Universität der Bundeswehr München, Werner-Heisenberg-Weg 39,
85577 Neubiberg, Germany
{verena.nitsch,berthold.faerber}@unibw.de
[2,4] Institute for Media Technology,
Technische Universität München, Arcisstraße 21, 80333 Munich, Germany
{kammerl,eckehard.steinbach}@tum.de

Abstract. The perceptual deadband (PD) data reduction scheme allows for a significant reduction of network load in real-time haptic communication scenarios. Aiming to ascertain how the optimum PD data reduction parameter k is best determined, an experiment was conducted in which a possible interaction of PD data reduction and visual feedback on haptic feedback quality and task performance was investigated. The results show that when haptic feedback is complemented with visual feedback, haptic data reduction affects haptic feedback quality at a lower data reduction rate than it affects task performance. When visual feedback is missing, however, this effect is reversed. These results imply that the perception of haptic feedback quality is markedly influenced by visual sensory input as well as task requirements; hence, it is recommended to consider feedback quality and task performance in the optimization of PD reduction before such schemes may be applied to industrial telepresence and teleaction systems.

Keywords: Perceptual data reduction, deadband approach, haptics, lossy compression, task performance.

1 Introduction

Telepresence and teleaction (TPTA) systems allow a human user to operate in environments that are physically distant, hazardous, scaled, or otherwise inaccessible (e.g. virtual) [1]. Specifically, in these systems, a human operator controls a teleoperator, typically a robot equipped with sensors and actuators, via a communication link [1]. In recent years, much research has focused on the added value of haptic feedback for task performance in TPTA systems [e.g. 2,3]. Here, mainly data regarding positions, angles, velocities, forces and torques are transmitted, which present high requirements

[*] This research was supported by the German Research Foundation (DFG) within the Collaborative Research Center on High-Fidelity Telepresence and Teleaction (SFB 453).

A.M.L. Kappers et al. (Eds.): EuroHaptics 2010, Part I, LNCS 6191, pp. 169–176, 2010.
© Springer-Verlag Berlin Heidelberg 2010

with respect to packet rate/signal update rate, time delay, and delay jitter [4]. When the remote teleoperator is accessed via a packet-based communication network (e.g. the Internet), minimizing the end-to-end delay with the goal of preventing instability of the involved control loops results in high packet rates. In this context, the integration of the perceptual deadband (PD) data reduction scheme proposed in [5] promises a significant reduction of packet rates without impairing the user experience. In contrast to early data reduction techniques [e.g. 6,7], which focus on the exploitation of statistical properties of the haptic signal, the PD data reduction approach exploits limitations of human haptic perception in order to keep introduced coding artifacts below haptic perception thresholds. For PD data reduction, sampled values are only considered to be relevant for transmission if they exceed the operator's just noticeable difference (JND) threshold as defined by Weber's Law [8].

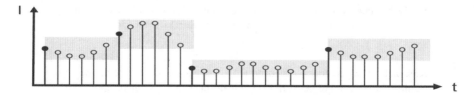

Fig. 1. Principle of the PD approach. Black samples violating the applied perception threshold (grey zones) are transmitted, grey samples are discarded. The perception thresholds are a function of the haptic stimulus intensity.

Hence, only if the difference between the most recently sent haptic signal value and the current input value exceeds an assumed perception threshold, a new transmission of a signal update is triggered. The receiver reacts to a missing sample by holding the value of the most recently received sample (see Fig. 1.). The size of the perception threshold describes the implication $\Delta I = kI$, where ΔI defines the JND threshold and k represents the Weber threshold parameter. Since the optimum amount of haptic data reduction in this approach is directly linked to human force perception thresholds, it is crucially important to ascertain which factors affect the user's perception of haptic feedback and to what degree these findings generalize to various TPTA-systems and –settings before this reduction scheme is employed in industrial settings.

1.1 Previous Work

The PD data reduction approach has been experimentally evaluated in a number of real-world and simulated TPTA systems. Previous work [5] reports force packet rate reductions of up to 85% for a 1-Degree-of-Freedom (DoF) TPTA system. Even higher reduction rates of up to 90% were reported for the multi-DoF extension of the PD data reduction approach [4].

Whilst the PD data reduction approach was found to be very successful in reducing network load, when it comes to the practical implementation of this approach in TPTA systems, the question remains, how the optimum Weber threshold parameter defining the size of the PDs may best be determined. Although, in theory, JNDs for force magnitude are approximately similar for all healthy human operators [9], configurations for the parameter k reported in the literature vary widely. For example, [5] found a threshold for the detection of PD-induced coding artifacts in the haptic signal of around k=2.5-7.5%, whereas [10] found no significant feedback quality deterioration with PD parameters of k<=15% and [11] reported thresholds to range between k=7.5% and k=20%. This suggests that the optimum size of the PD approach is not determined by a single JND of force magnitude, but influenced by various other factors as well. For instance, it seems reasonable to assume that detection thresholds of PD-induced coding artifacts are highly dependent on the system characteristics of the TPTA system used, as was suggested by [10]. In addition, cross-modal interactions, particularly those pertaining to visual sensory input, were also found to affect force perception JNDs [12], suggesting that haptic PD thresholds may also be influenced by the type of visual feedback received.

Finally, previous experiments were conducted in telepresence scenarios without consideration of contact force intensity. However, in many telepresence application scenarios such as dealing with dangerous materials or touching fragile objects, accurate representation of small contact forces is likely of great perceptual importance to the user. Hence it seems plausible that the characteristics of the haptic feedback signal, and consequently the effects of PD-based data reduction, strongly depend on the applied TPTA scenario. In this context, the threshold criterion in determining optimum PD sizes is also likely to make a difference. For example, until now, most studies on PD data reduction focused exclusively on the transparency of the applied signal processing steps in determining optimum PD detection thresholds [e.g. 5,11]. The rationale behind this approach is that as long as a loss of data is not noticeable, task performance should not be affected. However, as of yet, too few studies systematically investigated the effects of haptic PD data reduction on task performance so as to justify such a claim. For future applications of PD data reduction to specific TPTA systems it is therefore important to ascertain if and in what way task performance deterioration is linked to subjective impressions of the haptic feedback quality of TPTA systems and how this link might be influenced by other feedback modalities.

1.2 Research Questions

Based on this rationale, the present study aimed to systematically investigate the effects of PD data reduction on the perceived quality of haptic feedback and task performance in a TPTA scenario simulating a safety-critical application, in which minimal contact force is expected due to careful teleoperator navigation. Finally, it was to be investigated whether the effects of PD data reduction on task performance accuracy and/or perceived haptic feedback quality depend on the type of feedback employed. Specifically, since with visuo-haptic feedback, vision typically dominates the perceptual focus [e.g. 12], the present study aimed to establish whether the effects of PD data reduction on the experimental measurements would change if the perceptual focus was shifted to the haptic modality as visual feedback is withdrawn.

2 Methodology

2.1 Participants

A convenience sample of 13 female and 29 male (N=42) participants, aged 21-50 yrs. (mean age: 30.64 yrs., std. dev.: 7.22 yrs), took part in this experiment, all of whom were right-handed. A standardized motor performance test (Motor Performance Series© by Dr.G. Schuhfried GmbH) ensured that none of the participants were impaired in their tactile perception or motor performance.ï

2.2 Experimental Design and Setup

An 11 (PD parameter) x 2 (feedback modality) mixed-subjects design was employed, with PD data reduction as a within-subjects variable, which was manipulated on 11 levels (k=0%; 5%; 10%; 20%; 30%; 40%; 50%; 60%; 70%; 80%; 90%). Participants were assigned to one of two groups: one group received visuo-haptic feedback from the TPTA environment, the other performed with haptic feedback only. The groups were balanced in terms of gender, age and motor ability. Measured were data reduction performance, task performance defined as force control (variance in surface penetration depths and maximum surface penetration distances), as well as perceived haptic feedback quality. A Phantom Omni haptic device by SensAble Technologies[TM] was used for the experimental main task. For this task, participants were asked to move their cursor from a starting point through a three-dimensional, haptically rendered tunnel, to a pre-specified target position. The simulated stiffness of contact with the virtual tunnel was set to 15 N/m.

2.3 Procedure

Participants were naïve to the purpose of the experiment; they were merely told that "different settings of the Phantom device" would be tested. Participants were given the opportunity to familiarize themselves with the apparatus and the virtual environment without task performance constraints. They were then provided with standardized instructions asking them to traverse the virtual tunnel, while keeping in contact with its ground surface at all times with as little pressure as possible. Before main trials, participants underwent a stringent, methodical practice phase which had been established based on rigorous pilot testing. Purpose of this practice phase was to ensure that all participants performed the experimental task in a somewhat consistent manner so that measured variations in task performance could be confidently attributed to the experimental manipulation rather than individual style. Each person then performed the main task 11 times, each time at a different stage of PD data reduction, whereby the PD parameters were presented in randomized order to avoid practice and order effects. After each trial, participants rated haptic feedback quality.

3 Results

Possible differential PD data reduction effects of feedback on the data update rate, subjective haptic feedback quality and force control measures were investigated by conducting analyses of variance (ANOVA) for each feedback group, i.e, the group which had received visuo-haptic feedback and the group which had received haptic feedback only, individually. In cases where the assumptions for parametric tests had not been met, appropriate corrections were applied or non-parametric tests were used, as is specified in the following.

3.1 Data Reduction Performance

For both groups, the largest reductions in the number of sent data packets per second were observed for PD parameters of k>=20%. Figure 2 displays the median values for sent signal updates for each feedback group against the median values for force control measures.

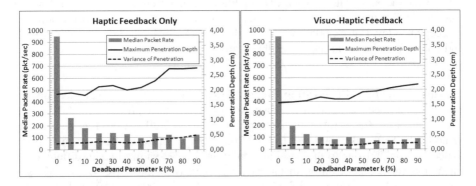

Fig. 2. Median number of data packets sent per second, penetration variance and maximum penetration depth for each PD parameter in each feedback group

3.2 Perceived Haptic Feedback Quality

Perceived deterioration of the haptic feedback quality was measured with a single 20-point Likert-type scale ("To what degree, if at all, did you perceive a disturbance in the haptic feedback") ranging from 1 (no disturbance was felt) to 20 (extremely large disturbance was felt). For the visuo-haptic feedback group, a parametric ANOVA revealed a significant deadband main effect on the quality of haptic feedback ($F(4.56, 91.24) = 17.19$, $p<.001$) (with Greenhouse-Geisser Correction, $\varepsilon = 0.46$), indicating that disturbance ratings differed significantly with different PD parameters. A similar effect was found for the haptic feedback group ($F(4.69, 93.82) = 5.93$, $p<.001$) (with Greenhouse-Geisser Correction, $\varepsilon = 0.47$). Bonferroni-adjusted post-hoc simple contrasts of disturbance ratings in each PD condition to the baseline (k=0%), revealed no sig. difference in disturbance ratings up to k=30% for the visuo-haptic group ($F(1,20)=10.47$, $p<.005$, part. $\eta^2 =.34$), and even up to k=80% for the group which only received haptic feedback ($F(1,20)=11.47$, $p<.005$, part. $\eta^2 =.36$).

3.3 Task Performance

Since one of the main purposes of haptic feedback is the intuitive control of forces applied to surfaces, penetration of the virtual tunnel's surface was deemed an appropriate measure of task performance accuracy. Here, two measures were considered: the variance in penetration depth and the maximum distances that participants penetrated into the surface, both measured in haptic device workspace scale (cm).

Surface Penetration Variance. With data of the haptic feedback group, Friedman's ANOVA showed a sig. effect of PD data reduction on penetration depth variance ($\chi^2(10)=61.53$, p<.001). The ANOVA also confirmed this effect on penetration variance for the visuo-haptic feedback group ($\chi^2(10)=33.92$, p<.001). Following-up the significant PD effect, Bonferroni-adjusted post-hoc signed-rank Wilcoxon comparisons of the measurements in each PD condition to the baseline measurement (k=0%) were made. For the haptic feedback group, none of the comparisons met the adjusted p-acceptance level of p<.005 up to a Deadband of k=60% (z=-3.04, p<.005, r=-.47) and above. For the visuo-haptic feedback group, the comparison to the baseline was significant at k=70% (z=-3.14, p<.005, r=-.47) and above.

Maximum Surface Penetration Depth. Friedman's ANOVA conducted on the maximum surface penetration distances for each feedback group individually confirmed sig. PD effects for both the haptic ($\chi^2(10) = 67.20$, p<.001) as well as the visuo-haptic feedback group ($\chi^2(10) = 43.76$, p<.001). Follow-up Bonferroni-adjusted Wilcoxon comparisons to the baseline condition (k=0%) showed a sig. difference in maximum surface penetration distances for k=60% (z = -3.04, p<.005, r=-.47) and above for the haptic group and for k=50% (z = -3.30, p<.005, r=-.50) and above for the visuo-haptic feedback group.

4 Discussion

Previous studies on PD data reduction focused on the transparency threshold of the applied signal processing routines. The underlying assumption was that as long as a loss of haptic information is not detectable, PD data reduction would not have a noticeable effect on the operator's control of the teleoperator. Aiming to ascertain how the optimum PD parameter k is best determined, the present study was conducted to investigate the performance of perceptual deadband coding with respect to perceived haptic feedback quality and force control as a measure of task performance. Furthermore, it was investigated whether these effects of haptic data reduction are influenced by visual feedback, or lack thereof.

The results show that, overall, the PD data reduction effects on task performance do not seem to change when the perceptual focus is shifted to the haptic modality, as similar thresholds, i.e. between k=50% and k=70%, are found for the force control measures of maximum surface penetration depth and penetration variance for both feedback groups. Interestingly, the detection thresholds varied widely between the two feedback groups. Participants who received visuo-haptic feedback from the task environment were more sensitive (threshold at k=30%) to the deteriorative effects of

PD data reduction than were those in the haptic feedback condition (threshold at k=80%). Presumably, participants who lacked this visual source of information were less able to distinguish coding artifacts from the intended haptic rendering, even though a stringent practice phase, in which PD data reduction was not applied, ensured that participants were familiar with the actual haptic rendition of the task environment. These results differ greatly from detected transparency thresholds in previous experiments. In contrast to previous PD-related experiments, in the present study, an application scenario was evaluated where small contact forces are expected. It seems that in TPTA scenarios with small expected contact forces, the artifacts introduced by PD data reduction are less disturbing as force-feedback intensity stays within small bounds.

For the implementation of PD-based haptic data reduction, the results indicate that the point of data reduction detection does not necessarily stipulate the on-set of task performance deterioration, at least not with respect to task performance criteria that relate to the operator's control of forces. Depending on the availability of additional feedback sources, data reduction may not even be consciously detected, even though the operator's control of the teleoperator is measurably affected. Furthermore, considering PD detection thresholds reported in the literature vary widely, this research clearly suggests that there is no single optimum PD threshold which may be universally applied to all TPTA-systems, but rather that its implementation into these systems needs to be adapted to the systems' capabilities and environmental demands, including specific task performance criteria.

On a final note, it should be mentioned that, concurring with previous studies on the PD data reduction approach [e.g. 5,10,11], the present study confirmed the effectiveness of this lossy data reduction scheme in terms of data reduction performance. In fact, for the specific set-up of the present study, an analysis of the packet rate reduction showed that PD parameters of k=10% already translated into packet rate reductions of 81% and 87 % with haptic feedback and visuo-haptic feedback, respectively, without significantly affecting perceived haptic feedback quality or operator force control. Further research is needed to investigate if and to what extent the findings of the present study generalize to other TPTA systems. In particular, a systematic investigation of the influence of limitations in mechanical bandwidth of deployed hardware components is needed. In addition, further evaluative studies are recommended which compare the PD data reduction approach to other types of haptic data reduction schemes in terms of their effects on haptic feedback quality and teleoperator force control.

References

1. Ferrell, W.R., Sheridan, T.B.: Supervisory Control of Remote Manipulation. IEEE Spectrum 4, 81–88 (1967)
2. Dennerlein, J.T., Martin, D.B., Hasser, C.J.: Force-feedback Improves Performance for Steering and Combined Steering-Targeting Tasks. In: CHI 2000 Conf. on Human Factors in Computing Systems, The Hague, Netherlands, pp. 423–429. ACM Press, New York (2000)

3. Debus, T., Becker, T., Dupont, P., Jang, T., Howe, R.: Multichannel Vibrotactile Display for Sensory Substitution during Teleoperation. In: SPIE 2001 Int. Symposium on Intelligent Systems and Advanced Manufacturing, Boston, USA, vol. 4570, pp. 42–49 (2001)
4. Hinterseer, P., Hirche, S., Chaudhuri, S., Steinbach, E., Buss, M.: Perception-Based Data Reduction and Transmission of Haptic Data in Telepresence and Teleaction Systems. IEEE Trans. on Signal Processing 56, 588–597 (2008)
5. Hinterseer, P., Steinbach, E., Hirche, S., Buss, M.: A Novel, Psychophysically Motivated Transmission Approach for Haptic Data Streams in Telepresence and Teleaction Systems. In: IEEE Int. Conf. on Acoustics, Speech, and Signal Processing, Philadelphia, USA, pp. 1097–1110 (2005)
6. Ortega, A., Liu, Y.: Lossy Compression of Haptic Data. In: McLaughlin, G.S.M., Hespanha, J. (eds.) Touch in Virtual Environments: Haptics and the Design of Interactive Systems, pp. 119–136. Prentice Hall, Englewood Cliffs (2002)
7. Borst, C.W.: Predictive Coding for Efficient Host-Device Communication in a Pneumatic Force-Feedback Display. In: First Joint Eurohaptics Conference and Symposium on Haptic Interfaces for Virtual Environment and Teleoperator Systems, pp. 596–599 (2005)
8. Gescheider, G.A.: Psychophysics. Lawrence Erlbaum, Mahwah (1985)
9. Jones, L.A., Hunter, I.W.: A Perceptual Analysis of Stiffness. Experimental Brain Research 79, 150–156 (1990)
10. Nitsch, V., Hinterseer, P., Faerber, B., Steinbach, E., Geiger, L.: An Experimental Study of Lossy Compression in a Real Telepresence and Teleaction System. In: HAVE 2008 IEEE International Workshop on Haptic Audio visual Environments and Games, pp. 75–80 (2008)
11. Hirche, S., Hinterseer, P., Steinbach, E., Buss, M.: Transparent Data Reduction in Networked Telepresence and Teleaction Systems. Part I: Communication without Time Delay. Presence: Teleoperators and Virtual Environments 16, 523–531 (2007)
12. Shi, Z., Hirche, S., Schneider, W.X., Müller, H.: Influence of Visuomotor Action on Visual-Haptic Simultaneous Perception: A Psychophysical Study. In: IEEE Symposium on Haptic Interfaces for Virtual Environments and Teleoperator Systems, pp. 65–70 (2008)

Stability Analysis of Mobile Robot Teleoperation with Variable Force Feedback Gain

Ildar Farkhatdinov[1] and Jee-Hwan Ryu[2]

[1] Institut des Systèmes Intelligents et de Robotique
Université Pierre and Marie Curie (Paris 06), CNRS UMR 7222, France
ildar@isir.upmc.fr
http://www.isir.upmc.fr
[2] Korea University of Technology and Education, School of Mechanical Engineering, Cheonan,
R. of Korea
jhryu@kut.ac.kr
http://robot.kut.ac.kr

Abstract. We analyze the stability of previously proposed mobile robot tele-operation system [7]. Unlike to other approaches human-operator dynamics is included for the stability analysis. Mobile robot teleoperation systems have two major differences when they are compared with conventional bilateral teleoperators: first, rate mode control is used; second, absence of physical interaction of the robot with the environment (except with the ground). Environmental force feedback based on measured distances to the obstacles is considered in the analyzed teleoperation system. Simulations showed advantages and disadvantages of teleoperation with environmental force feedback. It was shown that the quality of position control of mobile robot during teleoperation with previously proposed variable force feedback gain was better than with conventional approach.

Keywords: Teleoperation, mobile robot, force feedback, haptic interface.

1 Introduction

We consider mobile robot teleoperation (MRT) system, which mobile robot is remotely controlled by haptic master device. MRT systems have two major differences with conventional teleoperation systems for manipulators. First, rate mode control is used due to limited workspace of the master device and unlimited workspace of the slave (mobile) robot. Second, the force feedback displayed to the human-operator is not the reaction force from physical interaction of the slave robot with the environment. The goal of this study is stability analysis of such systems. There were several researches which addressed stability issues of MRT. In [1], it was shown experimentally that haptic feedback improves the safety of MRT. Passivity of such systems was studied in [2], but dynamics of operator and environment was not considered the model. More sufficient passivity and stability analysis of MRT was presented in [3]. However, the case of the environmental force feedback which is important for safety of MRT was not considered. In [4], authors proposed a collision vector based method for mobile robot teleoperation. The main contribution of this paper is proposing an analytical solution for designing

A.M.L. Kappers et al. (Eds.): EuroHaptics 2010, Part I, LNCS 6191, pp. 177–182, 2010.

the environmental force feedback gain. The disadvantages of MRT with constant force feedback gain are shown with the help of simulations.

2   Overview of Mobile Robot Teleoperation

In Fig. 1(a), configuration of a two link master manipulator and mobile robot are shown. The operator gives motion commands through the master haptic manipulator. Control inputs for the mobile robot are based on the position of the end-effecter (x_m, y_m). Linear and angular velocities of the robot are defined as V, ω, respectively. The force feedback is generated by the master device based on obstacle range information. The speed of the robot is changed with respect to the position of the master device. This control strategy is based on (1)

$$\begin{pmatrix} V \\ \omega \end{pmatrix} = \begin{pmatrix} k_V & 0 \\ 0 & k_w \end{pmatrix} \begin{pmatrix} y_m \\ x_m \end{pmatrix},$$ (1)

where k_V, k_w are scaling coefficients.

We consider feedback force based on the obstacle range information only (environmental force feedback). In conventional approach [1] the following basic law was used for calculating the force feedback:

$$f_e = \begin{cases} k(r_o - r), & r \leq r_o \\ 0, & r > r_o \end{cases}$$ (2)

f_e - force feedback, k - gain (stiffness), r - distance to the obstacle, r_o - distance from which generation of force feedback starts (See Fig. 1(b)). The force f_e is applied to operator through master device to the opposite direction of the obstacle. Experiments proved that the usage of environmental feedback force improves safety of teleoperation by reducing the number of collisions [1]. But, it was also shown that feedback force with constant feedback gain degrades the accuracy of mobile robot motion control [5]. In order to improve the accuracy of control while keeping it safe the authors proposed the variable force feedback which help the operator control the robot's position easily near the obstacle without collisions [7]. Here we give a brief explanation of the proposed approach. In cases, when it is required to perform accurate motion control, the mobile

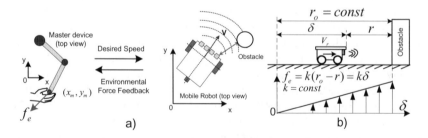

Fig. 1. Configurations of master manipulator and mobile robot (a). Conventional environmental force feedback rendering method (b).

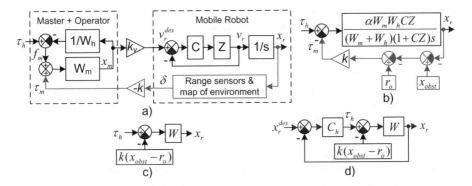

Fig. 2. Linear models for mobile robot teleoperation system

robot is teleoperated with low velocities. In this case, the distance between the robot and the obstacles decreases slowly and probability of collision is low. We propose to render force feedback with a variable gain based on relative speed of the mobile robot and obstacles. Main idea is modification of gain k in (2) based on distance to the obstacle r and its time derivative dr/dt. We define variable gain k^* for generating force feedback as follows:

$$k^* = \begin{cases} k_{\min}, & \frac{dr}{dt} \geq 0 \\ \frac{1}{-\gamma}(k_{\max} - k_{\min})\frac{dr}{dt} + k_{\min}, & -\gamma < \frac{dr}{dt} < 0 \ , \\ k_{\max}, & \frac{dr}{dt} \leq -\gamma \end{cases} \tag{3}$$

where k_{min} and k_{max} are minimum and maximum marginal values of feedback gain; γ is a boundary relative speed of mobile robot and obstacle. The values k_{min} and k_{max} should be designed with consideration of haptic device maximum force and stiffness capabilities and minimum distances between the mobile robot and the environment from which generation of the force feedback starts. In the next section we prove stability of MRT with the environmental force feedback and find the applicable range of feedback gain variation.

3   Stability Analysis

Usually, in MRT system the slave (mobile) robot does not interact with the environment and that is why the environmental force feedback displayed to the operator is calculated based on virtual potential force field. The potential force field does not effect the mobile robot directly, but it effects the operator who controls velocity of the mobile robot. We consider one-DOF case in stability analysis for easy explanation. Dynamics of operator, master device and slave robot (mobile robot) are described in similar way as it was done in [6]:

$$\begin{aligned} \tau_h - f_m &= m_h\ddot{x}_m + b_h\dot{x}_m + k_h x_m \\ \tau_m + f_m &= m_m\ddot{x}_m + b_m\dot{x}_m \\ \tau_r &= m_r\ddot{x}_r + b_r\dot{x}_r \end{aligned} \tag{4}$$

where x_m and x_r are positions of master device and mobile robot, respectively. m, b and k represent mass, viscous coefficient and stiffness, where lower indexes h, m and r correspond to operator's arm, master device and mobile robot, respectively. τ_h is the force generated by the operator's muscles; f_m denotes the force that the operator applies to the master device. τ_m and τ_r are actuator driving forces for master device and mobile robot, respectively. Note, that in MRT with environmental force feedback τ_m corresponds to the force feedback based on obstacle range information ($\tau_m = -f_e$). In Fig. 2(a), overall MRT system with force feedback based on obstacle range information is shown. W_h and W_m are transfer functions of operator and master device in s-domain; Z is impedance of the robot, C is the robot's velocity controller. The system in Fig. 2(a) can be transformed into the system in Fig. 2(b), where negative feedback represents f_e. Note that in our model we consider the cases when $(x_{obst} - x_r) \geq 0$ and $(x_r - x_{obst} + r_o) \geq 0$ which physically means that the distance to the obstacle can never be negative. In order to analyse system's stability we obtain closed loop system depicted in Fig. 2(c). Transfer function of this closed loop system can be represented as follows:

$$W = \frac{\alpha W_m W_h C Z}{(W_m + W_h)(1 + CZ)s + \alpha k W_m W_h CZ} = \frac{n_o}{d_4 s^4 + d_3 s^3 + d_2 s^2 + d_1 s + d_o}$$
$$n_o = \alpha C, d_o = \alpha k C, d_1 = (C + b_s)k_h, d_2 = (b_s + C)(b_m + b_h) + m_s k_h \qquad (5)$$
$$d_3 = (b_s + C)m_m + (b_m + b_h)m_s + (b_s + C)m_h, d_4 = (m_m + m_h)m_s$$

Using the Hurwitz stability criterion we get the following bounding conditions for the force feedback gain k:

$$0 < k < \frac{d_1(d_3 d_2 - d_4 d_1)}{d_3^2 \alpha C} \qquad (6)$$

If k satisfies the above condition then MRT system will be stable.

However, the system in Fig. 2(c) does not represent the real application of MRT. Usually, in MRT operator is given a task to move the robot to desired remote location. Visual information (image from remote cameras, interactive maps) is used to track the robot's position. Therefore, in MRT tasks human deals with position tracking control in which human's brain, vision, neural and muscle systems are used as tracking controller. In order to find the permissible range of feedback gain k, in which the overall teleoperation system remain stable, we analyze the system shown in Fig. 2(d). x_r^{des} is desired robots position defined by the task. C_h represents the human's brain and neural system as a position controller. For simplicity, we assume that C_h is a constant scalar value which means that operator does linear P-control of mobile robot's position. The closed loop system with consideration of position control is defined as follows:

$$W_{cl} = \frac{\alpha W_m W_h C Z C_h}{(W_m + W_h)(1 + CZ)s + (k + C_h)\alpha W_m W_h CZ} \qquad (7)$$

Hurwitz stability criterion gives the following bounding relation for gain k:

$$0 < k < \frac{d_1(d_3 d_2 - d_4 d_1)}{d_3^2 \alpha C} - C_h \qquad (8)$$

Admissible range of gain k is reduced by C_h. The range of C_h can vary a lot for different humans and conditions. That is why it is important to consider the uncertainty of human-based control during select the value of k.

4   Simulation

In simulation operator was given a task to move a mobile robot towards the obstacle to desired position x_{des} and to stop it near the obstacle. Scheme shown in Fig. 2(d) was used for simulation. The following values of parameters were used in all simulations: $m_h = 2 \ kg$, $b_h = 2 \ Ns/m$, $k_h = 10 \ N/m$, $m_m = 1 \ kg$, $b_m = 0.05 \ Ns/m$, $k_V = 0.3 \ s^{-1}$, $C_s = 30 \ Ns/m$, $m_s = 20 \ kg$, $b_s = 1 \ Ns/m$, $C_h = 7 \ N/m$, $x_{obst} = 1.2 \ m$, $x_{des} = 1.1$, $r_o = 0.5$ m. Based on (8) the value of force feedback gain was bounded: $0 < k < 25.0652 \ N/m$. Simulation results with $k = 0$ (no force feedback), $k = 20$ (with force feedback, stable), $k = 26$ (with force feedback, unstable) and with variable force feedback gain are shown in Fig. 3. In first case ($k = 0$), the mobile robot moved to desired position near the obstacle while the operator did not feel any force feedback. Absence of environmental force feedback could lead to collisions and teleoperation might not be safe [1]. In the case when $k = 26$, it was very difficult for the operator to stabilize position of the mobile robot due to the high impact from the force feedback. Therefore, position of the robot was oscillating and the teleoperation system was unstable. In the case when $k = 20$, the robot stopped at position about $0.4 \ m$ and could not move further because the force generated by operator's muscle and the force feedback from the master device compensated each other. Based on these simulation results we could see that existence of force feedback caused two effects. On the one hand force feedback prevented collisions of the robot with environment. On the other hand, force feedback reduced the accuracy of position control: the operator had no opportunity to approach the area near the obstacle due to the high values of the force feedback. Based on this conclusion we suppose that it is possible to improve the quality of position control by online modification of force feedback gain.

In simulation with variable feedback gain, $\gamma = 2.5 \ m/s$, $k_{max} = 20 \ N/m$, $k_{min} = 0$. The mobile robot reached the desired position and stopped near the obstacle. Velocity of the robot was lower near the desired position and that is why lower force feedback gain k^* was used. This led to a decrease of amount of force feedback displayed to operator. As a result, it was easy for operator to achieve the control goal. Preliminary experimental prove of effectiveness of variable force feedback gain was presented in [7].

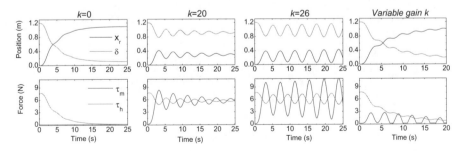

Fig. 3. Simulation results for MRT with constant and variable feedback gains

5   Conclusion

Stability criterion for the force feedback gain in the mobile robot teleoperation system was driven. A method for variation of force feedback gain based on the mobile robot's velocity was proposed and verified by simulation. One can say that the proposed variable force feedback can decrease the safety of teleoperation. However it improved the quality of motion control when the input from the human was not distorted by reflected forces. When it is compared with constant gain scheme, variable approach provides a better way for maintaining safety and accuracy of the motion control at the same time.

Acknowledgment

Authors wish to thank Prof. V. Hayward from Université de Pierre and Marie Curie (Paris 6) for taking part in helpful discussions and useful comments.

References

1. Lee, S., Sukhatme, G.S., Kim, G.J., Park, C.-M.: Haptic control of a mobile robot: a user study. In: Proc. of IEEE/RSJ IROS, Lausanne, Switzerland (October 2002)
2. Diolaiti, N., Melchiorri, C.: Haptic teleoperation of a mobile robot. In: Proc. of the 7th IFAC Symposium of Robot Control, pp. 2798–2805 (2003)
3. Lee, D., Martinez-Palafox, O., Spong, M.W.: Bilateral teleoperation of a wheeled mobile robot over delayed communication network. In: Proc. of IEEE ICRA (2006)
4. Ko, J.-P., Lee, J.-M.: Tactile tele-operation of a mobile robot with a collision vector. Robotica 24(1), 11–21 (2006)
5. Farkhatdinov, I., Ryu, J.-H., Poduraev, J.: A user study of command strategies for mobile robot teleoperation. J. on Intelligent Service Robotics 2(2), 95 (2009)
6. Yokokohji, Y., Yoshikawa, T.: Bilateral control of master-slave manipulators for ideal kinesthetic coupling - formulation and experiment. IEEE T. on Robotics and Automation 10(5), October
7. Farkhatdinov, I., Ryu, J.-H.: A Preliminary Experimental Study on Haptic Teleoperation of Mobile Robot with Variable Force Feedback Gain. In: Proc. of IEEE Haptics Symposium 2010, Waltham, Boston, USA, March 24-25 (2010)

Transparency of the Generalized Scattering Transformation for Haptic Telepresence

Iason Vittorias and Sandra Hirche

Institute of Automatic Control Engineering (LSR),
Technische Universität München
{vittorias,hirche}@tum.de

Abstract. In this paper we analyze the transparency of the generalized scattering transformation applied to teleoperation systems with constant time delay. Particularly, the human operator, the remote environment, and the robot manipulators are modeled as dissipative instead of just passive systems. By the application of this transformation delay-independent stability is guaranteed. It is shown that transparency can be substantially improved compared to the conventional scattering transformation approach. Simulations and experimental results on a three degree-of-freedom teleoperation system validate the presented approach.

Keywords: teleoperation, control, communication unreliabilities, transparency.

1 Introduction

A haptic telepresence system allows the human to manipulate in remote, inaccessible, dangerous, or scaled environments. From a control point of view, the haptic control loop, where motion and force data are exchanged, is very challenging as it is closed over a communication network, e.g. the Internet. The communication network introduces unreliabilities such as (time-varying) time delay and packet loss, which do not only distort the human haptic perception of the remote environment but potentially destabilize the overall system.

In [7] the authors propose to use the approximate knowledge on damping properties of the human arm, the controlled manipulators, and/or the remote environment. Using the *generalized* scattering transformation [3,6] which is suitable for dissipative systems delay-independent finite gain $\mathcal{L}_2$-stability can be ensured. The contribution of this paper is an extended transparency analysis of the proposed scheme. Simulations and experiments on a three degree-of-freedom (DoF) teleoperation system show that the performance in terms of displayed mechanical properties is improved compared to the standard scattering transformation.

2 Background

Generally, we assume that the human arm, the environment, and the manipulators can be represented by the second-order dynamics with unknown inertia, damping, and spring parameters in Cartesian space

$$M\ddot{x}(t) + D(x,\dot{x},t) + Kx(t) = f(t), \tag{1}$$

A.M.L. Kappers et al. (Eds.): EuroHaptics 2010, Part I, LNCS 6191, pp. 183–188, 2010.

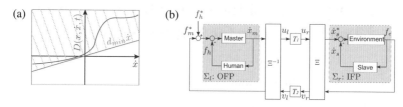

Fig. 1. (a) Nonlinear time-varying damping with lower bound d_{min}. (b) Teleoperation system with time delay and generalized scattering transformation.

with $x \in \mathfrak{R}^n$ the position vector in Cartesian space, $f \in \mathfrak{R}^n$ the Cartesian external force; $D(x, \dot{x}, t) \in \mathfrak{R}^n$ is the unknown damping term, $M \in \mathfrak{R}^{n \times n}$ and $K \in \mathfrak{R}^{n \times n}$ the unknown diagonal and positive-definite inertia and stiffness matrices, respectively. The components $D_i(x, \dot{x}, t)$ of the damping term vector $D(x, \dot{x}, t)$ are assumed to be continuous, and nonlinear functions for which the lower bound $d_{min} \geq 0$ is known such that $D_i(x, \dot{x}, t) \geq d_{min}\dot{x}$ holds $\forall i = 1...n$; see Fig. 1(a) for a visualization of the 1-DoF case. The system (1) belongs to the class of input-feedforward-output-feedback passive (IF-OFP) system as it is shown in [7]. Note that passive systems are a special case of IF-OFP systems. Due to space limitations we have to refer the reader to [4] for a more extensive treatment.

In this paper we will exemplarily study a velocity-force architecture with constant time delay as illustrated in Fig. 1(b). We further assume that master and slave manipulator are operated under an admittance control scheme with decoupled dynamics in Cartesian space, i.e. they can be represented by (1). It can be shown, that the controlled manipulators are output-feedback passive (OFP) systems with parameters $\varepsilon_m = d_{min}^m$ and $\varepsilon_s = d_{min}^s$, with subscript 'm', 's', representing the master and slave, respectively. Furthermore, the human arm and the environment are input-feedforward passive (IFP) systems with $\delta_h = d_{min}^h$ and $\delta_e = d_{min}^e$, with subscript 'h' referring to human arm and 'e' to environment. The negative feedback interconnection of the master manipulator and the human arm can be shown to be OFP(ε_l) system with $\varepsilon_l = \varepsilon_m + \delta_h$. Analogously, the negative feedback interconnection of the environment and the slave manipulator is IFP(δ_r) system with $\delta_r = min(\delta_e, \varepsilon_s + \delta_e)$ [7].

In order to prevent instability arising from a nonzero time delay between the local and remote side, the *generalized scattering transformation* (GST) is introduced. The GST, a linear input/output transformation, guarantees stability for arbitrary large constant, unknown time delay T_1, T_2, and it is represented by the matrix Ξ in Fig. 1(b). Instead of the lefthand output variable $\dot{x}_m$ the variable u_l is transmitted over the forward channel, and analogously υ_r instead of f_e via the backwards channel

$$\begin{bmatrix} u_l \\ \upsilon_l \end{bmatrix} = \Xi \begin{bmatrix} \dot{x}_m \\ f_m^* \end{bmatrix}, \begin{bmatrix} u_r \\ \upsilon_r \end{bmatrix} = \Xi \begin{bmatrix} \dot{x}_s^* \\ f_e \end{bmatrix} \quad (2)$$

with $u_r(t) = u_l(t - T_1)$ and $\upsilon_l(t) = \upsilon_r(t - T_2)$. The transformation is parametrized as a rotation R and a scaling matrix B

$$\Xi = R \cdot B = \begin{bmatrix} \cos\theta I & \sin\theta I \\ -\sin\theta I & \cos\theta I \end{bmatrix} \begin{bmatrix} b_{11}I & 0 \\ 0 & b_{22}I \end{bmatrix}, \quad \Xi = \begin{bmatrix} \xi_{11} & \xi_{12} \\ \xi_{21} & \xi_{22} \end{bmatrix} \quad (3)$$

where I represents the $n \times n$ unity matrix, $\det B \neq 0$ and $\theta \in [-\frac{\pi}{2}, \frac{\pi}{2}]$.

Proposition 1. *[3] Assume a system consisting of the networked negative feedback interconnection of an OFP(ε_l) and an IFP(δ_r) system with ε_l, $\delta_r > 0$, the bidirectional communication channel with constant time delay, and the input-output transformation (3). The overall system is finite gain delay-independently $\mathcal{L}_2$-stable if and only if for each B the rotation matrix parameter $\theta \in [\theta_l, \theta_r]$. Here θ_l and θ_r are one of the two solutions of*

$$\cot 2\theta_i = \varepsilon_{B_i} - \delta_{B_i}, \ i \in \{l, r\} \tag{4}$$

which simultaneously satisfy $a(\theta_i) = \sin \theta_i \cos \theta_i - \delta_{B_i} \cos^2 \theta_i - \varepsilon_{B_i} \sin^2 \theta_i \geq 0$, ε_{B_i} and δ_{B_i} are given by the matrix P_{B_i}

$$P_{B_i} = \begin{bmatrix} -\delta_{B_i}I & \frac{1}{2}I \\ \frac{1}{2}I & -\varepsilon_{B_i}I \end{bmatrix} = B^{-T} P_i B^{-1} = \begin{bmatrix} -b_{22}^2 \delta_i I & -\frac{1}{2} b_{11} b_{22} I \\ -\frac{1}{2} b_{11} b_{22} I & -b_{11}^2 \varepsilon_i I \end{bmatrix}, \ i \in \{l, r\}. \tag{5}$$

Hence, instead of choosing $\theta = 45°$ and $b_{11} = \sqrt{b}$, $b_{22} = \frac{1}{\sqrt{b}}$, as for standard scattering transformation [1], here θ can be chosen out of an interval.

3   Transparency Analysis

A teleoperation system is called transparent if the human user feels like directly interacting with the remote environment. In the following we will analyze the degree of transparency based on mechanical impedances (in contrast to position/force errors). Modeling the real environment as a mechanical linear time-invariant impedance $Z_e(s)$ and the impedance displayed to the human $Z_h(s)$ transparency is achieved if [5]

$$Z_h(s) = Z_e(s),$$

where s is a complex variable, representing the Laplace domain; it will be omitted when not needed. In practice, perfectly transparent teleoperation is difficult to achieve. The interesting question is the possible degree of transparency. The displayed impedance can be computed, here ignoring controller dynamics and robot compliance, based on the environment impedance and the generalized scattering transformation according to

$$Z_h = \frac{\xi_{21} - \xi_{11} R e^{-sT}}{-\xi_{22} + \xi_{12} R e^{-sT}}, \ R = \frac{\xi_{21} + \xi_{22} Z_e}{\xi_{11} + \xi_{12} Z_e} \tag{6}$$

where $T = T_1 + T_2$ the round trip time delay. In order to analyze and compare different impedances a Padé approximation is used for the time-delay, which is valid for low frequencies, i.e. $e^{-sT} \approx (1 - \frac{T}{2}s) \cdot (1 + \frac{T}{2}s)^{-1}$ for $\omega < \frac{1}{3T}$. The teleoperator dynamics are ignored for simplicity. The transformation angle is limited to $\theta \in [0, \frac{\pi}{2}]$ to simplify the following calculations and the requirement on stable transfer functions.

The displayed impedance in case of an spring-damper environment $Z_e = \frac{k_e}{s} + b_e$ is approximated for low frequencies by (6) as

$$Z_h^{LF}\big|_{Z_e = \frac{k_e}{s} + b_e} = \frac{\gamma \frac{k_e}{s} + b_h + m_h s}{1 + \gamma(\frac{T}{2} - \frac{b_{22}}{b_{11}} T b_e \sin\theta \cos\theta)s} \tag{7}$$

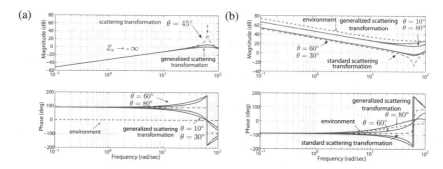

Fig. 2. Displayed impedance comparison in (a) free space (b) contact with the environment

with
$$\gamma = \frac{1}{1+Tk_e sin\theta cos\theta}, \qquad b_h = \gamma\left(b_e + \frac{T}{2}k_e\left(sin^2\theta - cos^2\theta\right)\right),$$
$m_h = \gamma\left(\frac{b_{11}}{b_{22}}T sin\theta cos\theta + \frac{T}{2}b_e\left(sin^2\theta - cos^2\theta\right)\right)$ and $\frac{b_{11}}{b_{22}} > 2b_e sin\theta cos\theta$; the latter resulting from the requirement on stable transfer functions in the approximation. The denominator of (7) can be shown to be a low pass filter which in the worst case, i.e. $\theta = 0°$ or $\theta = 90°$, has a cut-off frequency $\frac{2}{T} > \frac{1}{3T}$, therefore, it can be ignored. The resulting displayed impedance is then

$$Z_h^{LF}\Big|_{Z_e = \frac{k_e}{s} + b_e} \approx \gamma\frac{k_e}{s} + b_h + m_h s \qquad (8)$$

Similarly, it can be shown that for free space motion $Z_e = 0$ an inertia linearly increasing with the time delay is approximately displayed

$$m_h^{LF} \approx \frac{b_{11}}{b_{22}}T sin\theta cos\theta \qquad (9)$$

with the computation straightforward from (6).

We observe in (8) and (9) that the scaling matrix alters the performance of the system in a similar way the characteristic impedance of the standard scattering transformation configures the performance, cf. [2]. A small parameter $\frac{b_{11}}{b_{22}}$ will avoid large inertia in free space movement whereas a large one is required to display high stiffness; it can be chosen freely based on application.

Numerical Evaluation: The proposed approach is analyzed in simulation for a velocity - force admittance control scheme consisting of a linear time-invariant spring-damper environment $Z_e = \frac{500}{s} + 20$ and negligible slave dynamics, i.e. $\delta_r = \delta_e = 20$. The left-handside subsystem is assumed to be OFP(ε_l) with $\varepsilon_l = 10$ resulting from either the human or master dynamics' minimum damping. For comparison reasons a characteristic impedance $b = 1$ is chosen for the standard scattering transformation and the generalized scattering transformation is tuned with scaling components, $b_{11} = \sqrt{b} = 1$ and $b_{22} = \frac{2b_{11} sin\theta cos\theta}{b}$ such that in free space motion both methods display same inertia, i.e. have the same free space performance. The resulting system is delay-independently stable for all $\theta \in [3°, 85°]$. The time delay is set to $T_1 = T_2 = 50$ ms. The Bode plots of the environment impedance and the displayed impedance are depicted in Fig. 2(a)

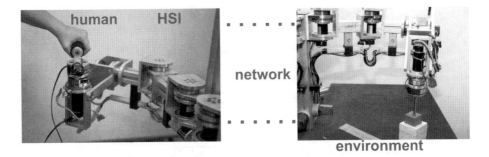

Fig. 3. Experimental setup

for free space motion and in Fig. 2(b) for the stiff environment. It is observed that the displayed impedance is closer to the environment impedance for the generalized scattering transformation. Particularly for the case $\theta = 30°$, $\theta = 60°$ a stiffness of 48.2 N/m is displayed, whereas for $\theta = 80°$, $10°$ a stiffness of 204 N/m is displayed. This by far closer to the real environment stiffness than with the standard scattering transformation, where a stiffness of 36.9 N/m is displayed, see Fig. 2(b).

4   Experiment

The experimental testbed consists of a real teleoperation system with two 4-DoF manipulators. Of the three translational and one rotational DoF only the translational are used resulting in a 3-DoF setup. A 6 DoF force/torque-sensors (JR3) is mounted at the tip of the manipulators to measure interaction forces with the human operator and the environment. The sampling rate of the haptic signals and the local control loops is 1 kHz. A position-based admittance control scheme is considered with a proportional-derivative joint controller; gravity is compensated. The master displayed 12 kg inertia, whereas the slave is rendered as a virtual tool with 40 kg inertia that could display 5000 N/m stiffness in all three degrees-of-freedom.

The master damping is 30 Ns/m in all three degrees-of-freedom, therefore $\varepsilon_m = 30$. On the slave side the virtual tool has 1000 Ns/m damping thus $\varepsilon_s = 1000$. A silicon cube is used as environment, having a damping 10 Ns/m thus $\delta_e = 10$. The human arm damping is considered unknown, i.e we just assumed passive behavior as typically done in the literature, $\delta_h = 0$. The scaling parameters are chosen such that the free-space motion displayed dynamics are similar in both methods, $b = 800$, $b_{11} = \sqrt{b}$, $b_{22} = \frac{2b_{11}\sin\theta\cos\theta}{b}$ and result in $\theta_l = 0.1°$ and $\theta_r = 46.2°$. The time delay is 50 ms in both channels. The system is stable throughout the experiment. During the experiment the silicon cube, which has a stiffness 1400 N/m, is haptically explored. The proposed scheme is tested with $\theta = 17°$, see Fig. 4 for a position and force tracking illustration. The displayed impedance is identified by a least-squares method. The generalized scattering transformation displays an impedance with $k_h = 492$ N/m and $b_h = 12$ Ns/m, obviously improved compared to that of the conventional scattering transformation, $k_h = 367$ N/m and $b_h = 68$ Ns/m. This generally results in more realistic contact, however, psychophysical studies have to be conducted in order to finally evaluate that.

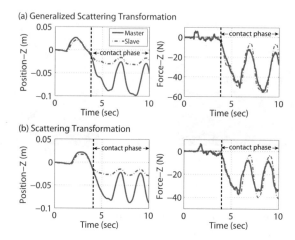

Fig. 4. Position and force tracking for (a) the generalized scattering transformation and (b) the standard scattering transformation

5   Conclusions

In this work, the transparency of the generalized scattering transformation applied to a teleoperation system with constant time delay is analyzed. Simulation and experimental results on a three degree-of-freedom teleoperation system indicate significant improvement, in terms of displayed mechanical impedances, compared to the conventional scattering transformation. In our future work psychophysical studies will aim to look deeper in the transparency results, analyzed in this paper.

References

1. Anderson, R.J., Spong, M.W.: Bilateral control of teleoperators with time delay. IEEE Transactions on Automatic Control 34(5), 494–501 (1989)
2. Hirche, S., Buss, M.: Human perception oriented control aspects of networked telepresence and teleaction systems. In: Proceedings of the International Conference on Instrumentation, Control and Information Technology, Okayama, Japan, pp. 3430–3435 (2005)
3. Hirche, S., Matiakis, T., Buss, M.: A distributed controller approach for delay-independent stability of networked control systems. Automatica 45(8), 1828–1836 (2009)
4. Khalil, H.K.: Nonlinear Systems. Prentice-Hall, Englewood Cliffs (1996)
5. Lawrence, D.: Stability and transparency in bilateral teleoperation. In: Proceedings of the 31st IEEE Conference on Decision and Control, vol. 3, pp. 2649–2655 (1992)
6. Matiakis, T., Hirche, S., Buss, M.: Networked control systems with time-varying delay - stability through input-output transformation. Automatisierungstechnik 56(1), 29–37 (2008)
7. Vittorias, I., Hirche, S.: Stable teleoperation with communication unreliabilities and approximate human/environment dynamics knowledge. In: Proceedings of the American Control Conference, ACC (2010)

VerroTouch: High-Frequency Acceleration Feedback for Telerobotic Surgery

Katherine J. Kuchenbecker[1], Jamie Gewirtz[1], William McMahan[1],
Dorsey Standish[1], Paul Martin[1], Jonathan Bohren[1],
Pierre J. Mendoza[2], and David I. Lee[2]

[1] Department of Mechanical Engineering and Applied Mechanics
[2] Department of Surgery, Division of Urology
University of Pennsylvania, Philadelphia, PA, USA
{kuchenbe,gewirtzj,wmcmahan,dorseys,pdmartin,jbohren}@seas.upenn.edu,
{pierre.mendoza,david.lee}@uphs.upenn.edu
http://haptics.seas.upenn.edu

Abstract. The Intuitive da Vinci system enables surgeons to see and manipulate structures deep within the body via tiny incisions. Though the robotic tools mimic one's hand motions, surgeons cannot feel what the tools are touching, a striking contrast to non-robotic techniques. We have developed a new method for partially restoring this lost sense of touch. Our VerroTouch system measures the vibrations caused by tool contact and immediately recreates them on the master handles for the surgeon to feel. This augmentation enables the surgeon to feel the texture of rough surfaces, the start and end of contact with manipulated objects, and other important tactile events. While it does not provide low frequency forces, we believe vibrotactile feedback will be highly useful for surgical task execution, a hypothesis we we will test in future work.

Keywords: vibrotactile feedback, robot-assisted surgery.

1 Introduction

The newest category of modern surgical practice is that of *robot-assisted minimally invasive surgery* (MIS) [17,7]. Rather than holding laparoscopic tools directly, the surgeon uses a master console to control the motion of several slave robot arms that are positioned above the patient. One robotic arm holds a stereoscopic camera, and the others wield long, thin, interchangeable instruments that enter the patient's body through tiny incisions. Unlike laparoscopy, the doctor can see a high-resolution stereoscopic image of the operating scene, and the surgical instruments are robotically controlled to precisely follow his or her hand motions. This innovative medical treatment approach (also known as telerobotic surgery) was pioneered at SRI International in the late 1980's, and it was successfully commercialized in the 1990's by Intuitive Surgical, Inc., in the form of the FDA-approved da Vinci Surgical System [1]. The da Vinci system is used to perform over 100,000 surgical procedures annually, primarily in prostatectomy, other deep pelvic surgeries, and various cardiac procedures [3].

Although robot-assisted MIS provides excellent visualization and a high level of tool dexterity, it suffers from a notable shortcoming: *the surgeon cannot feel the effects*

A.M.L. Kappers et al. (Eds.): EuroHaptics 2010, Part I, LNCS 6191, pp. 189–196, 2010.

of contact between the teleoperated instruments and the surgical environment. Under-standably, surgeons regularly complain about the lack of touch feedback in the da Vinci system, especially individuals first learning to use the system, e.g., [2,8]. Without appro-priate haptic feedback, operators cannot feel simple tissue properties such as stiffness and texture, nor can they detect subtle changes in tool contact state. To compensate, sur-geons must rely heavily upon visual feedback, which can increase cognitive load and error incidence [5].

As overviewed in the following section, researchers have investigated many ap-proaches to adding haptic feedback to robotic MIS, but none has yet emerged as being both clinically useful and technically feasible. In light of this challenge, we have de-veloped the VerroTouch system, a new approach to providing haptic feedback during telerobotic surgery. As described in Section 3, our fully functional prototype hapti-cally recreates the high-frequency contact accelerations experienced by a teleoperated da Vinci tool for the surgeon to feel.

2   Prior Approaches

Many experts believe that high-quality haptic feedback (forces and/or tactile sensations) will help surgeons quickly learn and adeptly perform robot-assisted minimally invasive procedures, e.g., [4,10,15,16]; however, the best method for providing this feedback re-mains unclear due to the wide variety of approaches being explored and the disparate requirements of the surgical tasks being studied. Furthermore, there are many technical challenges associated with adding haptic feedback to telerobotic MIS. For instance, the tool shaft must be very thin yet must also contain all of the mechanical cabling needed to drive the end-effector's degrees of freedom (typically yaw, pitch, roll, and grip). The electrical wires for any sensors or distal actuators must also pass through this narrow channel, which is often just 5 to 8 mm in diameter. These constraints make it difficult to integrate force sensors into tools, as do the additional requirements for low cost, long life, consistent performance, and sterilizability.

The most straightforward method for creating a bilateral connection between the master and the slave is that of *position-position control.* The devices continually trans-mit their positions to one another, and each robot is controlled to track the other's mo-tion, yielding a spring-like connection between the two. One early effort found that position-based haptic feedback (which includes the effects of the slave's friction and inertia) fatigued the operator during mock surgery and did not allow perception of soft tissue contact [9]. If parasitic forces are larger than contact forces, one can lower the gain of the position controller to reduce the slave's detrimental effect on the user, but this action also softens the feel of all touched surfaces. Many more sophisticated con-trollers have been developed for teleoperation in surgery, e.g., [15], as well as the one used in the commercial da Vinci, but most of these are fundamentally built on position measurements.

If a dynamic model of the slave robot can be obtained, one can estimate the propor-tion of the slave's actuator effort that is due only to contact with the environment and use this estimate as the haptic feedback command for the master. Mahvash and Oka-mura recently succeeded at using this model-based approach to cancel out a significant portion of the da Vinci slave tool forces that stem from friction [11] and inertia [10], thereby hiding the robot's natural dynamics from the user. However, the dynamic modeling process is intensive and highly configuration dependent, so these techniques may not be parametrically tractable or sufficiently robust for commercial deployment.

Another approach is to use separate sensors that are dedicated to the purpose of haptic feedback. Strain gauges can be positioned on the outside of the tool shaft to measure lateral tip forces, as in [15,16]. These sensors are small, but they are not sensitive to forces along the axis of the tool, and their placement and the associated wiring can interfere with insertion of the device into the trocar. A further option is to integrate a commercial force/torque sensor into the tool shaft, as in [18], but these are currently too bulky and expensive for clinical use. Others have developed novel, compact force sensors specifically for this purpose, e.g., [14], though these designs have not yet been commercialized. For all of these force sensor approaches, the data can be displayed to the surgeon haptically, through the motors on the master device, or through auditory or visual feedback. The loud environment of the operating room and the surgeon's attention to the stereoscopic display make graphical overlays of simplified force information an excellent option, e.g., [16]. Lastly, other researchers have designed new types of surgical slave robots which are typically smaller than the da Vinci arms, e.g., [19], but these have not yet been transitioned to clinical practice, so it is difficult to speculate on their ability to provide the operator with good haptic feedback.

The final body of research that is relevant to this problem is that of high-fidelity vibration feedback for industrial telemanipulation. In 1995, Kontarinis and Howe used a voice coil actuator mounted near the user's fingertips to superimpose acceleration waveforms measured at the slave's end-effector with force feedback from strain gauges [6]. Although the vibration feedback was not carefully controlled, user tests indicated that this hybrid feedback strategy increased user performance in inspection, puncturing, and peg-in-slot tasks. We recently refined this approach for use with two Phantom Omni robots in position-position control, installing a voice coil actuator in a custom handle and characterizing the system's dynamics to enable accurate acceleration matching between slave and master [12]. Tests with human subjects [13] showed that this high-frequency acceleration feedback significantly increases the realism of remote surfaces, and we believe it will have a similarly beneficial impact on telerobotic surgery.

3   System Design

We developed the VerroTouch system to enable surgeons to feel the structures they are touching during telerobotic surgery, specifically with the Intuitive da Vinci S surgical system. As diagrammed in Figure 1, VerroTouch continually measures the accelerations of the left and right teleoperated tools using small high-bandwidth accelerometers. These signals reflect the dynamic interaction that is instantaneously occurring between each tool and its environment, whether it is probing, cutting, sticking, or slipping. The system's main receiver filters and amplifies the two measured accelerations and uses a pair of vibration actuators (affixed to the sides of the master handles) to re-create these acceleration profiles at the fingertips of the surgeon. Like the tactile grasping system of [4], VerroTouch attaches to a fully functional da Vinci surgical system. Figure 2 provides a

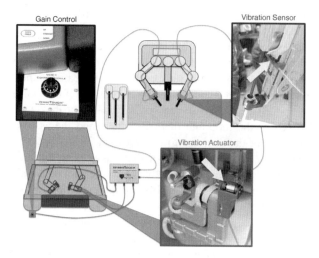

Fig. 1. VerroTouch installed on an Intuitive da Vinci S surgical system. The vibration sensors measure the high-frequency accelerations of the tool arms, and the central receiver drives the voice coil actuators on the master handles to let the surgeon feel these vibrations. The gain control knob adjusts the magnitude of the vibration feedback.

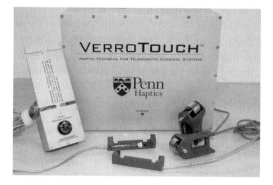

Fig. 2. The components of the VerroTouch system when not installed on a da Vinci surgical system. From left to right, one can see the gain control module, two vibration sensor clips, and two vibration actuator clips. The main receiver box is shown at the back.

photograph of the VerroTouch components when they are not installed on a da Vinci, and the subsections below explain their functionality.

Vibration Sensors. VerroTouch uses acceleration sensors to detect the vibrations occurring in the da Vinci tools. After considering many possible mounting locations, we chose to attach the sensors to the da Vinci S patient-side manipulators just below the interchangeable tool mounting point. This location does not interfere with tool or arm motion, and it allows measurement of significant vibrations along the long axis of the clip (perpendicular to the tool axis). Furthermore, this location is inside the da Vinci's plastic drapes, so the sensors would not need to be sterilized if used for actual surgery, thus reducing cost. Each clip contains an Analog Devices ADXL322 MEMS-based accelerometer, which is firmly held against the surface of the tool arm. This accelerometer has a range of ± 20 m/s^2, and we configure it with an on-board first-order low-pass filter set at 1000 Hz. The clips are 3D printed in ABS plastic, and the sensors are attached to the main controller via flexible shielded wire.

Vibration Actuators. VerroTouch's two actuator modules mount onto the da Vinci master handles on top of the platform wrist joints, as pictured in Figure 1. Early versions of our system placed the actuator on the rounded portion closer to the user's fingers, but we found that the weight of the actuator then constantly pulls down on the user's fingers, which is uncomfortable and fatiguing. Integration with the da Vinci controller would allow software gravity compensation, but we sought to create an independent system. Several other mounting positions were considered, and the current location was found to permit excellent signal transmission while minimizing interference with the user. The weight of the actuator does still create a moment around the elbow of the master arm; we alleviate this problem by adding a calibrated counterweight to the motor controlling this axis, which balances out the actuator's weight. Each actuator module is 3D printed from ABS plastic and contains an NCC04-10-005-1X voice coil actuator from H2W Industries.These actuators have a stroke of 10.4 mm with a maximum continuous force of 2.2 N and a peak force of 6.6 N; their force output is directly proportional to the applied current. The coil is rigidly attached to the plastic housing, and the magnet rides on a linear bearing and is centered in its workspace by a pair of compression springs. The actuators are connected to the main receiver using flexible shielded wire.

Main Receiver. The main receiver takes the measured acceleration signals from the sensor clips and drives the corresponding voice coil actuators to replicate these vibrations for the surgeon to feel. Figure 3 provides a flow chart for the analog circuit inside the receiver. A DC blocking capacitor removes the mean of the accelerometer's output, and a voltage amplification stage increases the magnitude of this signal according to the setting of the gain control knob. The signal is then band-pass filtered to remove low frequencies (not reproducible by our actuation method) and very high frequencies (beyond the bandwidth of human perception). The resulting signal is applied to the voice coil actuator as a current command.

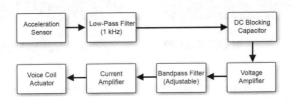

Fig. 3. The signal flow diagram for each channel of the VerroTouch system

4   Testing and Results

To benchmark its performance, we installed VerroTouch on a da Vinci S surgical system. Each actuator module was instrumented with an ADXL320 ±50 m/s^2 accelerometer to allow us to record the system's output. The acceleration feedback gain was set to a comfortable level, and several tasks were performed by the operator, as shown in Figure 4. The interaction was videotaped, and a National Instruments USB-6216 16-Bit analog input device was used to record tool accelerations, actuator currents, and actuator accelerations.

Figure 5 shows time-domain and frequency-domain views of ten seconds of data recorded during this session. The shape of the master acceleration waveform is seen to generally match the shape of the slave tool acceleration, scaled up by a factor of 15. The continuous vibrations of dragging and the sharp vibrations of contact events are

Fig. 4. The manipulation environment chosen for testing. The operator used a large da Vinci needle driver to interact with the practice suture pads, suture needles, small objects, rubber tubes, soft strings, and the hard plastic structure of the task board.

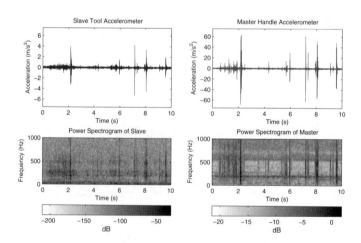

Fig. 5. Sample acceleration data recorded during VerroTouch testing with the setup shown in Figure 4. During these ten seconds, the operator stroked the practice suture pad, picked up the needle, and pricked the suture pad with the needle four times. This data was sampled at 20 kHz, and the spectrograms were calculated using a Blackman-Harris window of length 2048 in order to emphasize temporal events.

all transmitted for the operator to feel. Comparing the power spectrograms of the two signals reveals the ways in which the signals differ. The slave tool acceleration contains significant power at very low frequency, which was not being recreated on the master due to the settings of the adjustable bandpass filter. The master acceleration spectrogram is also seen to consistently contain significant power at 200 Hz and a moderate amount of power near 600 Hz and above 800 Hz; we believe these additional vibrations stem from either parasitic vibrations of the master or electrical noise. After correcting for the circuit's 1.75 ms time delay, the correlation between the depicted time-domain master and slave acceleration signals has a moderate R^2 value of 0.34, demonstrating a reasonable temporal match despite the addition of high-frequency noise and the presence of uncharacterized system dynamics. The correlation between the Fourier transforms of these master and slave accelerations has an R^2 value of 0.77, showing that frequencies are largely being preserved. Throughout the testing, the operator was able to easily feel these vibrations at their fingertips, including the texture of rough surfaces, the start and end of contact with manipulated objects, and other important tactile events. We were also pleased to find that the voice coil actuators produce collocated sounds that match the feel of these vibrations.

5   Conclusion

VerroTouch is the first work to add naturalistic high-frequency acceleration feedback to a commercial robot-assisted surgical system. Experimental analysis demonstrated that the accelerations VerroTouch creates at the da Vinci handles strongly resemble those measured at the tools. While VerroTouch does not provide low-frequency forces, we believe that its high-frequency acceleration feedback will be useful for surgical task execution. We plan to test this hypothesis with human subjects in future work.

While most previous approaches to haptic feedback require significant modification to the robotic system, VerroTouch is a simple augmentation that can easily be added to an existing teleoperator. Additionally, VerroTouch uses inexpensive off-the-shelf components, with the only custom hardware being the plastic mounts for the sensors and actuators. We believe these attributes are important in making VerroTouch practical as an addition to a clinical robot-assisted surgical system, such as the da Vinci S.

Acknowledgments. This work is supported by the National Science Foundation (grant #IIS-0845670) and the University of Pennsylvania.

References

1. Guthart, G.S., Salisbury, J.K.: The Intuitive telesurgery system: Overview and application. In: Proc. IEEE Conf. on Robotics and Automation, pp. 618–621 (2000)
2. Horgan, S., Vanuno, D.: Robots in laparoscopic surgery. Journal of Laparoendoscopic and Advanced Surgical Techniques 11(6), 415–419 (2001)
3. Intuitive Surgical, Inc., http://www.intuitivesurgical.com
4. King, C.H., Culjat, M.O., Franco, M.L., Bisley, J.W., Carman, G.P., Dutson, E.P., Grundfest, W.S.: A multielement tactile feedback system for robot-assisted minimally invasive surgery. IEEE Transactions On Haptics 2(1), 52–56 (2009)

5. Kitagawa, M., Okamura, A.M., Bethea, B.T., Gott, V.L., Baumgartner, W.A.: Analysis of suture manipulation forces for teleoperation with force feedback. In: Proc. Fifth Int. Conf. of Medical Image Computing and Computer Assisted Intervention (September 2002)
6. Kontarinis, D.A., Howe, R.D.: Tactile display of vibratory information in teleoperation and virtual environments. Presence: Teleoperators and Virtual Environments 4(4), 387–402 (1995)
7. Kumar, R., Hemal, A.K.: Emerging role of robotics in urology. Journal of Minimal Access Surgery 1(4), 202–210 (2005)
8. Lanfranco, A.R., Castellanos, A.E., Desai, J.P., Meyers, W.C.: Robotic surgery: A current perspective. Annals of Surgery 239(1), 14–21 (2004)
9. Madhani, A.J., Niemeyer, G., Salisbury, J.K.: The Black Falcon: A teleoperated surgical instrument for minimally invasive surgery. In: Proc. IEEE/RSJ Int. Conf. on Intelligent Robotic Systems, vol. 2, pp. 936–944 (1998)
10. Mahvash, M., Gwilliam, J., Agarwal, R., Vagvolgi, B., Su, L., Yuh, D.D., Okamura, A.M.: Force-feedback surgical teleoperator: Controller design and palpation experiments. In: Proc: IEEE Haptics Symposium, pp. 465–471 (March 2008)
11. Mahvash, M., Okamura, A.M.: Friction compensation for enhancing transparency of a teleoperator with compliant transmission. IEEE Transactions on Robotics 23(6), 1240–1246 (2007)
12. McMahan, W., Kuchenbecker, K.J.: Haptic display of realistic tool contact via dynamically compensated control of a dedicated actuator. In: Proc. IEEE/RSJ Int. Conf. on Intelligent RObots and Systems, pp. 3171–3177 (October 2009)
13. McMahan, W., Romano, J.M., Rahuman, A.M.A., Kuchenbecker, K.J.: High frequency acceleration feedback significantly increases the realism of haptically rendered textured surfaces. In: Proc. IEEE Haptics Symposium, pp. 141–148 (2010)
14. Peirs, J., Clijnen, J., Reynaerts, D., Brussel, H.V., Herijgers, P., Corteville, B., Boone, S.: A micro optical force sensor for force feedback during minimally invasive robotic surgery. Sensors and Actuators A: Physical 115, 447–455 (2004)
15. Preusche, C., Ortmaier, T., Herzinger, G.: Teleoperation concepts in minimal invasive surgery. Control Engineering Practice 10, 1245–1250 (2002)
16. Reiley, C.E., Akinbiyi, T., Burschka, D., Chang, D.C., Okamura, A.M., Yuh, D.D.: Effects of visual force feedback on robot-assisted surgical task performance. Journal of Thoracic and Cardiovascular Surgery 135, 196–202 (2008)
17. Salisbury, J.K.: The heart of microsurgery. Mechanical Engineering Magazine 120(12), 47–51 (1998)
18. Semere, W., Kitagawa, M., Okamura, A.M.: Teleoperation with sensor/actuator asymmetry: Task performance with partial force feedback. In: Proc. 12th Symp. on Haptic Interfaces for Virtual Environments and Teleoperator Systems, pp. 121–127 (March 2004)
19. Zemiti, N., Ortmaier, T., Vitrani, M.A., Morel, G.: A force controlled laparoscopic surgical robot without distal force sensing. In: Ang, M.H., Khatib, O. (eds.) Experimental Robotics IX. STAR, vol. 21, pp. 153–163. Springer, Heidelberg (2006)

A Turing-Like Handshake Test for Motor Intelligence

Amir Karniel, Ilana Nisky, Guy Avraham, Bat-Chen Peles, and Shelly Levy-Tzedek

The Computational Motor control Laboratory, Department of Biomedical Engineering,
Ben-Gurion University of the Negev, Beer-Sheva 84105, Israel
{akarniel,nisky,guyavr,pelesb,shelly}@bgu.ac.il

Abstract. In the Turing test, a computer model is deemed to "think intelligently" if it can generate answers that are not distinguishable from those of a human. This test is limited to the linguistic aspects of machine intelligence. A salient function of the brain is the control of movement, with the human hand movement being a sophisticated demonstration of this function. Therefore, we propose a Turing-like handshake test, for machine motor intelligence. We administer the test through a telerobotic system in which the interrogator is engaged in a task of holding a robotic stylus and interacting with another party (human, artificial, or a linear combination of the two). Instead of asking the interrogator whether the other party is a person or a computer program, we employ a forced-choice method and ask which of two systems is more human-like. By comparing a given model with a weighted sum of human and artificial systems, we fit a psychometric curve to the answers of the interrogator and extract a quantitative measure for the computer model in terms of similarity to the human handshake.

Keywords: Turing test, Human Machine Interface, Haptics, Teleoperation, Motor Control, Motor Behavior, Diagnostics, Perception, Rhythmic, Discrete.

1   Introduction

As long ago as 1950, Turing proposed that the inability of a human interrogator to distinguish between the answers provided by a person and those provided by a computer would indicate that the computer can think intelligently [1]. The so-called "Turing test" has inspired many studies in the artificial intelligence community; however, it is limited to linguistic capabilities. We argue that the ultimate test must also involve motor intelligence – that is, the ability to physically interact with the environment in a human-like fashion - encouraging the design and construction of a humanoid robot with abilities indistinguishable from those of a human being. However, this ultimate Turing-like test for motor intelligence involves an enormous repertoire of movements. In this paper we present the first step towards the ultimate test by using the handshake test proposed by G.E. Loeb as the basis for our test [2]. The handshake is of interest not merely as a reduced version of the ultimate humanoid test but also due to its bidirectional nature, in which both sides actively shake hands and explore each other. Moreover, motor control research has concentrated on hand movements [3], generating a variety of hypotheses which could be applied to generate a humanoid handshake.

A.M.L. Kappers et al. (Eds.): EuroHaptics 2010, Part I, LNCS 6191, pp. 197–204, 2010.
© Springer-Verlag Berlin Heidelberg 2010

Last but not least, the greatest progress in telerobotic technologies involves arm movements. The telerobotic interface is necessary to grant the human-computer discrimination significance, much as the teletype was necessary to hide the computer from the questioning human in the original Turing test.

Handshaking has been discussed in the social context [4, 5] but the development of artificial handshake systems is still in its infancy [6-10]. Nevertheless, research of human motor control has generated many theories as to the nature of hand movements, and the proposed Turing-like handshake test can be useful in identifying the aspects of these theories that are essential for producing a human-like handshake movement. In general terms, we assert that a true understanding of the motor control system could be demonstrated by building a humanoid robot that is indistinguishable from a human. Therefore, a measure of our distance from such demonstration could be most useful in evaluating current scientific hypotheses and guiding future neuroscience research.

We first describe the proposed one dimensional forced-choice Turing-like handshake test in section 2; we describe our experimental protocol in section 3; we analyze natural handshake movements in section 4; and demonstrate our experimental results for five simple handshake models in section 5. Finally, we introduce an international handshake test challenge in section 6.

2   The Turing-Like Handshake Test

In this study, a Turing-like handshake test is used in order to compare handshake models and extract a quantitative measure of their similarity to a human handshake.

In the classical Turing test, the human interrogator compares the answers of a human and a computer. In the proposed handshake test we followed the original concept of three entities (*a human*, *a computer*, and *an interrogator*) and defined a forced-choice protocol. We administered the test with two PHANToM® Desktop haptic devices by SensAble Technology Inc, operated using SenseGraphics H3D API. The *human* as well as the *interrogator* are each asked to hold the stylus of a haptic device and to generate handshake movements through the telerobotic interface (Fig. 1f). The force feedback to the interrogator is a linear combination of the forces generated by both the *human* and the *computer* (Fig. 1a-c). The *computer* is a simulated handshake model which generates force signal as a function of time and one dimensional position of the hand and its derivatives,

$$F_{model}(t) = \Phi\big[x(t), t\big] \quad 0 \le t \le T. \tag{1}$$

where $\Phi[x,t]$ stands for any causal operator, e.g., non-linear time-varying mechanical model of the one dimensional stylus movement generated by artificial handshake, and T is the duration of the handshake. The force feedback to the *human* is generated purely by the *interrogator*, in order to preserve the mutual and adaptive characteristics of the human handshake movement.

A *trial* consists of two handshakes, each lasting 5 seconds. In one of the handshakes in each trial – the *stimulus* – the interrogator interacts with a combination of forces that comes from the human and a *computer* handshake model:

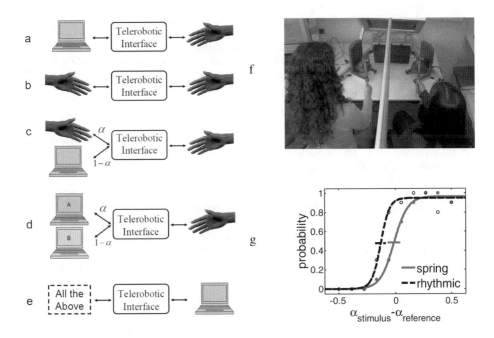

Fig. 1. Illustration of the handshake test. In the basic Turing-like handshake test the human interrogator has to distinguish between a simulated handshake (a) and a natural handshake (b). To extract a quantitative measure for the human-like behavior of simulated handshake we propose a forced-choice method in which the interrogator has to probe combinations of natural and simulated handshakes (c) and answer which one is more human-like. Using the same method one can compare between two simulated handshakes (d). Eventually, one can also consider an artificial interrogator (e) and test the reverse handshake hypothesis asserting that a simulated handshake indistinguishable from a natural handshake would be useful as an interrogator handshake to distinguish between other handshakes. The actual tests were performed using two haptic devices (f). The data was analyzed by fitting psychometric curves to the answers of subjects (g), where the vertical axis represents the probability of the subject to answer that the stimulus handshake felt more human-like. In the base curve (solid gray), both stimulus and reference models where passive springs, whereas in the test curve (dashed black), stimulus is based on a rhythmic handshake model and reference on a passive spring.

$$F = \alpha_{stimulus} \cdot F_{human} + (1 - \alpha_{stimulus}) \cdot F_{stimulusModel} \qquad (2)$$

$\alpha_{stimulus} = \{0, 0.11, 0.22, 0.33, 0.44, 0.55, 0.66, 0.77, 0.88, 1\}$

The other handshake – the *reference* – is a fixed combination of forces generated from the human and a reference model:

$$F = \alpha_{reference} \cdot F_{human} + (1 - \alpha_{reference}) \cdot F_{referenceModel} \quad ; \quad \alpha_{reference} = 0.5 \qquad (3)$$

At the end of each trial the interrogator is requested to choose the handshake that felt more human-like.

We fitted a psychometric curve to the answers of the interrogator (Fig. 1g) [16]. Such curve describes the probability of the interrogator to answer that a stimulus handshake is more human-like, as a function of $\alpha_{stimulus} - \alpha_{reference}$. The point of subjective equality (PSE), where the probability to answer that the stimulus is more human-like is at chance level is extracted from the curve and used to calculate a quantitative grade for each model's closeness to a human handshake – Model Human-Likeness Grade (MHLG) - according to:

$$MHLG = PSE + 0.5 \tag{4}$$

A model which is perceived to be as human-like as the reference model yields the MHLG value of 0.5. The models that are perceived as the least or the most human-like possible, yield MHLG values of 0 or 1 respectively.

3 The Handshake Experimental Protocol

In each of two experiments we performed, three *computer* handshake models were compared - two tested models and one base model. The comparison was performed by the following four tests: (1) Base vs. Base; (2) Base vs. Test #01; (3) Base vs. Test #02; and (4) Test #01 vs. Test #02.

Each experimental block consisted of 40 trials: 10 linear combinations of the stimulus and the human (eq. 2) for each of the four model combinations mentioned above. As described in section 2 each trial consisted of two handshakes: a stimulus and a reference handshake. The order of the trials within each block was random and predetermined. Each experiment consisted of 11 blocks, the first block was not analyzed and used for general acquaintance with the system and the task. For each test we fitted a psychometric curve and calculated the MHLG from the extracted PSE.

4 Smoothness and Harmonicity of a Natural Handshake

In approaching the challenge of creating a robotic model of the human handshake that will be indistinguishable from an actual human handshake we first assessed two of the quintessential properties of the human handshake: whether it is rhythmic or discrete in nature, and its relative smoothness. We hypothesized that a model which captures these properties will likely be more similar to the human handshake than one that did not account for the rhythmicity and smoothness of the handshake.

We asked five participants to hold the stylus of the haptic device and to generate handshake movements with the experimenter via a telerobotic system and recorded their position over time.

We evaluated the rhythmicity and the smoothness of the human handshake using two metrics: mean squared jerk ratio (MSJR), and harmonicity. The relative smoothness of a movement is obtained by dividing its mean squared jerk by the mean squared jerk of the corresponding maximally smooth movement [11]. This ratio would approach a value of one for a highly smooth movement, whereas a value much greater than one would imply the movement is highly fragmented. Harmonicity of the movement is determined by the features of the acceleration trace around movement reversals, and provides a measure of the harmonic or inharmonic nature of the movement [12]. A harmonicity value approaching one indicates a highly harmonic movement, whereas a value approaching zero implies mechanical energy is dissipated in the vicinity of movement reversal [13]. Detailed descriptions of the methods of calculating these metrics have been provided elsewhere [14, 15].

The average amplitude of the handshake movements was 10.0±1.0cm (mean±SD), and average frequency was 2.5±0.1Hz. MSJR values were close to unity (1.5±0.4), indicating a highly smooth movement. Harmonicity values from all analyzed trials almost uniformly equaled one (0.98±0.02), indicating a highly harmonic nature of the movement.

These results suggest that a model of the human handshake that produces a smooth, harmonic, movement is more likely to be perceived more human-like than one that produces a jerky, discrete movement.

5 Demonstrating the Turing-Like Handshake Test

One interrogator participated in two experiments. In each experiment we compared two test models and one base model (see Table 1). The following models were used as computer-generated handshake models:

Table 1. Experimental protocol parameters

Experiment	Base Model	Test Model #01	Test Model #02
I	K=50 N/m	K=50 N/m; B=2 N·sec/m	K=20 N/m; B=1.3 N·sec/m
II	K=50 N/m	Rhythmic	Discrete −sin(7t)

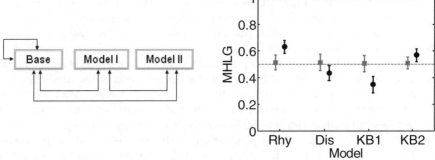

Fig. 2. Demonstrating the Turing-like Handshake test with human, interrogator and three models. In each experiment we compared three models by performing four model comparisons as illustrated in the left panel. The right panel depicts the results of the test using the Model Human-Likeness Grade (MHLG) Plot. The tested models, as appear in Table 1, are: Rhy- rhythmic; Dis- Discrete; KB1- spring K=50, damper B=2; KB2- spring K=20, damper B=1.3. Black circles and gray squares are the MHLG of the test and base models, respectively, each compared to the base model. Error bars are 95% confidence intervals of the MHLG.

$$F_1 = Kx \quad F_2 = Kx + Bv \quad F_3 = \sin(7t) \quad F_4 = \text{ceiling}(\sin(7t) - \sin(\pi/2 - 1)) \quad (5)$$

Where F_1, a simple passive model, was used as the Base model; F_2, a viscoelastic model, was used in experiment I with different values for the stiffness K and the viscosity B for Test Models #01 and #02; and F_3, F_4 were used in experiment **II** as the rhythmic and the discrete force generators.

Figure 2 displays the MHLG values of the four models that were tested. One can see that the interrogator perceived the rhythmic model and the second viscoelastic model as more human-like than the base model. On the other hand he perceived the discrete model as well as the first viscoelastic model as less human-like than the base model.

6 Discussion

In this study we propose a forced-choice Turing-like handshake test administered via a simple telerobotic system. We demonstrated the proposed handshake test by comparing four type of models: (i) a simple passive spring model (ii) passive viscoelastic models (iii) a rhythmic power source, and (iv) a discrete power source of the same frequency and amplitude (see equation 5, and Table 1). Using the Turing-like handshake test, and the proposed measure of Model Human-Likeness Grade (MHLG), we found that a rhythmic handshake model is perceived as more human-like than a discrete one. This preliminary finding is consistent with our analysis of rhythmicity: the human handshake is highly rhythmic. Moreover, this test is helpful in finding the parameters of the passive characteristics of motion that provide the most human-like feeling. Further studies are required to validate these results on a large group of subjects and, more importantly, to develop a model for a handshake which will be as human-like as possible. Here we provide a platform for comparing handshake models. The four models we propose are far from being indistinguishable from a natural human handshake as we did not consider the nonlinearities and time-varying nature of human impedance, mutual adaptation with the interrogator and many other aspects of a natural human handshake which should be tested and ranked using this forced-choice Turing-like handshake test.

There are many limitations to the proposed test which is one dimensional and consists of a telerobotic system and therefore hides many aspects of the handshake such as tactile information, temperature, moisture, and grasping forces. Moreover in this version of the test we didn't consider the duration of the handshake, the initiation and release times and the hand trajectories before and after the physical contact. There are also many types of handshakes depending on gender and culture of the person and therefore one cannot expect to generate a single optimal human-like handshake model. Nevertheless, we believe that the simplicity of the proposed test is an advantage, at least at this preliminary stage of the study. Once the key features of such one dimensional handshake are properly characterized we can move on to consider these limitations and extend the test accordingly.

It should be noted that a Turing-like handshake test could be reversed, with the computer instead of the person being asked about the identity of the other party (see Fig. 1e). In this framework, we consider the following reverse handshake hypothesis:

the purpose of a handshake is to probe the shaken hand; according to the reverse handshake hypothesis, the optimal handshake algorithm - in the sense that it will be indistinguishable from a human handshake – will best facilitate the discrimination between people and machines. In other words, once a model that best mimics the human handshake is constructed, it itself can then be used to probe handshakes generated by humans and/or other machines.

One should also note that the test discussed herein is a perceptual test and recent studies distinguish between perception and action [17,18]. Future studies should explore three versions of the test in order to accurately assess the nature of human-like handshake: (1) a psychometric test of the perceived similarity; (2) a motor behavior test that will explore the motor reaction of the interrogator which may differ from his/her cognitively perceived similarity; (3) an ultimate optimal discriminator which attempts to distinguish between human and machine handshakes based on the force and position trajectories.

In general terms, we assert that understanding the motor control system is a necessary condition for understanding the brain function, and that such understanding could be demonstrated by building a humanoid robot indistinguishable from a human. The current study focuses on handshakes via a telerobotic system. We assert that by ranking the prevailing scientific hypotheses about the nature of human hand movement control using the proposed Turing-like handshake test, we should be able to extract salient properties of human motor control or at least the salient properties required to build an artificial appendage that is indistinguishable from a human arm.

Acknowledgments. The first author wishes to thank Gerry Loeb for useful discussions about the proposed Turing-like handshake test. This research was supported by the Israel Science Foundation (grant No. 1018/08). SL was supported by a Kreitman Foundation postdoctoral fellowship. IN was supported by a Kreitman Foundation fellowship, and a Clore scholarship.

References

1. Turing, A.M.: Computing Machinery and Intelligence. Mind. A Quarterly Review of Psychology and Philosophy LIX (1950)
2. Loeb, G.E., Otten, B.: T-shirt logo human machine handshake Computational Neuroscience: Motor Control. Cold Spring Harbor, NY (1986)
3. Shadmehr, R., Wise, S.P.: The Computational Neurobiology of Reaching and Pointing: A Foundation for Motor Learning. MIT Press, Cambridge (2005)
4. Chaplin, W.F., Phillips, J.B., Brown, J.D., Clanton, N.R., Stein, J.L.: Handshaking, gender, personality, and first impressions. Journal of Personality and Social Psychology 79, 110–117 (2000)
5. Stewart, G.L., Dustin, S.L., Barrick, M.R., Darnold, T.C.: Exploring the handshake in employment interviews. Journal of Applied Psychology 93, 1139–1146 (2008)
6. Jindai, M., Watanabe, T., Shibata, S., Yamamoto, T.: Development of Handshake Robot System for Embodied Interaction with Humans. In: The 15th IEEE International Symposium on Robot and Human Interactive Communication, Hatfield, UK (2006)
7. Kasuga, T., Hashimoto, M.: Human-Robot Handshaking using Neural Oscillators. In: Internatioanl Conference on Robotics and Automation. IEEE, Barcelona (2005)

8. Ouchi, K., Hashimoto, S.: Handshake Telephone System to Communicate with Voice and Force. In: IEEE International Workshop on Robot and Human Communication, pp. 466–471 (1997)
9. Bailenson, J.N., Yee, N.: Virtual interpersonal touch and digital chameleons. Journal of Nonverbal Behavior 31, 225–242 (2007)
10. Miyashita, T., Ishiguro, H.: Human-like natural behavior generation based on involuntary motions for humanoid robots. Robotics and Autonomous Systems 48, 203–212 (2004)
11. Hogan, N., Sternad, D.: On rhythmic and discrete movements: reflections, definitions and implications for motor control. Exp. Brain Res. 181, 13–30 (2007)
12. Guiard, Y.: On Fitts's and Hooke's laws: simple harmonic movement in upper-limb cyclical aiming. Acta psychologica 82, 139–159 (1993)
13. Buchanan, J., Park, J., Shea, C.: Target width scaling in a repetitive aiming task: switching between cyclical and discrete units of action. Experimental Brain Research 175, 710–725 (2006)
14. Levy-Tzedek, S., Ben Tov, M., Karniel, A.: Early switching between movement types: indication of predictive control? (submitted)
15. Levy-Tzedek, S., Krebs, H., Song, D., Hogan, N., Poizner, H.: Non-monotonicity on a spatio-temporally defined cyclic task: evidence of two movement types? Experimental Brain Research 202(4), 733–746 (2010)
16. Wichmann, F.A., Hill, N.J.: The psychometric function: I. Fitting, sampling, and goodness of fit. Percept. Psychophys. 63, 1293–1313 (2001)
17. Goodale, M.A., Milner, A.D.: Seperate visual pathways for perception and action. Trends Neurosci. 15, 20–25 (1992)
18. Pressman, A., Nisky, I., Karniel, A., Mussa-Ivaldi, F.A.: Probing Virtual Boundaries and the Perception of Delayed Stiffness. Advanced Robotics 22, 119–140 (2008)

The Influence of Different Haptic Environments on Time Delay Discrimination in Force Feedback

Markus Rank[1], Zhuanghua Shi[2], Hermann J. Müller[2], and Sandra Hirche[1]

[1] Institute of Automatic Control Engineering, Technische Universität München, Munich, Germany
{m.rank,hirche}@tum.de
[2] Institute of Experimental Psychology, Ludwig-Maximilians-Universität München, Munich, Germany
{shi,hmueller}@psy.lmu.de

Abstract. Time delay in haptic telepresence arising from compression or communication alters the phase characteristics of the environment impedance. This paper describes how well a human operator can discriminate these changes in haptic environments. Three different environments are rendered on a haptic interface and manually excited by a human operator using sinusoidal movements. We find that time delay in haptic feedback can be discriminated starting from 15 ms in a pure damper environment, 36 ms in a spring system, and 72 ms when moving a damped inertia. We conclude that the discrimination thresholds increase with the absolute phase between velocity and force signals resulting from the remote environment characteristics. These results may benefit the human-centered design of high-fidelity haptic communication protocols and haptic filters.

Keywords: Time delay, telepresence, psychophysics.

1 Introduction

High-fidelity teleoperation requires sensory feedback from the remote environment with sufficient resolution and low latency [1]. While perceptual discrimination limits for different types of sensory information, e.g., force and position [2,3,4], and detection thresholds for latency in the visual and auditive modality [5,6,7,8,9] have been studied extensively, the perception of time delay in continuous haptic feedback has been largely neglected. However, time delay is an inherent artifact in long-distance telepresence [10] and in some compression techniques for haptic data [11], though there are haptic data reduction schemes without time delay [12,13]. In the few available studies on perception of time-delayed force feedback [5,14,15,16], detection and discrimination thresholds vary substantially, ranging from dozens to one hundred milliseconds, depending on the specific task and environment. To reveal potential common perceptual fundamentals capable of guiding engineers in dimensioning communication protocols, we embarked on a series of studies designed to systematically explore perceptual effects of haptic feedback latency. In a first study, we examined the impact of various manual excitation amplitudes and frequencies as well as different spring constants in a spring environment during performance of a sinusoidal movement [15]. It is found

A.M.L. Kappers et al. (Eds.): EuroHaptics 2010, Part I, LNCS 6191, pp. 205–212, 2010.

that increasing manual movement amplitude, and frequency, result in lower detection thresholds for time delays. By contrast, varying stiffness within a certain range does not influence the delay perception [15]. To our knowledge, however, the influence of different environment characteristics on delay perception is still an open issue.

The contribution of the present study lies in the analysis of human delay discrimination capabilities when interacting with a remote spring, damper, and, respectively, inertia environment. We find that discrimination thresholds for time delay increase with the absolute phase between velocity and force signals.

The remainder of this paper is organized as follows: In Section 2, we describe the experiment on delay discrimination; thresholds and just noticeable differences (JNDs) for phase shifts in the haptic feedback are presented in Section 2.2. The results and preliminary implications for data transmission and filter design for haptic signals are discussed in Section 3.

2   Delay Discrimination Experiment

The dynamic haptic environments examined in this study are a linear spring, a damper, and a damped inertia, described by the equations

$$f_e(t) = \begin{cases} -k \int_0^t v(\tau - T_d)d\tau, \\ -d_1 v(t - T_d), \\ -d_2 v(t - T_d) - m\dot{v}(t - T_d), \end{cases} \tag{1}$$

respectively. Here, $f_e(t)$ is the momentary force feedback from the remote environment, $v(t)$ is the velocity at time t, and T_d is the controlled variable – the time delay. The environment-specific parameter k denotes the spring constant, d_1, d_2 the damping factors, and m the inertia. The frequency characteristics of the spring, damping, and inertia (without time delay, $T_d = 0$) are characterized by their mechanical impedance $Z_e(j\omega) = \frac{F_e(j\omega)}{V(j\omega)}$ as depicted as in Fig. 1. Besides differences in the amplitude characteristics, the phase relation between velocity input and force feedback differs by $90°$ between inertia and damping, and spring and damping environment, respectively. Introducing time delay into the force feedback, i.e., $T_d > 0$ does not alter the environments' amplitude characteristics but the phase changes. This is observable from the force feedback response $F(j\omega)$ to an excitation with a specific trajectory of $v(t)$ with frequency response $V(j\omega)$

$$F_e(j\omega) = Z_e(j\omega)e^{-j\omega T_d} \cdot V(j\omega) = |Z_e(j\omega)| \cdot |V(j\omega)|e^{j(\angle Z_e(j\omega) - \omega T_d)}. \tag{2}$$

The larger the time delay for a given frequency, the larger is the phase difference between the velocity and force signal. Hence, the question as to the time delay discrimination threshold can equivalently be posed as a question as to the phase discrimination thresholds depending on the environment-induced phase between the velocity and force signal. To address this question, participants were required to make sinusoidal arm movements $x(t) = \int_0^t v(\tau)d\tau = A\sin(\omega t)$ of fixed amplitude $A = 15$ cm and frequency $\omega = 2\pi$ rad/s. To ensure good comparability between the conditions, the environment-specific constants were chosen to result in force feedback of equal amplitude: $k = 65\frac{N}{m}$, $d_1 = 65/(2\pi)\frac{Ns}{m}$, $d_2 = 43/(2\pi)\frac{Ns}{m}$, and $m = 22/(2\pi)^2\frac{Ns^2}{m} \approx 560$g.

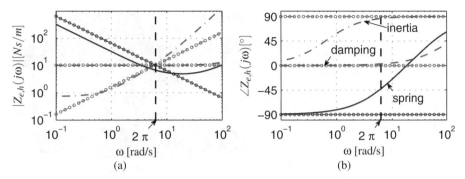

Fig. 1. Amplitude (a) and phase characteristics (b) of the ideal environment impedance $Z_e(j\omega)$ (light, circle markers) for inertia (dash-dotted), damper (dashed), and spring (solid), and the actually rendered $Z_h(j\omega)$ (bold)

2.1   Stimuli and Procedure

Ten university students (7 male; age range 20-27 years; 9 right-handed) participated in the experiment; they were paid at a rate of 10 Euros per hour. None of them reported any history of somatosensory disorders. Informed consent was obtained from all participants prior to the experiment. The haptic stimuli were rendered using a ServoTube linear motor module (Copley Controls Corp.), equipped with an optical encoder of 1μm resolution. A rubber-coated handle was used for user interaction with the device. Force and torque information was measured with a 6DoF force-torque sensor (JR3 Inc.). The device was controlled by a PC, equipped with a Sensoray 626 DAQ Card running Gentoo Linux. The haptic environment including the delay was realized using a force control scheme, depicted in Figure 2(a) and rendered in real-time with a sample rate of 1kHz by means of the RealTime Application Interface (RTAI). Visual information was displayed on a 22" LCD Monitor with a refresh rate of 60 Hz. To mask the noise produced by the haptic device, pink background noise was delivered to both ears of participants during the experiment via KOSS QZ99 Headphones. Participants sat in an upright position centered towards the middle of the linear actuator, and the forcefield was rendered in the users' transverse plane within a comfortable manual reaching range. Participants' responses were collected using a joystick. The setup is depicted in Figure 2(b). For an evaluation of the actually presented impedances $Z_h(j\omega) = \frac{F_h(j\omega)}{V(j\omega)}$ including the haptic interface dynamics, control and $Z_e(j\omega)$ as illustrated in Figure 2(a), we identified the haptic interface dynamics in the frequency domain. The uncontrolled linear actuator dynamics were found to be sufficiently well captured by a linear second-order system with the commanded force $f_c(t)$ as input and the endeffector position $x(t)$ as output. To determine the specific parameters, a standard least-squares system identification procedure was applied. By employing the implemented controller K_p used in the experimental procedure and the environmental dynamic equations in (1) as they were used in the actual experimental procedure, the respective frequency responses for $Z_h(j\omega)$ were calculated – see Fig. 1.

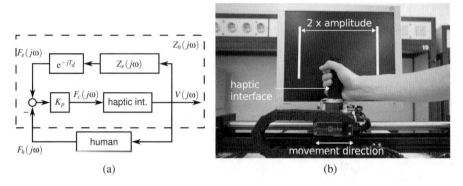

Fig. 2. (a) The force control scheme to render the impedance $Z_h(j\omega) = \frac{F_h(j\omega)}{V(j\omega)}$. (b) The experimental apparatus consisting of a linear actuator device with a rubber-coated handle and a TFT screen used for visual stimulus presentation.

As shown in the Bode diagram, inertia and damper were rendered quite accurately around the instructed movement frequency in terms of amplitude and phase characteristic. The influence of the actuator's mass and friction, however, changed the phase characteristic of the spring to approximately -45° at the movement frequency of 2π rad/s, instead of an ideal phase of -90°. All of the following results are based on the really rendered impedance $Z_h(j\omega)$, rather than the ideal environment impedance $Z_e(j\omega)$. The movement amplitude on a given trial was indicated by two vertical bars on the monitor, as can be seen in Fig. 2(b). The movement frequency was cued audibly by a rhythmic beep train, with each beep indicating the turning point in the direction of movement. An additional guidance dot moving in the desired sinusoidal way was shown on the monitor in the training session. After the participant had become familiar with the movement shape, the visual cue was removed to reduce potential distraction from the discrimination task to be performed in the formal experiment. To obtain an accurate estimate of the perceptual thresholds, the method of odd-one-out 3-alternative forced-choice (3AFC) was used in the experiment. Each trial was subdivided into three intervals of 3 seconds; one randomly chosen interval contained the target stimulus with a specific level of time delay introduced into the force feedback. In the remaining two intervals, the system responded with a non-delayed force feedback. In order to remove any abrupt-onset cues due to switching delay conditions, a transition phase of 1.5 seconds was added between delayed and non-delayed force feedback intervals. No feedback about the correctness of the answer was provided. Seven levels of time delay T_d, segmented equally between 0 ms and 50 ms, were tested for the spring environment, and seven delays between 0 ms and 80 ms for the mass and damping environments. These levels were determined in a pilot study and respected stability conditions for the experimental setup. Each delay level was tested 21 times, yielding a total of 441 trials. The experiment was conducted over three sessions, where each session contained 7 repetitions of all conditions in a random order.

2.2 Results

Three participants failed to follow the movement instructions accurately enough, so their data had to be excluded from further analysis. With the remaining data sets, an adjusted logistic function [17]

$$P(x) = \gamma + (1 - \gamma) \cdot \frac{1}{1 + e^{\frac{\alpha - x}{\beta}}} \tag{3}$$

is used for estimating the psychometric function, where the guessing rate γ is set to $1/3$ according to the 3AFC paradigm. Fig. 3(a) shows typical correct responses, produced by one participant, for the three different environments. Using equation (3), the discrimination threshold DT and the just noticeable difference JND at response level 67% can be easily obtained as DT= α and JND= $\beta \log 3$. In Fig. 3(b), the mean DTs and JNDs for spring, damper and inertia are presented. The results indicate that the discrimination threshold is the largest for the inertia, with a mean of 72 ms, corresponding to a phase shift of 25° as deriveable from equation (2). The threshold associated with the damper is the lowest, with a mean of 15 ms, equivalent to a phase shift of 5°. In the spring condition, time delay can be discriminated from a non-delayed spring starting at a threshold of 36 ms, corresponding to 13° phase lag. A repeated-measures ANOVA reveals the discrimination thresholds to be sensitive to the different environments, $F(2, 12) = 14.17, p < 0.01$. Follow-on comparison tests show the discrimination thresholds to differ reliably from each other ($p < 0.05$). This indicates that the different environments do indeed influence the subjective judgment of haptic feedback time delay. A further repeated-measures ANOVA for the JNDs of discrimination fails to reveal a significant effect of the environment, $F(2, 12) = 1.03, p > 0.1$. Further studies using more than three environmental conditions need to be performed in order to derive an analytic relationship between the environment induced phase $\angle Z_h(j\omega)$ and the time delay discrimination threshold DT. In general, it is observed that discrimination thresholds increase with the

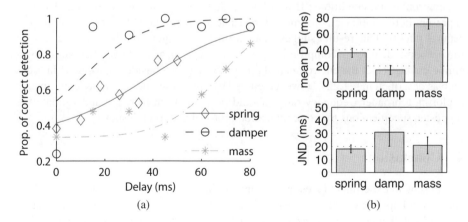

Fig. 3. (a) Estimated psychometric curves for the three environments for one typical participant. (b) Mean thresholds ($\pm$ standard error, $n = 7$) for the different environments.

absolute value of the phase difference between an arbitrary $\angle Z_h(j\omega)$ and the phase of a damper environment.

3 Discussion

The present study shows that discrimination thresholds of delayed force feedback from spring, damper, and, respectively, inertia are different. This supports our conclusion put forward in [15] that in a continuous haptic environment, the time delay detection mechanism is not based on a temporal correlation or an internal clock mechanism, e.g., as proposed in [18]. Considering equation (2), time delay shifts the phase characteristics independently of the environment type. Thus, there is a strong indication that the undelayed dynamical system properties play a role in discriminating the difference in phase. There are several effects potentially contributing to this observed perceptual performance. One of them is that JND of force discrimination is lowest when the limb is not moving [19,20]. Evidently, the force feedback from the various environments around the movement turning points, where $v(t) \approx 0$, differs significantly in terms of magnitude and slope: Inertia and spring with phases of $+90°$ and approximately $-45°$, respectively, have non-zero force feedback around these instances. High force levels are known to result in large discrimination thresholds [2]. Damping, by contrast, does not only combine low velocities with low force feedback, but additionally reverses force direction at the turning point of the movement. It is possible that this feature provides additional help for discriminating between delayed and undelayed force feedback. Further investigations may be considered to shed additional light on the mechanism responsible for the discrimination performance observed here.

Nevertheless, the present results have direct implications for the assessment and design of haptic communication protocols: If a time delay is introduced that shifts the phase by more than $5°$, perception of damping is compromised, while spring and mass can still be perceived unaffectedly. Schedulers, data compression techniques or filters – i.e. all potential measures inducing phase-lag – need to be dimensioned based on the environmental conditions: If it is known that no damping force, such as friction, is present in the remote environment, larger latencies are tolerable with respect to perceptual fidelity. Our results suggest that in order to achieve the best filter effect on force magnitude without compromising phase perception, an adaptive filter based on an online-estimation of the environmental properties may be considered, using techniques such as described in [21,22]. However, guided by our initial findings, more experiments exploring a broader frequency range should be carried out to refine and validate the suggested specifications for communication protocol and filter design.

4 Conclusion

We present an experiment investigating human time delay discrimination thresholds in continuous haptic environments, which, in our setup, is equivalent to the discrimination threshold of changes in the phase characteristic of the mechanical impedance. Discrimination thresholds are found to increase with the absolute value of the phase between velocity input and force of the environment. Based on these findings, we suggest that communication protocols and filters for haptic signals should take into account the environment's phase characteristic, e.g., by adapting the filter gains in accordance with the type of remote environment. Future research should test a greater range of frequencies and environments, composed of the elementary environment components spring, damper, and inertia, to contribute to the emerging picture on phase discrimination.

Acknowledgments. This work was supported in part by a grant from the German Research Foundation (DFG) within the Collaborative Research Centre SFB 453 on "High-Fidelity Telepresence and Teleaction". We thank Jimmy Butron for programming, Antonia Glaser for conducting the experiment, and Heng Zou for helpful discussions.

References

1. Chen, J.Y.C., Haas, E.C., Barnes, M.J.: Human performance issues and user interface design for teleoperated robots. IEEE Transactions on Systems, Man, and Cybernetics, Part C: Applications and Reviews 37(6), 1231–1245 (2007)
2. Weber, E.: Die Lehre vom Tastsinne und Gemeingefühle auf Versuche gegründet. Friedrich Vieweg und Sohn (1851)
3. Deml, B.: Human Factors Issues on the Design of Telepresence Systems. Presence: Teleoperators and Virtual Environments 16(5), 471–487 (2007)
4. Tan, H., Srinivasan, M., Eberman, B., Cheng, B.: Human factors for the design of force-reflecting haptic interfaces. Dynamic Systems and Control 55(1), 353–359 (1994)
5. Adelstein, B.D., Lee, T.G., Ellis, S.R.: Head tracking latency in virtual environments: psychophysics and a model. In: Proceedingsof the Human Factors and Ergonomics Society 47th annual meeting, pp. 2083–2087 (2003)
6. Arrighi, R., Alais, D., Burr, D.: Perceptual synchrony of audiovisual streams for natural and artificial motion sequences. Journal of Vision 6(3), 260–268 (2006)
7. Dixon, N.F., Spitz, L.: The detection of auditory visual desynchrony. Perception 9, 719–721 (1980)
8. Eid, M., Orozco, M., El Saddik, A.: A guided tour in haptic audio visual environments and applications. International Journal for Media and Communication 1(3), 265–297 (2007)
9. Frank, L.H., Casali, J.G., Wierwille, W.W.: Effects of visual display and motion system delays on operator performance and uneasiness in a driving simulator. Human Factors: The Journal of the Human Factors and Ergonomics Society 30(2), 201–217 (1988)
10. Peer, A., Hirche, S., Weber, C., Krause, I., Buss, M., Miossec, S., Evrard, P., Stasse, O., Neo, E., Kheddar, A., Yokoi, K.: Intercontinental multimodal tele-cooperation using a humanoid robot. In: Proceedings of the 2008 IEEE/RSJ International Conference on Intelligent Robots and Systems, pp. 405–411 (2008)
11. Shahabi, C., Ortega, A., Kolahdouzan, M.: A comparison of different haptic compression techniques. In: Proceedings of the International Conference on Multimedia and Expo (ICME), pp. 657–660 (2002)
12. Hirche, S., Hinterseer, P., Steinbach, E., Buss, M.: Transparent data reduction in networked telepresence and teleaction systems. Part i: Communication without time delay. Presence: Teleoperators and Virtual Environments 16(5), 523–531 (2007)
13. Hirche, S., Buss, M.: Transparent data reduction in networked telepresence and teleaction systems. Part ii: Time-delayed communication. Presence: Teleoperators and Virtual Environments 16(5), 532–542 (2007)

14. Jay, C., Glencross, M., Hubbold, R.: Modeling the effects of delayed haptic and visual feedback in a collaborative virtual environment. ACM Transactions on Computer-Human Interaction 14(2), 8/1–31 (2007)
15. Rank, M., Shi, Z., Müller, H.J., Hirche, S.: Perception of delay in haptic telepresence systems. In: Presence: Teleoperators & Virtual Environments (accepted 2010)
16. Shi, Z., Hirche, S., Schneider, W.X., Müller, H.J.: Influence of visuomotor action on visual-haptic simultaneous perception: A psychophysical study. In: Proceedings of the 2008 Symposium on Haptic Interfaces for Virtual Environment and Teleoperator Systems, pp. 65–70. IEEE Computer Society, Los Alamitos (2008)
17. Treutwein, B., Strasburger, H.: Fitting the psychometric function. Percept. Psychophys. 61(1), 87–106 (1999)
18. Fraisse, P.: Perception and estimation of time. Annual Review of Psychology 35, 1–36 (1984)
19. Yang, X.D., Bischof, W., Boulanger, P.: Perception of haptic force magnitude during hand movements. In: Proceedings of the 2008 IEEE International Conference on Robotics and Automation, pp. 2061–2066 (2008)
20. Zadeh, M.H., Wang, D., Kubica, E.: Perception-based lossy haptic compression considerations for velocity-based interactions. Multimedia Systems 13, 275–282 (2008)
21. Achhammer, A., Weber, C., Peer, A., Buss, M.: Improvement of model-mediated teleoperation using a new hybrid environment estimation technique. In: Proceedings of the 2010 IEEE International Conference on Robotics and Automation (2010)
22. Park, D.J., Jun, B.E.: Selfperturbing recursive least squares algorithm with fast tracking capability. Electronics Letters 28, 558–559 (1992)

Perception and Action in Simulated Telesurgery

Ilana Nisky[1], Assaf Pressman[1,2], Carla M. Pugh[3], Ferdinando A. Mussa-Ivaldi[2], and Amir Karniel[1]

[1] Biomedical Engineering, Ben Gurion University of the Negev, Beer-Sheva 84105, Israel,
{nisky,pressman,akarniel}@bgu.ac.il
[2] Sensory Motor Performance Program, Rehabilitation Institute of Chicago,
345E. Superior Street, Chicago IL
sandro@northwestern.edu
[3] Feinberg School of Medicine, Northwestern University, 201 E Huron St, Chicago, IL
cpugh@nmh.org

Abstract. We studied the effect of delay on perception and action in contact with a force field that emulates elastic soft tissue with a specific rigid nonlinear boundary. Such field is similar to forces exerted on a needle during teleoperated needle insertion tasks. We found that a nonlinear boundary region causes both psychometric and motor overestimation of stiffness, and that delay causes motor but not psychometric underestimation of the stiffness of this nonlinear soft tissue. In addition we show that changing the teleoperation channel gain reduces and can even cancel the motor effect of delay.

Keywords: delay, perception, action, telesurgery, needle insertion.

1 Introduction

Telesurgery can substantially improve patient care as well as surgical training by providing global access to surgical specialists [1, 2]. In telesurgery the surgeon determines the motion of a remote slave robot by moving a master robot and sensing the forces reflected from the slave to the master (Fig. 1a).

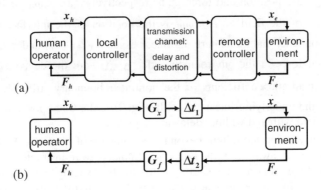

Fig. 1. Teleoperation system: (a) General case (b) Simplified ideal channel with delay and gain

A.M.L. Kappers et al. (Eds.): EuroHaptics 2010, Part I, LNCS 6191, pp. 213–218, 2010.
© Springer-Verlag Berlin Heidelberg 2010

Telesurgery requires transmission of information from a distance, and therefore delay is unavoidable. In the last few years, we have studied the effect of delay on perception of stiffness in linear spring like fields [3-6] and on action in contact with them [7]. Here we developed a new protocol to probe the effect on perception and action in the same experiment testing the effect of delay on a nonlinear environment which simulates needle insertion into soft tissue [8, 9]. We employed simulated telesurgery and focused on a simple teleoperation architecture which includes only delay and gains in the transmission channel (Fig. 1b) in order to highlight the effects of delay without additional control considerations [10, 11].

2 Methods

Subjects held the handle of a PHANTOM® Premium 1.5/6DOF haptic device, and looked at a screen which displayed start and target positions consistent with the haptic scene (see Fig. 2a). The haptic device exerted forces on the hand at 1 kHz and acquired its trajectory at 200 Hz. Lateral position of the hand was displayed by a line and provided subjects with partial position information, without revealing the penetration into a haptic virtual object.

In this study we wished to explore interactions with a force field that approximates the properties of biological tissue. This was, however, a simplified model, as the reaction forces were simulated to depend only on the position and direction of movement. Therefore the force $F_h(t)$ that was exerted in the x axis direction (away from the subject – see Fig. 2a) was a nonlinear function of the hand displacement $x_h(t)$, similar to the position dependent component in [9]:

$$x_e(t) = x_h(t - \Delta t_1) \cdot G_x$$

$$F_e(t) = \begin{cases} 0 & x_e(t) < x_0 \\ k_{b1}(x_e(t) - x_0) + k_{b2}(x_e(t) - x_0)^2 & x_0 < x_e(t) < x_b;\ \dot{x}_e(t) > 0 \\ k_t(x_e(t) - x_0) & x_e(t) > x_b \\ k_t(x_e(t) - x_0) & x_0 < x_e(t) < x_b;\ \dot{x}_e(t) < 0 \end{cases} \tag{1}$$

$$F_h(t) = F_e(t - \Delta t_2) \cdot G_F$$

where G_x, G_f are position and force gains respectively; $x_0 = 3mm$ is the position of the boundary of the field, $x_b = 20mm$ is the position of the interface between rigid nonlinear boundary and the underlying linear tissue, $x_e(t), \dot{x}_e(t)$ and $F_e(t)$ are position, velocity, and force at the environment side, $\Delta t_1, \Delta t_2$ are the delays, k_{b1}, k_{b2} are the linear and quadratic coefficients of the nonlinear boundary stiffness, and k_t is the stiffness of the underlying linear tissue. In Fig. 2b-c the force-position trajectories of such force field with and without delay are depicted.

The target was located 67mm beyond the boundary of the field, x_0; the start point was located 33mm away from the boundary. Subjects were instructed to quickly reach the target and then return to the starting point. Such a "slicing" movement completed a single trial. Performance feedback was provided as written text messages ("long", "short", and "exact").

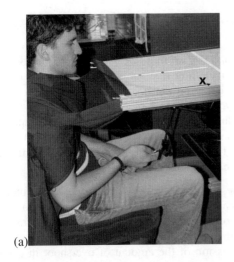
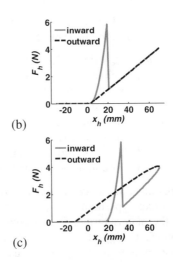

Fig. 2. Experimental setup: (a) Seated subject in setup. Dots on screen are start and end point. White line is partial position feedback. (b) Trajectory of nonlinear tissue force field in force position space. (c) Trajectory of nonlinear tissue force field with delay.

The experiment consisted of four phases: (i) Null training – 20 movements in free space allowing subjects to become acquainted with the dynamics of the haptic device and with the task. (ii) Base training – 40 movements with 10 randomly ordered blocks of force fields k_t stiffness levels chosen from k_t = 25, 35, 45, 55, 65, 75, 85, 95, 105, 115 N/m, 4 trials in each block, allowing subjects to become acquainted with the various tissue stiffness levels that were later presented during catch trials of the experiment. (iii) Task training – 20 movements with task force field. The exact values of the parameters of task and base force fields depend on the experiment. (iv) Test – the subject was introduced to a task or base field for a number of consecutive trials (5 to 7 – randomly chosen). Since the fast slicing movement involves mostly feedforward control [12], subjects who are trained to perform slicing movement to a certain point inside the surface are expected to miss the target (overshoot/undershoot) whenever the surface properties are unexpectedly changed [7]. Thus, following this series a catch trial was introduced in order to probe for adaptive changes in estimation [7]. We have introduced the term "motormetric" – as a contrast to "psychometric" analysis – to designate procedures based on observable motor actions for assessing the evolution of perceptual models. The catch trial was either followed by a question: "Which force field was stiffer – the current or previous?", or by another trial similar to the training block and then the question. This provided us also with a psychometric evaluation of stiffness perception. Feedback was not provided for trials in which the subject's response was required and for one randomly selected trial in each training block.

Experiment 1: Perception of stiffness of nonlinear tissue without delay. Seven subjects participated in this experiment. We aimed to test whether our combined motormetric and psychometric paradigm is applicable for comparing task nonlinear tissue force field (N) to base linear one sided elastic force field (L) using linear elastic force fields with different levels of stiffness as catch trials. The parameters of the experiment are specified in Table 1.

Experiment 2: Effect of delay on perception of stiffness of nonlinear tissue. Seven subjects participated in this experiment (including five subjects who participated in Exp. 1). Here we explored the effect of delay on the perception of the stiffness of nonlinear elastic force field. Since the psychometric task of comparing the stiffness of nonlinear tissue force field with linear elastic force field was difficult, we compared task delayed nonlinear (D) elastic force field and base nondelayed nonlinear (N) elastic force field. We introduced non delayed nonlinear elastic force fields with different levels of linear component of stiffness as catch trials (see Table 1).

Experiment 3: Canceling the motormetric effect of delay by use of gain. Two subjects from Exp. 2 participated in this experiment. We wished to test if it is possible to cancel the motormetric effect of delay by correctly choosing the gains of teleoperation channel, as suggested in [13]. The experiment was similar to Exp. 2, but position and force gains were changed. We used regression of the amount of overshoot in catch trial as a function of difference between the levels of linear components of stiffness between trained and catch fields to find the mean undershoot Δp for identical stiffness levels. To cancel the motormetric effect the position gain must be smaller than 1 such that the subject will make larger hand movements, yielding correct catch trials without delay. Thus, we calculated the position and force gains according to

$$G_x = (x_t - x_0)/(x_t - x_0 + \Delta p); \quad G_f = 1/G_x \qquad (2)$$

where x_t is target position and x_0 is as defined in Eq. 1.

We used a procedure that is described in detail in [4, 7] in order to fit psychometric functions to the probability of answering that training block field was stiffer as a function of the difference in k_t between catch field and trained field [14] and extract the point of subjective equality (PSE). The motormetric curve relates a subject's motor, not verbal, responses to the stimulus. We used a procedure that is described in [7] to fit motormetric functions to the probability to overshoot at catch trial relatively to the median of penetration in last three trials in training block as a function of the

Table 1. The parameters of **Eq. 1** in the different experimental setups. All stiffness levels are in [N/mm]. All delays are in [ms]. Icons are force-position trajectories similar to Fig. 2b-c.

Exp.	Task	Base	Catch
		$\Delta t_1 = \Delta t_2 = 0$ $G_x = G_f = 1$	
1	$k_{b1} = k_t = 0.06$ $k_{b2} = 0.02$	$k_{b1} = k_t = 0.06$ $k_{b2} = 0$	$k_{b1} = k_{ti}$ $k_{b2} = 0$
		$G_x = G_f = 1$	
2	$k_{b1} = k_t = 0.06$ $k_{b2} = 0.02$ $\Delta t_1 = \Delta t_2 = 25$	$k_{b1} = k_t = 0.06$ $k_{b2} = 0.02$ $\Delta t_1 = \Delta t_2 = 0$	$k_{b1} = k_{ti}$ $k_{b2} = 0.02$ $\Delta t_1 = \Delta t_2 = 0$
3	Similar to Experiment 2, but $G_x < 1$ $G_f = 1/G_x$		

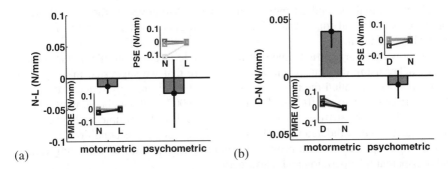

(a)   (b)

Fig. 3. Motormetric and psychometric differences in perception. Vertical axis is difference in PMRE (motormetric) and PSE (psychometric) values between task and base conditions. Negative difference is overestimation and positive difference is underestimation of the stiffness of task force field relative to base field. (a) Experiment 1 – overestimation of the stiffness of nonlinear force field. (b) Experiment 2 – delay causes underestimation in motormetric but not psychometric perception of nonlinear stiffness. Bars are differences in means and error bars are 95% confidence intervals for the difference means. Color insets show individual subjects' PSE (right) or PMRE (left).

difference in k_t between catch field and trained field, and extracted the point of motor response equality (PMRE) from them. Positive values of these PSE or PMRE indicate underestimation of the stiffness of the trained field, and negative values indicate overestimation.

3   Results and Conclusions

In this study we present, for the first time, psychometric and motormetric evaluation of the stiffness of nonlinear needle-insertion-like force field.

The psychometric component of the task in *Experiment 1* was difficult, and therefore two of the subjects failed to discriminate between the fields. The stiffness of the N field was overestimated relative to the stiffness of L field according to both motormetric (paired t-test t_6=-3.02, p=0.023, significant) and psychometric (paired t-test t_4=-1.32, p=0.26, nonsignificant) measures, as depicted in Fig. 3a.

The motormetric and psychometric effects of delay on perception of stiffness of nonlinear elastic force field were different. *Experiment 2* revealed that delay caused motormetric underestimation that was consistent across subjects (paired t-test t_6=6.86, p=0.0004) and no change in psychometric perception (paired t-test t_5=-1.66, p=0.16) of D field, as depicted in Fig. 3b. This gap is consistent with our findings about linear elastic force fields [7]. Here we report motormetric underestimation, which is consistent with absolute penetration in [7] which is relevant for telesurgery; however, it is interesting to explore in a future study why the delay did not affect the psychometric estimation unlike in the case of linear force fields [3-5]. The gap between perception and action that is demonstrated by different effects of delay supports our suggestion [13] that transparency of teleoperation systems in general, and telesurgery systems in particular, should be assessed using multidimensional transparency measures that include perceptual as well as motor components. Moreover, a focus on these two components is critical for additional aspects in surgery, such as training of surgeons and skills evaluation.

We show here for the first time that it is possible to eliminate the motormetric effect of delay using the transparentizing procedure that we suggested in [13]. In *Experiment 3* we cancelled the motormetric effect of delay, namely reduced the PMRE [N/mm] from 0.028 to -2×10^{-4} and from 0.043 to 0.007, without changing psychometric perception of the stiffness of nonlinear force field for both subjects. However, this finding needs to be validated with additional subjects in various conditions.

The results presented here provide an additional step towards achieving efficient and transparent teleoperation and telesurgery.

Acknowledgments. This research was supported by the Binational United States Israel Science Foundation and by NINDS grant 2R01NS035673. IN is supported by the Kreitman and Clore fellowships.

References

1. Schulam, P.G., Docimo, S.G., Saleh, W., Breitenbach, C., Moore, R.G., Kavoussi, L.: Telesurgical mentoring. Surgical Endoscopy 11, 1001–1005 (1997)
2. Marescaux, J., Leroy, J., Gagner, M., Rubino, F., Mutter, D., Vix, M., Butner, S.E., Smith, M.K.: Transatlantic robot-assisted telesurgery. Nature 413, 379–380 (2001)
3. Pressman, A., Welty, L.H., Karniel, A., Mussa-Ivaldi, F.A.: Perception of delayed stiffness. The International Journal of Robotics Research 26, 1191–1203 (2007)
4. Nisky, I., Mussa-Ivaldi, F.A., Karniel, A.: A Regression and Boundary-Crossing-Based Model for the Perception of Delayed Stiffness. IEEE Transactions on Haptics 1, 73–82 (2008)
5. Nisky, I., Karniel, A.: Proximodistal gradient in the perception of delayed stiffness. In: Virtual Rehabilitation 2009, Haifa, Israel (2009)
6. Nisky, I., Baraduc, P., Karniel, A.: Proximodistal gradient in perception of delayed stiffness. Journal of Neurophysiology (in press)
7. Pressman, A., Nisky, I., Karniel, A., Mussa-Ivaldi, F.A.: Probing Virtual Boundaries and the Perception of Delayed Stiffness. Advanced Robotics 22, 119–140 (2008)
8. Abolhassani, N., Patel, R., Moallem, M.: Needle insertion into soft tissue: A survey. Medical Engineering & Physics 29, 413–431 (2007)
9. Okamura, A.M., Simone, C., O'Leary, M.D.: Force modeling for needle insertion into soft tissue. IEEE Transactions on Biomedical Engineering 51, 1707–1716 (2004)
10. Niemeyer, G., Slotine, J.J.E.: Telemanipulation with time delays. International Journal Robotic Research 23, 873–890 (2004)
11. Lawrence, D.A.: Stability and Transparency in Bilateral Teleoperation. IEEE Transactions on Robotics and Automation 9, 624–627 (1993)
12. Miall, R.C., Wolpert, D.M.: Forward Models for Physiological Motor Control. Neural Networks 9, 1265–1279 (1996)
13. Nisky, I., Mussa-Ivaldi, F.A., Karniel, A.: Perceptuo-motor transparency in bilateral teleoperation. In: 9th biannial ASME conference on engineering systems design and analysis ESDA 2008, Haifa, Israel, vol. 2, pp. 449–456 (2008)
14. Wichmann, F.A., Hill, N.J.: The psychometric function: I. Fitting, sampling, and goodness of fit. Perception Psychophysics 63, 1293–1313 (2001)

Parallel Kinematics for Haptic Feedback in Three Degrees of Freedom: Application in a Handheld Laparoscopic Telemanipulation System

Sebastian Kassner[*] and Roland Werthschützky

Technische Universität Darmstadt, Institute of Electromechanical Design,
Merckstr. 25, 64283 Darmstadt, Germany
{s.kassner,werthschuetzky}@emk.tu-darmstadt.de
http://www.emk.tu-darmstadt.de

Abstract. In this paper parallel kinematic structures are analyzed to realize a haptic joystick with three translational degrees of freedom. The Chebychev–Grübler–Kutzbach criterion is applied to determine kinematic topologies. Resulting topologies are listed comprising prismatic, rotational, universal and cylindrical joints. Furthermore restrictions are compiled to enforce pure translational behaviour. An RUU mechanism is chosen as an applicable structure and adapted to be applied in a handheld control interface for a laparoscopic telesurgical system. An algorithm has been implemented to determine workspace size and shape. Three exemplary workspace shapes are shown and the occurring actor torques are calculated using the Jacobian matrix.

Keywords: minimally invasive surgery, parallel kinematic, topologies, translational parallel machines, workspace, force transmission.

1 Introduction

While being applied to more and more fields of minimally invasive surgery, laparoscopic[1] interventions are still accompanied by two major drawbacks:

1. *Limited degrees of freedom (DOF)* since laparoscopic instruments can be operated in only four DOF, given by the trocar[2].
2. *Poor haptic feedback* since the mass of the surgery tool has to be accelerated and high friction in the trocar has to be overcome [1].

1.1 The INKOMAN System

To approach these restrictions we introduced the concept of INKOMAN (intra corporeal manipulator), a handheld teleoperation system with multiple DOF and haptic feedback [2] (Figure 1).

---

[*] Corresponding author.
[1] Minimally invasive surgical technique in the abdomen (part of the body between the thorax (chest) and pelvis) using long rigid instruments through small incisions.
[2] Hollow cylinder, entry port through abdominal wall.

A.M.L. Kappers et al. (Eds.): EuroHaptics 2010, Part I, LNCS 6191, pp. 219–224, 2010.

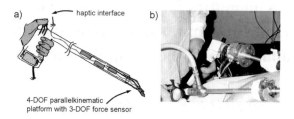

Fig. 1. a) concept of INKOMAN b) prototype in an animal experiment on a pig

This surgical tool consists of a intracorporeal parallel kinematic platform which provides four additional DOF, driven by position controlled piezoelectric actuators. The haptic feedback is based on a novel 3-DOF force sensor at the tip of the instrument [4]. The system is controlled in all four DOF by a man-machine interface which is operated by a single hand. Core part of the interface is a thumb-controlled joystick which will provide a spatial, pure translational haptic feedback to the surgeon. A more detailed description of the control strategy can be found in [3].

1.2 Scope of This Paper

This paper presents a preliminary study on applicable kinematic structures to realize the haptic joystick and transmit a spatial haptic feedback to the surgeon's thumb. An appropriate structure is chosen and adapted for the given application.

2 Kinematic Structures

Since parallel kinematic structures usually represent stiff structures with respect to their self-weight they are able to transmit high-dynamic force signals in multiple DOF. Therefore they are well suited to be applied in haptic applications. However they usually provide a smaller workspace and more inhomogeneous transmission behaviour in comparison to serial structures.

This section presents the topological synthesis of suitable mechanisms and the selection of an applicable kinematic structure.

2.1 Kinematic Topologies in 3 DOF

In order to obtain applicable parallel kinematic topologies the Chebychev-Grübler-Kutzbach criterion for mobility calculation of multi-loop mechanisms is applied to determine the sum f_g of joint DOF f_i with respect to the mechanism's DOF N:

$$f_g = \sum f_i = N + 6 \cdot (k - 1) \tag{1}$$

A fully parallel mechanism is obtained by $k = 3$ kinematic chains. Therefore one gets $f_g = 15$ DOF which have to be distributed in three kinematic chains, five DOF in each chain. In terms of actuation rotatory joints can be realized by rotatory motors as linear joints can be realized by linear motors. Compared to other publications (e.g. [5]) cylindrical joints where especially incorporated in the analysis. This was done in order to regard the actuation by a linear piston with a passiv rotatory degree of freedom as used in hydraulic drives for instance.

Hence the resulting topologies are listed in Table 1.

Table 1. Topologies for 3-DOF structures, joints: P prismatic (1 DOF), R rotational (1 DOF), U universal (2 DOF, R+R), C cylindrical (2 DOF, P+R)

Joints in one chain	Topologies
1x 1 DOF 2x 2 DOF	UUP, UPU, PUU, UUR, URU, RUU, CUP, CPU, CUR, CRU, RCU, UCP, UPC, PCU, UCR, URC, RUC, CCP, CPC, PCC, CCR, CRC, RCC
2x 1 DOF 1x 3 DOF	SPP, SRR, SPR, SRP, PSP, RSP, PSR, RSR, PPS, RRS, RPS, PRS
3x 1 DOF 1x 2 DOF	RRRU, RRUR, URRR, RRPU, RRUP, RURP, URRP, RPRU, RPUR, RUPR, URPR, PRRU, PRUR, PURR, UPRR, RPPU, RPUP, RUPP, URPP, PRPU, PRUP, PURP, UPRP, PPPU, PPUP, PUPP, UPPP, RRRC, RRCR, RCRR, CRRR, RRPC, RRCP, RCRP, CRRP, RPRC, RPCR, RCPR, CRPR, PRRC, PRCR, PCRR, CPRR, RPPC, RPCP, RCPP, PRPC, PCRP, PPPC, PPCP, PCPP, CPPP
5x 1 DOF	29 iterations of P and R joints

As mentioned above the haptic feedback should be provided in three translational DOF. Therefore further boundary conditions have to be introduced to obtain pure (x, y, z) behaviour at the mechanism's TCP platform. According to CARRICATO ET AL. [6] a TPM is obtained by using amongst others the following restrictions:

1. a single leg with three DOF which prevents all platform rotations
2. a leg with four DOF and one leg with five DOF, the former eliminating two DOF of rotation, the latter one DOF
3. three legs with five DOF, each one eliminating one rotational DOF

Applying the conditions to the topologies in Table 1 one obtains the applicable mechanisms to provide a haptic feedback in three pure translational DOF: UPU, PUU, RUU, RUC, CUR, CRU.

2.2 Actuation Principle and Topology Selection

The task of INKOMAN's man-machine interface is to display reasonably low mechanical impedances of soft liver tissue with visco-elastic properties. Therefore an impedance controlled (open-loop) structure was chosen as the appropriate system architecture. Rotational brushless DC-motors with a sinusoidal commutation will be used as the actuation principle.

Having a rotatory joint attached to the base platform the RUU and RUC mechanisms are the first topologies to look at. CUR and CRU imply the drawback of moved actuators with reasonable high self-weight and thus an unrequested impact on the device's dynamic behaviour.

The RUU mechanism creates translational motion only by using rotational joints. Thus it has only a small tendency to cant due to shear forces within the sliding motion of a C-joint as used in RUC. Therefore the RUU mechanism is chosen to be applied in INKOMAN's haptic interface.

3   Adapting a 3-RUU Mechanism

Figure 2 shows the RUU mechanism. Its kinematic relations were derived by TSAI and JOSHI [8]. To be applied as a haptic man-machine interface two major issues have to be analyzed: workspace and the force transmission behaviour.

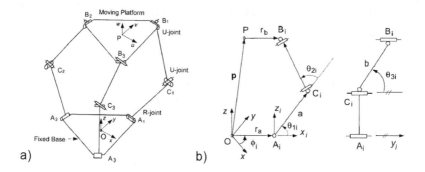

Fig. 2. a) RUU mechanism b) joint angles of one leg [8]

3.1   Workspace

The inverse kinematic

$$\mathbf{q} = f(\mathbf{p}) \tag{2}$$

is used to determine the joint angles $\mathbf{q} = [\theta_{1i}, \theta_{2i}, \theta_{3i}]^T$ of the ith leg with $\mathbf{p} = [p_x, p_y, p_z]^T$ the position of the TCP. Solutions for $\theta_{1i}(\mathbf{p})$, $\theta_{2i}(\mathbf{p})$ and $\theta_{3i}(\mathbf{p})$ are given in [8]. To determine size and shape of the workspace W a sample algorithm has been implemented which solves Equation 2 in a cube with edge lengths l_x, l_y, l_z and a resolution of Δl in each dimension. It is $\mathbf{p} \in W$ when the solution of Equation 2 is real.

Figure 3 shows an exemplarily variation of workspaces by changing limb lengths a and b (see Figure 2) as a basis for a future optimization process. The hull surface is approximated using a Delaunay tessellation algorithm.

During operation of the device equation 2 is implemented using LabView on a "cRIO" (PAC-system by National Instruments) and calculates the position of the joystick based on the joint angles $\mathbf{q}$ which are measured by hall sensors within the brushless DC motors. Hence the surgeon's input commands are based on equation 2.

3.2   Force Transmission

Force/torque transmission in a parallel kinematic structure is expressed by

$$\mathbf{t} = \mathbf{J}^T \cdot \mathbf{F} \tag{3}$$

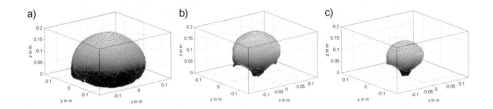

Fig. 3. RUU workspaces determined by the sample algorithm: a) $a = 8\,cm$ and $b = 12\,cm$, b) $a = 10\,cm$ and $b = 6\,cm$, c) $a = 12\,cm$ and $b = 8\,cm$, the size of the TCP platform is $r_b = 1\,cm$ and the size of base platform $r_a = 6\,cm$ for all cases, $\Delta l = 0.5\,cm$

with **t** the vector of actor forces/torques, **F** the vector of TCP forces/torques and the 3×3 Jacobian matrix $\mathbf{J}(\mathbf{q}) = \frac{\partial f}{\partial \mathbf{q}^T}$ whose elements are also given by [8] in closed form.

Previous works showed that in the case on hand a haptic feedback up to $F_{max} = 5\,N$ has to be presented to the user [9]. Hence another algorithm has been implemented which probes each point of the workspace with F_{max} exerted by the TCP in x, y and z direction. Results showed that in 91 % (case a)), 83 % (case b)) and 79 % (case c)) of the points a maximum feedback can be excited by actor torques $M_{actor} \leq 1\,Nm$. However, actor torques scale up to $1.2 \cdot 10^4\,Nm$ near singular positions.

Equation 3 is also implemented on the "cRIO" system and calculates the required actor torques with respect to the position of the joystick and the intracorporeal measured forces. Hereupon the corresponding currents are fed into the motors and the torques are generated.

4   Conclusions and Further Work

In this paper classes of parallel kinematic structures are discussed to realize a haptic joystick with three translational DOF. An applicable structure is determined and workspace and force transmission behaviour is calculated for three configurations. Future work comprises the optimization of the RUU structure and the determination of the mechanism's dimensions. Furthermore the analysis of the system's multibody behaviour is under way since it is essential to the quality of the haptic feedback.

The presented work embodies the basis for the realization of a unique man-machine interface which provides a high quality three dimensional feedback and easy usability in terms of the high demands of the surgical context.

References

1. van der Putten, E., Goossens, R., Jakimowicz, J., Dankelman, J.: Haptics in minimally invasive surgery-a review. Minim. Invasive Ther. Allied Technol. 17, 3–16 (2008)
2. Schlaak, H., Röse, A., Wohlleber, C., Kassner, S., Werthschützky, R.: A Novel Laparoscopic Instrument with Multiple Degrees of Freedom and Intuitive Control. In: 4th European Congress for Medical and Biomedical Engineering 2008, pp. 1660–1663. Springer, Heidelberg (2008)

3. Kassner, S., Röse, A., Werthschützky, R., Schlaak, H.: Operational Concept for a Handheld Laparoscopic Telemanipulation System: Design and Animal Experiment. In: World Congress on Medical Physics and Biomedical Engineering, Munich, Germany, September 7 - 12, pp. 317–320. Springer, Heidelberg (2009)
4. Rausch, J., Werthschützky, R.: Development of Piezoresisitve Strain Gauges for Multi-Component Force Measurement in Minimally Invasive Surgery. In: Proceedings of EuroSensors 2008 (2008)
5. Tsai, L., Joshi, S.: Kinematics and Optimization of a Spatial 3-UPU Parallel Manipulator. Journal of Mechanical Design 122, 439–446 (2000)
6. Carricato, M., Parenti-Castelli, V.: Singularity-Free Fully-Isotropic Translational Parallel Mechanisms. The International Journal of Robotics Research 21, 161–174 (2002)
7. Kassner, S., Rausch, J., Kohlstedt, A., Werthschtzky, R.: Analysis of mechanical properties of liver tissue as a design criterion for the development of a haptic laparoscopic tool. In: Proc. 4th European Congress for Medical and Biomedical Engineering 2008, pp. 2248–2251. Springer, Heidelberg (2009)
8. Tsai, L., Joshi, S.: Kinematic Analysis of 3-DOF Position Mechanisms for Use in Hybrid Kinematic Machines. Journal of Mechanical Design 124, 245–253 (2002)
9. Rausch, J., Röse, A., Werthschützky, R., Schlaak, H.: INKOMAN-Analysis of mechanical behaviour of liver tissue during intracorporal interaction. In: Gemeinsame Jahrestagung der Deutschen, Österreichischen und Schweizerischen Gesellschaften für Biomedizinische Technik (2006)

Mechanical Impedance: A Cobotic and Haptic Actuators Performance Criterion

Jonathan Van Rhijn[1,2], Alain Riwan[1], Ziad Jabbour[1], and Vigen Arakelyan[2]

[1] CEA, LIST, Interactive Robotics Laboratory,
Fontenay aux Roses, F- 92265, France
{jonathan.van-rhijn,alain.riwan,ziad.jabbour}@cea.com
[2] Departement de Génie Mécanique et Automatique
Institut National des Sciences Appliquées
20, av. Des Buttes de Coësmes, CS 14315
F-35043 Rennes Cedex, France
Vigen.arakelyan@insa-rennes.fr

Abstract. The Surgicobot is a cobot arm designed to generate high and low mechanical impedance though force feedback. We propose to use the impedance amplitude range in frequency domain as a comparision criterion to choose the best solution for the surgicobot actuation. We study different actuators to find the ones with best transparency and impedance capacity: low power electric motor combined with reconfigurable mechanical stops.

Keywords: Haptic, Cobotic, mechanical impedance, Surgicobot.

1 Introduction

The Surgicobot is a cobotic arm developed by the CEA (French : Commissariat of Atomic Energy). It will be able to secure and fasten the surgical tool's motion in the surgeon's hand. This cobot must be able to guide the surgeon's hand as well as preventing tool from entering in contact with some part of the patient. Those functions are performed thanks to haptic force feedback. To achieve the required level of performances the cobot must be able to generate extreme impedance with high effort capacity as well as optimal transparency in order not to add constraints to the surgeon movements when it is not needed.

To overcome this challenging tradeoff, we investigate the extreme impedance values reachable by different actuation systems to find the most efficient solution in the haptic and cobotic field.

The impedances modulations, in those systems, can be obtained by two ways: by changing the mechanical parameters of the robot (segments configuration and/or actuators properties [1],[2],[3]) or directly by simulating the desired behavior with the actuators control (motor control strategy). It is then easier to reach extreme impedance values if the mechanical structure of the robot has a wide impedance range by itself; regardless of the actuators control. It is possible to add elements in parallel or in series with actuators to change the mechanical characteristics of the actuating chain in order to bypass the weaknesses found in many actuators: The effort limits (electric motor's

A.M.L. Kappers et al. (Eds.): EuroHaptics 2010, Part I, LNCS 6191, pp. 225–232, 2010.

saturation torque for example) as inertia and dissipation losses which increase with actuator's effort capacity. This leads to a trade-off between transparency and maximum reachable impedance.

2   Mechanical Behavior and Limitations of Electric Actuators

Thanks to brushless Permanent Magnet Synchronous Motor (PMSM) coupled to a high precision encoder it is possible to simulate high stiffness [4]. The motor then reacts like a mass damper spring system (Fig. 1) with adjustable stiffness up to a maximum value (mainly depending on the encoder accuracy and controller performance) for input efforts under saturation torque.

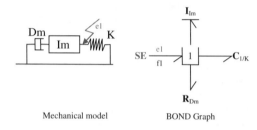

Mechanical model   BOND Graph

Fig. 1. PMSM simulating K stiffness with Dm the viscous damping and Im the rotor inertia

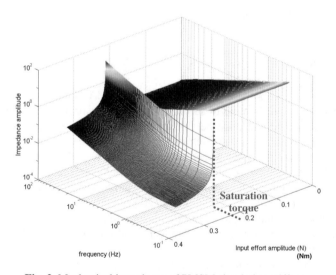

Fig. 2. Mechanical impedance of PMSM simulating stiffness

It is shown in (Fig. 2) that the stiffness falls down to zero when the input torque becomes greater than the saturation torque of the motor.

The mechanical impedance decreases as the input effort increases beyond the successive steps like dry friction torque and actuator saturation torque. In Haptic and moreover in cobotic the saturation torque is a strong limit: in order to stop efficiently the motion of the user, high torque capacity and high impedance are both needed simultaneously.

3 Comparison of Different Haptics and Cobotics Actuators Mechanical Impedance

The following study is a survey of several mechanical actuation systems used in haptics, cobotics and robots in contact with humans regarding the maximum and minimum impedance amplitudes that can be achieved.

This study includes :

Variable stiffness actuator (VSA) [2]. This system has impedance very close to the DM² [5] impedance with lower inertia.

Systems using magneto rheological fluid brake alone [6] or in series with a motor (Series Damper Actuator) [1] or in parallel with motor.

System with variable inertia (Continuously Variable Transmission : CVT) [7].

System with mechanical stop [8].

Stand alone electric actuator.

All systems are normalised to have the same torque capacity of 50 Nm, which corresponds to the maximal requirement for the project "surgicobot" and use the Maxon ECmax 40 (saturation torque 0.212 Nm) everywhere an electrical motor is needed. The mechanical parameters for each system are gathered in Table 1 and Table 2.

Table 1. Parameters of the stand alone ECmax40, the ECmax40 in parallel with CVT, the ECmax40 in series with variable stiffness and ECmax in parallel with magneto-rheological

	Variable Stiffness (min)	Variable Stiffness (max)	CVT (min)	CVT (max)	Parallel MR brake (min)	Parallel MR brake (max)	ECmax40
Dm (Ns/m)	$1.18.10^{-4}$	$1.18.10^{-4}$	$1.18.10^{-4}$	$1.18.10^{-4}$	$1.18.10^{-4}$	$1.18.10^{-4}$	$1.18.10^{-4}$
Im (kg.m²)	$1.01.10^{-5}$	$1.01.10^{-5}$	$1.01.10^{-5}$	$1.01.10^{-5}$	$1.01.10^{-5}$	$1.01.10^{-5}$	$1.01.10^{-5}$
N	236	236	1	1000	236	236	10
K (Nm/rad)	2	50	2000	2000	2000	2000	2000
Ib (kg.m²)	0	0	$1.6.10^{-4}$	$1.6.10^{-4}$	$1.6.10^{-4}$	$1.6.10^{-4}$	0
Da (Ns/m)	2.10^{-4}	2.10^{-4}	2.10^{-4}	2.10^{-4}	0.159	23	2.10^{-4}

3.1 Variable Stiffness, Variable Inertia (CVT), Magneto-Rheological Brake in Parallel or Stand Alone Electric Actuator Model

The Fig. 3 shows the model used to calculate the impedance. The mechanical impedance is given by equation (1).

$$Z(s) = \frac{e_1(s)}{f_1(s)} = \frac{K.N^2\left(I_m.s + D_m\right)}{N^2 I_m.s^2 + N^2 D_m.s + K} + I_b.s + D_a \tag{1}$$

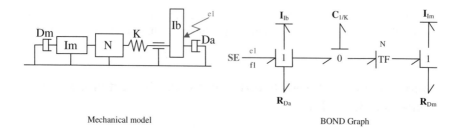

Mechanical model   BOND Graph

Fig. 3. Model of actuators using ECmax40 motor alone or with CVT reducer or magneto-rheological brake in parallel or with variable stiffness in series. With K the transmission stiffness, Dm the motor's viscous damping, N the reducer, Im the rotor's inertia and Da the arm's viscous damping.

3.2 Model of Passive System Driven by Magneto Rheological Brake Alone

The passive magneto-rheological fluid brake is the Lord RD-2068-10. Its torque capacity is 5 Nm so a $N=10$ ratio is chosen. The mechanical impedance is given by equations (2).

$$Z(s) = \frac{e_1(s)}{f_1(s)} = \left(I_b + N^2.I_m\right)s + D.N \tag{2}$$

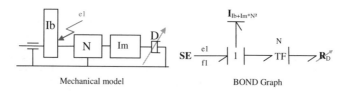

Mechanical model   BOND Graph

Fig. 4. Passive actuator using magneto-rheological fluid brake alone with N the transmission ratio, Im the brake's inertia and D the brake's viscous damping

3.3 SDA System Model: Magneto-Rheological Brake in Series with Actuator

The Fig. 5 presents the mechanical model of the Series Damper Actuator. We use a Lord RD-2068-10 brake. So $N_2=10$ and $N=23.6$ to comply with torque capacity requirement. The mechanical impedance is given by equations (3).

$$Z(s) = \frac{e_1(s)}{f_1(s)} = I_b.s + D.N_2^2 - \frac{D^2.N_2^2}{I_m.N^2.s + D + N^2.D_m} \tag{3}$$

3.4 Mechanical Stops Model

Using Mechanical stop produces unilateral high mechanical impedance with an optimal speed of transition from low to high impedance. When the stop is not in contact, all the components involved in high mechanical impedance are decoupled and thus do

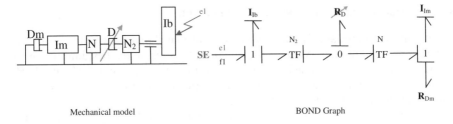

Mechanical model   BOND Graph

Fig. 5. Series Damper Actuator with *Dm* the motor's viscous damping, *D* the brake's viscous damping, *N* and N_2 the transmission ratios and *Im* the rotor's inertia

not affect the transparency. Contrary to PADyC system [8], the architecture considered is a mechanical stop driven through irreversible transmission which can safely generate very high passive torque with just small actuator.

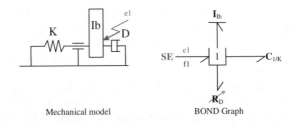

Mechanical model   BOND Graph

Fig. 6. Mechanical stops in contact with *K* the stop's stiffness and *D* the joint's viscous damping

The Fig. 6 presents the mechanical model of mechanical stop in contact; the mechanical impedance is given by equations (4).

$$Z(s) = \frac{e_1(s)}{f_1(s)} = I_b.s + D + \frac{K}{s} \qquad (4)$$

Table 2. Parameters of magneto-rheological fluid break alone (*MRB*), Series Damper Actuator (*SDA*) and mechanical Stop 1 : in series with cable transmission, and stop 2 : on arm's joint

	SDA (min)	SDA (max)	MRB(min)	MRB (max)	Stop 1	Stop 2
Dm (Ns/m)	$1.18.10^{-4}$	$1.18.10^{-4}$	--	--	--	--
Im (kg.m²)	$1.01.10^{-5}$	$1.01.10^{-5}$	$1.6.10^{-4}$	$1.6.10^{-4}$	--	--
N	23.6	23.6	10	10	--	--
N₂	10	10	--	--	--	--
K	--	--	--	--	2000	200 000
Ib (kg.m²)	$1.6.10^{-4}$	$1.6.10^{-4}$	0	0	--	--
D (Ns/m)	0.159	23	0.159	23	0.0002	0.0002

3.5 Extreme Mechanical Impedance Comparison

The mechanical impedance's amplitudes were calculated and drawn for the different systems presented in their extreme configurations to compare the best impedance and the best achievable transparencies. The range of frequencies, from 0.1 Hz to 100 Hz, enables to classify the systems responses in the frequencies range of the disturbance torque that can be applied by a human user.

The Fig. 7 shows the benefit of mechanical stop to obtain the greatest impedance value. The best transparency (lowest impedance) can be obtained with electric motor without reducer (without torque capacity required). It is particularly true for low frequencies. For higher frequencies, the systems allowing a decoupling of inertial elements such as variable stiffness actuator or CVT take precedence.

To design COBOT, other criteria must be taken into account to refine the selection such as the capacity to generate unilateral impedances and the speed of transition between maximum and minimum impedance. Systems with variable stiffness or reducer (CVT) use moving mechanical parts to change impedance which introduces a mechanical time constant in addition to the command that penalizes the reaction rate and decrease the realism of shock and contact simulation. Both systems generate bilateral efforts that do not create accurate impressions of contact while using the haptic interface in comparison with the performance of an electric motor with torque control simulating stiffness.

The results show the advantages of using drivable mechanical stop in parallel with electric motor. The presence of the mechanical stops enable to use low torque active actuator in parallel thus significantly improve transparency. When output effort increases, in high impedance configuration, the contact with the stops increases the mechanical impedance (Fig. 8) rather than reducing it as seen in classically actuated systems (Fig. 2).

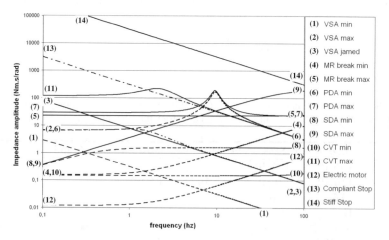

Fig. 7. Maximum and minimum impedance amplitude of *VSA* (variable stiffness actuator), *MR Break* (Magneto-rheological break alone), *PDA* (parallel damper actuator), *SDA* (series damper actuator), CVT (variable inertia), *Electric motor* (low torque capacity ECmax40), *Compliant Stop* (mechanical stop in series with cable transmission) and Stiff Stop (irreversible mechanical stop in direct contact with the output)

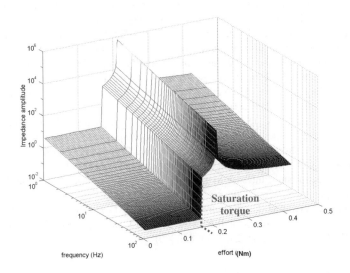

Fig. 8. Mechanical impedance of PMSM simulating stiffness in parallel with mechanical stop

6 Conclusion

The achievable impedances range in the frequency domain by the actuation systems in haptic and COBOT interfaces should be as wide as possible to faithfully reproduce haptic sensations to the user. Electric actuators can cover a very large impedance spectrum but unfortunately are penalized by efforts restrictions. The proposed solution to circumvent these tradeoffs between effort capacity and transparency quality is to use reconfigurable mechanical stop in parallel with low power electric actuator engines to guaranty optimal effort capacity in high impedance as well as good transparency.

This patented system is already studied in CEA-LIST to be implanted in the future "Surgicobot". This robot will be able to physically and passively bloc the motions of a surgeon to prevent any damage to the patient. The optimal transparency and the intrinsic effort capacity will enable to reduce the operation duration while increasing safety.

References

[1] Chew, C.-M., Hong, G.-S., Zhou, W.: Series damper actuator: a novel force/torque control actuator. In: 4th IEEE/RAS International Conference on Humanoid Robots, vol. 2, pp. 533–546 (2004)
[2] Schiavi, R., Grioli, G., Sen, S., Bicchi, A.: VSA-II: a Novel Prototype of Variable Stiffness Actuator for Safe and Performing Robots Interacting with Humans, Pasadena, CA, USA (2008)

[3] Faulring, E., Colgate, J., Peshkin, M.: High performance Cobotics. In: 9th International Conference on Rehabilitation Robotics, ICORR 2005, pp. 143–148 (2005)

[4] Jabbour, Z., Moreau, S., Riwan, A., Champenois, G.: Speed estimation comparison between full order state observer & Kalman filter for a haptic interface. In: IEEE International Symposium on Industrial Electronics, ISIE 2009, pp. 1482–1487 (2009)

[5] Zinn, M., Khatib, O., Roth, B.: A new actuation approach for human friendly robot design. In: Proceedings of IEEE International Conference on Robotics and Automation, ICRA 2004, vol. 1, pp. 249–254 (2004)

[6] Scilingo, E., Bicchi, A., De Rossi, D., Scotto, A.: A magnetorheological fluid as a haptic display to replicate perceived biological tissues compliance. In: 1st Annual International Conference On Microtechnologies in Medicine and Biology, pp. 229–233 (2000)

[7] Faulring, E., Colgate, J., Peshkin, M.: Control and Performance of the Rotational-to-Linear Cobotic Transmission. In: 14th Symposium on Haptic Interfaces for Virtual Environment and Teleoperator Systems 2006, pp. 103–107 (2006)

[8] Schneider, O., Troccaz, J., Chavanon, O., Blin, D.: PADyC: a synergistic robot for cardiac puncturing. In: Proceedings of IEEE International Conference on Robotics and Automation, ICRA 2000, vol. 3, pp. 2883–2888 (2000)

Online Intention Recognition in Computer-Assisted Teleoperation Systems

Nikolay Stefanov, Angelika Peer, and Martin Buss

Institute of Automatic Control Engineering, Technische Universität München
Theresienstrasse 90, 80333 München, Germany
{nikolay.stefanov,angelika.peer,mb}@tum.de
http://www.lsr.ei.tum.de

Abstract. Limitations of state-of-the-art teleoperation systems can be compensated by using shared-control teleoperation architectures that provide haptic assistance to the human operator. This paper presents a new approach for computer-assisted teleoperation, which recognizes human intentions and dependent on the classified task activates different types of assistances. For this purpose, time series haptic data is recorded during interaction, passed through an event-based feature extraction, and finally used for task classification by applying a Hidden Markov Model approach. The effect of the assistance function on human behavior is discussed and taken into account by training multiple classifiers for each type of assistance. The introduced approach is finally validated in a real hardware experiment. Results show an accurate intention recognition for assisted and non-assisted teleoperation.

Keywords: teleoperation, human intention recognition, shared control, computer assistance.

1 Introduction

Despite recent advances in the design and control of haptic teleoperation systems, they are still characterized by a high execution time, failure rate, and low performance when compared to direct human manipulation. Because of hardware or software limitations existing teleoperation systems cannot satisfy objectives like robustness, transparency, performance, and high degree of presence at the same time. Providing assistance when executing a teleoperation task is considered a valuable strategy to overcome some of these limitations. To provide, however, a suitable assistance at the right moment in time, knowledge about the actual executed task is required. Thus, an automated, online intention recognition algorithm must be implemented, which is able to recognize and classify tasks at the moment in time they are executed by the human operator. While reliable classifications are achievable in case no assistance is provided, the provision of assistance leads to a drastic change of human behavior which again results in a high probability of misclassification. A reliable classification for both, computer-assisted as well as direct teleoperation is, however, a prerequisite for a correct activation of the assistance function. In this paper we present an intention recognition algorithm which shows a high recognition rate for both types of teleoperation.

A.M.L. Kappers et al. (Eds.): EuroHaptics 2010, Part I, LNCS 6191, pp. 233–239, 2010.

1.1 Related Work

Haptic assistants are well known in the field of autonomous robot assistants where the scenario of collaboratively carrying an object has been studied intensively. Corteville et al. [1] e.g. proposed a robot assistant that actively supports the human while transporting an object from a given start to a prespecified target position. Their approach clearly goes beyond classical leader-follower architectures by implementing a robot that estimates human intentions from haptic signals and that contributes actively to the collaboration. Unterhinninghofen et al. [2] suggest a shared control assistance for bilateral teleoperation. The approach infers human intentions, predicts the trajectory of the operator, and based on this information applies corrections on the position signal at the remote side as well as activates forces of a virtual potential field at operator side.

Although the importance of identifying human intention and distinguishing between tasks is mentioned in both studies, Corteville et al. do not approach this problem online, but rather use methods for offline task segmentation and Unterhinninghofen et al. concentrates on a single task only such that no task classification is required.

Human intention recognition received more attention in fields like robot imitation, programming-by-demonstration, see [3], [4] and [5], or human-robot skill transfer [6] where mostly motion signals are studied and human intentions are represented on different levels of abstraction [7]. These kind of studies, however, do not consider any contact between human and robot and thus, intention recognition is unaffected by the actual robot behavior. This is not the case for haptic assisted teleoperation where human and assistant closely interact with each other.

In this work, we present an assistance control architecture which i) online[1] classifies the actual task by analyzing haptic data and ii) provides different types of haptic assistances. The presented approach takes into account changing human behavior in case assistance is applied and reaches a good task classification for both, computer-assisted as well as direct teleoperation.

2 Control Architecture for Computer-Assisted Teleoperation

This section provides an overview of the implemented control architecture for computer-assisted teleoperation. As illustrated in Fig. 1 a) a classical bilateral teleoperation architecture (solid line) is extended by introducing new building blocks for the computer assistance (dashed line). Since human operator and assistant share the control over the telerobot, a classical shared control architecture is realized.

2.1 Main Building Blocks of Computer Assistant

A detailed illustration of the computer assistant is given in Fig. 1 b). Its building blocks are briefly discussed in the following paragraphs. It generally consists of two main components, intention recognition and assistance function. The intention recognition block again contains two main building blocks, feature extraction and classifier. For a detailed description of these last two components please refer to our previous work [8]. Here only a short summary will be provided.

---

[1] An **online** algorithm receives its input incrementally and responses to each input portion.

Feature Extraction. The feature extraction algorithm uses haptic data as input signals and generates a highly compressed one-dimensional, discrete observation vector. The algorithm is event-triggered and emits a symbol if the input data crosses a certain threshold. This has a big advantage over sampling with fixed sampling rate as the resulting observation sequence is time-warping invariant and robust against noise and small variations in the human behavior ([8]).

Classifier. Since human intentions cannot be measured directly, but can be estimated by observing human behavior by means of a sequence of output symbols [9], multiple discrete Hidden Markov Models (HMM) are used for online intention recognition. For each HMM (each represents a certain task) the forward probability is computed and thus the first canonical problem over HMMs is solved: Given the HMM λ and an observation sequence $O = \{o_1, o_2, \ldots, o_\tau\}$ with $o_i \in V$, the probability that O is produced by λ is calculated. Finally, the HMM with the highest probability is assumed to have emitted the observed sequence and to represent the task the human is going to perform, respectively her/his intention.

Assistance Function. Assistance functions are highly task dependent and often introduced to enhance task performance in terms of precision or task completion time. Assistance can either concentrate on a single modality by providing visual, auditory, or haptic feedback or be multimodal when providing a combination of these. As the focus of this paper lies on the haptic modality, only haptic assistance functions suitable for the usage in shared control architectures are considered.

2.2 Intention Recognition in Computer-Assisted Teleoperation Systems

When activating the assistance function the human behavior changes, which leads to new patterns in haptic signals measured during execution of the task. Accordingly, the observation sequences generated by the feature extraction module change as well and thus, the previously trained classifier is not longer able to correctly classify these sequences. On this account, the influence of the assistance function has to be taken into account in the design of the intention recognition algorithm. A natural approach would be to compensate the influence of the assistance function on the recorded signals before passing them to the intention recognition algorithm. This could be achieved by applying the inverse of the assistance function on the recorded data. This approach assumes that the adjusted haptic signals used as input signals for the feature extraction block would have the same form as in the non-assisted case. Unfortunately, however, assistance functions affect the whole human interaction behavior and thus, patterns change significantly for the assisted and non-assisted case, compare e.g. Fig. 3. Consequently, when applying assistances the observed oberservation sequence contains symbols that are arranged in a different way than in the non-assisted case, which makes the classification fail. Finally, such an approach would also assume that the assistance function can be modelled mathematically, which can be difficult in certain cases. On this account, we follow an alternative approach to compensate the effect of the assistance function on the intention recognition. Instead of compensating the influence of the assistance function on the extracted features, we switch between different classifiers. For the non-assisted case as well as for each type of assistance function an own classifier has to

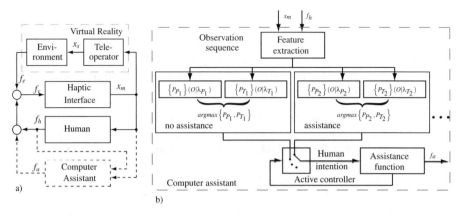

Fig. 1. Schematic view of: a) Control architecture for computer-assisted teleoperation; b) Computer assistant

be trained, see Fig. 1 b) for the case of only one assistance function. Since the information about the currently active assistance function is known, this information can be used to switch between the single trained classifiers. The drawback of this solution is obvious: it assumes that the task can still be performed even when having activated the wrong assistance function, because such training trials are necessary to train the single classifiers.

3   Experimental Evaluation

Scenario. For evaluation of the presented approach of online intention recognition, a scenario consisting of typical point-to-point movements is chosen, which requires repeated transferring of an object from a starting to a target position, see Fig. 2 a). In doing so, the subject applies a force f_h to overcome the inertia of the object and operates against friction f_r. The exercise consists of two randomly concatenated tasks: i) the transportation task (transportation of the object from the starting to the target position) and ii) the positioning task (positioning the object at the target location). Instead of using a teleoperation system with a real slave device, we used a haptic interface to interact with a virtual, haptically rendered object. In doing so, we are able to avoid artifacts originating from the communication channel and can easily perform experiments with various objects and environment dynamics.

To simulate the virtual object a haptic rendering algorithm was used which implements a rigid object with a mass of 3 kg that can be slided horizontally over a rigid ground. In order to increase the realness of the simulation, the following friction model was implemented:

$$f_f = f_{st} + f_k + f_v \quad \text{with} \quad f_{st} = \begin{cases} -f_h \text{ for } f_h < \mu_s f_N \\ 0 \quad \text{ for } f_h \geq \mu_s f_N \end{cases}, \quad f_k = \mu_k sgn(f_h), \quad f_v = \mu_v \dot{x},$$

where f_{st} is the static, f_k the kinetic and f_v the viscous friction and $\mu_s = 0.5$, $\mu_k = 0.2$ and $\mu_v = 0$ are the corresponding friction coefficients. The human interaction force

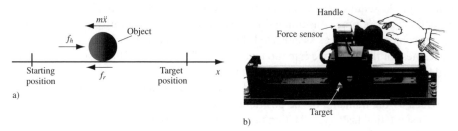

Fig. 2. Scenario and experimental setup: a) Object transportation and positioning; b) Admittance-type haptic interface

is denoted with f_h, the normal force with f_N. No visual feedback of the object was provided.

Experimental Setup. Experiments are performed using a 1 DOF haptic interface controlled by position-based admittance control, see Fig. 2 b). The interface is equipped with a force, position, and acceleration sensor and uses a linear actuator Thrusttube 2504 of Copley Controls. Its control is implemented in Matlab/Simulink and executed on the Linux Real Time Application Interface RTAI. The haptic rendering runs on another computer, and communication is realized by a UDP connection in a local area network.

Assistance Function. In the experiments an assistance function is used which aims at compensating static friction to ease the positioning of the object. A possibility to realize such a compensation is achieved by amplifying the force f_h applied by the human when she/he tries to move the object:

$$f_v = \begin{cases} k f_h & \text{for } \dot{x} \leq \varepsilon_{\dot{x}}, \\ 0 & \text{for } \dot{x} > \varepsilon_{\dot{x}}; \end{cases}$$

where k is a predefined fixed gain. This assistance function virtually reduces the weight of the object and thus results into an easier and faster manipulation, see Fig. 3. During transportation, however, the assistance is switched off, which allows the human to feel the real mass and friction between object and environment.

Experimental Results. The presented approach for intention recognition was evaluated by an experiment, where a subject who was familiar with the setup performed 10 trials (each two minutes long), consisting of random sequences of positioning and transportation tasks. The sequence of the tasks was determined by the subject and no special instructions were given how to concatenate them. The result of the intention recognition was visualized on a screen during runtime in form of text messages. Using a button the subject was asked to indicate whether the recognized intention was in agreement with her/his own intention. The used classifiers were trained offline by means of the Baum-Welch algorithm. To produce training data the subject performed each task 30 times in both, assisted and non-assisted mode.

In total 251 intentions were evaluated by the human, out of them 30.68% for positioning and 69.32% for transportation. The larger number of transportation tasks can be explained by the fact that transportation tasks consist of a single fast motion, while positioning tasks require several iterations even when assistance is applied and thus, their execution is more time consuming. Moreover, tasks were randomly performed following the subject preferences as indicated above. Please note that the human only rated the correctness of the identified intention while the effectiveness of the assistance function lied beyond the focus of the performed study.

In 70.73% of all cases, the recognized intention was in agreement with the feedback provided by the human. For the positioning task a recognition rate of 96.35% and for the transportation task a recognition rate of 59.6% was achieved.

As the probability of correct recognition by chance for our experiment is 50%, the overall recognition can be regarded as good. The lower recognition rate for transportation tasks can be explained by similar human behavior and thus observed patterns in both, positioning and transportation tasks, in case assistance is provided. This effect, however, can be reduced by dynamic adaptation of the symbol sequence length.

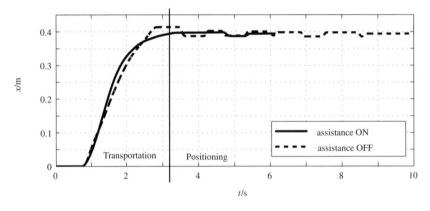

Fig. 3. Comparison of computer-assisted and direct manipulation in a transportation and positioning task

Discussion. The presented algorithm for intention recognition doesn't use any prior knowledge, like e.g. the sequence of tasks and thus, is most efficient when the behavior of the human is totally random. For such situations it clearly outperforms context-dependent methods that evaluate the second problem over HMMs to predict the next task to be executed.

Moreover, the proposed method is able to recognize human intentions, even in case assistance functions are activated. In such situations, intention recognition algorithms without compensation of the assistance function are doomed to failure, because of the changes in the observed patterns.

4   Conclusion and Future Work

In this work we presented an online intention recognition algorithm for computer-assisted teleoperation, which is able to reliable recognize the type of task the human is currently performing in case of assisted and non-assisted teleoperation. The approach is based on analyzing time domain haptic data recorded during execution of the task. The effect of the assistance function on human behavior is taken into account by training multiple classifiers for each type of assistance. The experimental results show good classification for stable human interaction behavior. Changing human behavior over time, however, reduces the recognition accuracy of the developed algorithm, and thus, a method for dynamic feature extraction to reduce this effect is currently under development.

So far the proposed approach requires an intensive training phase and provides reliable estimations only for the person who has provided the training data. Future work will consequently focus on reducing the required training data and fast adaptation of the classifiers to different human operators. Finally, the extension of the presented approach to tasks requiring more degrees of freedom is envisaged.

Acknowledgments

This work is supported in part by the German Research Foundation (DFG) within the collaborative research center SFB453 "High-Fidelity Telepresence and Teleaction".

References

1. Corteville, B., Aertbelien, E., Bruyninckx, H., Schutter, J.D., Brussel, H.V.: Human-inspired robot assistant for fast point-to-point movements. In: 2007 IEEE International Conference on Robotics and Automation, pp. 3639–3644. IEEE, Los Alamitos (2007)
2. Unterhinninghofen, U., Freyberger, F.K., Buss, M.: Study on computer assistance for telepresent reaching movements. In: Ferre, M. (ed.) EuroHaptics 2008. LNCS, vol. 5024, pp. 745–754. Springer, Heidelberg (2008)
3. Lee, D., Kulic, D., Nakamura, Y.: Missing motion data recovery using factorial hidden markov models. In: IEEE International Conference on Robotics and Automation, ICRA 2008, May 2008, pp. 1722–1728 (2008)
4. Aarno, D., Kragic, D.: Motion intention recognition in robot assisted applications. Robot. Auton. Syst. 56(8), 692–705 (2008)
5. Zollner, R., Rogalla, O., Dillmann, R., Zollner, M.: Understanding users intention: programming fine manipulation tasks by demonstration. In: IEEE/RSJ International Conference on Intelligent Robots and System, vol. 2, pp. 1114–1119 (2002)
6. Castellani, A., Botturi, D., Bicego, M., Fiorini, P.: Hybrid hmm/svm model for the analysis and segmentation of teleoperation tasks. In: Proceedings of IEEE International Conference on Robotics and Automation, ICRA 2004, April-1 May, vol. 3, pp. 2918–2923 (2004)
7. Aarno, D., Kragic, D.: Layered HMM for motion intention recognition. In: 2006 IEEE/RSJ International Conference on Intelligent Robots and Systems, pp. 5130–5135 (October 2006)
8. Stefanov, N., Peer, A., Buss, M.: Online intention recognition for computer-assisted teleoperation. In: IEEE International Conference on Robotics and Automation (to appear, 2010)
9. Duda, R., Hart, P., Stork, D.: Pattern Classification. Wiley-Interscience Publication, Hoboken (2000)

Evaluation of a Coordinating Controller for Improved Task Performance in Multi-user Teleoperation

Thomas Schauß, Raphaela Groten, Angelika Peer, and Martin Buss

Institute of Automatic Control Engineering, Technische Universität München
Theresienstrasse 90, 80333 München, Germany
{schauss,r.groten,angelika.peer,mb}@tum.de
http://www.lsr.ei.tum.de

Abstract. In virtual reality as well as teleoperation the interaction between multiple users is impaired by the mediated signal exchange between partners. To answer challenges of such scenarios assistance functions taking the interaction into account need to be developed. In this work, a coordinating controller implementing a virtual coupling between the participants is evaluated. Goal of the controller is to improve movement synchronization between partners leading to higher overall performance. As the coupling may cost additional effort, the evaluation considers an efficiency measure which relates performance to effort. An experiment is conducted with 20 participants. Contrasting the presented approach to relevant control conditions shows that the proposed virtual coupling results in a significantly higher efficiency: the relative growth in performance exceeds the increase in effort. Hence, the coordinating controller can be concluded to be a beneficial assistance for haptic collaboration.

Keywords: teleoperation, telepresence, collaboration, multi-user, coordinating controller, evaluation, performance, effort, efficiency.

1 Introduction

Manipulating objects over a teleoperation system or within a virtual environment is per se challenging. Joint manipulation of an object in a shared remote environment poses an additional challenge: interacting partners must coordinate their actions although the signal exchange between them may be impaired by the technical system. Thus, perception of the partner and environment, and joint action of the partners may not be as realistic as in everyday life. This is especially problematic when the task involves precise movements, or the object is valuable or sensitive. Adding a coordinating controller can help to overcome these difficulties and significantly improve coordination and thus, facilitate joint manipulation.

A known approach in this direction based on an adaptive controller was published in [1]. In their work stable interaction with the object is achieved by using an internal force controller. The object dynamics in the remote environment is canceled and replaced by a virtual object. This results in several drawbacks: Dynamic properties of the object are not observable any more by the operators, and forces applied to the object are predefined by the desired internal force. Furthermore, the effect of these issues on

A.M.L. Kappers et al. (Eds.): EuroHaptics 2010, Part I, LNCS 6191, pp. 240–247, 2010.

human performance, coordination ability, and feeling of presence was not studied since no evaluation was performed.

In [2] two new algorithms were presented for haptic interaction in virtual environments: a) a virtual spring is pulling both users towards the object and b) a virtual damping is guiding the partners towards equivalent speed of the individual movements. However, the results do not indicate that the newly developed algorithms lead to higher user-performance than approaches providing classical force feedback resulting from the interaction with the virtual environment only.

In [3] we introduced a new coordinating controller: it adds a virtual coupling between the two interacting partners, which consists of a damper acting on the relative speed of the two systems. The goal of this paper is to investigate the potential of this controller to improve task performance in multi-user setups.

1.1 Coordinating Controller

Fig. 1 depicts the coordinating control structure developed in [3]: Two single-user teleoperation systems (system 1/2) are connected using a *virtual coupling* $Z_{cm}(c)$ which generates a force f_{cm} proportional to the relative desired motion $x_{d1} - x_{d2}$ of the single systems. The virtual coupling is only active in contact. Contact phases ($c = 1$) are distinguished from non-contact phases ($c = 0$) by a force threshold: if the two teleoperator arms push against each other with a force of 1 N or above this is determined as contact, if the force is below this threshold this is determined as non-contact[1]. As virtual coupling we consider the impedance

$$Z_{cm} = c\, b_{cm} s. \tag{1}$$

Therefore, the two systems are coupled via a virtual damping b_{cm}. The force f_{cm} generated by the virtual coupling is fed into the virtual admittance Y_v of each system together with the respective measured forces f_{m1} / f_{m2} from master side and f_{s1} / f_{s2} from slave side. For the virtual admittance Y_v a mass-damper system

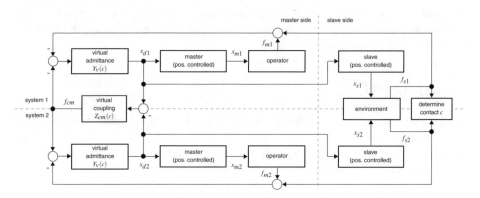

Fig. 1. Control structure of coordinating controller

---

[1] The threshold of 1 N was determined as suitable with pre-studies.

$$Y_v = \frac{1}{m_d s^2 + c\, b_{dc} s + (1-c)\, b_{df} s} \qquad (2)$$

is used in which m_d is the desired mass and damping can be switched depending on the contact situation, i.e. the damping is b_{df} during free-space motion and b_{dc} in contact. The desired positions x_{d1} / x_{d2} generated by the two admittance models are used as input for position-controlled haptic interfaces on master side and teleoperator arms on slave side[2].

1.2   Research Questions

The research questions raised in the experimental evaluation consider the efficiency (relation between performance and physical effort) of haptic interaction. This is motivated by the fact that we want to relate performance benefit to the increased physical effort which may accompany higher damping parameters.

Virtual coupling: If the two partners, who jointly perform the haptic interaction task are coupled via a damper, asynchronous movements of the two partners are prevented. This should avoid mistakes like dropping the object. Furthermore, we assume that the coupling does not provoke additional physical effort (forces) during task completion, as long as the two partners move in synchrony. Hence, we expect a higher performance if virtual coupling is provided ($b_{cm} > 0$). In addition, we will examine the effect of virtual coupling on physical effort and efficiency.

Damping: We want to determine whether an increase in task performance and efficiency is caused by higher damping in general or specifically by the virtual coupling between the two partners. Therefore, we vary damping b_{df} and b_{dc} of the separate systems to access this effect. Higher damping is expected to increase the effort necessary to perform movements. However, additional damping can also be seen as a low pass filter for movements which may lead to a more stable interaction, i.e. the partner's movements become more predictable which might lead to better performance.

Repetition: A well-trained dyad could benefit less than unfamiliar partners from the coordinating controller. As a preliminary investigation, we analyze repetitions of the same task to check for learning effects.

2   Experiment

Two partners manipulated a 4 degrees of freedom (DOF) haptic interface each, which allowed them to control two teleoperator arms with 4 DOF (see Fig. 2). The devices provide all three translational DOF and rotations around the vertical axis. As rotation was not necessary to perform the task the devices were controlled to always have the same orientation of the end-effectors. The task was to move two objects (7.5 cm $\times$ 3.0 cm $\times$ 2.5 cm blocks made of polystyrene) sequentially in an instructed order to

---

[2] Computed-torque controllers with gravity compensation are used in the inner control loop, where PD-controllers compensate remaining modelling errors.

master 1   slaves 1 & 2   master 2

Fig. 2. *Experimental Setup:* One partner controlled the left teleoperator arm (slave 1) by using the haptic interface depicted on the left (master 1) while the other partner controlled the right teleoperator arm (slave 2) by using master 2

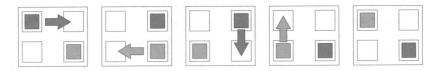

Fig. 3. *Instructions for one trial of the experiment:* The five images above were shown from left to right during one trial of the experiment. The two colored squares mark the positions of the objects at the beginning of the current manipulation, the arrows show the desired movement of the objects. Participants had to perform 4 moving operations, thereby swapping the position of the two objects.

four different positions marking the corners of a rectangle (compare Fig. 3). The objects had to be placed on top of pedestals (two cubes with an edge length of 2.0 cm, see Fig. 2) accurately enough so they did not fall down (an accuracy of approx. 1 cm was necessary). The teleoperator arms did not provide any grippers, which increased the difficulty of the task. Thus, it was essential that the two partners found a shared strategy to maneuver the object by pressing the end-effectors against each other. In addition to haptic feedback, visual mono feedback was provided over a camera image displayed on a monitor[3]. The participants were shown the task they had to execute by a presentation (see Fig. 3) which was shown on a second monitor. Haptic interfaces and teleoperator arms were located in the same room, leading to negligible time-delay. To increase the internal validity of the experiment participants wore headphones to prevent oral communication and a wall was placed between them.

We were interested in the effect of virtual coupling and "general" damping on performance and related effort. Therefore, we examined the two factors **damping** and **virtual coupling**. See Table 1 for the different conditions and related parameters (determined by pre-studies)[4]. As shown in [3] these values result in a robustly stable system.

---

[3] The camera covered the area in which the task was performed from a 45° degree viewing angle (relative to the horizontal plane) from the front.

[4] As mixed condition we consider the case with high damping in contact (b_{dc}) and low damping in free-space (b_{df}) only, as this could improve handling of the object while not introducing additional effort in free-space.

Table 1. Experimental conditions based on two factors (see section 1.1 for details)

Condition No.		Damping		Virtual coupling	
		$b_{df}[\mathrm{Nsm}^{-1}]$	$b_{dc}[\mathrm{Nsm}^{-1}]$	$b_{cm}[\mathrm{Nsm}^{-1}]$	
1	**low**	10	10		
2	**mixed**	10	100	**off**	0
3	**high**	100	100		
4	**low**	10	10		
5	**mixed**	10	100	**on**	100
6	**high**	100	100		

Although switching (when coming into contact and loosing contact with the partner via the object) was not considered in the stability analysis, no instabilities were observed during the experiments. In addition, a **repetition** factor (repetition number 1, 2, 3) is investigated to check for a possible interaction with the assistance functions. This results in a three (damping) × two (coupling) × three (repetition) completely crossed experimental plan which was realized with a repeated measurement design. The experimental conditions where executed in three repetition blocks within which the other two factors where presented counterbalanced. The experiment was performed voluntarily by 20 participants[5]. All had normal or corrected-to-normal vision and were right-handed. Partners did not know each other. The participants were instructed to perform the task as fast as possible.

The data is analyzed on the dyadic level. The performance of each trial is measured as the time from the beginning of the first contact phase until the end of the last contact phase (task completion time, TCT). This measure not only takes the speed into account but also penalizes dropping of objects by the time it takes to pick them up. The necessary precision to accomplish the task is constant over all experimental conditions. In addition, we investigate the physical effort with the mean absolute force (MAF), which is computed as mean of the Euclidean norm of the force vector over a complete trial. To understand the relation between performance and effort an efficiency measure is used which is introduced for haptic interaction in [4,5]. The (across the whole sample) z-standardized values (standard deviation = 1, mean = 0) of effort and performance can be utilized to examine the *relative* efficiency of conditions compared *within* the sample.

3   Results and Discussion

Descriptive results of the evaluation are depicted in the following: We show the performance measured in task completion time (TCT), the physical effort it took to complete the task (measured as the mean absolute force across each trial, MAF), and the resulting efficiency [4]. This is done for the three experimental factors: virtual coupling (Fig. 4), damping (Fig. 5), and repetition (Fig. 6).

We executed a 3-factorial repeated measurement ANOVA (analysis of variance, see e.g. [6]) separately for each of the three measures. As TCT was not normally distributed it was logarithmized before running the statistic test which is common practice [6].

---

[5] Mean age: 23.9 years, age range: 19 to 32 years; 3 female, 3 male, and 4 mixed dyads.

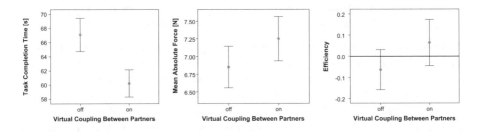

Fig. 4. Comparison between the two levels of the **virtual coupling** factor on the three measures TCT, MAF, and efficiency. Mean and standard error are depicted.

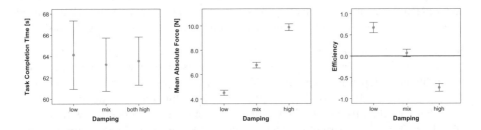

Fig. 5. Comparison between the three levels of the **damping** factor on the three measures TCT, MAF, and efficiency. Mean and standard error are depicted.

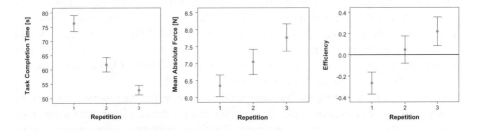

Fig. 6. Comparison between the three levels of the **repetition** factor on the three measures TCT, MAF, and efficiency. Mean and standard error are depicted.

Allocation of **virtual coupling** significantly (tested on a 5% significance level) increases performance compared to conditions where this feature is not provided ($F(1,9)=16$; $p<0.01$; partial $\eta^2=0.63$). It can be assumed that the coupling simplifies the task execution by preventing dropping of the object and avoiding asynchronous motion between the two partners. This leads to a lower task completion time. The fact that virtual coupling leads to higher mean effort ($F(1,9)=21$; $p<0.01$; partial $\eta^2=0.70$) shows that this assistance is actually active during the given task (partners moved in asynchrony). However, some of the additional effort may be caused by the shorter task execution time, which results in higher speeds and therefore a larger force. The time saving is such a big advantage compared to the risen effort that the efficiency is significantly higher with virtual coupling ($F(1,9)=6.0$; $p=0.04$; partial $\eta^2=0.40$).

Damping does not significantly influence task performance. However, with higher damping the applied effort increases as well ($F(2,18)=256$; $p<0.01$; partial $\eta^2=0.97$). The difference in effort reaches significance between all three levels (p-values of Bonferroni adjusted pairwise comparisons: low vs. mixed: <0.01; low vs. high: <0.01; mixed vs. high: <0.01). High damping can principally have two different effects: a) either participants perform slower movements or b) participants increase their effort to execute the given task: obviously participants tend to increase the effort to keep the performance on an equal level. Due to the effort differences, the resulting efficiency measure is significantly influenced by damping ($F(2,18)=98$; $p<0.01$; partial $\eta^2=0.92$) where all three levels are significantly different from each other (p-values of Bonferroni adjusted pairwise comparisons tests: low vs. mixed: <0.01; low vs. high: <0.01; mixed vs. high: <0.01): the higher the damping the lower the efficiency in the given task.

Repetition positively affects performance, i.e. with each repetition performance increases ($F(2,18)=39$; $p<0.01$; partial $\eta^2=0.81$). This effect reaches significance between all three repetitions (p-values of Bonferroni adjusted pairwise comparisons: 1vs.2: <0.01; 1vs.3: <0.01; 2vs.3: <0.01). In the effort measure significant differences between the first and third repetition are found, i.e. growing effort with training ($F(2,18)=10$; $p<0.01$; partial $\eta^2=0.54$; p-values of Bonferroni adjusted pairwise comparisons: 1vs.2: 0.11; 1vs.3: 0.01; 2vs.3: 0.15). We explain the higher effort by two effects: on the one hand participants learned that pushing their end-effectors together more strongly was a valuable strategy to prevent the object from falling down, on the other hand participants executed the task more quickly, thereby making a higher effort necessary to overcome the damping. Based on the performance and effort measures, there is a significant effect of repetition on efficiency ($F(2,18)=7.6$; $p<0.01$; partial $\eta^2=0.46$), where an increasing trend can be found with the number of repetitions. Only the first and third repetition are significantly different (p-values of Bonferroni adjusted pairwise comparisons: 1vs.2: 0.11; 1vs.3: 0.03; 2vs.3: 0.23).

There is a significant **interaction** between the damping and the repetition factors for the effort measure ($F(4,36)=3.6$; $p=0.02$; $\eta^2=0.29$): the differences between the three damping levels increase with more training. This finds an explanation in physics: as the task completion time decreases with the number of repetitions (thus velocity increases) the relation between the damping factor and the amount of force, which is necessary to overcome it, becomes more evident.

4 Conclusion

The evaluation of haptic collaboration in the multi-user teleoperation system shows that in the given task a coordinating controller, here virtual coupling, between partners increases performance. However, the costs in physical effort increase as well: whenever the virtual coupling generates a force facilitating coordination, this leads to higher forces, and thus to an overall higher effort. Relating both measures results in an increased efficiency for virtual coupling relative to task execution without that feature.

Contrasting the new controller to other damping-based controllers shows that higher damping leads to more applied forces (effort) whereas performance remains at a constant level. Hence, the increase in efficiency when applying virtual coupling is indeed caused by the coordinating controller and not only by adding more damping to the overall system. Performance also increases with training, and as this only causes relatively small additional effort, efficiency increases as well. This can have several explanations e.g. participants adapt to their partner and develop shared strategies or they adapt to the teleoperation system and task.

Virtual coupling was identified as promising coordinating controller for multi-user teleoperation systems. Future studies will focus on generalizing these results to other setups, tasks (e.g. for training or rehabilitation) and coupling parameters (e.g. spring-damper coupling). Furthermore, we are considering the possibility of functions which take the adaptation between partners into account. Finally the effects of additional oral communication could be investigated.

Acknowledgement

This work is supported in part by the German Research Foundation (DFG) within the collaborative research center SFB453 "High-Fidelity Telepresence and Teleaction".

References

1. Sirouspour, S., Setoode, P.: Adaptive nonlinear teleoperation control in multi-master/multi-slave environments. In: Proc. of the IEEE Conf. on Control Applications, Toronto, Canada, pp. 1263–1268 (2005)
2. Ullah, S., Richard, P., Otmane, S., Naud, M., Mallem, M.: Haptic guides in cooperative virtual environments: Design and human performance evaluation. In: Haptics Symposium (2010)
3. Tanaka, H., Schauß, T., Ohnishi, K., Peer, A., Buss, M.: A Coordinating Controller for Improved Task Performance in Multi-User Teleoperation. In: Eurohaptics (2010)
4. Groten, R., Feth, D., Klatzky, R., Peer, A., Buss, M.: Efficiency analysis in a collaborative task with reciprocal haptic feedback. In: The 2009 IEEE/RSJ International Conference on Intelligent Robots and Systems (2009)
5. Groten, R., Feth, D., Peer, A., Buss, M.: Binary shared decision making and efficiency in a collaborative task with reciprocal haptic feedback. In: IEEE International Conference on Robotics and Automation (2010)
6. Field, A.: Discovering Statistics Using SPSS. Sage Publications Ltd., Thousand Oaks (2009)

Effects of Force Feedback and Arm Compliance on Teleoperation for a Hygiene Task

Chih-Hung King, Marc D. Killpack, and Charles C. Kemp

Healthcare Robotics Laboratory, Georgia Institute of Technology
828 West Peachtree Street NW, Atlanta, Suite 204, GA 30308
aaking@hsi.gatech.edu
http://www.healthcare-robotics.com/

Abstract. Teleoperated assistive robots with compliant arms may be well-suited to tasks that require contact with people and operation within human environments. However, little is known about the effects of force feedback and compliance on task performance. In this paper, we present a pilot study that we conducted to investigate the effects of force feedback and arm compliance on the performance of a simulated hygiene task. In this study, each subject (n=12) teleoperated a compliant arm to clean dry-erase marks off a mannequin with or without force feedback, and with lower or higher stiffness settings for the robot's arm. Under all four conditions, subjects successfully removed the dry-erase marks, but trials performed with stiffer settings were completed significantly faster. The presence of force feedback significantly reduced the mean contact force, although the trials took significantly longer.

Keywords: force feedback, compliant arm, teleoperation, assistive robots.

1 Introduction

Safety is an important design consideration for human-centered robotics [1]. Many industrial robot arms utilize high stiffness and high speed actuation to increase precision and efficiency. While appropriate for controlled settings, these design choices can exacerbate the consequences of unintended collisions with people and the environment [2]. Many researchers have proposed the use of compliant arms to increase the safety of robots operating within human environments [3, 4, 5]. In addition, arm compliance has the potential to improve task performance [6].

For teleoperated robots, haptic feedback can enable operators to perform manipulation tasks using less force [7, 10]. It can also reduce task error [10], increase safety [9], and enable the operator to perform new tasks [8].

Given their individual benefits, combining haptic feedback and arm compliance would seem to be a promising combination for teleoperated assistive robots. However, little is known about the effects of force feedback and compliance on task performance. Haptic feedback has primarily been studied with stiff arms, such as surgical robots like the da Vinci System (Intuitive Surgical Inc.) [7, 10], or with arms that have only a little compliance, such as link flexion in surgical robots [11]. While a variety of compliant robots have been teleoperated, such as the Stanford/Willow Garage PR1 [12], and some have

A.M.L. Kappers et al. (Eds.): EuroHaptics 2010, Part I, LNCS 6191, pp. 248–255, 2010.

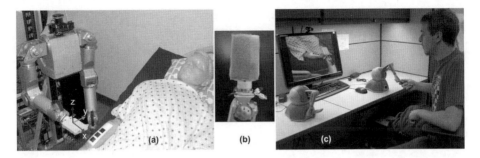

Fig. 1. The teleoperation system used during the experiment: (a) the compliant assistive robot Cody annotated with the end effector's coordinate system; (b) the customized end-effector used in this study; and (c) the master console with a PHANToM Omni and video

provided haptic feedback to the operator, such as DLR's Justin [13], formal user studies to assess the effects of haptic feedback and compliance on task performance do not appear to have been conducted.

We expect that haptic teleoperation of compliant arms would be especially important for assistive robots that are designed to help older adults and persons with disabilities perform activities of daily living (ADL). Research has shown that brushing teeth, shaving, cleaning and washing are high priority hygiene tasks for people with disabilities [14, 15]. Since this type of assistive task involves the robot operating near or in contact with a person, haptic feedback and arm compliance could be especially advantageous. As such, we chose to perform our study with respect to the task of cleaning a person's body. Although researchers have previously developed robots that assist with tooth brushing [14] and face washing [16], there has been relatively little work on robots that clean a person's body or provide other forms of hygiene assistance.

In this paper, we describe a teleoperated assistive robot that uses compliant arms and provides force feedback to the operator. We also present one of the first user studies to look at how force feedback and arm stiffness influence task performance when teleoperating a very low stiffness arm. Finally, we present evidence that teleoperated assistive robots could be used to clean a person's body for hygiene.

2   Teleoperation System

The teleoperation system consists of a master console and a slave robot. The slave robot is Cody (Fig. 1a), a statically stable mobile manipulator assembled at the Healthcare Robotics Laboratory (HRL). It consists of two MEKA A1 arms (MEKA Robotics), an omni-directional mobile base (Segway RMP 50 Omni), and a 1-DoF linear actuator (Festo DGE-SP-KF) that can raise and lower the torso. The arms are 7-DoF anthropomorphic arms that use series elastic actuators (SEAs) in all joints. The wrist is equipped with a 6-axis force/torque sensor (ATI Mini40). In addition, we mounted a video camera (Logitech Pro 9000) above the torso to provide video feedback. Two computers running Ubuntu GNU/Linux control the robot. The control software, operating at 100 Hz, was

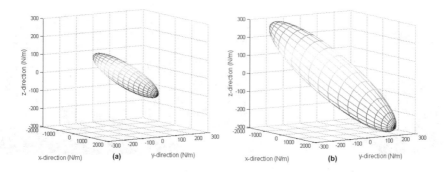

Fig. 2. Calculated stiffness ellipsoids based on manufacturer-provided specifications for (a) the more compliant setting and (b) the stiffer setting of the arm in its initial configuration (shown in Fig. 1(a))

written in Python using various open source packages, including the Kinematics and Dynamics Library (KDL, The Orocos Project) and the Robot Operating System (ROS, Willow Garage). We also designed and attached a flat, 3D-printed, spatula-like end effector (7.8 cm x 12.5 cm, Fig. 1b) to resemble an extended human hand. We attached white board eraser felt to the bottom of this end effector.

The master console (Fig. 1c) consists of two PCs and a pair of PHANToM Omni (Sensable Technology) haptic interfaces that provide force feedback in position only. Information between the master and the slave is transmitted over the network using ROS at 50 Hz to: (1) transfer the position and the joint angle information from the Omni to Cody; and (2) return the force/torque sensor data on Cody's wrist to the Omni. The Omni controller operates at 1 kHz and provides force feedback to emulate the force measured by the robot's force/torque sensor with a gain of two. For example, a force magnitude of 1N from the robot's wrist-mounted sensor will result in 2N of feedback to the operator. We implemented a first-order hold approximation on the measured force values to improve stability in the feedback loop. This resulted in smoother motion of the arm. The master console uses Skype to display video (640x480 pixels) at 30 fps on average, but occasionally drops frames.

We scaled and mapped the position of the Omni's wrist to a cuboid workspace that corresponds to the workspace of Cody's 7-DoF arm. We use the KDL to determine the configuration for Cody's shoulder and elbow joints so that the position of Cody's wrist matches the scaled position of the Omni's wrist. The system controls the orientation of Cody's end effector to match the global orientation of the Omni's stylus.

Our code controls Cody's arm using equilibrium point control for all arm motions except two joints in the wrist [6]. For these joints (pitch and yaw) Cody uses position control, which relates the motor output to joint encoder values and ignores torque estimates from the deflection of the SEA springs.

We used manufacturer-provided stiffness values for the joints of the robot with a kinematic model to compute the expected stiffness matrix of the end effector. In Fig. 2, we show a visualization of the the stiffness ellipsoid for each of the two stiffness settings used in our study [17]. These ellipsod correspond with the arm configuration and coordinate system shown in Fig. 1(a).

We also empirically measured the compliance in the upward direction (z-direction, see Fig. 1(a)) at the end effector. Since the orientation of the surface to be cleaned in our experiments was approximately normal to gravity, we expected the end effector to be mostly displaced in this direction when making contact with the mannequin during cleaning.

We measured the approximate force per unit displacement for the two stiffness settings of the arm using a spring scale and a tape measure. Our results show that the stiffer arm (M=61.7 N/m; SD=0.781 N/m) was only 1.45 times greater than the compliant arm (M=42.5 N/m; SD=0.660 N/m), which differs from our model-based estimate.

3   Methods

For this study, we designed an experiment to investigate the effects of force feedback and arm stiffness on a dry-erase cleaning task. The protocol was approved by the Georgia Institute of Technology Institutional Review Board.

Each subject used his/her right hand to clean off three squares on a dry-erase sheet colored by a black dry-erase marker. We attached the dry-erase sheet to the top of the right forearm of a medical mannequin that was lying down. The sheet's flexible surface conformed to the shape of the mannequin's arm. The mannequin was lying down on a hospital bed in a separate room to simulate a hospital or home-care environment and we secured its arm to its body to prevent large displacement during the experiment. A total of 12 subjects (age range 21-32 years), which consisted of male (n=11) volunteers and female (n=1) volunteers participated in the study.

We gave subjects 5 minutes to familiarize themselves with the dry-erase cleaning task and the teleoperation system. During the experiment, we allowed subjects to use any technique they wished to perform the task. Fig. 3 shows images from a typical example of the dry-erase cleaning task.

The dry-erase cleaning task consists of four consecutive blocks of trials with the independent variables of force feedback and arm compliance. In each block, a subject performed one trial of the cleaning task on three approximately 1" x 1" squares on the dry-erase sheet. In Block FC, we tested the subject using the compliant arm with force feedback. In Block FS, we tested the subject using the stiffer arm setting with force feedback. In Block NC, we tested the subject using the compliant arm without force feedback. In Block NS, we tested the subject using the stiffer arm settings without force feedback.

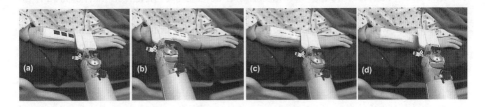

Fig. 3. Images of the robot during the dry-erase cleaning task: (a) the initial position of the arm; (b) swiping to the left; (c) swiping to the right; and (d) task completion

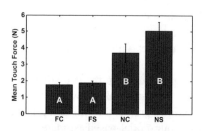

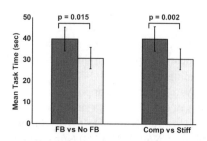

Fig. 4. The mean contact forces for each block: FC block uses the compliant arm with force feedback; FS block uses the stiffer arm with force feedback; NC block uses the compliant arm without feedback; and NS block uses the stiffer arm without feedback. Error bars show standard error of the mean. Bars with the same letter were not significantly different, while A and B were (p<0.01).

Fig. 5. Histogram of the mean completion time: all trials with force feedback (FB) versus without force feedback (No FB); all trials using the compliant setting (Comp) versus trials using the stiffer setting (Stiff). Error bars show standard error of the mean.

Before each trial, we informed the subjects whether they would receive feedback or not, but we did not inform them about the compliance setting. In order to reduce the impact of learning, we counterbalanced the trial order across the four blocks, with each subject receiving a unique presentation order using three partial Latin squares.

We stationed the robot at the same location near the hospital bed throughout the experiment. We initialized the robot to the standby mode, in which the forearm was positioned parallel to the bed with the elbow bent at 90 degrees. Before each trial began, we cleaned the dry-erase sheet before drawing new squares with a black dry-erase marker using a square stencil. We used a tripod-mounted camera to take an image of the forearm with the dry-erase sheet before the trial began (Fig. 6a), and we imaged the same area again after the trial was completed (Fig. 6b). In addition, we recorded the force/torque sensing data at the robot's wrist and the time to complete the task.

3.1 Data Analysis

For this study, contact force, task completion time, and the uncleaned marker area from the dry-erase cleaning test were the dependent variables. Since we were interested in the contact forces, we estimated when the end effector was in contact with the mannequin's arm. First, we recorded the magnitude of the total force vector measured by the wrist-mounted force/torque sensor while the end effector was not in contact with anything. We then defined a threshold (0.5N) based on this data that was equal to the mean of these recorded force magnitudes plus one standard deviation. For the rest of our analysis, we assumed that the end effector was in contact with the arm whenever the measured force magnitude was above this threshold, and was not in contact with the arm when the measured force magnitude was below or equal to this threshold.

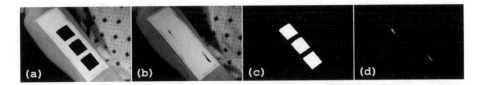

Fig. 6. (a) pre-trial image and (b) post-trial image of the dry-erase sheet on the mannequin's arm; binary image of (c) pre-trial image and (d) post-trial image where white pixels mean dry-erase marks remaining and black pixels mean no dry-erase marks

We defined the time to complete a task as the time between when the magnitude of the measured force first exceeded this threshold, and when it last transitioned from above this threshold to below this threshold. For each task, we calculated the mean contact force by averaging the above-threshold force magnitudes during the task.

We used an image taken before and an image taken after the task to quantify success at performing the cleaning task. Using standard machine vision techniques, we converted these two color images to binary images for which the white pixels represent dry-erase marks on the arm, and the black pixels represent the absence of dry-erase marks (see Fig. 6 (c) and (d)). Ideally, the image taken after the trial would have no white pixels, indicating perfect cleaning. We defined the marks-left ratio as the number of white pixels in the second image divided by the number of white pixels in the first image. Hence, perfect performance would result in a marks-left ratio of zero, while not cleaning anything would result in a marks-left ratio of one.

4   Results

We used within-subject, two-way analysis of variance (ANOVA) and Tukey's Post-Hoc test to analyze the mean contact forces, time for task completion, and the marks-left ratio. We consider a p-value less than 0.05 to be statistically significant.

Fig. 4 shows the overall mean contact force of all four blocks. The results indicate that the addition of force feedback reduced the mean contact force by a factor of 2 or more. ANOVA showed that there were interaction effects $[F(1,11) = 8.89, p = 0.01]$ between the independent variables on the dependent variable of force, and therefore we used Tukey's test to analyze the difference between blocks. The overall mean contact force during Block FS (stiffer arm setting with force feedback) was significantly less than during Block NS (stiffer arm setting without force feedback) ($p < 0.01$, Tukey's tests), while the overall mean force for Block FC (compliant arm with feedback) was also significantly less than for Block NC (compliant arm without feedback)($p < 0.01$, Tukey's tests). However, we did not find a significant difference between the overall mean force during Block FC and the overall mean force during Block FS ($p = 0.99$, Tukey's tests). The overall mean of the contact force during Block NC was less than during Block NS, but we did not find it to be a statistically significant difference ($p = 0.10$, Tukey's tests).

ANOVA of completion time showed no interaction effects. Subjects used significantly more time (Fig. 5) when using the more compliant arm $[F(1,11) = 17.03, p$

$\ll 0.01$]. Subjects also used significantly more time when force feedback was present [$F(1,11) = 8.30$, $p = 0.01$].

The marks-left ratios of all trials in all four blocks were much less than 0.01. So in every single trial, the subject successfully removed over 99% of the dry-erase marks. ANOVA and Tukey's tests showed no interaction effects for this dependent variable, and we did not find a significant difference between blocks ($p \gg 0.05$).

5 Discussion and Conclusion

For this pilot study, we developed a system to investigate the effects of force feedback and arm compliance on task performance with teleoperated low stiffness arms. When no force feedback was present, subjects used significantly higher force to accomplish the task. This result is comparable to results obtained for teleoperation of stiff arms with haptic feedback [7, 10]. This suggests that a teleoperator may use unnecessary force when performing hygiene cleaning tasks without force feedback, and that force feedback might reduce negative effects due to hyperforce, such as bruising and discomfort. Further study will be required to understand the implications of contact force in this task. For example, applying too little force may cause undesirable tickling sensations, while excessive force may cause discomfort or injury. We did not find a significant difference between the mean contact force associated with the two compliance settings. This may be due to the two stiffness settings being too similar, and due to a lack of data from our small number of subjects. A follow-up study with larger differences between the stiffness settings would be beneficial. A study involving stiffnesses comparable to stiff robot arms, such as the PUMA arm or the da Vinci System, would be especially interesting. It would also be worthwhile to consider providing additional haptic feedback from the robot's compliant joints, since important contact might occur anywhere along the arm.

Our time analysis showed that the task with force feedback required significantly more time to complete. One possible explanation is that subjects became more careful about the applied force when receiving feedback. For example, they may have reduced their speed to better control the forces. Another possibility is that reduced contact forces resulted in the removal of less dry-erase marking per stroke, resulting in more total. Time analysis also showed that the task with a stiffer arm setting was completed significantly faster, which may be due to similar reasons. All subjects were novices to the task, so further research into the impact of long-term use and expertise could be worthwhile.

We designed our simulated task in order to objectively quantify performance of the task, and avoid complexities such as water, which could damage Cody. Future work with more subjects cleaning real people over larger surface areas of skin would be worthwhile. Moreover, it would be worthwhile to perform a study to better understand interactions between the person being cleaned, the robot, and the robot's operator.

We believe this paper presents one of the first studies to characterize the effects of force feedback and compliance on task performance when using a teleoperated compliant arm. We expect for these factors to become increasingly important as more robots enter human environments and provide assistance.

Acknowledgments

We thank Advait Jain and Tiffany Chen for their help. We gratefully acknowledge support from NSF grant IIS-0705130 and Willow Garage.

References

1. Zinn, M., Khatib, O., Roth, B., Salisbury, J.: Playing it safe [human-friendly robots]. IEEE Robo. and Auto. Mag. 11(2), 12–21 (2004)
2. Haddadin, S., et al.: The role of the robot mass and velocity in physical human-robot interaction - part ii: Constrained blunt impacts. In: ICRA, pp. 1339–1345 (2008)
3. Pratt, G., Williamson, M.: Series elastic actuators. In: IEEE/RSJ Int. Conf. Intelligent Robots and Systems, vol. 1, pp. 399–406 (1995)
4. Shin, D., Khatib, O., Cutkosky, M.: Design methodologies of a hybrid actuation approach for a human-friendly robot. In: ICRA, pp. 4369–4374 (2009)
5. Schiavi, R., et al.: Vsa-ii: a novel prototype of variable stiffness actuator for safe and performing robots interacting with humans. In: ICRA, pp. 2171–2176 (2008)
6. Jain, A., Kemp, C.C.: Pulling Open Novel Doors and Drawers with Equilibrium Point Control. In: Proc. IEEE-RAS Int. Conf. Hum. Robo. (2009)
7. King, C.H., et al.: Tactile feedback induces reduced grasping force in robot-assisted surgery. IEEE T. Haptics 2, 103–110 (2009)
8. Tholey, G., Desai, J.P., Castellanos, A.E.: Force feedback plays a significant role in minimally invasive surgery. Annals of Surgery 241(1), 102–109 (2005)
9. Wagner, C., Stylopoulos, N., Howe, R.: The role of force feedback in surgery: analysis of blunt dissection. In: Haptics Symp., pp. 68–74 (2002)
10. Gwilliam, J.C., et al.: Effects of haptic and graphical force feedback on teleoperated palpation. In: ICRA, pp. 677–682 (2009)
11. Tavakoli, M., Howe, R.D.: Haptic Effects of Surgical Teleoperator Flexibility. Int. J. Robot. Res. (2009) 0278364909101231
12. Wyrobek, K., et al.: Towards a personal robotics development platform: Rationale and design of an intrinsically safe personal robot. In: ICRA, pp. 2165–2170 (2008)
13. Kremer, P., et al.: Multimodal telepresent control of dlr's rollin' justin. In: IEEE Int. Conf. Robo. Auto., pp. 1601–1602 (2009)
14. Hammel, J., et al.: Clinical evaluation of a desktop robotic assistant. J. Rehabil. Res. Dev. 26(3), 1–16 (1989)
15. Romilly, D., et al.: A functional task analysis and motion sim. for the development of a powered upper-limb orthosis. IEEE T. Rehab. Eng. 2(3), 119–129 (1994)
16. Topping, M.: The development of handy 1. a robotic system to assist the severely disabled. In: Int. Conf. Rehab. Robo., pp. 244–249 (1999)
17. Friedman, J., Flash, T.: Task-Dependent Selection of Grasp Kinematics and Stiffness in Human Object Manipulation. Cortex 43, 444–460 (2007)

Telepresence Technology for Production: From Manual to Automated Assembly

Marwan Radi[1], Andrea Reiter[1], Michael F. Zäh[1],
Thomas Müller[2], and Alois Knoll[2]

[1] Institute for Machine Tools and Industrial Management (*iwb*)
{marwan.radi,andrea.reiter,michael.zaeh}@iwb.tum.de
http://www.iwb.tum.de
[2] Robotics and Embedded Systems, Institut für Informatik VI
{muelleth,knoll}@in.tum.de
http://www6.in.tum.de/
Technische Universität München, D-85748 Garching, Germany

Abstract. In this paper a telepresence system for micro- and macroscopic assembly is presented. The proposed system integrates haptic devices on the operator side for reflecting gripping and collision forces as well as artificial scene information. Scaling of the position and force information is implemented to overcome the physical constraints of micro- as well as macroassembly tasks.

Furthermore, the paper introduces a flexible automation framework for teaching in action primitives, which the operator can then compose to incrementally complex assembly tasks.

This combination of a haptic telepresence approach with a user-friendly automation framework allows the manufacturer to cope with the challenges of todays industrial requirements.

Keywords: Telepresence Technology, Manual Assembly, Flexible Automated Assembly.

1 Introduction

Regarding the production process, assembly takes usually up to 70 percent of costs [1]. This is why efficient assembly strategies are an important issue in many industrial sectors. Efficiency is often achieved by automation, which is preferable compared to manual assembly regarding time, repeatability and accuracy.

Nevertheless, automation is just suitable for a very specific range of products, which can easily be handled and produced in high quantities. It may not be cost-efficient for production of small batches, which is meanwhile one of the important growing production trends to meet the demand of individualization and customization. Some of the challenges in production of such goods are flexibility and reconfigurability (e.g. the need of tool changeover and reprogramming the machines after each batch). In spite of significant advances in the field of artificial intelligence and industrial automation [2], human intelligence is far superior in terms of reasoning, language comprehension, vision, and ingenuity [3]. Therefore, people are still necessary to manage complex assembly activities for personalized and customized products.

A.M.L. Kappers et al. (Eds.): EuroHaptics 2010, Part I, LNCS 6191, pp. 256–261, 2010.

However, the ability of the human is hindered in some cases by physical barriers. For instance, the production of micro products demands fine motor skills and good visual perception to deal with highly precise components. Moreover, some materials can have adverse health effects on humans, e.g. radioactive materials or ones being too bulky to be ergonomically handled.

Considering these and other production trends in society and economy, it becomes evident that new assembly techniques are required. A promising solution to cope with the aforementioned challenges in manual assembly is the telepresence technology. Up to now, telepresence is rarely used in industrial applications, however recently researchers started to investigate the implementation of telepresence technology in these environments.

Okazaki et al. [4] designed a portable micro factory and an operator workplace equipped with a standard joystick without force feedback. For handling nano-objects a remotely controlled nano-manipulation system with haptic feedback [5,6] was developed. For other industrial sections, different robotic assist systems were designed with or without force feedback to manually guide industrial robots [7,8].

Considering small batch sizes, intuitively, performing an assembly task in a telepresent approach once while recording it, and replaying it several times makes sense. In contrast to a standard automation system, which requires time-consuming reprogramming, this flexible automation approach with telepresent teach-in takes just as long as the manually controlled telepresence task and exploits the superior human abilities.

In this paper, a novel promising approach to telepresent assembly applications ranging from individual prototypes to small lot sizes is proposed.

2   Manual Telepresent Assembly Systems

In this section, a generic telepresence system for the assembly of both micro- and macroscopic products is described (see Figure 1). The dominant characteristic is the reliance on readily available commercial components (e.g. personal computers and cameras) and standard industrial equipment (e.g. force/torque sensors (FTS) and manipulators).

Thus, the operator workplace consists of a haptic device and a monitor for visual feedback (see Figure 1). In order to make it easier for the human operator to understand the device's movement [9], it is preferred to have a simple input device, by which task-relevant degrees of freedom are enabled. Therefore, a 2-DOF force feedback joystick is

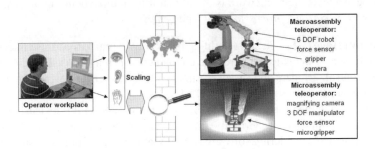

Fig. 1. Telepresence Systems for Micro and Macroscopic Assembly

used in this setup as an Input/Output device. This device receives the motion commands from the human operator and sends them to the teleoperator side via a communication link. The signals are scaled bidirectionally, i.e., the displacement of the device to motions of the teleoperator and haptic feedback information back to the operator. To allow the human operator to steer the teleoperator in three degrees of freedom, a mapping strategy is implemented. The user can select which DOF to be moved by switching in between.

The teleoperator for the micro assembly, which is located in a clean room environment, consists of a high precision planar table (x- and y-axis) and a linear drive (z-axis) with an accuracy of 1.0 μm. A vacuum gripper and a magnifying camera are mounted onto the linear axis moving in the vertical direction. A one degree of freedom force sensor, positioned on the planar table, is used to measure forces in z-direction and thus detect contact between the microgripper and the table.

For the macroscopic assembly, an industrial robot is used as a teleoperator (see Figure 1). It is a 6-DOF articulated robot with a nominal payload of 6 kg. The robot has a position controller with a real time communication interface, Ethernet Remote Sensor Interface (RSI). This RSI is used to connect the teleoperator with the central controller via the Ethernet TCP/IP protocol. For a pick and place task, a pneumatic gripper is mounted at the tool center point of the robot. A pan-tilt camera is used to give the human operator the visual feedback needed to accomplish the task.

3   Towards Automation of Assembly Systems

Although telepresence technology is considered a promising solution for manual assembly, it is not as profitable when switching from unique individual products to small batch sizes. Here, an approach combining the advantages of telepresence technology and automation techniques forms an efficient solution. Therefore, in this section a generic framework for flexible automation in the field of robot-assisted telepresent assembly is introduced.

3.1   Framework Overview

The framework presented here hence comprises a telepresence interface for convenient teach-in, and a graphical, user-friendly task automation facility. From a software engineering perspective, the framework is mainly built from three building blocks, namely the *information storage*, *processing unit*, and *generic interface*.

Generic Interface (GI). The first building block provides an easy-to-use interface abstraction for accessing external hardware components such as the real time connectors for robot control, grippers and servos, or image sensors, user IO-devices (mouse, keyboard, etc.), or other sensory devices, e.g. FTS.

However, implementing a generic interface is not limited to IO-devices, but indeed one can write an interface to virtually any external component, be it software or hardware. For instance considering software libraries, at the time of publication, the framework already provides predefined interfaces to the robust model-based realtime tracking library *OpenTL* [10] and the library underlying the efficient *EET* (exploring / exploiting tree) planner [11] for advanced industrial robot control. Additionally, in order to support seamless integration with external applications, interfaces for accessing socket connectors for remote control, data exchange, and remote procedure calls are supplied by the framework, as well as an interface for running arbitrary executables.

Processing Unit (PU). The base class for processing data, the PU, provides a configuration, control and feedback facility as well as a possibility to share information with other PU's. Furthermore, each processing unit is designed as a thread and supplies a description of the action it performs to the automation system (see Section 3.2).

Typically, an application comprises a set of PUs, where PUs perform their action either continuously or they are triggered by an event. While most hardware interfaces need a cyclic, continuous update/retrieval (such as the robot joint values or the camera interface), higher-level actions wrapped into a PU, e.g. moving the end-effector from A to B, handing over a workpiece to the next robot, or finding a grasping point in a visual scene, most commonly need a trigger-event in the assembly workflow.

Information Storage (IS). In order to map a complex assembly workflow, exchanging data between PUs is essential. For example, the input device unit maps to the target pose generation unit, which again maps to the joint values corresponding to a robotic end-effector.

The singleton information storage supplied by the framework is the building block designed for this purpose. Figure 2 shows the workflow for data registration, storage, and retrieval modalities as a diagram.

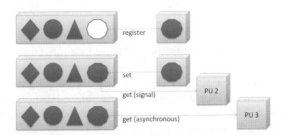

Fig. 2. Dataflow for a data item in the information storage

As shown in the figure, after registering a data-item, synchronous and asynchronous data access is possible, i.e. PUs can either listen for the event generated, when a data item has changed in the storage, or poll the data only on demand.

3.2 Task Automation

Tasks are generally described as a set of connected actions, where each processing unit defines a such action. In order to combine actions to a complex task, a generic action description comprising an identifier, IO- and configuration parameters, etc., was developed. Utilizing this action description, it is possible to specify a complex task by combination of primitive actions. These primitive actions, e.g., operations like "grasp", "screw", or "move-to *xy*", are taught in using the telepresence system described in Section 2.

Furthermore, the framework supplies an automation unit, which enables a user to transform a task into an action and generate a new processing unit (see Figure 3) from it through graphical interaction.

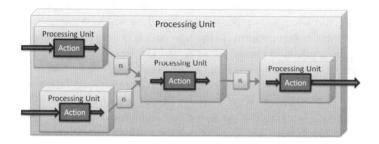

Fig. 3. Processing units can be generated online to combine a set of arbitrary actions into a more complex one for automation

These composite actions are then provided to the user interface for further combination, hence increasingly complex tasks can be automated. This enables the user to conveniently adapt a production system to a novel product variant requiring different assembly steps.

4   Conclusion

Addressing the challenges of manufacturing highly customized products, this paper presents a telepresence system tailored to micro- and macroscopic assembly tasks. The system integrates haptic feedback devices for reflecting gripping and collision forces as well as artificial scene information (virtual walls, etc.). Furthermore, the proposed system incorporates facilities to generate automation functions for small lot sizes, using the presented telepresence system for teach-in.

One can expect that the presented combination of the complementary techniques, namely telepresent assembly and flexible automation, will satisfy todays and future industrial requirements for highly adaptive production systems.

Acknowledgements

This work is supported by the German Research Foundation (DFG) within the Collaborative Research Center SFB 453 on "High-Fidelity Telepresence and Teleaction".

References

1. Chollet, S.K., Benmayor, L., Uehlinger, J.M., Jacot, J.: Cost effective micro-system assembly automation. In: Proceedings of 7th IEEE International Conference on Emerging Technologies and Factory Automation, ETFA 1999, vol. 1, pp. 359–366 (1999)

2. Brooks, R.A., Aryananda, L., Edsinger, A., Fitzpatrick, P., Kemp, C., O'Reilly, U.M., Torres-Jara, E., Varshavskaya, P., Weber, J.: Sensing and manipulating built-for-human environments. International Journal of Humanoid Robotics 1(1), 1–28 (2004)
3. Nichol, Z., Liu, Y., Suchyta, P., Prokos, M., Goradia, A., Xi, N.: Super-media enhanced internet-based real-time teleoperation. In: Hands-On International Mechantronics and Automation Conference (2005)
4. Okazaki, Y., Mishima, N., Ashida, K.: Microfactory and micro machine tools. In: 1st Korea-Japan Conference on Positioning Technology, Daejeon, Korea, pp. 150–155 (2002)
5. Fahlbusch, S., Fatikow, S.: Micro force sensing in a micro robotic system. In: IEEE International Conference on Robotics and Automation, Seoul, Korea, pp. 3435–3440 (2001)
6. Kortschack, A., Shirinov, A., Trueper, T., Fatikow, S.: Development of mobile versatile nanohandling microrobots: design, driving principles, haptic control. Robotica 23(4), 419–434 (2005)
7. Schraft, R., Meyer, C., Parlitz, C., Helms, E.: Powermate – a safe and intuitive robot assistant for handling and assembly tasks. In: IEEE Proceedings of the Robotics and Automation, ICRA 2005 (2005)
8. Krüger, J., Bernhardt, R., Surdilovic, D.: Intelligent assist systems for flexible assembly. CIRP Annals 2006 55(1), 29–32 (2006)
9. Deml, B.: Human factors issues on the design of telepresence systems. Presence 16(5), 471–487 (2007)
10. Panin, G., Lenz, C., Nair, S., Roth, E., Wojtczyk, M., Friedlhuber, T., Knoll, A.: A unifying software architecture for model-based visual tracking. In: Proc. of the 20th Annual Symposium of Electronic Imaging (2008)
11. Rickert, M., Brock, O., Knoll, A.: Balancing Exploration and Exploitation in Motion Planning. In: Proc. of the IEEE International Conference on Robotics and Automation (2008)

High Fidelity Haptic Rendering for Deformable Objects Undergoing Topology Changes

Hoeryong Jung[1], Stephane Cotin[2], Christian Duriez[2], Jeremie Allard[2], and Doo Yong Lee[1]

[1] Department of Mechanical Engineering, KAIST, Yuseong-gu Daejeon, Korea
[2] INRIA Lille-North Europe, Villeneuve d'Ascq, France
{jungh180,leedy}@kaist.ac.kr,
{stephane.cotin,christian.duriez}@inria.fr

Abstract. The relevance of haptic feedback for minimally invasive surgery has been demonstrated at numerous counts. However, the proposed methods often prove inadequate to handle correct contact computation during the complex interactions or topological changes that can be found in surgical interventions. In this paper, we introduce an approach that allows for accurate computation of contact forces even in the presence of topological changes due to the simulation of soft tissue cutting. We illustrate this approach with a simulation of cataract surgery, a typical example of microsurgery.

Keywords: haptics, biomechanics, simulation, surgery, soft tissue, cutting.

1 Introduction

High fidelity haptic rendering of deformable objects undergoing topology changes is a fundamental requirement in surgery simulation, in particular for the simulation of dissection or other processes involved in the separation of soft tissues. However, topological changes introduce several challenges, related to re-meshing of the domain, real-time simulation of the deformation, contact computation, and haptic rendering. Several approaches have been proposed for re-meshing the domain while maintaining a relatively good mesh quality [1]. Considering the deformation aspect, handling topological changes essentially requires the update of the stiffness matrix (assuming the deformation is modeled using a finite element approach). As most recent real-time deformation methods are based on non-linear models (geometrical and/or material) [2][3], which require an update of the stiffness matrix at every time step, the handling of topological changes adds little overhead to the process. The main difficulty comes from haptic rendering, in particular in applications where multiple complex contacts occur. Examples of such applications are common in surgery simulation. In this paper we consider the particular case of cataract surgery, an example of microsurgery where haptics can play a key role during training. Approaches for providing haptic feedback in the case of soft tissue interactions often rely on a simple contact point rather than an actual area of contact, and rarely account for friction. While such simplifications can produce plausible results in certain contexts, it can lead to incorrect results in some applications, such as surgery, where multiple anatomical structures can be in contact simultaneously.

A.M.L. Kappers et al. (Eds.): EuroHaptics 2010, Part I, LNCS 6191, pp. 262–268, 2010.

This paper introduces a new method for providing high-fidelity force feedback during soft tissue manipulation involving topological changes. The proposed approach can be seen as an extension of previous works on contact modeling [4] or haptics [5]. These works rely on the computation of a compliance matrix and resolution of a linear complementary problem (LCP). Although more computationally expensive than other approaches, such a method guarantees that all interpenetrations are solved at the end of each time step in the simulation while providing stable and efficient haptic feedback. The following sections present our contribution. Section 2 introduces the surgical context and background material regarding our simulation method. Section 3 describes the main contribution of this paper, i.e. an efficient numerical approach for updating a compliance matrix even during topological changes. Finally, section 4 presents some results in the context of cataract surgery simulation and section 5 discusses possible future directions.

2 Simulation Overview

2.1 Cataract Surgery

Cataract surgery, along with glaucoma surgery and vitro-retinal surgery, is one of the more frequent and difficult procedures of ophthalmic surgery. A cataract is an opacification in the natural lens of the eye. It represents an important cause of visual impairment and, if not treated, can lead to blindness. Cataract surgery has made important advances over the past twenty years, but remains technically challenging. The objective of our simulation is to reproduce with great accuracy the three main steps of cataract surgery: capsulorhexis, phacoemulsification and implantation of an intraocular lens. In this paper we focus on the phacoemulsification, which consists in using a microscopic surgical device which tip vibrates at an ultrasonic frequency (40,000 Hz) to locally fragment the natural lens of the eye. This progressively leads to the separation of the lens into several small parts, which can then be sucked out of the eye through a small incision.

Fig.1. *Left*: detailed anatomy of the eye, with the retina (in red), the cornea, and the lens. *Right*: the different anatomical models used in our simulation, and an illustration of the phacoemulsification device interacting with the tetrahedral mesh of the lens (the particular rendering of the lens is only for the purpose of showing the size of the tetrahedral elements).

2.2 Deformable Model

The dynamics of the eye lens is modeled using the FEM based differential equation:

$$M\dot{v} = F(u, v) + R \qquad (1)$$

Where v and u are velocity and displacement vector of the nodes. M is the mass matrix, R the vector of contact forces and F(u,v) is the sum of external and internal forces. In our case, we model the eye lens as a linear elastic material, which undergo large displacements. To model this behavior we rely on a co-rotational finite element method [3]. At each time step, we compute a linearization of the finite element model: $F(u + du, v + dv) = F(u, v) - Kdu - Bdv$, where K=K(u), the tangent matrix is non constant. As we will see in the following section, we can take advantage of this particular model to optimize the computation of the compliance matrix required in the contact solver and haptic rendering loop.

2.3 Contact Model

To solve for contacts occurring between the microsurgical instruments and the different anatomical structures of the eye (such as the lens, lens capsule and cornea) we rely on the method introduced in [4]. This method computes the forces required to solve all interpenetrations within a single time step, thus guaranteeing a contact-free configuration at the beginning of the next time step. The core computation of the algorithm involves solving a linear complementary problem (LCP).

$$\delta = HCH^T f + \delta^{free} \quad \text{with} \quad 0 \le \delta \perp f \ge 0 \qquad (2)$$

Where $C = \left(\frac{1}{h^2} M + \frac{1}{h} B + K \right)^{-1}$ is called the compliance matrix which needs to be re-

computed and every time step. Obviously the computation of C can quickly become prohibitive when the number of nodes in the mesh increases. To solve this issue, it is possible to take advantage of the co-rotational formulation, where non-linearities are mainly related to rotations. The computation of C is only performed for the rest configuration and updated at each time step based on a local estimation of the rigid motion at each node (see [4] for more details).

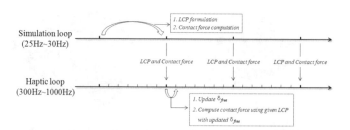

Fig. 2. Multi-rate haptic rendering technique. The inter-sampled force is computed using the LCP given by the simulation loop with updated δ_{free} at every time step of haptic loop.

2.4 Haptic Rendering

For the haptic rendering, which requires high rate (300Hz~1000Hz) force computation, we employ multi-rate haptic rendering technique [5], separating the haptic loop from the simulation loop. At every time step of the simulation loop, we build the LCP using the given compliance matrix, and compute the contact force from the LCP. And the LCP and the contact force are transmitted to the haptic loop so that those can be used to compute inter-sampled force between time steps of the simulation loop. In the haptic loop, the interpenetration depth δ^{free} is updated using new position of haptic device, and the inter-sampled contact force is computed using the given LCP with updated δ_{free} at every time step of haptic loop.

3   Topology Modifications

One of the basic tasks in the simulation of phacoemulsification procedure is locally fragmenting the lens of the eye with the microscopic surgical device. We simulate the action of the device on the eye lens by consecutively removing tetrahedra intersected by the tip of the device.

3.1   System Matrix Modification

When the tetrahedron is removed from the current mesh of the model, the local system matrix of the tetrahedron should be subtracted from the current system matrix:

$$\left(\frac{1}{h^2}\mathbf{M}+\frac{1}{h}\mathbf{B}+\mathbf{K}\right)_{i+1} = \left(\frac{1}{h^2}\mathbf{M}+\frac{1}{h}\mathbf{B}+\mathbf{K}\right)_i - \mathbf{G}_e\left(\frac{1}{h^2}\mathbf{m}_e+\frac{1}{h}\mathbf{b}_e+\mathbf{k}_e\right)\mathbf{G}_e^T \qquad (3)$$

Where, $\left(\frac{1}{h^2}\mathbf{m}_e+\frac{1}{h}\mathbf{b}_e+\mathbf{k}_e\right)$ is the local system matrix of the removed tetrahedron, and $\mathbf{G}_e$, $\mathbf{G}_e^T$ are the globalization matrices which map the rows and the columns of the local system matrix to the global system matrix.

3.2   Compliance Matrix Update Algorithm

As stated in section 2.3, the contact model relies on a pre-computation of the compliance matrix on the rest shape configuration. But the removal of tetrahedron makes this matrix no more valid as all values are affected. Since an element removal alters only a few entries of the original system matrix, low rank inverse update algorithms, such as Sherman-Morrison-Woodbury formula [7], can be a reasonable solution for real-time computation [6]. The modified compliance matrix can be computed from the current compliance matrix as follows.

$$\mathbf{C}_{i+1} = \mathbf{C}_i - \mathbf{C}_i\mathbf{G}_e\left(\mathbf{S}_e^{-1}+\mathbf{G}_e^T\mathbf{C}_i\mathbf{G}_e\right)^{-1}\mathbf{G}_e^T\mathbf{C}_i = \mathbf{C}_i - \mathbf{P}_i\mathbf{Q}_i^{-1}\mathbf{P}^T \qquad (4)$$

Where $\mathbf{S}_e = -\left(\frac{1}{h^2}\mathbf{m}_e+\frac{1}{h}\mathbf{b}_e+\mathbf{k}_e\right)$, $\mathbf{P}_i = \mathbf{C}_i\mathbf{G}_e$ and $\mathbf{Q}_i = \mathbf{S}_e^{-1}+\mathbf{G}_e^T\mathbf{C}_i\mathbf{G}_e^T$. The matrix $\mathbf{P}_i$ and $\mathbf{G}_e^T\mathbf{C}_i\mathbf{G}_e^T$ are simply constructed by extracting corresponding rows and columns of the matrix $\mathbf{C}_i$. While the above formula is computationally less expensive than re-computing the inverse of the modified system matrix from scratch, the matrix multiplication $\mathbf{P}_i\mathbf{Q}_i^{-1}\mathbf{P}^T$ has a complexity of $O(n^2)$, where n is the dimension of the compliance matrix, which is still too demanding to be performed in real-time.

Building the LCP used to compute the contact force in the haptic loop, only involves the part of compliance matrix related to the nodes in contact. Consequently, we do not have to compute all entries of the compliance matrix, and it leads us to update only the necessary part of the compliance matrix rather than complete update. Once we obtain the matrix $\mathbf{Q}_i^{-1}$, one entry of the compliance matrix $\mathbf{C}_{i+1}$ can be computed with (m^2+m) operations, where m is the dimension of $\mathbf{Q}_i$. Even though m is a very small number (12 in case of one tetrahedron removal), we should minimize the number of operations because $(n \times m)$ entries of $\mathbf{C}_{i+1}$ should be computed in the next modification to construct the matrix $\mathbf{P}_{i+1}$. We diagonalize the matrix $\mathbf{Q}_i$ using $\mathbf{Q}_i = \mathbf{W}_i\, \ddot{\mathbf{E}}_i\, \mathbf{W}_i^T$ ($\ddot{\mathbf{E}}_i$ is a diagonal matrix). It reduces the number operations to $2m$.

$$
\begin{aligned}
\mathbf{C}_{i+1} &= \mathbf{C}_i - \mathbf{P}_i \left(\mathbf{W}_i\, \ddot{\mathbf{E}}_i\, \mathbf{W}_i^T\right)^{-1} \mathbf{P}_i^T \\
&= \mathbf{C}_i - \mathbf{L}_i\, \ddot{\mathbf{E}}_i^{-1}\, \mathbf{L}_i^T
\end{aligned}
\tag{5}
$$

Where $\mathbf{L}_i = \mathbf{P}_i \mathbf{W}_i$. Whenever tetrahedra are removed during the simulated phacoemulsification procedure, we compute the matrices $\mathbf{L}_i$ and $\ddot{\mathbf{E}}_i^{-1}$, and save them as follows.

$$
\mathbf{C}_k = \mathbf{C}_0 = \mathbf{L}_0\, \ddot{\mathbf{E}}_0^{-1}\, \mathbf{L}_0^T = \mathbf{L}_1\, \ddot{\mathbf{E}}_1^{-1}\, \mathbf{L}_1^T = \cdots = \mathbf{L}_{k-1}\, \ddot{\mathbf{E}}_{k-1}^{-1}\, \mathbf{L}_{k-1}^T
\tag{6}
$$

Where $\mathbf{C}_0$ is the initial compliance matrix and k is the number of modification. One entry of the modified compliance matrix whose row and column index is i, j, is computed quickly as follows.

$$
\mathbf{C}_k(i,j) = \mathbf{C}_0(i,j) - \sum_{q=0}^{k-1}\left(\sum_{l=1}^{m} \mathbf{L}_q(i,l)\mathbf{L}_q(j,l)\ddot{\mathbf{E}}_i^{-1}(l,l)\right)
\tag{7}
$$

4   Results

We have evaluated our method in the framework of the cataract surgery simulation. The experiments were performed on a 2.33GHz Xeon processor with 3GB of memory. Fig. 3 shows a simulation of the phacoemulsification step of the cataract surgery, where the eye lens is fragmented by a microsurgical device. The eye lens model consists of 4862 tetrahedra and 1113 nodes.

We measured the computation time spent to update the compliance matrix, and compared it with the previous method which completely updates the compliance matrix. As shown in Fig. 4, the proposed algorithm achieves better performance than the previous method when the number of removed elements is small, however, the computation time linearly increases as the number of removed elements increase. The growth in the computation time is caused by construction of the matrix $\mathbf{P}_k = \mathbf{C}_k\mathbf{G}_k$. The computation time required to construct $\mathbf{P}_k$ is linearly dependent on the number of modification as shown in equation (8). However when the number of removed elements per time step remains small, we obtain fast update.

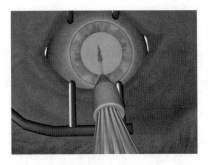
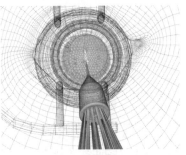

Fig. 3. Cataract surgery simulation: the eye lens is progressively fragmented using a phacoemulsification device while realistic visual and haptic feedbacks are provided

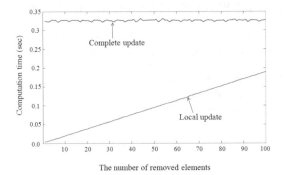

Fig. 4. Computation time necessary to update the compliance matrix as a function of the number of removed elements

5   Conclusion

In this paper we introduce a numerical technique for accurately computing contact forces during soft tissue manipulation, even in the presence of topological changes. The method is based on a local update of the compliance matrix, compatible with geometrically non-linear elastic models. Our approach allows for accurate contact force computation and realistic haptic rendering. Future work will be directed toward more precise cutting simulation involving element subdivision. While element removal only induces the modification to the system matrix, subdivision induces an extension of the matrix dimension, making it more difficult to update the compliance matrix.

Acknowledgement

This research was supported by the Basic Science Research Program through the National Research Foundation of Korea (NRF) funded by the Ministry of Education, Science and Technology (No. R01-2007-000-11353-0) and the Brain Korea 21 Project in 2009.

References

1. Sifakis, E., Der, K.G., Fedkiw, R.: Arbitrary Cutting of Deformable Tetrahedralized Objects. In: Proceeding of Eurographics, pp. 73–80. ACM, San Diego (2007)
2. Comas, O., Taylor, Z., Allard, J., Ourselin, S., Cotin, S., Passenger, J.: Efficient nonlinear FEM for soft tissue modelling and its GPU implementation within the open source framework SOFA. In: Bello, F., Edwards, E. (eds.) ISBMS 2008. LNCS, vol. 5104, pp. 28–39. Springer, Heidelberg (2008)
3. Felippa, C.A.: A systematic approach to the element independent corotational dynamics of finite elements: Technical Report CU-CAS-00-03, Center for Aerospace Structures (2000)
4. Saupin, G., Duriez, C., Cotin, S., Grisoni, L.: Efficient Contact Modeling using Compliance Warping. In: Computer Graphics International Conference (2008)
5. Saupin, G., Duriez, C., Cotin, S.: Contact Model for Haptic Medical Simulations. In: Bello, F., Edwards, E. (eds.) ISBMS 2008. LNCS, vol. 5104, pp. 157–165. Springer, Heidelberg (2008)
6. Lee, B., Popescu, D.C., Joshi, B., Ourselin, S.: Efficient Topology Modification and Deformation for Finite Element Models Using Condensation. In: Medicine Meets Virtual Reality, vol. 14, pp. 299–304. IOS Press, Los Angeles (2006)
7. Sherman, J., Morrison, W.J.: Adjustment of an Inverse Matrix Corresponding to Changes in the Elements of a Given Column or a Given Row of the Original Matrix. Annals of Mathematical Statistics 20, 621 (1949)

PART III
Novel Approaches

Basic Properties of Phantom Sensation
for Practical Haptic Applications

Hiroshi Kato[1], Yuki Hashimoto[1], and Hiroyuki Kajimoto[1,2]

[1] University of Electro-Communications, Department of Human Communication
[2] Japan Science and Technology Agency
1-5-1 Chofugaoka Chofu, Tokyo 182-8585, Japan
{hiro.kato,hashimoto,kajimoto}@kaji-lab.jp

Abstract. Phantom sensation (PhS) is a pseudo-tactile sensation that occurs when two or more mechanical or electrical stimuli are presented simultaneously to the skin. PhS has two well-known characteristics. First, the location of PhS can be changed by changing the strength of stimuli. Second, the intensity of stimulation can influence the resulting PhS. This illusion has the potential to greatly reduce the number of stimulators required in wearable tactile interfaces. Although it has been shown that PhS is perceived more clearly with shorter pulses, currently only rough quantitative evaluation has been performed. In addition, the subjective qualities of the sensation have not previously been examined. We first summarize the basic characteristics of PhS, including the relationship between the duration of stimuli and the clarity of the illusion.

Keywords: Phantom sensation, funneling illusion, tactile illusion, haptic I/O and tactile display.

1 Introduction

Two major problems are inherent in the development of tactile displays. First, tactile receptors are distributed over the entire body. Second, it is difficult to stimulate tactile receptors from remote locations, typically requiring physical contact. As such, most tactile displays designed to present spatially specific tactile stimulation have been composed of dense pin arrays activated by small actuators.

However, apparatus involving numerous actuators directly contacting the skin are typically bulky and complex. Moreover, these systems are generally costly, making them inappropriate for many research settings. The necessity of numerous actuators directly contacting the skin requires a large array of wire harnesses, further reducing the practicality of these systems.

One potential solution to this problem involves the use of a tactile illusion called 'phantom sensation' (PhS). PhS was initially discovered by von Bekesy as a form of 'funneling' illusion [1] (Fig.1), and is an illusory tactile sensation that arises between two points of simultaneous vibration or electric stimulation [2] [3].

The subjective strength and clarity of the illusory sensation in comparison to the sensation of the two actual stimuli, is dependent on the duration of the actual stimuli. If constant stimulation is applied, PhS becomes relatively weak compared with the

A.M.L. Kappers et al. (Eds.): EuroHaptics 2010, Part I, LNCS 6191, pp. 271–278, 2010.

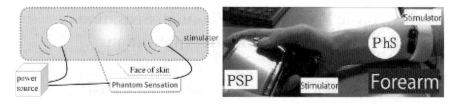

Fig. 1. PhS is induced by tactile stimuli in two locations. The location in which PhS is experienced is determined by the ratio between the strength of the two stimuli. The image on the right shows an example of one potential application of PhS. This system stimulates the palm and forearm, in conjunction with a handheld videogame. PhS can be elicited at any location of the forearm with a very simple setup, and could be used to produce tactile sensations as part of a videogame.

actual stimuli. Stimuli of a short duration, on the other hand, produce a stronger PhS and a weaker perception of the two actual stimuli.

Following von Bekesy's initial report, many studies have examined the basic properties of PhS. Several studies have shown that the position and strength of the illusory sensation can be controlled by changing the strength ratio of the actual stimuli [2] [3] [4] [5] [6] [7] [8] (Fig.1 (left)).

Fig.1 (right) shows our exploratory study of a novel application of PhS, aiming to test the use of PhS in conjunction with portable gaming devices including PSP and iPhone.

We used tactile stimulators on the palm and forearm to generate PhS at an arbitrary position on the forearm. This method enabled the subjective sensation of game characters and objects 'dancing' on the arm of the gamer. The ability to adjust and quantify the position, strength, and 'clarity' of the PhS are necessary elements of such a system. We defined the 'clarity' of the PhS as the ratio between the strength of the sensation of the experienced PhS, and the sensation of the two real stimuli.

$$(clarity) = (PhS\ strength) / (real\ stimuli\ strength)$$

We adjusted two stimulation parameters and examined their effects. The first parameter was the duration of stimulus presentation. It has been previously established that stimuli of shorter durations generate clearer sensations[1]. However, no previous research has examined the effects of the duration of the resting period between the stimulus pulses on the clarity of repeated stimulation. The present study evaluated the effects of rest-period duration on PhS, allowing the selection of appropriate stimulus durations.

The second parameter in question was the spatial location of stimuli. It was previously established that a large distance between the stimuli could cause the location of the experienced PhS to become ambiguous. Therefore, we tested the effects of an additional third stimulator between the original two stimulators. Previous work has shown that two-dimensional arrangements of three or more identical stimuli can generate a PhS in the center of the array[4]. However, it is unclear how PhS is affected by differences in the stimuli. In addition, the effect of a single stimulus on the PhS generated by the other two is not well understood. This knowledge will enable the design of systems with an appropriate spatial distribution for producing a PhS with the desired properties.

We conducted three experiments. The first was conducted to confirm that our system generated a PhS, and to evaluate the basic properties of the illusion induced by our setup. The second experiment evaluated the relationship between the duration of the rest interval of the stimuli and the clarity of PhS induced. The third experiment evaluated three stimulus paradigms.

2   Methods

2.1   Set up

We presented PhS induction stimuli to the left forearm. Mechanical vibration was used as tactile stimulation. We asked participants to place their forearm onto two stimulators. (Fig. 2)

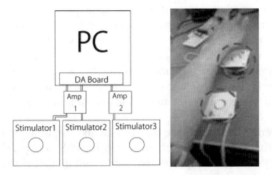

Fig. 2. System setup: PhS was generated by using two stimulators (audio speakers). In the third experiment, we used three stimulators.

The distance between two stimulation points was 130 mm (based on previous work [2])

We used audio speakers as vibrating stimulators (ES-06603/8Ω MAX14W, S.J). A contactor (ABS plastic,Φ20 mm) was attached to each speaker. As the maximum amplitude of vibration was 2 mm, the contactor was set 2 mm higher than the edge of the speaker, so that it continuously contacted the skin during stimulation.

Our system output tactile stimulation controlled by a waveform generated by a D/A board (PCI-3523A, Interface Corp.; Fig. 2). We used headphones to play white noise to mask the sound of the vibration stimulators.

2.2   Waveforms for Stimulation

Because PhS is not generated by static pressure, and constant vibration induces only very weak PhS, we used pulse wave stimulation like that shown in Fig. 3 to maintain a clear PhS. The pulse width was fixed to 5 ms (based on preliminary testing), while the amplitude and cycle were varied as experimental manipulations.

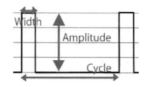

Fig. 3. Waveform for stimulation. The width was fixed to 5 ms; amplitude and cycle were manipulated experimentally.

3   Experiments

3.1   Experiment 1: Basic Properties of PhS with Different Types of Pulse Stimulation

Experiment 1 was conducted to confirm that our experimental setup could generate PhS on the forearm. We measured basic aspects of the experience of PhS, including location and strength. In addition, we tested the effects of varying spatial and temporal aspects of the tactile induction stimuli.

An LCD monitor was located on the right side of the left forearm and a visual representation of the PhS was displayed, in the form of square (a 'PhS image'; Fig. 4) Participants could move and resize three squares using horizontal scroll bars on the right side of the screen.

Participants were asked to indicate the position and size of any PhS experienced, by moving and resizing the white square on screen for PhS, and purple squares for real stimulations. They submitted responses pressing a button. Participants were also asked to indicate the strength of experienced PhS from 0 to 100 using a moving scale bar. A rating of 100 represents the subjective strength of the sensation of a single stimulator driven with 100% amplitude. A rating of 0 indicates that no tactile stimulation was perceived. Pulse cycle and width were fixed to 1,000 ms and 5 ms respectively.

In the first test, the amplitude of the two stimuli was changed from 12.5% to 100% of the maximum stimulation strength, while the PhS size and strength were measured separately. In the second test, the ratio of the amplitude of the two stimuli was changed from 0.125 to 8, and PhS position was measured. Each participant completed five trials. The 100% amplitude was set by each participant so that they could perceive PhS easily and reliably. In the second test, the larger amplitude was set to 100%. For example, if the ratio of two amplitudes was 8.0 or 0.125, the larger amplitude was set to 100%, while the smaller amplitude was set to 12.5%. Participants were three adults familiar with PhS. (22-23 years old, all males)

As shown in Fig. 4, the location and strength of PhS indicated by tactile image adjustments changed in response to changes in the ratio and amplitude of the stimuli, which are well known from previous researches.

Interestingly, we found that the 'size' of the experienced PhS was altered by changes in stimulus strength (Fig. 4, top right). To the best of our knowledge, this change in the subjective size of PhS has not been reported in any previous studies. We instructed participants to distinguish size and clarity. However, the upper right and lower left graphs are similar in shape, indicating that participants might not be able to distinguish between size and clarity.

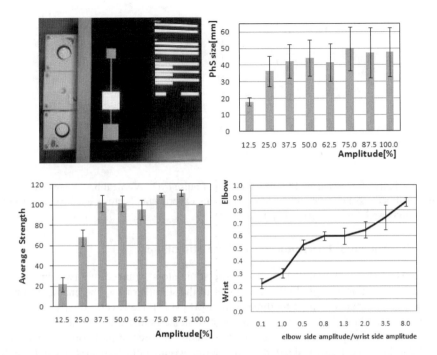

Fig. 4. Upper left: Experimental setup. Upper right and lower left: PhS size and strength as a function of amplitude. Lower right: PhS location as a function of the ratio of the two actual stimuli strength. Each vertical bar represents the standard error. All participants gave similar answers in all three experiments.

3.2 Experiment 2: Change in PhS Clarity with Change in Pulse Cycle

It has been previously shown that constant stimulation can generate a constant PhS, but because actual input stimuli are also perceived, this can result in a relatively ambiguous PhS experience. The trade-off between continuity and clarity has not yet been explored quantitatively.

To this end, we changed continuity by using different cycles. We used stimulation of 100, 50, 5, 2, and 1 pps (pulses per second). The pulse width was fixed to 5 ms. We calibrated and fixed amplitudes for each participant so they could perceive PhS easily and reliably.

Participants responded according to the strength of the PhS they experienced, and the strength of the two real stimuli, using the same setup as in Experiment 1.

Participants were three adults familiar with PhS. (22-23 years old, all males). Five trials were conducted for each stimulation type. The results are shown in Fig. 5.

Our results clearly showed that stimulation over 5 pps produced an ambiguous PhS. To the best of our knowledge, this is the first quantitative report of a relationship between continuity and clarity in the PhS. This result indicates that stimulation under 5 pps should be used in systems designed to induce PhS.

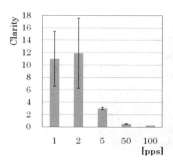

Fig. 5. Clarity of experienced PhS as a function of pulse cycle. Vertical bars represent standard error. All participants gave similar answers in this experiment. There is a statistically significant difference between 2pps and 5pps (p<0.05).

3.3   Experiment 3: PhS Induced by Three Stimulators

Previous work has shown that three or more stimulators arranged in a two-dimensional space can generate a single PhS at the center of the stimulator set, and enable it to move in the triangular area formed by three stimuli [3] [4] [7]. However, no study has examined the generation of PhS with three or more stimulators in a straight line.

In our third experiment, we tested the effects of three stimulators arranged in a straight line. We hypothesized that this setup would either generate two PhSs, or would produce a single PhS. We investigated this issue because such an ambiguous situation is likely to arise in practical applications of PhS involving the use of multiple stimulators simultaneously. As demonstrated by the second experiment, the clarity of PhS can be changed by the continuity of the stimuli. Therefore, we used two types of stimuli: a continuous 120 Hz sine wave (referred to as 'sine mode'), and a 5 ms pulse with 1,000 ms cycle (referred to as 'pulse mode'). We calibrated amplitudes for each participant so they could perceive PhS easily and robustly. We prepared four combinations as follows.

(1)   All stimulators driven by sine mode. (mode: sin-sin)
(2)   Two terminal stimulators driven by sine mode, and one central stimulator driven by pulse mode.(mode:sin-pul)
(3)   Two terminal stimulators driven by pulse mode, one central stimulator driven by sine mode.(mode:pul-sin)
(4)   All stimulators driven by pulse mode.(mode:pul-pul)

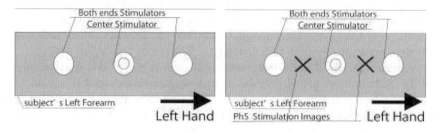

Fig. 6. Experiment 3 setup. Right figure shows a 'divided' tactile image.

Initial testing revealed that participants reported four types of tactile sensation:

Augmented: Augmented PhS felt at the central stimulator.
Blended: PhS sensation and real sensation of central stimulator mixed at the central stimulator.
Divided: Two PhSs perceived between the two pairs of stimulators.
Lost: No PhS elicited.

Participants were three adults familiar with PhS (22-23 years old, all male). The trials were conducted ten times for each combination. Participants were asked to categorize the sensation they experienced as Augmented, Blended, Divided, or Lost for each trial. The results are shown in Fig. 7.

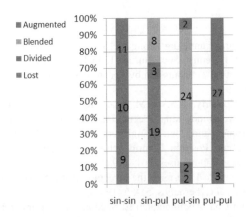

Fig. 7. Percentage of reported sensation types, sorted into combinations. The number on each column indicates the total number of answers. All participants experiments. The number on each column The results showed statistically significant differences (χ^2 test, p<0.01).

When the two terminal stimulators were driven in sine mode (sin-sin and sin-pul), responses were highly variable and inconsistent, implying that PhS generated by terminal stimulators was vague and difficult for participants to categorize.

When the two terminal stimulators were driven by pulse mode (pul-sin and pul-pul), responses were more consistent. This was likely due to pulse stimuli inducing stable PhS. Interestingly, the central stimulator in sine mode clearly induced a 'blended' sensation of sine wave and pulse stimuli.

4   Conclusion

This study examined the effects of temporal and spatial properties of stimulation on the clarity of subjectively experienced PhS, in an attempt to aid the development of practical applications for the tactile illusion.

In terms of the temporal aspects of PhS, we revealed that the clarity of PhS is drastically reduced when pulse stimuli are presented at a frequency higher than 5 pps.

Clarity in our paradigm was defined as a ratio of subjective strength between the sensation of PhS and the sensation of actual tactile stimuli.

Regarding the spatial aspects of PhS, the fusion of the experience of real stimuli and PhS occurred only when two terminal stimuli were presented as pulses. This finding is consistent with previous research. However, we also reported a novel way of 'blending' PhS pulses and sinusoidal stimuli (pul-sin). We propose that the development of a tactile display composed of a central 'shape' display and a peripheral 'impulse' display may have practical applications.

Having summarized the temporal and spatial features of PhS, we now hope to apply our findings in the development of a portable tactile stimulation device.

References

1. von Bekesy, G.: Neural Funneling Along the Skin and Between the Inner and Outer Hair Cells of the Cochlea. J. Acoust. Soc. Am. 31, 1236-1249 (1959)
2. Alles, D. A.: Information Transmission by Phantom Sensations. IEEE Trans. Man-Machine Syst. MMS-11, 85 (1970)
3. Tanie K, Tachi S, Komoriya K, Abe M, Asaba K, Tomita. Y: Information Transmission Characteristics of Two-Dimensional Electrocutaneous Phantom Sensation. Transactions of the Society of Instrument and Control Engineers. 16 (5), 732-739 (1980)
4. Mann R.W.: Force and Position Proprioception for Prostheses. The Control of Upper-Extremity Prostheses and Outhouses, 201–219 (1974)
5. Chorzempa A.: Attempt to Determine the Structure of the Nervous System Serving Mechanoreceptors. Biological Cybernetics. 51-56 (1981)
6. Lara Rahal, Jongeun Cha, Abdulmotaleb El Saddik., Julius Kammerl, and Eckehard Steinbach: Investigating the Influence of Temporal Intensity Changes on Apparent Movement Phenomenon Proceedings of the 2009 IEEE international conference on Virtual Environments, Human-Computer Interfaces and Measurement Systems. 310-313 (2009)
7. Fukuyama K, Mizukami Y Sawada H: A Novel Micro-vibration Actuator and the Presentation of Tactile Sensations, 12th IMEKO TC1 & TC7 Joint Symposium on Man Science & Measurement, 141-146 (2008)
8. Ahmad Barghout, Jongeun Cha, Abdulmotaleb El Saddik, Julius Kammerl, and Eckehard Steinbach, "Spatial Resolution of Vibrotactile Perception on the Human Forearm when Exploiting Funneling Illusion," International Workshop on Haptic Audio-Visual Environments and Games(HAVE), Lecco,Italy,(2009)

Evaluation of Transmission System for Spatially Distributed Tactile Information

Katsunari Sato[1] and Susumu Tachi[2]

[1] Graduate School of Information Science and Technology, The University of Tokyo, Japan
sato@tachilab.org
[2] Graduate School of Media Design, Keio University, Japan
tachi@tachilab.org

Abstract. Spatially distributed tactile information is essential for dexterous operation in telexistence. We propose a transmission system for spatially distributed tactile information using a finger-shaped GelForce and an electrotactile display. Both devices are suitable for integration with multi-fingered tele-operation system because these devices are compact. In this study, we evaluate the performance of a one-fingered transmission system for spatially distributed tactile information by conducting recognition experiments. We discuss the efficiency and limitations of the proposed transmission system.

Keywords: finger-shaped force sensor, electrotactile display, spatially distributed tactile information, and telexistence.

1 Introduction

The transmission of haptic information in tele-operation systems is essential for interaction with remote objects. In particular, spatially distributed tactile information is essential for dexterous operation [1]. Thus far, several systems have been developed for the transmission of spatially distributed tactile information [2] [3]. For example, Methil et al. [3] have developed a tele-diagnostic system that can be used to detect tumors in remote patients. Unfortunately, because this system was developed for use as a diagnostic tool for breast pathology, users are unable to grasp objects. The size of the tactile device limits the finger workspace, making it all the more difficult to fabricate a multi-fingered transmission system. Therefore, compact sensors and displays are required to achieve dexterous grasping of remote objects in tele-operation systems.

To achieve dexterous tele-operation, we have developed the following compact tactile devices: a finger-shaped force sensor named as finger-shaped GelForce [4] and an electrotactile display [5]. Because these devices are small in size and light in weight, they can be easily mounted on any multi-fingered tele-operation systems (Fig. 1). Furthermore, the spatial resolution of these devices can be easily improved because of their simple structures. In this study, we fabricated a one-fingered transmission system and evaluated the contact area recognition efficiencies of the system.

A.M.L. Kappers et al. (Eds.): EuroHaptics 2010, Part I, LNCS 6191, pp. 279–284, 2010.

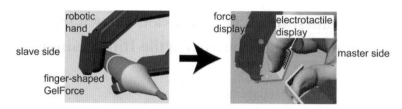

Fig. 1. Transmission system for spatially distributed tactile information using finger-shaped GelForce and electrotactile display

2 Transmission of Spatially Distributed Tactile Information

2.1 Finger-Shaped GelForce

A finger-shaped GelForce sensor [4], which was developed in-house, was used to obtain spatially distributed tactile information. The finger-shaped GelForce consists of a transparent elastic body, red and blue marker matrices, and a color charge-coupled device (CCD) camera that captures the movements of the markers. These movements are used to calculate the distribution of the force vector (magnitude and angle) applied on the sensor surface. Thus, we easily realized a high-resolution sensor that has a design, such as shape and impedance, similar to that of the human fingertip.

We use a human skin gel (Exseal Corp., Young's modulus: 50.0 KPa) for the transparent elastic body of the finger-shaped GelForce to match the impedance of the human finger. We set 15 force sampling points at intervals of 2.5 mm. In this case, the spatial, magnitude, and temporal resolutions of the constructed finger-shaped GelForce are 5.0 mm, 0.15 N, and 16 ms, respectively.

2.2 Electrotactile Display

The developed electrotactile display [5] produce spatially distributed tactile stimulus. It comprises pin electrode matrices and directly activates nerve fibers under the skin by passing electric current through surface electrodes. The current flows from an electrode to adjacent electrodes through the skin. By periodically changing the pin used for stimulation, electrotactile stimuli can be presented at any point. Because the electrotactile display does not require the use of any mechanical actuators, the displays can be easily attached to each fingertip.

In this study, we use an electrotactile display that has 15 electrodes. The diameter of each electrode and the distance between the centers of the electrodes are 1.25 mm and 2.5 mm, respectively. A square wave having a pulse width and maximum pulse amplitude of 20 μs and 5.0 mA, respectively, is used for stimulation. The frequency of pulses applied at the electrode is 30 Hz. The line-width, two-line, and amplitude discrimination thresholds are 2.5 mm, 7.5 mm, and 0.1 mA, respectively.

2.3 Methods for Information Transmission

In the proposed system, spatially distributed tactile information is transmitted from the finger-shaped GelForce to the electrotactile display (Fig. 2). The magnitude and

distribution of the force vectors are related to the amplitude and position of the electrotactile stimuli. The electrotactile display can only indicate the magnitude and distribution of the force vectors, not their orientation. The magnitude of the force vector
$|f_i|$ is calculated as follows:

$$|f_i| = \sqrt{f_{ix}^2 + f_{iy}^2 + f_{iz}^2} \qquad (1)$$

where i denotes the number of force sampling points. When the magnitude of force
at a point is less than half its value at adjacent sampling points, we set the magnitude of force at that point to 0.0. This elimination technique seems to virtually improve the spatial resolution of the finger-shaped GelForce from 5.0 mm to 2.5 mm
[4]. The amplitude of the electrotactile stimulus at a pin electrode, $|A_i|$, is given as
follows:

$$|A_i| = \alpha |f_i| + \beta \qquad (2)$$

where i, α and β denote the number of pin electrodes, gain, and bias, respectively.
Each value of α and β is pre-examined by a user.

3 Experiment

We evaluate the transmission system for spatially distributed tactile information from
the view-point of contact area recognition efficiency.

3.1 Material and Method

Material. We employed PHANToM Omni (SensAble, Technologies) to touch the
remote object in the transmission system for spatially distributed tactile information.
We mounted the electrotactile display and the finger-shaped GelForce on the end-
effectors of the master PHANToM and slave PHANToM, respectively (Fig. 3). The
participants had to place the tip of their index finger on the electrotactile display and
move the end-effector of the master PHANToM to control the finger-shaped
GelForceon the slave PHANToM. In this experiment, we used the simplest symmetric
position servo type control algorithm for robotic master-slave control, which can be
represented by the following equations:

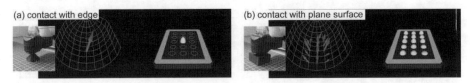

Fig. 2. Transmission of spatially distributed tactile information. Contact with (a) edged object
and (b) flat object. The lengths of the arrows represent the magnitude of the measured force,
whereas the size of the sphere represents the amplitude of the electrostimulus.

Fig. 3. Experimental setup: one-fingered transmission system for spatially distributed tactile information employing PHANToM master-slave system

$$f_s = (x_m - x_s)K_p \quad f_m = -f_s \tag{3}$$

where f_s and f_m denote the forces of the slave and master systems, respectively; x_s and x_m, the positions of the slave and master systems, respectively; K_p, the gain. We limited the participant's finger movement to a single direction (along the y-axis, as indicated in Fig. 3). Participants were instructed to push the object, but not to stroke the surface of the object or to change the contact position.

Method. Participants conducted three recognition experiments: position, width and angle. In the position experiment, the participants touched the edge of a circular cone at an arbitrary position (Fig. 4a). The circular cone is made from plastic and its diameter and height are 20.0 mm and 10.0 mm, respectively. The contact position of the cone was selected randomly from five positions, namely, the center of the sampling point, 2.5 mm away from the center and toward to left, toward the right, forward, and backward. Subsequently, participants reported the position in which they made contact with the cone. In the angle experiment, the participants touched at rectangular prism that was oriented at 0°, 45°, 90°, or 135° (Fig. 4b). The rectangular prisms are made from plastic, and they have a width and length of 2.5 mm and 20.0 mm, respectively. The angle of orientation of the prism was selected randomly. Then, the participants reported the orientation of the prism that they touched. In the width experiment, the participants touched closely-arranged rectangular prisms (Fig. 4c) using the transmission system. The number of prisms was randomly selected as 1, 2, 3, and 4, and therefore, their total widths were 2.5 mm, 5.0 mm, 7.5 mm, and 10.0 mm, respectively. Then, participants reported on the number of prisms they had touched.

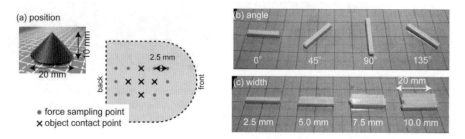

Fig. 4. Conditions of object for each position, width, and angle recognition experiment

One male and two female participants in the age-group of 23-26 volunteered for the experiments. In each discrimination experiment, each experimental condition was performed ten times. Throughout the experiment, there was no visual or audio feedback for the participants.

3.2 Result

The experimental results are shown in Fig. 5. In the position experiments, the averaged correct answer ratio was 0.75. Using ANOVA, we determined that there is no significant difference in the results obtained for the different contact positions on the circular cone ($F(4,14)=1.33$, $p=0.34$). In the angle experiments, the averaged correct answer ratio was 0.74. There is no significant difference in the results obtained for different orientation of the rectangular prism ($F(3,11)=2.37$, $p=0.17$). Finally, in the width experiments, the averaged correct answer ratio was 0.53. There is a significant difference in the results obtained by changing the widths of the rectangular prisms ($F(3,11)=6.51$, $p<0.05$). Furthermore, the results of multiple comparisons demonstrate that there are significant differences in the results when the widths of the prisms are 2.5 mm and 7.5 mm ($t(11)=4.11$, $p<0.05$).

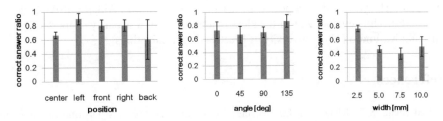

Fig. 5. Experimental results. The graphs on the left, at the center, and on the right represent the results of the position, angle, and width experiments, respectively. The horizontal axis represents the experimental condition, whereas the vertical axis represents the ratio of correct answers. The bars represent the averages of all participants. The error bar represents standard deviation.

3.3 Discussion

In this evaluation, we employed a finger-shaped GelForce and an electrotactile display. These devices have similar spatial resolutions as those employed in previous studies. From the spatial resolutions of these devices, we expected that participants would correctly discriminate the 2.5 mm differences more than 75% of the time. The results of the experiment involving the position and angle demonstrate that the proposed system is capable of effectively determining the contact position and orientation of the object. Therefore, we expect that an improvement in the spatial resolutions of our tactile devices would result in the improvement in the efficiency of the transmission system.

However, it appeared that participants were unable to discriminate the 2.5 mm difference in the width experiment. A previous study [5] showed that the participants can discriminate this difference using the electrotactile display. Therefore, we assume that the measurement error of the finger-shaped GelForce causes a decrease in the accuracy of the transmission system. It is believed that the measurement error can be decreased by increasing the resolution of the CCD camera [4].

4 Conclusion

In this study, we fabricated a one-fingered transmission system for spatially distributed tactile information using a finger-shaped GelForce and an electrotactile display. The results of the contact area recognition experiment showed that our system is efficient for transmission for spatially distributed tactile information.

However, the transmission of other haptic information such as compliance or texture is also essential for tele-operation systems. Therefore, in the future, we would aim to conduct a comprehensive evaluation of our system as a haptic transmission system. Then, we will design a multi-fingered transmission system and evaluate its efficiency from the viewpoint of achieving dexterous grasping.

Acknowledgement

This research was partly supported by CREST and Grant-in-Aid for JSPS Fellows (20·10009). The development of the electrotactile display was partly supported by Dr. Hiroyuki Kajimoto (The University of Electro-Communications).

References

1. Lederman, S.J., Klatzky, R.L.: Sensing and Displaying Spatially Distributed Fingertip Forces in Haptic Interfaces for Teleoperator and Virtual Environment Systems. Presence 8(1), 86–103 (1999)
2. Khatchatourov, A., Castet, j., Florens, J.-L., Luciani, A., Lenay, C.: Integrating tactile and force feedback for highly dynamic tasks: Technological, experimental and epistemological aspects. Interacting with Computers 21, 26–37 (2009)
3. Methil, N.S., Shen, Y., Zhu, D., Pomeroy, C.A., Mukherjee, R., Xi, N., Mutka, M.: Development of supermedia Interface for Telediagnostics of Breast Pathology. In: Proceedings of IEEE ICRA 2006, pp. 3911–3916 (2006)
4. Sato, K., Kamiyama, K., Kawakami, N., Tachi, S.: Finger-shaped GelForce: Sensor for Measuring Surface Traction Fields for Robotic Hand. IEEE Transaction on Haptics 3(1), 37–47 (2010)
5. Sato, K., Kajimoto, H., Kawakami, N., Tachi, S.: Electrotactile Display for Integration with Kinesthetic Display. In: Proceedings of 16th IEEE RO-MAN 2007, pp. 3–8 (2007)

Electro-tactile Display with Real-Time Impedance Feedback

Hiroyuki Kajimoto[1,2]

[1] The University of Electro-Communications
1-5-1 Chofugaoka, Chofu, Tokyo 182-8585 Japan
[2] Japan Science and Technology Agency
kajimoto@kaji-lab.jp

Abstract. An electro-tactile display is a tactile interface composed of skin surface electrodes. Such displays comprise many useful features such as durability and energy efficiency, but their use is limited by the variability of the elicited sensation. One possible solution to this problem involves monitoring skin electrical impedance. Previous studies established the existence of a correlation between impedance and threshold, but did not construct true real-time feedback loops. In this study, we constructed a system with a 1.45-μs feedback loop, and evaluated the feasibility of the system.

Keywords: Electro-tactile Display, Impedance, Real-time Feedback.

1 Introduction

An electro-tactile (electrocutaneous) display is a tactile interface that uses surface electrodes to directly activate sensory nerves under the skin. Its merits include small and thin size, low cost, energy efficiency and durability, and many works proposed applications utilizing the merits, such as a wearable tactile display for visually handicapped people [1-3] and multi-touch interface with tactile feedback [4]. However, the variability of the elicited sensation has hindered its practical use.

This variability results from two problems (Fig. 1). *Temporal changes* occur when the contact conditions are altered by sweat and motion. The sweat reduces sensation, while abrupt motion of the skin generates an electric shock sensation.

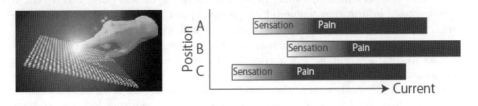

Fig. 1. Two factors contributing to the sensation variability of electro-tactile displays. (Left) Temporal changes caused by sweat and contact. (Right) Spatial variation of thresholds.

A.M.L. Kappers et al. (Eds.): EuroHaptics 2010, Part I, LNCS 6191, pp. 285–291, 2010.

Spatial variation also contributes to variability. The threshold for tactile sensation (absolute threshold) is quite close to the pain threshold. Furthermore, the spatial variation of the threshold is large. Thus, if hundreds of electrodes are used, and the stimulating currents are the same, it is impossible to exceed the absolute threshold at all electrodes, without also exceeding the pain threshold at some.

1.1 Previous Studies

Several solutions aimed at stabilizing the sensations generated by electro-tactile displays have been proposed. These can be classified into three categories.

The first category is to increase the difference between the absolute and pain thresholds. Collins [3] found that using a smaller pulse width (20–50 μs) was effective, while Polleto and van Doren [5] suggested applying a low-level pulse before the main pulse. Kaczmarek et al. [6] optimized several parameters such as number of pulses/burst to obtain maximal dynamic range. These methods represent important advances, but their effectiveness is limited.

The second category involves adjusting the stimulation in response to the user's explicit feedback [7]. A pressure sensor is placed under the electrode, and the electrical current is controlled by the sensor value. This simple method is quite effective for one finger and might be applied to multi-touch situation if multi-touch sensor is used, but requires user to control each finger pressure independently.

The third category measures the electrical impedance of the skin and controls the pulse using the measured value. This was originally done using an analog circuit. There are two main types of techniques for electrical stimulation: voltage regulation [8], and current regulation [1-5], while another type regulates energy [9]. These variations can provide different strategies to deal with impedance fluctuation using analog circuits.

In order to tackle the problem in a more general way, it is necessary to construct a measurement-stimulation control loop, such that the electrode can be used for both stimulation and measurement. Tachi et al. [9] regulated pulse width, based on the finding that perceived strength is related to input energy (current × voltage × pulse width). Watanabe et al. [10] found a correlation between skin resistance and absolute threshold. Gregory et al. [11] applied similar technique for fingertip. Takahashi et al. [4] monitored contact conditions by measuring impedance, and used the results to develop an electro-tactile touch panel.

1.2 Real-Time Feedback

Although feedback using skin impedance has been attempted in the previous studies, these have not been used real-time. In some of them the current pulse was regulated by impedance information acquired by a previous pulse (Fig. 2 (left)). It works if the finger is fixed to the electrodes, but it is not applicable to touch panel situation.

In some other studies, pre-pulse was used for measurement, with small enough values not to elicit a sensation (Fig. 2 (right)). The main pulse was applied after the initial measurement, *under the assumption that conditions did not change during this short period of time*. However, when hundreds of electrodes are used, this assumption is not justified. Analog switches are commonly used to construct low-cost systems with hundreds of electrodes [12]. A pair of top/bottom switches is connected to an electrode (Fig. 3). If the top switch is on, the electrode works as an anode, while if the bottom switch is on, it works as a cathode. The system only requires a single current source, thus significantly reducing the hardware costs. Using this system, only one point is stimulated at a time, and a two-dimensional pattern is produced by scanning.

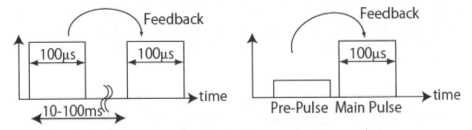

Fig. 2. Previous Methods. (Left) Current pulse is regulated by impedance information acquired by a previous pulse. (Right) Combination of measuring pre-pulse and stimulating main pulse.

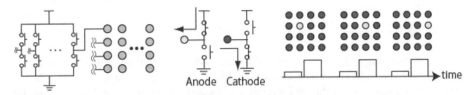

Fig. 3. Each electrode is connected to a pair of switches and can work as either an anode or a cathode. A two-dimensional pattern is produced by scanning.

Assuming a system with 100 electrodes and a refresh rate of 50 Hz, the allowed time period for one point stimulus is just 200 μs (= 20 ms/100 points), while the typical stimulating pulse width is 100 μs. However, if the contact conditions are altered by an abrupt skin movement, then an electric shock sensation lasting for 50% of the length of a stimulus (100 μs) may be generated, because it is not possible to feedback change during stimulation.

Measurement of skin impedance using pre-pulses also presents problems. Skin impedance is known to be highly dependent on applied voltage [13]. Therefore, if the pre-pulse is well below the absolute threshold, then the acquired data may not contain the full threshold information.

In light of these problems, we aimed to stabilize electro-tactile stimulation using true real-time impedance feedback. This involves dividing single stimulation into numerous sub-pulses, each containing a measurement and a feedback control (Fig. 4).

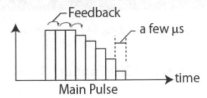

Fig. 4. Proposed method. A single stimulation is divided into numerous pulses, each containing a measurement and a feedback control.

2 System Structure

Fig. 5 and Fig. 6 illustrate the system structure. To achieve high-speed feedback, the measurement and control loops should be less than a few microseconds. The system used a microprocessor (SH-7144F, Renesas Technology) as a main controller, and included a D/A converter (TLV5619, Texas Instruments, 12 bit, 1 Msps) and an A/D converter (LTC1851, Linear Technology, 12 bit, 1.25 Msps), both with parallel data input/outputs.

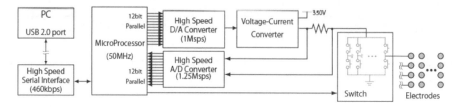

Fig. 5. System structure

The stimulating pulse was generated by the D/A converter and converted to a current pulse by a voltage/current converter, driven by a high-voltage source (350 V). The current pulse passed through a resistor to measure the voltage and current. As the stimulating pulse was regulated by current, it was not usually necessary to measure the current, except when the voltage became saturated.

As described in Section 1.2, the switches (HV507, Supertex) controlled by the microprocessor selected a stimulating electrode one at a time.

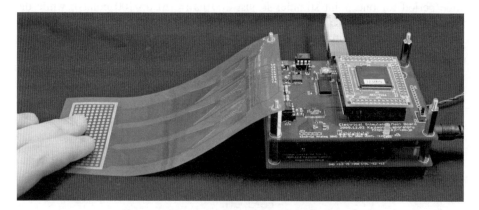

Fig. 6. Control circuit and electrodes

3 Hardware Evaluation and Preliminary Experiments

We evaluated the hardware and conducted two preliminary experiments to test the feasibility of the system. The author was the participant in all the experiments.

3.1 Feedback Loop Speed

The speed of the feedback loop was measured based on 30 control-measurement loops (Fig. 7 (left)). D/A signal was set and A/D value was acquired for each loop. The output was 5 mA for the first 15 measurements and 0 mA for the second 15. The subject's left index finger touched the electrode during the measurements.

Fig. 7 (right) shows the voltage data acquired by the A/D and the true voltage waveform measured using a digital oscilloscope (TPS2024, Tektronix). The two sets of data were in good agreement and confirmed that the duration of the feedback loop was about 1.45 μs, which fulfilled the requirements of the system.

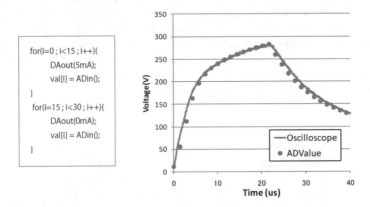

Fig. 7. (Left) Pseudo code for feedback loop measurement. (Right) Voltage waveform measured using an oscilloscope and the A/D converter.

3.2 Contact Detection

Similar measurements to those described in Section 3.1 were repeated six times under different contact conditions. In five of the six trials, one of five fingers contacted the electrode, while one measurement was done without contact.

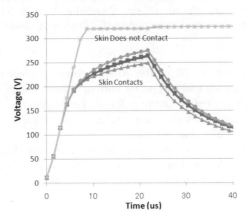

Fig. 8. Voltage waveforms when skin does or does not contact the electrodes

Fig. 8 shows the acquired voltage waveform. As the current was regulated (5 mA), a higher voltage meant higher impedance. It was possible to distinguish between measurements made with and without contact, as the voltage became saturated in the absence of contact. The system was able to distinguish between the two conditions after about 6 μs. This was fast enough to avoid an electric shock sensation caused by abrupt motion.

3.3   Correlation between Impedance and Threshold

To confirm the presence of a correlation between skin impedance and threshold, we measured the absolute thresholds and voltage waveforms. The absolute thresholds were obtained by the method of adjustment. A 20-μs current pulse was applied to one electrode, and the participant adjusted the amplitude of the pulse to find the absolute threshold. Just after the threshold was reached, a 5-mA, 20-μs current pulse was applied and the voltage waveform was obtained (as in Sections 3.1 and 3.2). The stimulating position was changed for each trial. Five finger pads were used as the stimulating locations. Trials were performed 70 times.

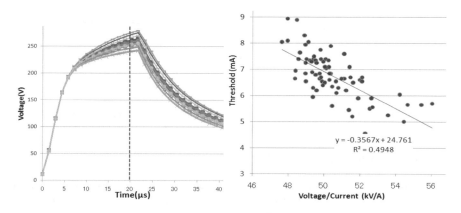

Fig. 9. (Left) Voltage waveforms of finger skin when current pulses were applied. Typical 20 of the 70 waveforms were plotted. (Right) Correlation between skin impedance (voltage/current) and threshold. Voltage values obtained at 20μs were divided by the current value (5 mA).

Fig. 9(left) shows typical 20 of the 70 waveforms produced. As these voltage waveforms were generated under constant current pulses, higher voltage waveforms corresponded to higher resistive components of skin impedance. Voltage values obtained at 20 μs were divided by the current value (5 mA), to demonstrate the relationship with absolute threshold (Fig. 9(right)).

The graph shows a clear negative correlation (R^2=0.49). The horizontal axis is roughly equivalent to skin resistance, indicating that skin with a higher resistance requires a smaller electrical current. This result is in agreement with the results of previous studies [9] [10].

4 Conclusion

This study investigated the problem of stabilizing electro-tactile displays. Although previous studies found a correlation between skin impedance and threshold, they failed to fully integrate the measurement and control phases.

We proposed to apply true real-time impedance feedback by dividing the stimulating pulse into numerous sub-pulses, each containing a measurement and a feedback control. We constructed a system that enables this high-speed feedback, evaluated the system and concluded that skin impedance (voltage/current) has sufficient information for the prediction of absolute threshold.

Future studies will involve the construction of a control algorithm and the application of the electro-tactile display to various fields.

References

1. Bach-y-Rita, P., Kaczmarek, K.A., Tyler, M.E., Garcia-Lara, J.: Form perception with a 49-point electrotactile stimulus array on the tongue. J. Rehabilitation Research Development 35, 427–430 (1998)
2. Kajimoto, H., Kanno, Y., Tachi, S.: Forehead Electro-tactile Display for Vision Substitution. In: Proc. EuroHaptics (2006)
3. Collins, C.C.: Tactile Television: Mechanical Electrical Image Projection. IEEE Trans. Man-Machine System MMS-11, 65–71 (1970)
4. Takahashi, M., Kuroki, S., Nii, H., Kawakami, N., Tachi, S.: Environmental Type Electro-Tactile Display for Touchpanel Interface. In: JSME Conference on Robotics and Mechatronics, 1P1-G05 (2009)
5. Poletto, C.J., Van Doren, C.L.: Elevating pain thresholds in humans using depolarizing prepulses. IEEE Trans. BME 49(10), 1221–1224 (2002)
6. Kaczmarek, K.A., Webster, J.G., Radwin, R.G.: Maximal Dynamic Range Electrotactile Stimulation Waveforms. IEEE Trans. BME 39(7), 701–715 (1992)
7. Kajimoto, H., Kawakami, N., Maeda, T., Tachi, S.: Electro-tactile display with force feedback. In: World Multi conf. on Systemics, Cybernetics and Informatics, Orlando (2001)
8. Journée1, H.L., Polak1, H.E., de Kleuver, M.: Influence of electrode impedance on threshold voltage for transcranial electrical stimulation in motor evoked potential monitoring. Medical & Biological Engineering & Computing 42(4) (2004)
9. Tachi, S., Tanie, K., Komiyama, K., Abe, M.: Electrocutaneous Communication in a Guide Dog Robot (MELDOG). IEEE Trans. Biomedical Engineering BME-32(7), 461–469 (1985)
10. Watanabe, T., Watanabe, S., Yoshino, K., Futami, R., Hoshimiya, N.: A Study of Relevance of Skin Impedance to Absolute Threshold for Stabilization of Cutaneous Sensation Elicited by Electric Current Stimulation. Biomechanisms 16, 61–73 (2002)
11. Gregory, J., Xi, N., Shen, Y.: Towards on-line fingertip bio-impedance identification for enhancement of electro-tactile rendering. In: Proc. IEEE/RSJ Int. Conf. Intelligent Robots & Systems (IROS), pp. 3685–3690 (2009)
12. Jones, K.E., Normann, R.A.: An advanced demultiplexing system for physiological stimulation. IEEE Trans. BME 44(12), 1210–1220 (1997)
13. Yamamoto, T., Yamamoto, Y.: Non-linear Electrical Properties of Skin in the Low Frequency Range. Med. & Biol. Eng. & Comput. 19, 302–310 (1981)

Life Log System Based on Tactile Sound

Yasutoshi Makino[1] , Masakazu Murao[2], and Takashi Maeno[2]

[1] Center for Education and Research of Symbiotic, Safe and Secure System Design,
Keio University, 4-1-1, Hiyoshi, Kohoku-ku, Yokohama, 223-8526, Japan
[2] Graduate School of System Design and Management, Keio University,
4-1-1, Hiyoshi, Kohoku-ku, Yokohama, 223-8526, Japan
makino@sdm.kcio.ac.jp, murao@z7.keio.jp, maeno@sdm.keio.ac.jp

Abstract. In this paper, we propose a new life log system which estimates touching object based on a contact sound. A life log system records our behaviors for recommending appropriate information depending on logs. There are some devices including a camera, a microphone and a GPS for recording our actions. However, those devices record too rich information to be accepted in terms of privacy. In this research we focus on the sound when we touch/manipulate objects. A piezoelectric device on a fingernail records touching sound propagating through a fingertip. Since the recorded sound depends on touching objects, we can record what we touched. This can be used as a new life log which assures secrecy. We show that our prototype system recognizes 12 different actions with 94.4% accuracy.

Keywords: Tactile sensor, Life log, Sound recognition.

1 Introduction

In this paper, we propose a new "life log" system. Our method is based on a "tactile sound" that is recorded with piezoelectric device, attached on a fingernail, when human touches objects. With the tactile sound, we can record touching objects in our daily lives. Since we use our fingers for manipulation such as clicking a button, opening/closing doors, wearing clothes, and so on, the tactile sound can be used as a life log.

A life log is a log that captures human daily life as a digital data. There are many proposed life logs which use a camera [1], a microphone [2], a GPS [3] and sensor networks [4] and so on. In general, we can record a plenty amount of data with cameras, and microphones. However, people may feel lack of secrecy because of too rich visual/auditory information. People especially dislike to be recorded "WHO" is involved in his/her behaviors. The privacy issue prevents life log from being accepted. In contrast, the tactile sound has small amount of information. We can know what we touched. We cannot know "WHO" is involved only based on the tactile sound. This makes people accept using the tactile sound as a new type of life log system.

The tactile sound life log can be used as follows.

Ex. 1: We can use the log for obliviousness. For example, imagine that you usually lock an entrance door just after closing the door. If the key-insertion sound is not

A.M.L. Kappers et al. (Eds.): EuroHaptics 2010, Part I, LNCS 6191, pp. 292–297, 2010.

detected after the entrance-closed sound and the other sound like a car-engine-start sound is detected instead, the system can estimate that the entrance key has not been locked yet and it can tell you that.

Ex.2: When we record brushing teeth sound, for example, an appropriate way of brushing may cause different sound from the inappropriate way of it. The log can be used for correcting people's actions.

Ex.3: Numbers of mouse clicks and keyboard types can be used to estimate how hard you are working on computer. In this case, tactile sound cannot recognize what types of article you wrote or what you have been watching on web site.

Ex.4: Since our proposed life log has high anonymousness, we can share the data of our daily behaviors through network for a statistical survey.

Ex.5: Off course, our system can be used with the other existing life log system. For visual life log system, for example, it is hard to cut out meaningful sections only based on movie data. Our system can be complementary to the visual data.

In this paper, we show how to detect a tactile sound. Then we demonstrate that we can recognize 12 different touching events based on the tactile sound.

2　Tactile Sound Detection

Figure 1 shows our tactile sound detection system. The piezoelectric device is attached onto the fingernail of the index finger with double-faced adhesive tape. When we touch objects with attaching this device, vibrations around the contact point propagates to the device through the finger tissue and the fingernail. That sound is recorded as a life log. This method has following advantages.

1) Both electrical-device-related information (mouse clicks, keyboard types) and non-electrical-device-related information (opening/closing a door, brushing of teeth) can be recorded with single device. Though we can measure electrical device-related information when we connect all appliances to network, it is hard to detect non-electrical-device-related information with such system.

2) The sensor output is not affected by external noises, since the tactile sound propagates inside the finger. This system is robust against noises compared with visual and auditory system.

3) It is easy to pick up a significant sound period from the whole data. Because almost all the part of the data is soundless. Unless we touch objects, no sound is detected.

4) Only based on the tactile sound, it is hard to tell who the operator is. This feature is suitable for life log.

Figure 2 shows the detected tactile sound. The left side shows the click of a mouse button and the right side shows the insertion of a key to a keyhole. We can see the difference between two sounds. Also we can see that the signal magnitude is significantly large compared with no-sound level even though the tactile sound propagates through the visco-elastic fingertip.

There are some previous studies that tried to detect contact condition without inserting sensors between a finger and a touching object. Mascaro [5] et al. focused on a color of a fingernail. The change of it represented contact conditions. Fukumoto [6] et al. attached an accelerometer on a wrist to detect tapping sounds of fingers. Iwamoto [7] used ring-shaped interface to detect tapping of fingers for a human-machine interface. Martinot [8] recorded touch sound and its vibration for understanding perceptional characteristic of touch.

Our approach is different from these researches. We especially focus on a contact sound so as to recognize what the touching object is.

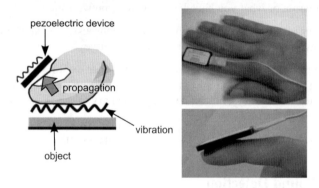

Fig. 1. Prototype tactile sound detection system. The piezoelectric device attached on the fingernail receives vibrations through fingertip.

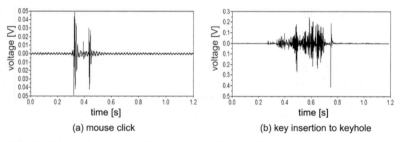

Fig. 2. Observed tactile sounds. (a) mouse click and (b) key insertion to keyhole.

3   Experiments

3.1   Experiment 1: Recognition of 12 Daily Actions

In this research, we focused on the tactile sound which was emitted in our daily lives. Figure 3 shows the 12 types of objects and related actions we used in our experiment as representative daily behaviors.

In order to recognize these 12 objects, we used the Hidden Markov Model (HMM) which is usually used in speech recognition. Twelve models of the tactile sounds were created using HTK (The Hidden Markov Model Toolkit) [9]. In the HTK algorithm, we used 25-dimensional data as characteristic values which were calculated from Mel Frequency Cepstrum Coefficient (MFCC).

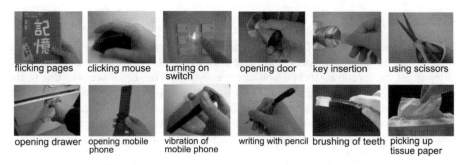

flicking pages   clicking mouse   turning on switch   opening door   key insertion   using scissors

opening drawer   opening mobile phone   vibration of mobile phone   writing with pencil   brushing of teeth   picking up tissue paper

Fig. 3. Twelve daily actions used in recognition experiments

For constructing training data of the tactile sound, 7 subjects (6 males: 20s~30s and 1 female: 20s) participated in our experiment. Subjects manipulated 12 objects 50 times each. As a result, we obtained 350 (7 subjects times 50 trials) data in total for each objects. In the experiment, we used the same mouse or mobile phone. A sampling frequency for tactile sound detection was 16 kHz which was determined based on our pilot experiment.

We conducted two recognition tests. One was offline recognition test and the other was online (real time) recognition test. The recognition does not need to be in real time when you review your actions after a while. On the other hand, if you want to use the log for preventing obliviousness as described in Ex.1, the system has to work in real time.

For constructing the appropriate HMM for the recognition, we tried to change the number of states of the HMM so as to know the proper number of them. We experimentally confirmed that the recognition rate increased as the number of the states increased. In the pilot experiment, the recognition rate converged when the number of states was larger than 20. Therefore, we decided that the number of the states was 20.

For offline recognition, we used cross-validation method for calculating a recognition rate. We divided 350 data into 5 groups. Thus each group has 70 data (10 data each from 7 subjects). Four groups of 5 were used as training data and the rest one group was used as test data. We altered test data so that every group became test data once. Finally we calculated the recognition rate by averaging all the results.

For the online recognition, we additionally used the Julius [10]. The algorithm automatically cut out sound section based on its amplitude. In the case of 20 HMM states, the required time for recognition is not so long (about 1second after the action finished). That can be accepted as real time recognition. The same 7 subjects were participated in the experiment. The training models were constructed from above 350 data. Each subject was asked to do 12 actions 20 times each as test data. Then we calculated the average recognition rate of 20 data.

3.2 Experiment 2: Recognition of Different Mouse Devices

In the previous section, we used an identical mouse device for training data set for mouse button click. Then we used different two mouse devices for checking their recognition rates. Eight subjects (6 males and 2 females) were asked to click them 20 times each. Then we calculated their recognition rates with real time system.

4 Results

Figure 4 shows the results of recognition rate for 12 different daily actions. For offline recognition, the averaged recognition rate was 94.4%. On the other hand for online recognition, the averaged recognition rate was 84.6%. The difference was due to the cut out process of recorded sound. We manually cut out sound section for offline recognition, while it was done automatically for online one. The both rates were relatively high even though we did not take individual differences into account for constructing the models. This means that the tactile sound does not strongly depend on person but on objects.

In the experiment, subjects did only the registered 12 actions. If they did different actions instead, the system will mistake those actions for one of these 12 actions.

Figure 5 shows the averaged recognition rates for another two different mouse devices. The mouse A is the one used as the training data in the experiment 1. The averaged recognition rates for the mouse B and the mouse C were 84.4% and 71.3 % respectively while it was 89.3% for the mouse A. We realized that the different mouse devices had relatively similar tactile sound characteristic.

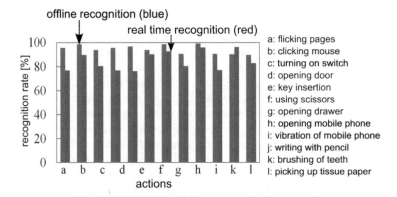

Fig. 4. Averaged recognition rates of 12 different actions

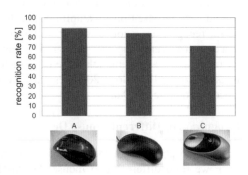

Fig. 5. Averaged recognition rates of 3 different mouse devices. The mouse A is used for constructing recognition model.

After the experiment, we showed the action histories to subjects and asked them whether this information can be used to review their own actions. Almost all the subjects answered that the tactile sound was useful for remembering their daily behaviors.

5 Summary

In this paper, we proposed a new life log system which records a sound of manipulation. Our method is superior to conventional life log systems in terms of privacy issue since it only records what you touch in your daily lives. We showed our prototype which records tactile sound with piezoelectric device attached on a fingernail. Then we demonstrated that our prototype can recognize 12 different actions using conventional speech recognition scheme. The average recognition rates of 12 actions were 94.4 % for offline recognition and 84.6% for real time recognition. We also showed the recognition rates of different mouse devices, which were not used for training. Those recognition rates were more than 70% in average. These experimental results indicated that our method is suitable for the life log which considers privacy issue.

Acknowledgements

This work was supported in part by Grant-in-Aid for the Global Center of Excellence Program for "Center for Education and Research of Symbiotic, Safe and Secure System Design" in Japan.

References

1. Ueoka, T., Kawamura, T., Kono, Y., Kidoe, M.: I'm Here!: A Wearable Object Remembrance Support System. In: Proc. of the Fifth International Symposium on Human-Computer Interaction with Mobile Devices and Services, pp. 422–427 (2003)
2. Veuri, S., Schmandt, C., Bender, W., Tellex, S., Lassey, B.: An Audio-Based Personal Memory Aid. In: Proc. 6th International Conference on Ubiquitous Computing, pp. 400–417 (2004)
3. Ashbrook, D., Starner, T.: Using GPS to Learn Significant Locations and Prodict Movement Across Multiple Users. Personal and Ubiquitous Computing 7(5), 275–286 (2003)
4. Mori, T., Hayama, N., Noguchi, H., Sato, T.: Informational support in distributed sensor environment sensing room. In: 13th IEEE International Workshop on Robot and Human Interactive Communication, ROMAN 2004, pp. 353–358 (2004)
5. Mascaro, S., Asada, H.: Measurement of Finger Posture and Three-Axis Fingertip Touch Force Using Fingernail Sensors. IEEE Transactions on Robotics and Automation 20(1), 26–35 (2004)
6. Fukumoto, M., Tonomura, Y.: Whisper: A Wristwatch Style Wearable Handset. In: Proc.of CHI 1999, pp. 112–119 (1999)
7. Iwamoto, T., Shinoda, H.: Finger Ring Tactile Interface Based on Propagating Elastic Waves on Human Fingers. In: Proc. World Haptics, pp. 145–150 (2007)
8. Martinot, F., Plenacoste, P., Chaillou, C.: Haptic Sounds and Vibrations of Human fingerprints. In: Proc. International Conference on Sensing Technology, pp. 615–620 (2005)
9. http://htk.eng.cam.ac.uk/
10. http://julius.sourceforge.jp/

What Is It Like to Be a Rat? Sensory Augmentation Study

Avraham Saig, Amos Arieli, and Ehud Ahissar

Neurobiology Department, Weizmann Institute of Science,
Rehovot 76100, Israel
{avraham.saig,amos.arieli,ehud.ahissar}@weizmann.ac.il

Abstract. The present study examined the human ability to learn a new sensory modality, specifically "whisking". An experimental apparatus containing artificial whiskers, force sensors, position sensors and computer interface was developed. Twelve participants took part in an experiment containing three tasks: pole localization in the radial dimension, roughness estimation, and object recognition. All tasks were performed only through use of the artificial whiskers which were attached to participants' fingers. With little or no practice humans were able to localize objects, recognize shapes and assess roughness with accuracy equal to or greater than that of rats in equivalent tasks, though with longer times. While the number of available whiskers significantly affected shape recognition, it did not affect radial localization accuracy. Introspection by participants revealed a wide range of motor-sensory strategies developed in order to solve the tasks.

Keywords: Sensory augmentation, vibrissa, perception, whiskers, object recognition, localization.

1 Introduction

The question "what is it like to be a bat" was raised by the philosopher Thomas Nagel in a classical paper carrying that name [1]. The work argues for the unavoidably subjective nature of perception and experiences. The rats' vibrissa (whisker) system, which has no human equivalent, is a part of their somatosensory system. The vibrissae are extremely sensitive [2]; their sensitivity is comparable to that of primate fingertips [3]. Rats can independently move their whiskers across surfaces to make fine tactile discriminations [3, 4]. For many years researchers have been looking into the precise nature of information conveyed by the whiskers to the brain (see [5-10] for current reviews). However, the more information we gain about rats' vibrissa system, the more Nagel's claim becomes relevant, since we humans lack first-hand knowledge of a whisker-like system. In order to gain "first hand" knowledge of the vibrissa system, we augmented the sense of touch in human volunteers by creating a new sense of 'whisking' and tested the volunteers in a variety of perceptual tasks. An advantage of studying 'whisking' in human subjects, in the study of the mechanisms of sensory perception, is that we already possess good models of sensory coding in the rat. Specifically, we have acquired a basic understanding of the computational constraints on

A.M.L. Kappers et al. (Eds.): EuroHaptics 2010, Part I, LNCS 6191, pp. 298–305, 2010.

several of the algorithms and on some of the neuronal implementations that area involved in the execution of active tasks by the rats' vibrissa system.

Sensory augmentation is a developing area of research in which human sensation is augmented in order to create new sensory capabilities (e.g. sensing magnetic fields [11]). This approach can give insights into both the way the brain learns to use a new sensory modality and the subjective experience of the learner during this process by measuring the change in performance capabilities with practice.

Our experimental goals were: (1) to study mechanisms of perception in an augmented tactile sense, and (2) to gain information through human introspection about plausible internal processes in a whisking rat. Preliminary results on 3 different tasks are presented.

2 Methods

2.1 Apparatus

Twelve adult human participants were dressed with long elastic rods on their fingers that mimic rats' whiskers (Fig. 1).

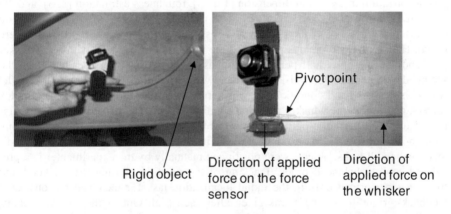

Fig. 1. Left: The artificial whiskers apparatus used in the experiments. The whisker is pressed against a rigid object. Right: The "button" of the v-scope system and the plastic whisker attached to force sensor.

The whiskers were made from transparent PVC rods that were molded into a conical shape by heating and stretching. The diameter of each whisker changed gradually from 1.8mm at the base to 1.2mm at its end and their length was 34.5cm. The whiskers' stiffness was slightly softer than that of a drinking straw, and they did not bend under their own weight when held horizontally. The base of each whisker was glued to an electronic force sensor (FS20 load cell, measurement specialties, USA). The force sensor (along with the whisker) was glued to a narrow Velcro ® strip which was used to connect the apparatus to the finger (see Fig. 1). A small piece of PVC rod was glued to the whisker base in front of (and in contact with) the finger pad. The movements and forces of the whisker were transmitted by the PVC rod to the entire length of the finger pad – this arrangement simulated the interaction between the whisker and its elongated follicle in rats. The rod also served as a pivot point – i.e. when the finger pad was pressed against it, the base part of the whisker was pressed against the force sensor. Therefore, the forces applied by the whisker on the fingertip could be recorded via the electronic force sensor. In addition, a 3D tracking "button" was connected to the Velcro® on the opposite side of the force sensor. The button is part of the v-scope tracking system (V-scope, LVS-11-pro, Litek, Tel-Aviv, Israel). Each button's position (and therefore the fingers' positions) was tracked via the system every 30ms with a spatial resolution of 0.1mm. The force sensors were connected to a computer via an analog-to-digital card (DaqBoard/100, ioteck, USA). In the experiment room, a video camera was positioned on the ceiling and an upper view of the human volunteer performing the different tasks was captured. All electronic monitoring devices (whisker force sensors, position trackers and video camera) were connected to a single computer. Data acquisition was handled through a specialized real-time program written in Matlab.

2.2 The Tasks

Three perceptual tasks, mimicking published rat whisker-related tasks, were chosen: pole localization in the radial dimension [12, 13], roughness estimation [2, 3], and 3D shape recognition [14]. The experiment consisted of 2 sessions of ~1 hour each on two different days (24-48 hours between sessions). In each session, all tasks were tested. Half of the participants performed the tasks on the first day with one whisker per hand and the other half performed the task with two whiskers per hand. On the second day the number of whiskers per hand was switched between the groups. In the two whiskers per hand condition the whiskers were affixed to the middle and index fingers, and in the one whisker per hand condition they were affixed to the index fingers. During all tasks the participants were blindfolded and wore earphones playing white-noise superimposed on classical music in order to block any assistance by auditory cues. In all tasks, objects were positioned manually by the experimenter in a predefined counter balanced order. Tracking of the position of fingers (whiskers) and force was performed only in the radial localization task for technical reasons. Oral feedback ("right" / "wrong") was given after each trial. Out of the 12 participants, only 8 performed the task twice.

2.2.1 Radial Discrimination Task

Two Small Tables were positioned to the right and left of the participant, equidistant from the midline of the chair where the participant sat. A metal pole wrapped with cotton cloth (in order to eliminate contact sounds between poles and whiskers) was positioned on each table (fig 2).

Poles were located in different radial distances and the participant's task was to determine which pole was located closer to him or her along the radial axis (i.e., which pole is closer to the base of the whisker). No further instructions on how to solve the task were given.

The difference in position between the poles at the beginning of each trial was 16 cm. This difference was stepped down in logarithmic increments following a staircase paradigm as in Knutsen et al 2006 [15]. The radial position differences between the poles were rounded-up to the nearest integer number in centimeters, and therefore the smallest difference tested was 1 cm (1 cm was also the measuring error in the experimental apparatus). For all distances, the poles were within reach only of the whiskers and not within reach of the participant's fingers. Before the beginning of the session the participant was given *one* practice trial (of 16 cm difference).

2.2.2 Roughness Estimation

The participant sat in front of a table. In each trial he or she needed to palpate a pair of sandpaper sheets and to say which one was more "rough". The sandpapers' roughness measure, the grit, represents the average number of particles per inch of sandpaper. Within the range we used, the lower the grit, the rougher was the sandpaper (the diameter of the particles and the intervals between them were larger). The grits used in these trials are 120 vs. 1200, 60 vs. 24, 60 vs. 1200 and 1200 vs. smooth transparency sheet.

2.2.3 Three-Dimensional Shape Recognition

Four 3D geometrical objects (pyramid, prism, small box and elongated box, Fig. 2) made from cardboard were first presented visually to the participants. Then the participants were asked to palpate the objects with their whisker(s) and determine which of the four objects was placed on the table in front of them (the shapes were presented in a random order).

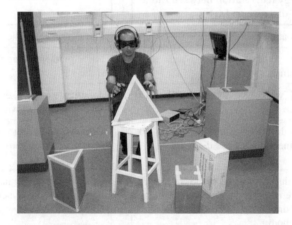

Fig. 2. The 3D shape recognition task. The two poles used in the radial discrimination task are seen on both sides of the participant. Notice, two 'towers' of the v-scope tracking system are seen on the wall behind the participant.

3   Results

Interestingly, with little or no practice humans were able to localize objects and estimate roughness as accurately as, and in some cases even better than, rats in equivalent tasks. Here we present the psychophysical results and introspective reports by the participants. The sensor data (force and location) have not yet been analyzed.

3.1   Radial Discrimination Task

In this task participants were asked to tell which one of the two bilaterally presented poles was closer to them in the radial dimension. We did not find any effect of the number of whiskers per hand on participants' performance or psychophysical threshold (paired T-test, n = 8, P-Value = 0.82). Comparison of the performance between the first and the second session shows a weak experience effect. In the second session the thresholds were lower, but with borderline statistical significance (paired T-test, n = 8, P-Value = 0.053).

At the beginning of the first session, the participants found it difficult to know which pole was closer to them (notice that participants were not given any instruction on how to solve the task). Thus, at the beginning of the first session participants were in search of correlations between the correct answer in the trial and some physical or sensory variable mediated through the whiskers (via motor action). Interestingly, the 12 participants reported 5 different strategies for correlating the radial distance with some motor-sensory behavior. The strategies, according to self-reports of the participants are summarized in Table 1.

Table 1. Strategies used by participants in the radial discrimination task according to participants' introspection, and possible analogous rats' strategies

Human strategy (correlation between radial distance and...)	#	Analogous rat strategy
Force-moment at the whisker base.	7	Force-moment at the whisker base.
Force-gradient along the finger-pad area touching the whisker.	2	Force-gradient along the whisker follicle.
Amplitude of whiskers vibration following contact with the poles.	1	Amplitude of whiskers vibration following contact with the poles.
Detach time during synchronized forward whisker movement that passes the poles.	1	Detach time during synchronized forward whisker movement that passes the poles.
Detach time during synchronized retraction whisker movement in the coronal plane (movement from fully stretched hands to hands close to body).	1	Detach time during lateral head movements (non synchronous comparison).

The first 4 strategies can be employed in a similar manner by humans and rats while the 5th strategy must be implemented differently. There is evidence suggesting that radial distance is encoded in rats by the force-moment at the base of the whisker [16-18]; interestingly, the majority of participants chose this strategy by themselves. However, in contrast to the rats' behavior in the experiments reported by Krupa et al. [12], human participants in our experiments did not improve their performance with additional whiskers (as mentioned above). Multiple whisker palpation might be helpful in radial localization in rats due to the limited resolution of single mechanoreceptors [19], which might not be the case in human skin sensation.

All in all, participants' performance was very good in the test (average threshold around 2.5cm). Two participants even reached the minimum discrimination distance in the system: 1cm. These threshold values are better than rats' ones [12] when taken in relation to the distance between the two poles (2.5 / 190 vs 3 / 65) and comparable when taken in relation to whisker length (2.5 / 34.5 vs 3 / 50).

3.2 Shape Recognition Task

In this task, participants were asked to identify geometrical shape through palpation by the whiskers. Human success rates (Fig. 3) were comparable to those of rats [14]. In contrast to the radial task, the number of whiskers did significantly affect the results. In sessions performed with two whiskers per hand participants were more accurate relative to sessions performed with one whisker per hand (Fig. 3, paired T-test P-Value<0.05).

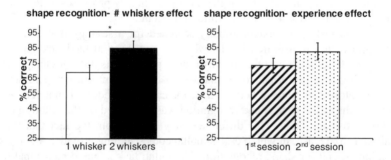

Fig 3. Success rate (percent correct) in the shape recognition task as a function of whiskers number (left) and experience (right). The error bars represent the s.e.m.

As in the radial discrimination task, the experience of the participants seems to affect their performance (Fig. 3). However, in this task the effect was small and was not found to be statistically significant.

3.3 Roughness Estimation

In this task all participants in all conditions were 100% correct – all of them were always able to discriminate correctly the rough from the less rough sand-paper in less than 30 seconds of palpation. Obviously, the task was too easy for humans. This is in contradiction to rats, which even in a much easier task – of discriminating totally smooth surface from a sandpaper – do not reach 100% correct performance [2]. Note however that rats rarely spend more than half a second on such tasks, possibly because 100% perfection is rarely their obsession.

4 General Discussion

In this research we have shown a proof of principle. Humans were able to learn to use a new sense of 'whisking', and to use this new sense to solve different perceptual tasks. The perceptual thresholds reached were as good as, and sometimes even better than, rats in similar tasks. Using humans as a 'model animal' for rats can provide insights, via introspection, on perceptual strategies that might be employed by rats and mice – insights that cannot be obtained otherwise. Although rodent and human touch biomechanics differ, the motor-sensory strategies, and the use of re-afference and ex-afference signals might be comparable [9, 20]. Studying tactile augmentation in humans can facilitate development of efficient sensory augmentation and substitution devices for the blind and deaf. Another consequence of this kind of research is gaining knowledge of how the brain learns to use a sense. When performing research on existing human senses, humans can be considered experts in their use. With such high level expertise, it is almost impossible to unravel *why* participants tend to use a specific motor-sensory strategy and *how* this strategy was developed. Introspection in this case cannot help, since perceptual learning of regular tasks by existing senses occurs in the early stages of life and thus cannot be reliably reported. In contrast, sensory-augmentation both facilitate the isolation of sensory variables, as has been previously shown [21, 22], and allows for the most preliminary processes of learning to be recorded, analyzed and self-reported while they occur.

In the radial task, participants initially searched for a strategy that correlated the sensory information transmitted by the whisker, and the oral feedback given by the experimenter. Once such correlation was found, participants did not change strategy, but tried to improve performance by sharpening the relevant sensory parameters, using their developed strategy. Whether this is the case with rodents is not yet clear.

Unlike in the radial task, shape recognition was facilitated by the addition of a second whisker to each hand. This difference may derive from the fact that the shape recognition is a 3D task, in which case simultaneous scanning provides relative spatial information crucial for shape recognition. The radial task is one dimensional task for which relative information between whiskers is not crucial. Bilateral palpation of frontal objects, which is occasionally observed in freely exploring rats and mice (unpublished observations), probably further facilitates shape recognition.

Acknowledgments. We thank Ms. Tess Oram for reviewing this article. This work was supported by the EU FP7 BIOTACT project (ICT-215910). A.S. is supported by the Adams Fellowship Program of the Israel Academy of Sciences and Humanities.

References

1. Nagel, T.: What is it like to be a bat? Philosophical Review 83, 435–450 (1974)
2. Arabzadeh, E., Zorzin, E., Diamond, M.E.: Neuronal encoding of texture in the whisker sensory pathway. PLoS Biol. 3, 17 (2005)
3. Carvell, G.E., Simons, D.J.: Biometric analyses of vibrissal tactile discrimination in the rat. J. Neurosci. 10, 2638–2648 (1990)
4. Guic-Robles, E., Valdivieso, C., Guajardo, G.: Rats can learn a roughness discrimination using only their vibrissal system. Behav. Brain Res. 31, 285–289 (1989)
5. Ahissar, E., Kleinfeld, D.: Closed-loop neuronal computations: focus on vibrissa somatosensation in rat. Cereb. Cortex 13, 53–62 (2003)
6. Kleinfeld, D., Ahissar, E., Diamond, M.E.: Active sensation: insights from the rodent vibrissa sensorimotor system. Curr. Opin. Neurobiol. 16, 435–444 (2006)

7. Ahissar, E., Knutsen, P.M.: Object localization with whiskers. Biol. Cybern. 98, 449–458 (2008)
8. Brecht, M.: Barrel cortex and whisker-mediated behaviors. Curr. Opin. Neurobiol. 17, 408–416 (2007)
9. Diamond, M.E., von Heimendahl, M., Knutsen, P.M., Kleinfeld, D., Ahissar, E.: 'Where' and 'what' in the whisker sensorimotor system. Nat. Rev. Neurosci. 9, 601–612 (2008)
10. Petersen, C.C.: The functional organization of the barrel cortex. Neuron 56, 339–355 (2007)
11. Nagel, S.K., Carl, C., Kringe, T., Martin, R., Konig, P.: Beyond sensory substitution–learning the sixth sense. J. Neural Eng. 2, R13–R26 (2005)
12. Krupa, D.J., Matell, M.S., Brisben, A.J., Oliveira, L.M., Nicolelis, M.A.: Behavioral properties of the trigeminal somatosensory system in rats performing whisker-dependent tactile discriminations. J. Neurosci. 21, 5752–5763 (2001)
13. Shuler, M.G., Krupa, D.J., Nicolelis, M.A.: Integration of bilateral whisker stimuli in rats: role of the whisker barrel cortices. Cereb. Cortex 12, 86–97 (2002)
14. Harvey, M.A., Bermejo, R., Zeigler, H.P.: Discriminative whisking in the head-fixed rat: optoelectronic monitoring during tactile detection and discrimination tasks. Somatosens Mot. Res. 18, 211–222 (2001)
15. Knutsen, P.M., Pietr, M., Ahissar, E.: Haptic object localization in the vibrissal system: behavior and performance. J. Neurosci. 26, 8451–8464 (2006)
16. Kaneko, M., Kanayama, N., Tsuji, T.: Active antenna for contact sensing. IEEE Transactions on Robotics and Automation 14, 278–291 (1998)
17. Solomon, J.H., Hartmann, M.J.: Biomechanics: robotic whiskers used to sense features. Nature 443, 525 (2006)
18. Birdwell, J.A., Solomon, J.H., Thajchayapong, M., Taylor, M.A., Cheely, M., Towal, R.B., Conradt, J., Hartmann, M.J.: Biomechanical models for radial distance determination by the rat vibrissal system. J. Neurophysiol. 98, 2439–2455 (2007)
19. Szwed, M., Bagdasarian, K., Blumenfeld, B., Barak, O., Derdikman, D., Ahissar, E.: Responses of trigeminal ganglion neurons to the radial distance of contact during active vibrissal touch. J. Neurophysiol. 95, 791–802 (2006)
20. Knutsen, P.M., Ahissar, E.: Orthogonal coding of object location. Trends Neurosci. 32, 101–109 (2009)
21. Gamzu, E., Ahissar, E.: Importance of temporal cues for tactile spatial- frequency discrimination. J. Neurosci. 21, 7416–7427 (2001)
22. Levy, M., Bourgeon, S., Chapman, C.E.: Haptic discrimination of two-dimensional angles: influence of exploratory strategy. Exp. Brain Res. 178, 240–251 (2007)

Innovative Real-Time Communication System with Rich Emotional and Haptic Channels

Dzmitry Tsetserukou[1] and Alena Neviarouskaya[2]

[1] Toyohashi University of Technology,1-1 Hibarigaoka, Tempaku-cho,
Toyohashi, Aichi, 441-8580 Japan
t.setserukou@erc.tut.ac.jp
[2] University of Tokyo, 7-3-1 Hongo, Bunkyo-ku, Tokyo, 113-8656 Japan
lena@mi.ci.i.u-tokyo.ac.jp

Abstract. The paper focuses on a novel system iFeel_IM! that integrates 3D virtual world Second Life, intelligent component for automatic emotion recognition from text messages, and innovative affective haptic interfaces providing additional nonverbal communication channels through simulation of emotional feedback and social touch (physical co-presence). The core component, Affect Analysis Model, automatically recognizes nine emotions from text. The detected emotion is stimulated by innovative haptic devices integrated into iFeel_IM!. Users can not only exchange messages but also emotionally and physically feel the presence of the communication partner (e.g., family member, friend, or beloved person).

Keywords: Affective Haptics, haptic display, tactile display, haptic communication, online communication, Instant Messaging, 3D world.

1 Introduction

"All emotions use the body as their theater..."
Antonio Damasio

Nowadays, companies providing media for remote online communications place a great importance on live communication and immersive technologies. Along with widely used Instant Messengers (such as Yahoo IM, AOL AIM, Microsoft Windows Live Messenger, Google talk, Skype), such new web services as Twitter, Google Wave, Google Buzz gain notability and popularity worldwide. Such applications allow keeping in touch with friends in real-time over multiple networks and devices. Recently mobile communication companies launched Instant Messenger service on cellular phones (e.g. AIM on iPhone). 3D virtual worlds (e.g., Second Life, OpenSim) are also embedded with chat and instant messenger. Such systems encourage people to establish or strengthen interpersonal relations, to share ideas, to gain new experiences, and to feel genuine emotions accompanying all adventures of virtual reality. However, conventional mediated systems usually (1) support only simple textual cues

A.M.L. Kappers et al. (Eds.): EuroHaptics 2010, Part I, LNCS 6191, pp. 306–313, 2010.

like emoticons; (2) lack visual emotional signals such as facial expressions and gestures; (3) support only manual control of expressiveness of graphical representations of users (avatars); and (4) completely ignore such important channel of social communication as sense of touch.

Tactile interfaces could allow users to enhance their emotional communication abilities by adding a whole new dimension to mobile communication [1]. Besides emotions conveyed through text, researchers developed an additional modality for communicating emotions in Instant Messenger (IM) through tactile interfaces with vibration patterns [2], [3]. However, in the proposed methods users have to memorize the vibration or pin matrix patterns and cognitively interpret the communicated emotional state. Demodulation of haptically coded emotion is not natural for human-human communication, and direct evocation of emotion cannot be achieved in such kind of systems. Moreover, the rest of shortcomings of conventional communication system hold true.

2 Affective Haptics. Emerging Frontier

All our senses play significant role in recognition of emotional states of communication partner. Human emotions can be easily evoked by different cues, and sense of touch is one of the most emotionally charged channels.

Affective Haptics is the emerging area of research which focuses on the design of devices and systems that can elicit, enhance, or influence on emotional state of a human by means of sense of touch. We distinguish four basic haptic (tactile) channels governing our emotions: (1) physiological changes (e.g., heart beat rate, body temperature, etc.), (2) physical stimulation (e.g., tickling), (3) social touch (e.g., hug), (4) emotional haptic design (e.g., shape of device, material, texture).

Driven by the motivation to enhance social interactivity and emotionally immersive experience of real-time messaging, we pioneered in the idea of reinforcing (intensifying) own feelings and reproducing (simulating) the emotions felt by the partner through specially designed system iFeel_IM!. The philosophy behind the iFeel_IM! (intelligent system for **Feel**ing enhancement powered by affect sensitive **I**nstant **M**essenger) is "*I feel* [therefore] *I am!*".

3 Architecture of the System

In the iFeel_IM! system, great importance is placed on the automatic sensing of emotions conveyed through textual messages in 3D virtual world Second Life (artificial intelligence), the visualization of the detected emotions by avatars in virtual environment, enhancement of user's affective state, and reproduction of feeling of social touch (e.g., hug) by means of haptic stimulation in a real world. The architecture of the iFeel_IM! is presented in Fig. 1. As a media for communication, we employ Second Life, which allows users to flexibly create their online identities (avatars) and to play various animations (e.g., facial expressions and gestures) of avatars by typing special abbreviations in a chat window.

The control of the conversation is implemented through the Second Life object called EmoHeart attached to the avatar's chest [4]. In addition to communication with the system for textual affect sensing (Affect Analysis Model), EmoHeart is responsible for sensing symbolic cues or keywords of 'hug' communicative function conveyed by text, and for visualization of 'hugging' in Second Life.

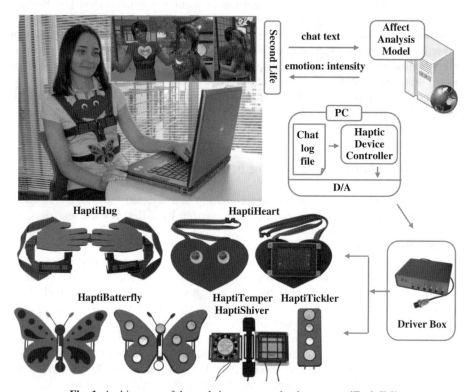

Fig. 1. Architecture of the real-time communication system iFeel_IM!

Haptic Devices Controller analyses these data in a real time and generates control signals for Digital/Analog converter (D/A), which then feeds Driver Box for haptic devices with control cues.

4 Affect Recognition

The Affect Analysis Model [4] senses nine emotions conveyed through text ('anger', 'disgust', 'fear', 'guilt', 'interest', 'joy', 'sadness', 'shame', and 'surprise'). The affect recognition algorithm, which takes into account specific style and evolving language of online conversation, consists of five main stages: (1) symbolic cue analysis; (2) syntactical structure analysis; (3) word-level analysis; (4) phrase-level analysis; and (5) sentence-level analysis. Our Affect Analysis Model (AAM) was designed based on the compositionality principle. An empirical evaluation of the AAM algorithm showed promising results regarding its capability to accurately (achieves accuracy in 81.5 %) classify affective information in text from an existing corpus of informal online communication.

5   Affective Haptic Devices

In order to support the affective communication, we implemented several novel haptic gadgets embedded in iFeel_IM!. They make up three groups. First group is intended for emotion elicitation implicitly (HaptiHeart, HaptiButterfly, HaptiTemper, and HaptiShiver), second type evokes affect in a direct way (HaptiTickler), and third one uses sense of social touch (HaptiHug) for influencing on the mood and providing some sense of physical co-presence.

5.1   HaptiHug: Realistic Hugging over a Distance

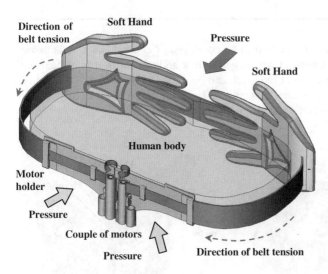

Fig. 2. Structure of the wearable HaptiHug device

Among many forms of physical contact, hug is the most emotionally charged one. When people are hugging, they generate pressure on the chest area and on the back of each other by the hands, simultaneously. The key feature of the developed Hapti-Hug is that it physically reproduces the hug pattern similar to that of human-human interaction. The couple of oppositely rotating motors (Maxon RE 10 1.5 W with gearhead GP 10 A 64:1) are incorporated into the holder placed on the user chest area. The Soft Hands, which are aligned horizontally, contact back of the user. Once 'hug' command is received, couple of motors tense the belt, pressing thus Soft Hands and chest part of the HaptiHug in the direction of human body (Fig. 2). The duration and intensity of the hug are controlled by the software in accordance with the emoticon or a keyword, detected from text.

5.2   HaptiHeart Enhancing User Emotions

Each emotion is characterized by a specific pattern of physiological changes. We selected four distinct emotions having strong physical features [5]: 'anger', 'fear', 'sadness', and 'joy'. The precision of AAM in recognition of these emotions is considerably higher ('anger' – 92 %, 'fear' – 91 %, 'joy' – 95 %, 'sadness' – 88 %) than of other emotions. Table 1 shows the affiliation of each haptic device and emotion being induced.

Of the bodily organs, the heart plays a particularly important role in our emotional experience. The ability of false heart rate feedback to change our emotional state was reported in [6]. We developed the heart imitator HaptiHeart to produce special

Table 1. Each affective haptic device is responsible for stimulation of particular emotion

Haptic device	Emotions				Social Touch
	Joy	**Sadness**	**Anger**	**Fear**	
HaptiHeart		V	V	V	
HaptiButterfly	V				
HaptiShiver				V	
HaptiTemper	V		V	V	
HaptiTickler	V				
HaptiHug	V				V

heartbeat patterns according to emotion to be conveyed or elicited (sadness is associated with slightly intense heartbeat, anger with quick and violent heartbeat, fear with intense heart rate). False heart beat feedback can be directly interpreted as a real heart beat, so it can change the emotional perception. The HaptiHeart consists of two modules: flat speaker FPS 0304 and speaker holder (Fig. 3).

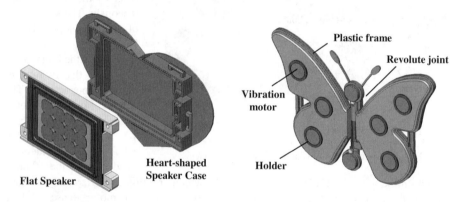

Fig. 3. HaptiHeart layout   **Fig. 4.** Structure of HaptiButterfly

The flat speaker sizes (66.5 x 107 x 8 mm) and rated input power of 10 W allowed us to design powerful and relatively compact device. It is able to produce realistic heartbeating sensation with high fidelity. The pre-recorded sound signal generates the pressure on the human chest through vibration of the speaker surface.

5.3 Butterflies in the Stomach and Shivers on Body's Spine

HaptiButterfly was developed with the aim to evocate joy emotion. The idea behind this device is to reproduce effect of "*Butterflies in the stomach*" (fluttery or tickling feeling in the stomach felt by people experiencing love) by means of the arrays of vibration motors attached to the abdomen area of a person (Fig. 4).

We conducted the experiment aimed at investigation of the patterns of vibration motor activation that produce most pleasurable and natural sensations on the abdomen area. Based on the results, we employ 'circular' and 'spiral' vibration patterns.

The temperature symptoms are great indicators of differences between emotions. The empirical studies [5] showed that (1) fear and (in a lesser degree) sadness, are characterized as 'cold' emotions, (2) joy is the only emotion experienced as being 'warm', while (3) anger is 'hot' emotion.

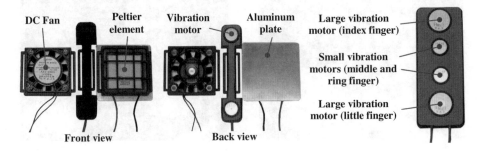

Fig. 5. Structure of HaptiShiver/HaptiTemper   **Fig. 6.** HaptiTickler device

Fear is characterized by the most physiological changes in the human body. Driven by the fear, blood that is shunted from the viscera to the rest of the body transfers heat, prompting thus perspiration to cool the body.

In order to boost fear emotion physically, we designed HaptiShiver interface that sends *"Shivers down/up human body's spine"* by means of a row of vibration motors (HaptiShiver), and *"Chills down/up human body's spine"* through both cold airflow from DC fan and cold side of Peltier element (HaptiTemper, TES1-12705 thermoelectric module, I_{max}=5 A; P_{max}=57 W, ΔT=76 °C). The structure of HaptiShiver/HaptiTemper device is shown in Fig. 5. HaptiTemper is also intended for simulation of warmth on the human skin to evoke either pleasant feeling or aggression (it was proved that uncomfortably hot temperatures arouse anger feelings [7]).

5.4 HaptiTickler: Device for Positive Emotions

A reflex view suggests that tickle requires the element of unpredictability or uncontrollability. The experimental results from [8] support a reflex view and reveal that ticklish laugher evidently does not require that stimulation be attributed to another person. However, the social and emotional factors in ticklishness affect the tickle response greatly (interpersonal explanations of tickling effect).

We developed HaptiTickler with the purpose to evoke positive affect (joy emotion) in a direct way by tickling the ribs of the user. The device includes four vibration motors reproducing stimuli that are similar to human finger movements during rib tickling (Fig. 6). The uniqueness of our approach is in (1) combination of the unpredictability and uncontrollability of the tickling sensation through random activation of stimuli, (2) high involvement of the social and emotional factors in the process of tickling (positively charged on-line conversation potentiates the tickle response).

6 User Study

Recently we demonstrated the iFeel_IM! system with HaptiHeart, HaptiHug, HaptiButterfly, and HaptiTickler at CHI Media Showcase (April 2010) (Fig. 7).

Fig. 7. Demonstration of iFeel_IM! at CHI 2010 Media Showcase

In total 64 persons had experienced our system in a real time. Most of them reported that the haptic modalities (i.e., heartbeating, hugging, and tickling) produced highly realistic sensations. Subjects enjoyed wearing the HaptiHug. The simultaneous observation of hugging animation and experiencing of the hugging sensation evoked surprise and joy in all participants. We randomly selected six participants and conducted a preliminary user study aimed at the evaluation of the effectiveness of emotion elicitation and hug reproduction. The results of the user study revealed that the devices generated the corresponding emotion successfully (see Table 2, where 100% stands for six positive replies). We assume that anger emotion would be reinforced by the HaptiTemper device, if it was activated along with HaptiHeart.

Table 2. Results of the user study

Haptic device	Emotions				Social Touch
	Joy	**Sadness**	**Anger**	**Fear**	
HaptiHeart		*83.3%*	*66.7%*	*100%*	
HaptiButterfly	*83.3%*				
HaptiTickler	*100%*				
HaptiHug	*100%*				*100%*

During the demonstration we had been observing that HaptiButterfly and HaptiTickler forced the majority of participants to smile and, in some cases, to laugh. The participants expressed anxiety, when fear was evoked through fast and intensive heartbeat pattern. The atmosphere between the participants and exhibitors was very relaxing and joyful during iFeel_IM! demonstration, thus indicating that the developed system contributed to the successful elicitation of emotions.

7 Conclusions

While developing the iFeel_IM! system, we attempted to bridge the gap between mediated and face-to-face communications by enabling and enriching the spectrum of senses such as vision and touch along with cognition and inner personal state.

In the paper we described the architecture of the iFeel_IM! and the development of novel haptic devices. The emotional brain of our system, Affect Analysis Model, can sense emotions and intensity with high accuracy. Moreover, AAM is capable of processing the messages written in informal and expressive stile of IM (e.g., "LOL" for "laughing out loudly", "<3" for love, etc.). Haptic devices were designed with particular emphasis on natural and realistic representation of the physical stimuli, modular expandability, ergonomic human-friendly and emotional haptic design. User can perceive the intensive emotions during online communication, use desirable type of stimuli, comfortably wear and easily detach devices from torso. Our primary goal for the future research is to conduct extensive user study on iFeel_IM!. Additional modalities aimed at intensifying affective states will be investigated as well.

The demonstration of the iFeel_IM system was very captivating for the participants and resulted in keen discussions of possible applications for future research (e.g., therapy, affective game, psychological testing). We believe that iFeel_IM! system has great potential to impact on the communication in 'sociomental' (rather than 'virtual') online environments that facilitate contact with others and affect the nature of social life in terms of both interpersonal relationships and the character of community.

References

1. Chang, A., O'Modhrain, S., Jacob, R., Gunther, E., Ishii, H.: ComTouch: Design of a Vibrotactile Communication Device. In: Conference on Designing of Interactive Systems, pp. 312–320. ACM Press, New York (2002)
2. Rovers, A.F., Van Essen, H.A.: HIM: a Framework for Haptic Instant Messaging. In: ACM Conference on Human factors in Computing Systems, pp. 1313–1316. ACM Press, New York (2004)
3. Shin, H., Lee, J., Park, J., Kim, Y., Oh, H., Lee, T.: A Tactile Emotional Interface for Instant Messenger Chat. In: Smith, M.J., Salvendy, G. (eds.) HCII 2007. LNCS, vol. 4558, pp. 166–175. Springer, Heidelberg (2007)
4. Neviarouskaya, A., Prendinger, H., Ishizuka, M.: EmoHeart: Conveying Emotions in Second Life Based on Affect Sensing from Text. Advances in Human-Computer Interaction, Special Issue on Emotion-Aware Natural Interaction, 1–13 (2010)
5. Wallbott, H.G., Scherer, K.R.: How Universal and Specific is Emotional Experience? Evidence from 27 Countries on Five Continents. In: Scherer, K.R. (ed.) Facets of Emotion: Recent Research, pp. 31–56. Lawrence Erlbaum Inc., Hillsdale (1988)
6. Decaria, M.D., Proctor, S., Malloy, T.E.: The Effect of False Heart Rate Feedback on Self Reports of Anxiety and on Actual Heart Rate. Behavior research & Therapy 12, 251–253 (1974)
7. Anderson, C.A.: Temperature and Aggression: Ubiquitous Effects of Heat on Occurrence of Human Violence. Psychological Bulletin 106(1), 74–96 (1989)
8. Harris, C.R., Christenfeld, N.: Can a Machine Tickle? Psychonomic Bulletin & Review 6(3), 504–510 (1999)

Tactile vs Graphical Authentication

Ravi Kuber[1] and Wai Yu[2]

[1] UMBC, 1000 Hilltop Circle, Baltimore, MD, 21250, USA
[2] Thales, Alanbrooke Road, Belfast, BT6 9HB, UK
rkuber@umbc.edu

Abstract. This paper describes a novel approach to authenticate entry to a system using tactile feedback. The user is required to remember a sequence of pre-selected pin patterns. A study has been undertaken to determine the feasibility of the tactile authentication mechanism, through a comparison with a graphical scheme. Findings from a within-subjects study have revealed that both tactile and graphical authentication sequences could be entered at specific points over the course of a five month period. While graphical sequences could be entered on average 28.5 seconds faster than tactile sequences, participants believed the tactile mechanism offered greater levels of security from observers. As pins are presented underneath the fingertips, they are concealed from the view of third parties. As tactile sensations are difficult to describe, it is less likely that they will be disclosed to others, thereby reducing the chances of unauthorized access.

Keywords: Authentication, haptics, human factors, photographs, tactile.

1 Introduction

Haptic technologies can be used to enhance interaction with a wide variety of interfaces, ranging from virtual museum applications to medical training software [1]. More recently, touch has been applied to the design of authentication mechanisms, providing an alternative to traditional systems requiring both a username and alphanumeric password. The VibraPass system [2] presents vibrations via the user's own mobile telephone when entering a Personal Identification Number (PIN) into a public terminal. The vibrations indicate whether the user should 'lie' and enter a different digit from the numbers contained within his/her PIN. The aim is to confuse 'shoulder surfers' seeking to record their victim's PIN. Deyle and Roth [3] have developed an authentication system using eight solenoids, which are either raised or lowered. To enter the system, the user must accurately indicate the state of the solenoids corresponding to his/her personal authentication sequence. Orozco Trujillo et al. [4] have integrated biometric data as part of their authentication procedure. The software extracts key information including the force exerted using the stylus, the torque and the orientation. These features can be used to verify that the user's authenticity. In contrast with these solutions, the Tactile Authentication System [5] enables the user to authenticate entry through the ability to remember a sequence of pre-selected patterns of raised pins. Pins are presented to users via cells (contactor pads) on top of the VT Player tactile mouse (Figure 1-left). Four different pin patterns are selected and memorized by users as their 'tactile password' to a system, similar to a four digit PIN for an ATM (Figure 1-right).

A.M.L. Kappers et al. (Eds.): EuroHaptics 2010, Part I, LNCS 6191, pp. 314–319, 2010.
© Springer-Verlag Berlin Heidelberg 2010

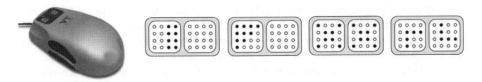

Fig. 1. VT Player (Virtouch Ltd) (left) with sequence of tactile stimuli forming 'tactile password' (right). The filled circles indicate which pins are raised.

Benefits of the Tactile Authentication System (TAS):

- TAS capitalizes on our abilities to remember arrangements of raised pins. This is evidenced by Braille readers, who are able to successfully associate tactile patterns with alphanumeric characters.
- Stimuli are perceived underneath the fingertips, occluding the feedback from view, thereby protecting the user from the threat of third parties observing and recreating the authentication sequence.
- Up to thirty-two pins can be raised to form a variety of patterns on the tactile mouse. Pins can be presented in a timed sequence forming 'animated' stimuli, in conjunction with 'static' raised arrangements.
- The interface has been designed enabling the user to recognize his/her pre-selected stimuli, rather than recalling information. The process of recognition is known to be less cognitively intensive compared with the process of recall.

Fig. 2. Sequence of facial photographs adapted from Passfaces™ [6]

A study has been designed to determine the feasibility of TAS, by comparing it with an alternative authentication mechanism. Graphical schemes have grown in popularity in recent years, capitalizing on our abilities to remember images. Passfaces™ has been designed to enable users to enter a system, by recognizing a series of pre-selected stimuli (facial photographs) in a prescribed order (Figure 2). Studies have shown Passfaces™ to be memorable and recognizable over a long-term period [7,8,9].

2 Tactile Authentication System

A web-based authentication interface has been designed using HTML, ASP, Javascript, VBScript and the VT Player SDK. It is hosted on a local server. In order to enter the system, the user firstly selects his/her full name from a drop-down box, and then selects his/her personal authentication sequence by choosing four tactile stimuli from a wider range presented. The TAS interface consists of four grids, each of which contains nine

316   R. Kuber and W. Yu

visually-identical squares arranged in a 3x3 format (Figure 3), similar to the layout used by Brostoff and Sasse [7] in their study. Each square is associated with a unique tactile stimulus [10], presented via the VT Player mouse. By actively exploring the interface, the user will be able to locate the first stimulus from his/her 'tactile password'. The process is repeated on the remaining three grids, until four stimuli have been selected (Figure 4). Tactile sensations are randomly arranged within each grid, so that an observer cannot distinguish the spatial position of the stimulus chosen. A more detailed explanation of the design of TAS is presented in [10].

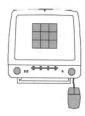

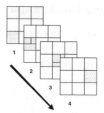

Fig. 3. TAS system displaying grid of tactile stimuli

Fig. 4. Example of authentication sequence to enter system

For purposes of the comparison study, TAS was modified to either present tactile information or facial photographs. The photographs were selected both from the Passfaces™ demonstration software and other sites containing headshots. Photographs were selected to ensure that attention would not be unduly drawn to them (e.g. monochrome backgrounds, limited facial jewelry). Similar to entering a 'tactile password', in the graphical condition, the user locates and selects one photograph from each of the four grids presented (Figure 2). After four stimuli have been chosen, entry can be granted, providing the photographs match the user's pre-selected stimuli. The chance of a third party guessing either a tactile or graphical sequence at random would be 1 in 6561 (9^4 combinations [7]).

3 Experiment Design

An experiment was designed where sixteen participants were exposed to two conditions. Participants were first asked to select a tactile authentication sequence consisting of four static and/or animated stimuli. They were asked to log-in to the system from Monday to Friday only for two weeks, and once at the end of the fourth week, following a procedure adapted from Valentine [8,9]. Participants were then asked to select a graphical authentication sequence, consisting of either male or female faces. These would be entered using the same schedule. Sixteen weeks after participating in each condition, participants were asked to enter their authentication sequences for one last time, to determine their ability to remember secure information over a long term period without rehearsal. In order to determine the feasibility of both the tactile and graphical approaches, measures such as task time taken, failed authentication attempts and resets made were recorded and analyzed.

4   Results and Discussion

Fourteen out of the original sixteen participants completed both conditions of the study. Findings revealed that fewer errors were made by the fourteen participants on their first attempt entering a system under the graphical condition (90.0% rate of success) compared with the tactile condition (86.4% rate of success). Results are presented in Table 1. Levels of accuracy entering the system on the first attempt appeared to reduce when sequence entry could not be rehearsed (e.g. Day 8 after a gap of two days, Day 28 after a gap of sixteen days, and Day 140 after a gap of four months).

Table 1. Accuracy of entry and time taken to enter system for both by condition

	Accuracy of first entry attempt (Tactile)	Average time Taken (Tactile)	Accuracy of first entry attempt (Graphical)	Average time taken (Graphical)
Day 1	100.0%	35.4 s	100.0%	8.6 s
Day 8	87.5%	50.1 s	100.0%	9.4 s
Day 12	92.3%	33.0 s	90.0%	11.0 s
Day 28	83.3%	39.9 s	100.0%	15.0 s
Day 140	58.3%	58.0 s	90.0%	20.0 s

Graphical sequences could be entered on average 28.5 seconds faster (SD 13.4 seconds) compared to entering tactile sequences. Results from a paired t-test revealed that this difference was significant ($p < 0.005$). Reasons were attributed to the presentation of tactile information. Participants were observed moving cautiously through each grid, perceiving each of the tactile stimuli presented, prior to choosing their pre-selected stimulus. A greater level of deviation was also experienced under the tactile condition (16.6 seconds) compared to the graphical condition (3.2 seconds).

There were more incorrect authentication attempts when entering a tactile sequence (20 out of 137 recorded attempts – 14.6 %) over the five month period, compared to when entering a graphical sequence (3 out of 112 recorded attempts – 2.7%). Fourteen of the twenty-three incorrect attempts were made on Day 140 (i.e. four months later). While this in part may have also been attributed to limitations of both the tactile and graphical memory, some participants suggested that they were able to remember their respective authentication sequences but had selected the mouse button twice in quick succession. As a result, two stimuli were entered instead of one (e.g. one stimulus from one grid, another from a second grid). Findings from the study have indicated that participants were able to recover from errors made, and authenticate entry by the fourth attempt. The levels of self-initiated resets were also judged as comparable, with a total of seven resets made for the tactile condition, and a total of five made for the graphical condition.

In terms of perceived security, seven out of fourteen participants stated that they felt more secure using tactile authentication compared to conventional alphanumeric passwords and PINs. When using an ATM, participants remarked that they often shielded the keypad using their hand or wallet when entering their PINs, to reduce the threat of observer attacks. However, as tactile stimuli are occluded from view in TAS, they suggested that they would not need to perform this task when using the tactile mechanism. Participants agreed that as the sense of touch is difficult to describe and is personal to each user, stimuli would be tougher to disclose to others. Even if the tactile sequence was disclosed, there would be no guarantee that a verbal explanation of a tactile pattern could be replicated easily by a third party, as descriptions would vary from person to person. While the graphical condition was not thought to offer the same level of perceived security, eight participants suggested that it was a less cognitively intensive process to visually-scan each grid and recognize graphical stimuli, compared with tactile identification. Participants suggested that concentration was needed for tactile perception, as it was a relatively unpracticed skill, in contrast with facial recognition. As a result, the graphical scheme was found to be more usable than the touch-based mechanism by half the group of participants.

When questioned upon their selections of graphical stimuli, nine participants selected facial photographs from a mixture of racial groups, which they described as being a key factor to help them distinguish between faces. Participants also remarked that accessories within photographs such as glasses and shirt collars offered them a cue to remember and recognize their selected photograph. Analysis of tactile stimuli selected revealed that popular choices included patterns containing a small number of raised pins, or pins arranged in geometric patterns (e.g. formed into lines or shapes). Animated patterns were less widely chosen by participants compared with static patterns. Reasons for this were most likely due to our limited spatial and temporal resolution abilities, making distinguishing between animations a more time-consuming and cognitive intensive process.

5 Conclusion

This paper has described the results of a study to determine the feasibility of a pin-based authentication approach through a comparison with a graphical scheme. Both sets of authentication sequences could be committed to memory, and entered at points over a five month period. However, results showed that the process of identifying and selecting tactile stimuli was slower compared to graphical stimuli. The tactile channel offers the benefits of presenting information underneath the fingertips, away from prying eyes. As the sense of touch is personal to each user, it is harder to externalize or to share with others [10]. Future work will focus upon investigating challenges facing TAS, which also pertain to mechanisms requiring alphanumeric passwords/PINs. Research will examine the impact of infrequent tactile authentication sequence usage, and the problems associated with remembering multiple 'tactile passwords'.

Acknowledgements

The authors would like to thank Passfaces Corporation for the use of the Passfaces™ demonstration software [6].

References

1. Brewster, S.A.: Chapter 30: The impact of haptic 'touching' technology on cultural applications. In: Digital Applications for Cultural Heritage Institutions, pp. 273–284. Ashgate Press, UK (2005)
2. De Luca, A., von Zezchwitz, E., Hußman, H.: VibraPass-Secure Authentication Based on Lies. In: Proceedings of ACM SIGCHI 2009, pp. 913–916 (2009)
3. Deyle, T., Roth, V.: Accessible Authentication via Tactile PIN Entry. Computer Graphics Topics 2, 24–26 (2006)
4. Orozco Trujillo, M., Shakra, I., El Saddik, A.: Haptic: The New Biometric-Embedded Media to Recognizing and Quantifying Human Patterns. In: Proceedings of the 13th Annual ACM International Conference on Multimedia (2005)
5. Kuber, R., Yu, W.: Tactile Authentication. Patent No 0603581.0 (Patent Applied For) (2006)
6. PassfacesTM Demonstration Software, Passfaces Corporation (2009), http://www.passfaces.com
7. Brostoff, S., Sasse, M.A.: Are PassfacesTM more usable than passwords? A field trial investigation. In: Proceedings of HCI 2000, pp. 405–424 (2000)
8. Valentine, T.: An Evaluation of the Passface Personal Authentication System (Technical Report), London, UK (1998)
9. Valentine, T.: Memory for PassfacesTM after a Long Delay (Technical Report), London, UK (1999)
10. Kuber, R., Yu, W.: Feasibility Study of Tactile-based Authentication. International Journal of Human Computer Studies 68, 158–181 (2010)

Haptics Can "Lend a Hand" to a Bionic Eye

Barry Richardson and George Van Doorn

Bionics and Cognitive Science Centre
School of Humanities, Communications and Social Sciences
Monash University, Churchill, Australia, 3842
{Barry.Richardson,George.Vandoorn}@arts.monash.edu.au

Abstract. Here we argue that haptics (touch and kinaesthesis) can play a key role in the development of a bionic eye. Tactile displays can supplement and complement the incomplete information that a visual prosthetic will offer the brain in early stages of the prosthetic's development. Kinaesthetic inputs give the brain feedback about motor activities that correlate with both visual and tactile inputs, and are critical for perceptual competency. Haptic inputs can also help "teach" the new visual sense to respond to stimuli that are initially indiscriminable and enable cross-calibration of inputs to strengthen multimodal cortical connections. By using haptics to supplement and complement inputs from a visual prosthetic, a bionic eye can develop more quickly than did the Bionic Ear.

Keywords: Haptics, bionic eye, sensory integration.

1   Introduction

Regardless of the approach taken in the design and development of a visual prosthetic, haptics can play a critical role. We say this because *normal* vision, a predominantly spatial sense, relies on interactions with haptics. Artificial vision will need the help of other senses even more than does normal vision. One reason for this is that no visual prosthetic currently available can compete with normal vision. Pezaris and Eskandar [1] argue that, because of the fovea's exquisite ability to capture detail, high-resolution artificial vision may be a fantasy. Similarly, Suaning, Lovell, Schindhelm, and Coroneo [2] suggest that, for the foreseeable future, visual prostheses will provide limited stimulation and "act only as aids to mobility with the hope being that obstacles and moving objects may be detected and avoided" (p. 197). While there is support for such pessimistic views, there are also grounds for optimism if we adopt a multimodal approach and allow haptics to "lend a helping hand" during early stages of bionic eye development.

There are several ways in which non-visual senses can help a visual prosthetic. For example, when a response to a visual stimulus is found to depend largely on the presence of another sense, that can help pinpoint a weakness in the prosthetic which can then perhaps be addressed with a modified design, or training protocol. It has been noted that people fitted with Bionic Ears "learn" to compensate for input deficiencies. In fact, speech recognition has been shown to improve long after implantation to a point where one in five people can converse over the telephone [3]. These improvements involve visual cues (e.g., lip movement) in combination with auditory inputs when listening to the

A.M.L. Kappers et al. (Eds.): EuroHaptics 2010, Part I, LNCS 6191, pp. 320–325, 2010.
© Springer-Verlag Berlin Heidelberg 2010

speech of others [4]. Moreover, non-auditory cues (visual and haptic) can combine with an initially inadequate signal to eventually enable users of the auditory prosthetic to discriminate hitherto "unheard" sounds. An analogous process can be expected to apply to a visual prosthetic - sub-threshold visual stimuli will be seen following training with tactile displays. In short, haptics can provide information "missed" by the prosthetic, "teach" vision how to work with other senses, enhance mutimodal cortical connections, and alert researchers to areas in need of improvement.

2   Haptics Can Complement and Supplement Vision

The basic building block of prosthetic vision is, often, the electrically evoked phosphene [5] which is commonly experienced as a small spot of light at a localised point in the visual field [6]. Discreet phosphenes may generate a patterned visual experience when spatiotemporal parameters allow integration [7]. Perception of the environment using such patterns will require that they are correlated with better spatial information, and this can be provided in a tactile display that allows "joining of dots" correctly. What is, at first, merely an array of light spots can become a coherent pattern if perceptual organization is facilitated (see [8] for figures illustrating this principle).

Phosphenes, at first discreet, may thus resemble incomplete figures that invite Gestalt principles of integration [9]. This would be analogous to the brain "filling in" or interpolating frequencies not actually coded by a Bionic Ear, or the eye filling in the blind spot on the basis of what surrounds it. Jervis [10] showed that Gestalt principles work in touch, as well as vision, suggesting that tactile displays can indeed help a new visual system integrate stimulus elements into meaningful wholes.

3   Tactile Displays Can Inform Vision

Multimodal inputs also permit intersensory calibration. That is, one sense "learns" about the environment when "taught" by another. Held and Hein [11] argued that motor feedback (kinaesthesis/proprioception) that accompanies inputs from vision, hearing and touch, are critical for the development (e.g., calibration) of these major senses. Thus, sophisticated visual mechanisms such as size constancy may depend on early haptic experience in which the hand informs the brain that objects do not, in reality, get smaller (as they appear to do visually) when they are moved away from the eye. Such a role for haptics in visual development is supported by the finding that children under eight years of age rely on haptics for size judgments, and vision is calibrated against haptics for this attribute [12]. Shape, on the other hand, is an attribute that haptics "learns" about from vision. These senses operate somewhat independently up to age eight, after which visual and haptic inputs are integrated [12]. Because the senses tend to operate individually rather than collectively at early stages of development, the progress of a visual prosthetic offers a unique opportunity to study these processes.

The implications of these cross-calibration findings are significant for congenitally blind users of a visual prosthetic since they will have missed the early experiences during which such calibration normally occurs. Deficits are likely to mirror those observed for congenitally deaf users of the Bionic Ear who were not privy to auditory inputs at critical (early) stages of development. However, tactile displays that accompany the new visual experiences can compensate for early deprivation whether complete, or partial.

4   Tactile Displays Can Enhance Cortical Connections

For people with severe, early-onset visual handicaps, the visual cortex is not a spare computer waiting to be turned on. Blindness causes the visual cortex to be recruited to a role in somatosensory processing [13][14] - a role that could explain superior tactile abilities in the blind. Functional imaging studies of early-onset, blind individuals show that their visual cortical areas are activated by Braille reading [14]. Further, transcranial magnetic stimulation studies have shown that stimulation of the visual cortex of blind individuals interferes with their perception of tactile stimuli, something not found in sighted people [13]. The fact that the visual cortex of blind subjects has been co-opted for non-visual functions implies that touch is already privileged in the brains of the sight-impaired and, for that reason, we can expect enhanced salience of tactile information for all users of a bionic eye.

In addition, when some part of the visual stimulus is too weak to register, haptics can act as a support mode until multimodal mechanisms allow withdrawal of that support (i.e., when the visual system can cope alone). The principle of a support mode was shown when hearing aids, initially unable to allow users to discriminate some speech sounds, came to do so following support from vibrotactile cues to code the speech features "missed" (i.e., that could not be lip-read and were not well-coded) by the hearing aid [15]. After a few weeks, the correlated tactile and auditory information enhanced cortical connections to the extent that speech features could then be heard with the hearing aid alone. Tactile stimulation functionally changed the responsivity of the auditory system [16].

There is every reason to expect similar advantages when adding touch to a visual prosthetic. Macaluso, Frith, and Driver [17] have already shown that a sudden touch on one hand improved vision near that hand. In their experiment it appears as though tactile stimulation enhanced activity in the visual cortex. It is assumed that a tactile display would form part of the haptic information that, with *normal* vision, serves to form sensorimotor links and intersensory connections that typify efficient perception.

Although sensory modalities feed into brain areas that primarily analyse inputs from the different sources, they also all project into association areas that are involved in integrating multisensory information [18]. Some of these areas contain bimodal neurons that are stimulated both by visual and by tactile inputs; these neurons are also likely to play a role in processes of spatial integration [19]. In theory, any network connections receiving frequent concomitant activation produce progressively stronger synaptic connections, and thus become more "modular" with development, while those that receive less concomitant activation may either drop out or become weaker [20].

The enhancement of cortical connections is a function for haptics that goes beyond its potential role in supplementing and complementing certain aspects of visual inputs. Although these roles are important in themselves, the contribution of haptics moves to another level when the sensitivity of the visual cortex is enhanced to the point that previously non-discerned stimuli become discernable.

5   Technical Considerations

Tactile inputs can be "incorporated" into a bionic eye in a number of ways. The output of a camera, or any optical device the prosthetic uses (e.g., an array of photoelectric cells), could be "split" between, or fed to, two displays, one visual (e.g., artificial retina) and the other tactile (e.g., vibrotactors), which could compensate for impoverished or low-fidelity visual inputs. Bach-y-Rita, Collins, Saunders, White and Scadden [21] demonstrated that the skin can be used to "see" shapes impressed on it as points of vibration corresponding to areas of light and dark picked up by a television camera. Interestingly, subjects could externalize the percepts, thus challenging the idea that touch is just a "proximal" sense [22]. The function resembles redundancy according to which perception benefits from two or more channels of information which can have additive or multiplicative benefits [23]. Far from representing superfluous information, perceptual redundancy is a well recognized principle on which effective perception relies [20].

Although fingertip displays take full advantage of cutaneous sensitivity when proximal stimuli are explored, it may be inconvenient to use fingertips to assist vision in the perception of distal objects - because of the need to interact with objects, via the hands, when exploring an environment. Fortunately, skin surfaces other than the fingertips (e.g., torso) have been used successfully in substituting touch for hearing [7][24] and vision [21]. The use of skin surfaces can be optimized by exploring how different mechanoreceptors can be targeted and recruited. This could be achieved by varying the frequency of vibration of specific tactors in a cutaneous display. For example, Summers and Chanter [25] have shown that object perception (when using tactile renditions of "visual" scenes) can be improved if one frequency (e.g., 40 Hz) represents the figure and another frequency (e.g., 320 Hz) represents the ground - a dichotomy that can be depicted as different both spatially and temporally in a tactile display. In the case of basic features such as figure and ground, the matching process, according to which figure is associated with one frequency and ground another, can be done by computer software. Alternatively, the user of the visual prosthetic could manually alter the supplementary information by varying the respective frequencies until they were subjectively optimal for object discrimination. Suitable spacing, and other parameters, could be determined empirically and would depend in part on the skin site chosen.

A major advantage of giving a second channel of information to skin sites is that distal objects, those out of the range of the hand but picked up by a camera, can be perceived via the skin [22]. This additional channel of spatial information has the potential to significantly improve, what we know will be, a less-than-perfect visual percept provided by the prototype visual prosthesis.

6   Conclusion

In summary, we believe that a newly introduced sense cannot immediately expect dialogue with senses that have developed without it. We argue that cutaneous and/or kinaesthetic information can significantly enhance the prospects of success in the development and testing of a bionic eye, or any artificial visual system. This is partly because the spatial nature of haptics is ideally suited to roles it can play as a substitute for, or complement of, vision. However, haptics can also help by facilitating appropriate cortical connections, and by identifying features of a prosthetic in need of improvement. How a bionic eye will work with existing sensory processes is unclear, although lessons learned during the development of the Bionic Ear indicate that the age (level of development) at which a sensory prosthetic is fitted has profound effects on its usefulness. This is because the human senses grow together. They cross-calibrate during infancy, and they end up as an efficient team of inputs providing the brain with information about the outside world. There are critical periods during which the brain is maximally sensitive to these inputs. For these reasons, young children should be given a visual prosthetic as early as possible. The inescapable conclusion of the evidence presented here is that a bionic eye, or equivalent, must operate in a multimodal context in which haptics will be a major player. In that case, why not use haptics in the developmental stages of a visual prosthetic?

References

1. Pezaris, J.S., Eskandar, E.N.: Getting Signals into the Brain: Visual Prosthetics Through Thalamic Microstimulation. Neurosurg. Focus. 27(1), 1–11 (2009)
2. Suaning, G.J., Lovell, N.H., Schindhelm, K., Coroneo, M.T.: The Bionic Eye (Electronic Visual Prosthesis): A Review. Aust. NZ. J. Ophthalmol. 26, 195–202 (1998)
3. Cohen, N.L., Waltzman, S.B., Shapiro, W.H.: Telephone Speech Comprehension with use of the Nucleus Cochlear Implant. Ann. Otol. Rhinol. Laryngol. Suppl. 142, 8–11 (1989)
4. Grant, K.W., Seitz, P.F.: The use of Visible Speech Cues for Improving Auditory Detection of Spoken Sentences. J. Acoust. Soc. Am. 108(3), 1197–1208 (2000)
5. Dowling, J.A.: Artificial Human Vision. Expert Review of Medical Devices 2(1), 73–85 (2005)
6. Brindley, G.S., Lewin, W.S.: The Sensations Produced by Electrical Stimulation of the Visual Cortex. J. Physiol. 196, 479–493 (1968)
7. Richardson, B.L., Frost, B.J.: Sensory Substitution and the Design of an Artificial Ear. J. Psych. 96, 259–285 (1977)
8. Leeper, R.: A Study of a Neglected Portion of the Field of Learning - The Development of Sensory Organization. J. Genet. Psychol. 46, 41–75 (1935)
9. Quinlan, P.T., Wilton, R.N.: Grouping by Proximity or Similarity? Competition Between the Gestalt principles in Vision. Perception 27(4), 417–430 (1998)
10. Jervis, C.: Gestalt Principles in Tactile Pattern Perception (Unpublished master's thesis). Monash University, Churchill (2004)
11. Held, R., Hein, A.: Movement-produced Stimulation in the Development of Visually Guided Behaviour. J. Comp. Physiol. Psych. 56(5), 872–876 (1963)
12. Gori, M., Del Viva, M., Sandini, G., Burr, D.C.: Young Children do not Integrate Visual and Haptic form Information. Curr. Biol. 18(9), 694–698 (2008)
13. Cohen, L.G., Celnik, P., Pascual-Leone, A., Corwell, B., Faiz, L., Dambrosia, J., Honda, M., Sadato, N., Gerloff, C., Catala, M.D., Hallett, M.: Functional Relevance of Cross-modal Plasticity in Blind Humans. Nature 389, 180–183 (1997)
14. Gizewski, E.R., Gasser, T., de Greiff, A., Boehm, A., Forsting, M.: Cross-modal Plasticity for Sensory and Motor Activation Patterns in Blind Subjects. NeuroImage 19(3), 968–975 (2003)
15. Perier, O., Boorsma, A.: A Prosthetic Device Utilizing Vibro-tactile Perception of Profoundly Deaf Children. Brit. J. Audiol. 16, 277–280 (1982)

16. Richardson, B.L.: Tactile Hearing Aids Enhance Cortical Connections. Brit. J. Audiol. 20, 173–174 (1986)
17. Macaluso, E., Frith, C.D., Driver, J.: Modulation of Human Visual Cortex by Crossmodal Spatial Attention. Science 289, 1206–1208 (2000)
18. Burgess, N., Jeffery, K.J., O'Keefe, J.: Integrating Hippocampal and Parietal Functions. In: Burgess, N., Jeffery, K.J., O'Keefe, J. (eds.) The Hippocampal and Parietal Foundations of Spatial Cognition, pp. 4–29. Oxford University Press, Oxford (1999)
19. Graziano, M.S., Gross, C.G.: The Representation of Extrapersonal Space: A Possible Role for Bimodal, Visual-tactile Neurons. In: Gazzaniga, M.S. (ed.) The Cognitive Neurosciences, pp. 1021–1042. MIT Press, Cambridge (1995)
20. Millar, S.: Network Models for Haptic Perception. Infant Behav. Dev. 28(3), 250–265 (2005)
21. Bach-y-Rita, P., Collins, C.C., Saunders, F.A., White, B., Scadden, L.: Vision Substitution by Tactile Image Projection. Nature 221, 963–964 (1969)
22. Guarniero, G.: Experience of Tactile Vision. Perception 3, 101–104 (1974)
23. Klatzky, R.L., Lederman, S., Reed, C.: Haptic Integration of Object Properties: Texture, Hardness, and Planar Contour. J. Exp. Psychol. Human 15, 45–57 (1989)
24. Brooks, P.L., Frost, B.J., Mason, J.L., Gibson, D.M.: Continuing Evaluation of the Queen's University Tactile Vocoder 1: Identification of Open Set Words. J. Rehabil. Res. Dev. 23, 119–128 (1986)
25. Summers, I.R., Chanter, C.M.: A Broadband Tactile Array on the Fingertip. J. Acoust. Soc. Am. 112(5), 2118–2126 (2002)

Analysis of Active Handrest Control Methods

Mark A. Fehlberg, Brian T. Gleeson, and William R. Provancher

Haptics and Embedded Mechatronics Lab, University of Utah
50 S. Central Campus Drive, Salt Lake City, UT, 84112-9208
m.fehlberg@utah.edu, brian.gleeson@gmail.com, wil@mech.utah.edu

Abstract. People use fixed handrests to complete routine dexterous activities such as providing a signature or making a sketch. Because the hand's workspace for very fine motions is limited, we have developed an Active Handrest that extends a user's dexterous workspace while providing ergonomic support. Our current Active Handrest prototype is a planar, computer controlled support for the user's hand and wrist that allows complete control over a grasped tool. The device determines handrest motions by interpreting isometric (force) input from the user's wrist, isotonic (position) input from a grasped manipulandum, or a blend of both inputs. Circle tracing experiments measuring task precision and completion time were conducted to investigate each control mode under various velocity limits for both experienced and novice users.

Keywords: Haptic devices and technology, dexterous manipulation, precision manipulation, isometric and isotonic control, velocity limit.

1 Introduction and Background

People often desire ergonomic support for their hands while performing dexterous tasks. For example, people will brace their wrist or arm against fixed objects or even their own bodies to increase precision. Static handrests have been used to improve precision and reduce fatigue over small workspaces in applications such as painting details in a portrait. Repositionable handrests require time for repositioning and create multiple small workspaces rather than a large continuous dexterous workspace. A continuously repositionable handrest like the Active Handrest (Fig. 1), could aid in obtaining high precision and improved support over a workspace several orders of magnitude larger than that of a static handrest. In this paper we present analysis of various control methodologies for the Active Handrest, a device that continuously repositions itself so that the user's hand remains near the center of its dexterous workspace. Our device could be useful, as other robotic devices have been shown to be (e.g., [1-3]), for assisting a user in performing a variety of precision tasks over large workspaces, such as surgery, rehabilitation assistance, pick-and-place tasks, or any task requiring dexterous control of tools.

Background. Use of handrests has been shown to aid in reducing user muscle fatigue [4] and devices such as Steady Hand [5] and Cobots [6] have been shown to aid a user in performing precision tasks. Experiments with haptic devices placed in serial with admittance devices have allowed for expanded workspaces [7]. The Active Handrest

A.M.L. Kappers et al. (Eds.): EuroHaptics 2010, Part I, LNCS 6191, pp. 326–331, 2010.

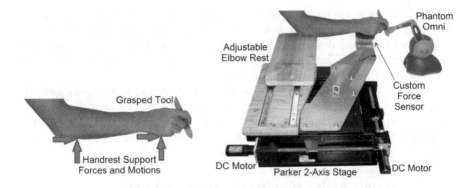

Fig. 1. Active Handrest concept (*left*) and Active Handrest prototype (*right*)

attempts to provide all of these benefits, while allowing the user to maintain complete control of any grasped tool.

Two major factors were considered in tuning the control of the Active Handrest: *input mode* and *velocity limits*. In examining the input mode from the user to our device, we designed the controller to output desired motions based on isotonic (position) input, isometric (force) input, or a blend of isotonic and isometric inputs. Previous work has shown that while isotonic controllers lead to shorter task completion times, their movements are less precise than isometric controllers [8]. Other work has shown that elastic (blended) rate control initially increases task completion times over isometric control alone, but that learning eventually equalizes completion times regardless of the control strategy used [9]. The second factor examined was the effect of limiting the device's velocity and acceleration. In [10] it was shown that velocity limits determine force control precision. In an attempt to eliminate any difficulties in maintaining force control precision during start up and termination of individual device movements, as observed both in [10] and in our pilot testing, we added acceleration limiting to our controller.

2   Device Description and Controller

The motion of the Active Handrest is provided by a Parker two-axis linear stage (Fig. 1 right). While interacting with the device, users sit with their right arm in contact with an adjustable elbow rest. The user grasps a Phantom Omni stylus and rests their hand or wrist on a support pad, which contains our custom 3-axis force sensor.

To accomplish our goal of continuously repositioning the user's hand at the center of its dexterous workspace, our controller as detailed in [11] must determine the user's intent and provide support in that location. The controller receives position input from the grasped stylus and force interaction input between the user's hand and the force sensor embedded in the support pad. Each of these inputs is able to control the device independently or they can be blended to implement hybrid control.

Both inputs are subject to deadbands to prevent device movement due to hand tremor or small stylus repositioning. The force input is processed by a 1.6 Hz low-pass filter to prevent feedback instabilities caused by stage motion relative to the input. The position input is multiplied by a gain to equate its scale to that of the force input. The inputs are then prorated by their desired input percentages and summed. Output motion of the stage is then controlled by a 1 kHz servo rate proportional admittance controller with average error in output velocity less than 5%.

Hardware and software limits were installed for protection of the device and to better match the workspace of the Omni stylus. Before outputting the desired velocity, the signal is processed through acceleration and velocity limits. These saturation limits dramatically smooth the motion of the Active Handrest and allow higher gains to be used without the system becoming unstable.

3   Experiment: Active Handrest Control Methods

For this paper, we conducted a circle tracing experiment (Fig. 2) using the Active Handrest to examine the effects of control method, velocity limit, completion time, and user experience. In previous circle tracing experiments, the Active Handrest was shown to provide an increase in accuracy of 36.6% over an unsupported condition and 26% over a fixed support condition [11]. Circle tracing was chosen for simplicity, the relative ease in task error calculation (e.g. compared to [12]), and the ability to scale uniformly from small, localized tasks to large, distributed tasks. 7.5 mm and 40 mm radii circles and arcs of 100 mm radius were chosen to test a range of precisions tasks with varying curvatures. The various circle sizes also created task spaces ranging from motion of only the fingers to motions of the hand and arm. The tracing task was somewhat difficult due to the non-collocated stylus input [13] and screen output as well as stick-slip friction within the Omni device. These factors affected all test cases equally and were not a concern in our analysis.

The experiment was conducted in 3 test blocks; one for each control method. 24 circles (2 circles of 3 sizes using each of 4 velocity limits) were displayed, one at a time, on a computer monitor and subjects were asked to trace each circle as accurately as possible within a reasonable amount of time. The blocks required approximately 30 minutes to complete (90 min. total). Test blocks were ordered using a Latin Squares technique to reduce the effects of learning and fatigue. Headphones played white noise to mask sound from the device and to aid in eliminating distractions. All tests were completed under Institutional Review Board approved human subjects protocol.

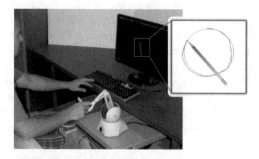

Fig. 2. Experiment setup and graphical user interface. Note: the color in the monitor's close-up is inverted for clarity.

The experiment was completed by 12 volunteer subjects ranging from 21 to 37 years old. The subjects were classified in two groups: 5 subjects with prior experience using the Active Handrest (from pilot testing) and 7 with no prior experience. For the group with prior experience using the device, all were male and 2 were authors of this paper - one of which was left hand dominant. For the group with no prior experience, 4 subjects were males, 3 were females, and all were right hand dominant.

Drawing error was calculated based on a radial projection of points from the drawn circle onto the displayed circle. Median error was computed as a measure of performance for each circle. Circle drawing time was measured as the time between the first click of the drawing button to its release at the completion of the circle.

Observations from Pilot Studies. We first conducted pilot studies with velocity limits ranging from 1 to 30 mm/s, while using each of three control methods to control the Active Handrest. To mitigate feedback instabilities with the device under force control, we implemented a low-pass filter with 1.6 Hz corner frequency on the force sensor input and an acceleration limit of 0.5 m/s^2 on the stage's motion.

Pilot study subjects also noted that the stage did not feel like it was moving when the velocity limit was set to 1 mm/s, and consequently the average error generally increased with this limit. Additionally, [14] indicates that when users are forced to work slower than they desire, they generally tend to expend more energy than is required. Our pilot study results also showed that error did not significantly change for velocity limits above 15 mm/s. We speculate that this trend was caused, in part, because users did not desire to perform the tracing tasks at speeds above some velocity. The tracing completion time data supports this conclusion. Therefore, in our experiment, we decided to examine velocity limits between 2.5mm/s and 15mm/s.

Analysis of Control Input. An ANOVA was conducted on the difference between drawing error data and the overall drawing error mean using the predictors of velocity limit, circle size, and control type. All of these predictors were found to have a significant effect on drawing error [control type: $F(259,2) = 3.91$, $p = 0.0204$; velocity limit: $F(259,3) = 10.9$, $p < 0.0001$; circle size: $F(259,2) = 6.51$, $p = 0.0016$]. No significant interactions were found.

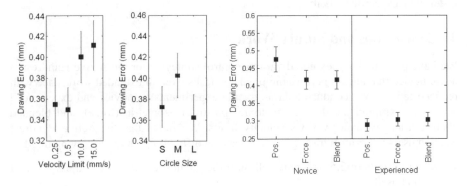

Fig. 3. Drawing error grouped by velocity limit (*left*), circle size (*middle*), and experience and control type (*right*). Error bars represent 95% confidence intervals.

Velocity limit had the greatest effect (Fig. 3 (left)). Error was greater with velocity limits 10 and 15 mm/s and less with 2.5 and 5 mm/s (effect size = 0.054 mm, or ~12%). This difference was observed through Tukey's HSD ($\alpha = 0.05$) and confirmed with a paired t-test [$t(858) = 5.56$, $p < 0.0001$]. Circle size, related to task complexity, also had an effect (Fig.3 (middle)). Medium circles were more difficult than large circles, resulting in 0.040 mm more error (~9% increase) [$t(573) = 3.36$, $p = 0.0008$]. Accuracy data from blended and force control trials were combined and tested against position control data. Position control resulted in a slightly larger 0.028 mm error (~6%) than force or blended control [$t(858) = 2.702$, $p = 0.007$].

Analysis of User Experience. An ANOVA on drawing error showed error to differ significantly between experienced and novice subjects [$F(859,2) = 1.71$, $p = 0.016$]. On average, experienced subjects completed the drawing tasks with 0.14 mm less error (~32% reduction in error). When separating the data by control type, the difference between experienced and novice performance remains significant for all control types [$t > 6.3$, $p < 0.0001$], as seen in Fig. 3 (right). Interestingly, the ANOVA also showed an interaction between control type and user experience [$F(859,2) = 4.84$, $p = 0.0081$]. As can be seen in Fig. 3 (right), novice users had significantly more difficulty with position control [$t(333) = 2.55$, $p = 0.011$], but experienced users showed no significant change in performance between the control types.

Analysis of Drawing Time. As would be expected velocity limit and circle size both had an effect on drawing time [$F(859,3) = 318.02$, $p < 0.0001$; $F(859,2) = 1580$, $p < 0.0001$, respectively]. However, control method did not affect drawing time [$F(859,2) = 2.17$, $p = 0.115$]. The medium circles took the longest to draw, as they had the longest arc length. Large circles, then small circles took progressively less time. [$time_{medium} > time_{large}$: $t(573) = 18.47$, $p < 0.0001$; $time_{large} > time_{small}$: $t(570) = 17.85$, $p < 0.0001$; these results valid after Bonferroni correction for non-orthogonal comparisons]. The 2.5 mm/s velocity limit resulted in the slowest drawing times [$time_{2.5} > time_{(5\&10\&15)}$, $t(858) = 12.52$, $p < 0.0001$], followed by the 5 mm/s limit [$time_5 > time_{(10\&15)}$, $t(643) = 6.25$, $p < 0.0001$)]. Interestingly, there was no significant difference between the drawing times resulting from the 10 and 15 mm/s limits [$t(430) = 0.71$, $p = 0.481$]; which again implies that users did not desire to draw faster than a specific velocity.

4   Conclusions and Future Work

We have presented and explored various control strategies for the Active Handrest, a novel device that aids in performing precision tasks over an extended workspace with reduced fatigue. We conducted circle tracing experiments on novice and experienced users that explored the device's isotonic (position), isometric (force), and blended control strategies under various velocity limits. We found that the Active Handrest enabled users to perform tracing tasks of varying difficulty with the following trends:

- velocity limits of 2.5 or 5 mm/s allowed the greatest accuracy regardless of input method used;
- a 32% reduction in error for users having prior experience with our device;
- greater difficulty using position control for novices.

Through further exploration of the Active Handrest's utility, we believe that the device will be shown to be useful in assisting medical personnel, artists, machinists, and others in performing precision tasks that require dexterous manipulation of tools over a large workspace.

We will continue optimizing the controller by adding enhancements such as visual cues for stage position and virtual interaction forces. Experiments will also be conducted on practical task performance such as pick-and-place tasks. It would be useful to compare the Active Handrest to additional methods of support, other devices, and other control methods. Finally, a third motion axis could be added to allow performance of dexterous tasks in a 3-DOF space.

Acknowledgements. This work was supported, in part, by the National Science Foundation under awards IIS-0746914 and DGE-0654414.

References

1. Okamura, A.: Methods for Haptic Feedback in Teleoperated Robot-Assisted Surgery. Industrial Robot. 31(6), 499–508 (2004)
2. Hogan, N., et al.: Motions or Muscles? Some Behavioral Factors Underlying Robotic Assistance of Motor Recovery. Jnl. Rehab. Res. Devel. 43, 605–618 (2006)
3. Kumar, R., et al.: Performance of Robotic Augmentation in Microsurgery-Scale Motions. In: Taylor, C., Colchester, A. (eds.) MICCAI 1999. LNCS, vol. 1679, pp. 1108–1115. Springer, Heidelberg (1999)
4. Ito, S., Yokokohji, Y.: Maneuverability of Master Control Devices Considering the Musculo-Skeletal Model of an Operator. In: Proc. of World Haptics. IEEE Society, Los Alamitos (2009)
5. Taylor, R., et al.: A Steady-Hand Robotic System for Microsurgical Augmentation. The International Journal of Robotics Research 18(12), 1201–1210 (1999)
6. Colgate, J., Wannasuphoprasit, W., Peshkin, M.: Cobots: Robots for Collaboration with Human Operators. In: Proc. ASME Dyn. Sys. Cont. Div., vol. DSC-58, pp. 433–440 (1996)
7. Barrow, A., Harwin, W.: High Bandwidth, Large Workspace Haptic Interaction: Flying Phantoms. In: Symp. Haptic Interfaces for Virt. Environ. and Teleop. Sys., pp. 295–302 (2008)
8. Zhai, S., Milgram, P.: Quantifying Coordination in Multiple DOF Movement and Its Application to Evaluating 6 DOF Input Devices. In: Proc. of SIGCHI conf. (1998)
9. Zhai, S.: Investigation of Feel for 6DOF Inputs: Isometric and Elastic Rate Control for Manipulation in 3D Environments. Human Factors & Ergonomics Society Proc. 37, 323–327 (1993)
10. Wu, M., Abbott, J., Okamura, A.: Effects of Velocity on Human Force Control. In: Proc. of First Joint World Haptics (2005)
11. Fehlberg, M., et al.: Active Handrest for Precision Manipulation and Ergonomic Support. In: Proc. of 2010 Haptics Symposium (2010)
12. Morris, D., Tan, H., Barbagli, F., Chang, T., Salisbury, K.: Haptic Feedback Enhances Force Skill Learning. In: Proc. of IEEE World Haptics (2007)
13. Ware, C., Arsenault, R.: Frames of Reference in Virtual Object Rotation. In: Proc. of 1st Symp. on Appld. perception in graphics and visualization. ACM, Los Angeles (2004)
14. Wise, S., Shadmehr, R.: Motor Control. In: Encyclopedia of the Human Brain, vol. 3. Elsevier Science, Amsterdam (2002)

Roly-poly: A Haptic Interface with a Self-righting Feature

Seung-Chan Kim[1], Byung-Kil Han[1], Soo-Chul Lim[1],
Andrea Bianchi[1], Ki-Uk Kyung[2], and Dong-Soo Kwon[1]

[1] Human Robot Interaction Research Center, KAIST
335 Gwahangno, Yuseong-gu, Daejon 305-701, Republic of Korea
{kimsc,hanbk,limsc,andrea}@robot.kaist.ac.kr, kwonds@kaist.ac.kr
http://robot.kaist.ac.kr, http://touch.kaist.ac.kr
[2] POST-PC Research Group,
Electronics and Telecommunications Research Institute
138 Gajeongno, Yuseong-gu, Daejeon, 305-700, Republic of Korea
kyungku@etri.re.kr

Abstract. In this paper, a human-computer interface equipped with self-uprighting feature and haptic feedback functionality as a PC peripheral is proposed. Device motion triggered by a user is sensed through embedded inertial sensors. Taking advantage of a mechanical structure incorporating a weighted bottom and mass symmetry, the device uses restorative uprighting force to right itself, making erratic motion once tipped over. The acceleration values are counterbalanced once yaw motion is applied by a user. The haptic feedback in this system is intended for both the realization of subtle detent effects and surface transmitting vibrations. Providing impulse tactile feedback according to gestural input, the device can function as a rotatable knob which is mechanically ungrounded. Moreover, surface transmitting vibration generated by linear actuators provides notifications of events important to the user in the form of ambient haptic feedback. With the utilization of the proposed features, it is expected that both intuitive information input and practical use of haptics in a desktop environment can be achieved.

Keywords: haptic interface, self-centering interface, ambient haptic feedback.

1 Introduction

Allowing users to perform a task with the appropriate mapping of captured sensor data using gestures such as strokes, shaking, tilting and twisting, gestural interface systems have been utilized in a variety of application fields. Sreedharan et al. proposed a method for interaction with a 3-D virtual world using a commercial interface [1]. For social interaction in the virtual world, gestures by virtual characters, such as waving, were controlled from a hand-held device. Additionally, based on the gestural information, numerous life-log systems were proposed for a context-based service [2] and for abnormality detection [3]. For gesture-based affective communication, haptic functionality was recently embedded [4]. However, because haptic feedback requires

A.M.L. Kappers et al. (Eds.): EuroHaptics 2010, Part I, LNCS 6191, pp. 332–339, 2010.
© Springer-Verlag Berlin Heidelberg 2010

visual attention while physical contact is established and cognitive attention while transmitting the physical feedback, it ironically results in heavy user loads at times, despite the fact that the objective of haptic feedback is to help users. This inherent contradictive problem of haptics has prevented the applications related to haptics from being developed in practice. In this paper, inspired by typically perceived phenomena such as the vibration from a mobile phone located on a desk without any attention in the event a notification call arrives, notification using tactile feedback in the form of surface transmitting vibration is proposed. This paper introduces and explains the features of the gesture-based human-computer interface with both direct and indirect haptic feedback functionality.

2 Motion Input

In this section, the proposed human-computer interface with restorative uprighting force which can be used for desktop work is described. Having a center of mass located below its geometrical center, it returns to its undisplaced configuration when released. Fig. 1 shows the mechanical structure of the developed device. The system follows the structure of a roly-poly toy which rocks when touched due to the weighted and rounded bottom. This feature has several advantages during user input, each of which will be explained in turn.

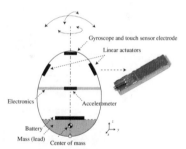

Fig. 1. Developed system which can be categorized as an inertial proprioceptive device [5] and corresponding mechanical diagram in an undisplaced configuration

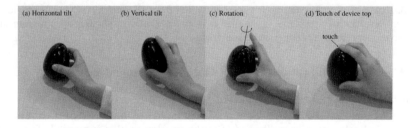

Fig. 2. Different types of motion that can be sensed

2.1   Return to the Original Position

As the proposed system tends to return to its original home position once tilted, the accumulative drift error of the acceleration signals can be easily offset in a repeated manner. Providing subtle kinesthetic feedback caused by the restoration movement, the returning functionality also allows a user to input 2-DoF signals as an isometric joystick which senses the force and adopts a returning function using mechanical grounding [6]. Owing to the absence of additional external structures, akin to an isometric joystick, the entire system can remain small and move freely on a desk or even in space.

2.2   Various Patterns

As gestures are stylized motions that contain meaning, various patterns can be created in an HCI context using a gesture-based interface. These patterns are generally utilized as control input data. Due to the limited capability of humans [7], however, the spectral feature of the gesture signal is limited in terms of its bandwidth. Moreover, it has a single dominating frequency. With the utilization of the proposed system, a wide variety of patterns can be achieved with the benefit of irregular device motions such as rolling, spinning, oscillating and wobbling. Information with both intentional and unintentional frequency components can be used for entertainment applications. Fig. 3 shows an example of a pattern generated from a system with an initial external force.

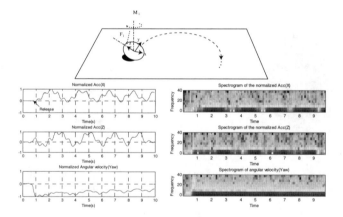

Fig. 3. Example of erratic motion triggered by initial force (F_i) and moment (M_i) provided by the user. Resultant motion signal in the time domain and the corresponding spectrogram shows that two or more frequency components dominate.

2.3   Coordinate Calibration for Input-Output Correspondence

Once rotated with respect to the inertial vertical line (z-axis), the coordinates of the sensors are changed. As this problem raises the issue of kinesthetic correspondence [6, 8], the coordinates must be calibrated after the rotation motion is applied. This section introduces a counterbalancing method that resolves the described usability issue. Acceleration data at a specific time is utilized for the estimation of rotated angle, α, rather

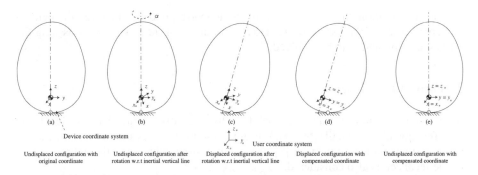

(a)   (b)   (c)   (d)   (e)

Device coordinate system

User coordinate system

Undisplaced configuration with original coordinate

Undisplaced configuration after rotation w.r.t inertial vertical line

Displaced configuration after rotation w.r.t inertial vertical line

Displaced configuration with compensated coordinate

Undisplaced configuration with compensated coordinate

Fig. 4. After counterbalancing, a user can manipulate the device in its initial state

than using data from a gyroscope due to the accumulative measurement error that arises with a gyroscope. The proposed calibration method starts with the predefined actions of tilting to the y-axis in user coordinate followed by the touching of the device top.

Given that the rotation occurs with respect to the z-axis of the accelerometer, the inertial vertical axis, the calibration of the coordinate can be expressed by Eq. (1).

$$Rot_z(\alpha) A = \tilde{A} \tag{1}$$

To estimate the rotation angle, α, instantaneous acceleration data at a predefined position, the positive y-direction of the user coordinates is utilized.

$$\begin{pmatrix} \cos\alpha & -\sin\alpha & 0 \\ \sin\alpha & \cos\alpha & 0 \\ 0 & 0 & 1 \end{pmatrix} \begin{pmatrix} a_x \\ a_y \\ a_z \end{pmatrix} = \begin{pmatrix} 0 \\ \tilde{a}_y \\ \tilde{a}_z \end{pmatrix}, \ \alpha = \arctan(a_x / a_y)$$

$$\tilde{a}_y = a_x \sin\alpha + a_y \cos\alpha$$
$$= a_x \sin\left(\arctan\left(a_y / a_x\right)\right) + a_y \cos\left(\arctan\left(a_y / a_x\right)\right)$$

(2)

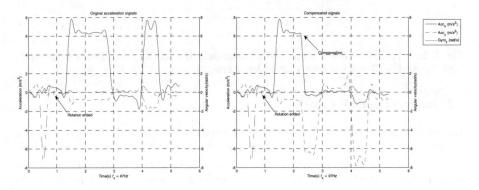

Fig. 5. An example of the calibration process

Once the rotation angle, α, is determined, noncorrespondence between the perceptual coordinates of the user and the actual coordinates of the device when issuing the tilt-based commands can be resolved.

3 Haptic Feedback

In this system, haptic feedback is mainly delivered in the form of tactile feedback. One functionality of tactile feedback in this system involves providing information about gestures issued by the user [9]. For attention-free interaction, the indirect use of tactile feedback is also considered.

3.1 Ungrounded Haptic Wheel

Numerous haptic effects have been researched, such as detents, ridges, friction and snaps to a specific position in the form of a haptic dial or a rotary knob [10]. The concept of tactile feedback for detents in a rotary configuration is similar to that of a haptic grid [11], which divides the workspace using haptic planes. The virtual detents faced while making a gesture allows a user to acquire a sense of velocity if the spatial interval is constant, although the amount of this content is uncountable. Providing impulse tactile feedback with an actuation time of approximately 10ms, a subtle detent effect was represented. The objective of the detent effects according to the gesture information is to give a user sense of tilting. The graph below shows the gesture patterns and corresponding tactile pulses.

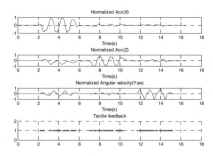

Fig. 6. Issued tactile feedback according to the gesture. The red dot in the fourth graph represents the fired tactile feedback for a subtle detent effect.

3.2 Indirect Haptic Feedback

Inspired by phenomena that are commonly perceived, such as the vibration from a mobile phone located on a desk without any attention in the event a phone call arrives, notification using indirect tactile feedback is proposed in this section. These types of haptic feedback events can be categorized as *indirect haptic feedback*. As feedback can be transmitted to the wrists, which are typically resting on the desk, it can be considered that implementing the indirect haptic functionality is an alternative means of providing additional information to users. The transmitted information has advantages in that the form of the information is private [12] and can be perceived by any part of the body. Moreover, it also allows low-attention interaction, as addressed in previous research [13]. Considering that the integration of a desk system with haptic feedback is complicated, inducing the surface transmission of vibrations using an external interface on the surface may be advantageous. Fig. 7 illustrates the concept of indirect haptic feedback using a desktop interface.

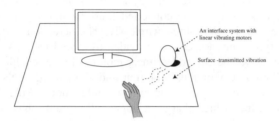

Fig. 7. Concept of indirect haptic feedback. Surface-transmitted vibrations are perceivable even when users are not concentrating on the incoming stimulus.

Utilizing the tendency of the vibrotactile threshold on the palm, or the thenar eminence, which is most sensitive at around 250Hz in general [14] (although the contact area affects the sensitivity), the frequency of the vibrotactile feedback in this system was set to 250 Hz.

4   System

The figure below shows the electronics architecture and developed electronics system.

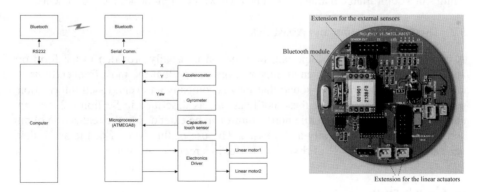

Fig. 8. The developed electronics system. Actuators and some sensors are attached through an extension cable, as shown in the mechanical diagram.

The sensor parts consist of an accelerometer, a gyroscope, and a capacitive touch sensor. The gyroscope, model IDG-300 of InvenSense Inc., is located along the z-axis. It uses an extension cable to measure the yaw motion of the device. The onboard accelerometer, model MMA7260Q by Freescale Semiconductor, Inc., located on the center of the electronics board, measures the amount and direction of the tilting. For the detection of touch and/or near-proximity, a sensing electrode used for charge-transfer touch sensor, model QT113 by Quantum Research Group Ltd., is attached underneath the top of the device. Data is measured at 15ms intervals, which is sufficient for measuring human movement [5] using an onboard microprocessor (AT-mega8L). Signal processing of the converted four-channel data is then done in the host PC after the data is transmitted wirelessly. The actuation parts consist of two linear motors (L-type Force Reactor ^{TM} provided by Alps Electric Co.) with a source current transistor array. The embedded linear motors show a reliable broad frequency response up to 250Hz. Continuous vibration and short tactile pulses can be represented using linear actuators. A recharging module, model MAX1555 by Maxim Integrated Products, Inc., which charges a single-cell lithium-ion (Li+) battery, is also included in the system, allowing its continuous use as a PC peripheral.

5   Applications

5.1   Bimanual Input

While users typically use their dominant hand for mouse control in a desktop environment, the non-preferred hand is also actively used when key inputting is required in a functional combination with the mouse. For example, pressing the space bar key for panning action and pressing the ctrl key for zooming are frequently used with the mouse. Considering that people use both hands for everyday tasks, this can be considered as a natural phenomenon, although the task load should be measured. Given that the proposed system can complement the mouse by providing additional input modalities in a comfortable manner, it can be used with current desktop environments.

5.2   Tactile Notification and Assist tick

A considerable amount of important information is usually provided in the form of audio feedback in a desktop environment. Considering that the most frequently used cue is an alert or a notifying sound that may accompany an event, touch information can be alternatively used for these notifications, as described in Section 3.2. For an entertainment application, tactile notifications can be extended to the realization of an assist tick, which is generally audio-based. The use of this type of tactile assist tick can also enhance the sense of rhythm of a user in a realistic manner.

6   Conclusion

In this paper, a human-computer interface with a self-centering feature and tactile feedback functionality was proposed. Utilizing a mechanically ungrounded structure with low structural damping and a rounded and weighted bottom, the device produces erratic patterns in the event it is tipped over. Available input means such as tilting, rotation, and touch allow a user to give commands in a comfortable manner. The system also embraces the functionality of tactile feedback using linear actuators for both direct and indirect contact conditions. While the haptic information provides a type of notification as the device is being manipulated, it can also provide indirect tactile feedback that can notify a user of events from a computer. Mapping vibration patterns with events from the computer, the proposed system could be extended as a desktop ambient haptic display. For the implementation of robotic feedback, dynamic allocation of the center of mass will be researched as a further work.

Acknowledgments. This work was supported by the IT R&D program of MKE/KEIT, [2009-S-035-01, Contact-free Multipoint Realistic Interaction Technology Development].

References

1. Sreedharan, S., Zurita, E., Plimmer, B.: 3D input for 3D worlds. In: OzCHI, Adelaide, Australia (2007)
2. Abe, M., et al.: A Life Log Collector Integrated with a Remote-Controller for Enabling User Centric Services. IEEE Transactions on Consumer Electronics 55(1), 295–302 (2009)
3. Lee, M., et al.: Unsupervised Clustering for Abnormality Detection Based on the Tri-axial Accelerometer. In: ICROS-SICE International Joint Conference, Fukuoka International Congress Center, Japan (2009)
4. Brown, L., Williamson, J.: Shake2Talk: Multimodal Messaging for Interpersonal Communication. In: Oakley, I., Brewster, S. (eds.) HAID 2007. LNCS, vol. 4813, pp. 44–55. Springer, Heidelberg (2007)
5. Verplaetse, C.: Inertial proprioceptive devices: Self-motion-sensing toys and tools. IBM Systems Journal 35(3), 639–650 (1996)
6. Hinckley, K.: Input technologies and techniques. In: The human-computer interaction handbook: fundamentals, evolving technologies and emerging applications, pp. 151–168 (2002)
7. Stiles, R.N.: Frequency and displacement amplitude relations for normal hand tremor. Journal of Applied Physiology 40(1), 44–54 (1976)
8. Britton, E., Lipscomb, J., Pique, M.: Making nested rotations convenient for the user. ACM SIGGRAPH Computer Graphics 12(3), 222–227 (1978)
9. Norman, D.A.: The design of everyday things. Basic Books, New York (2002)
10. Swindells, C., MacLean, K.: Capturing the Dynamics of Mechanical Knobs. In: Proceedings of the Second Joint EuroHaptics Conference and Symposium on Haptic Interfaces for Virtual Environment and Teleoperator Systems. IEEE Computer Society, Washington (2007)
11. Kim, S., Kwon, D.: Haptic and sound grid for enhanced positioning in a 3-D virtual environment. In: Oakley, I., Brewster, S. (eds.) HAID 2007. LNCS, vol. 4813, p. 98. Springer, Heidelberg (2007)
12. Luk, J., et al.: A role for haptics in mobile interaction: initial design using a handheld tactile display prototype.
13. Oakley, I., Park, J.: Designing Eyes-Free Interaction. In: Oakley, I., Brewster, S. (eds.) HAID 2007. LNCS, vol. 4813, p. 121. Springer, Heidelberg (2007)
14. Verrillo, R.: Psychophysics of vibrotactile stimulation. The Journal of the Acoustical Society of America 77, 225 (1985)

HaptiHug: A Novel Haptic Display for Communication of Hug over a Distance

Dzmitry Tsetserukou

Toyohashi University of Technology,1-1 Hibarigaoka, Tempaku-cho,
Toyohashi, Aichi, 441-8580 Japan
tsetserukou@erc.tut.ac.jp

Abstract. The motivation behind our work is to enrich social interaction and emotional involvement of the users of online communication media. The paper focuses on a novel haptic display HaptiHug for the representation of hug over a distance by means of online communication system supporting haptic feedback. The system integrates 3D virtual world Second Life, intelligent component for automatic recognition of hug cue from text messages, and innovative affective haptic interface providing additional nonverbal communication channel through simulation of social touch. Based on the real data (the pressure and duration of the interpersonal hug), the control system generates a signal that produces the feelings similar to the real hugging sensations. User study revealed that social pseudo-touch was successful in increasing the hugging immersion as well as hugging sensation.

Keywords: Affective haptics, computer-mediated communication, haptic display, sense of touch, 3D world.

1 Introduction

In a real world, whenever one person interacts with another, both observe, perceive and interpret each other's emotional expressions communicated through a variety of signals. Valuable information is also transferred by non-verbal communication (e.g., social touch). It is well known that touching is one of the most powerful means for establishing and maintaining social contact. The fact that two people are willing to touch implies an element of trust [1]. Expressive potential of touch is the ability to convey and elicit strong emotions.

Computer-mediated on-line interactions heavily rely on senses of vision and hearing, and there is a substantial need in mediated social touch [2]. Among many forms of physical contact, hug is the most emotionally charged one. It conveys warmth, love, and affiliation. DiSalvo et al. [3] introduced "The Hug" interface. When person desires to communicate hug, he/she can squeeze the pillow, so that such action results in the vibration and temperature changes in the partner's device. The Hug Shirt allows people who are missing each other to send physical sensation of the hug over distance [4]. User can wear this shirt, embedded with actuators and sensors, in everyday life.

A.M.L. Kappers et al. (Eds.): EuroHaptics 2010, Part I, LNCS 6191, pp. 340–347, 2010.

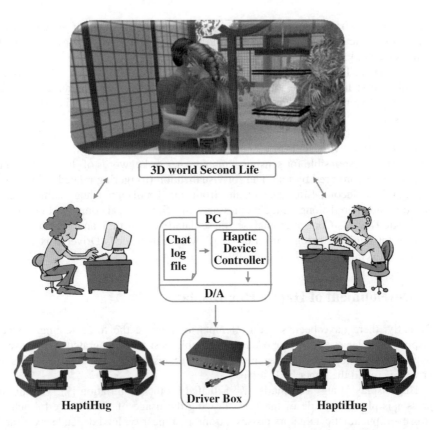

Fig. 1. Architecture of computer-mediated communication system with hug display HaptiHug

However, these interfaces suffer from inability to resemble natural hug sensation and, hence, to elicit strong affective experience (only slight pressure is generated by vibration actuators) [5]; lack the visual representation of the partner, which adds ambiguity (hugging in a real life involves both visual and physical experience), and do not consider the power of social pseudo-haptic illusion (i.e., hugging animation is not integrated). Moreover, real-time online application, open to public and supporting hug feedback, has not been developed.

Driven by the motivation to enhance social interactivity and emotionally immersive experience of real-time messaging, we developed a novel haptic hug display producing realistic force feedback through online communication system. The interpersonal relationships and the ability to express empathy grow strongly when people become emotionally closer through disclosing thoughts, feelings, and emotions for the sake of understanding.

2   Architecture of the System

We placed great importance on the automatic sensing of keywords through textual messages in 3D virtual world Second Life, the visualization of the hugging animation by avatars in virtual environment, and reproduction of feeling of social touch by means of haptic stimulation in a real world. The architecture of the developed system is presented in Fig. 1.

As a media for communication, we employ Second Life, which allows users to flexibly create their online identities (avatars) and to play various animations (e.g., facial expressions and gestures) of avatars by typing special abbreviations in a chat window.

The control of the conversation is implemented through the Second Life object called EmoHeart (invisible in case of 'neutral' state) attached to the avatar's chest. EmoHeart is responsible for sensing symbolic cues or keywords of 'hug' communicative function conveyed by text, and for visualization (triggering related animation) of 'hugging' in Second Life. The results from and EmoHeart ('hug' communicative function) are stored along with chat messages in a file on local computer of each user.

Haptic Devices Controller analyses these data in a real time and generates control signals for Digital/Analog converter (D/A), which then feeds Driver Box for haptic device with control cues (Hug intensity and duration).

3 Development of Haptic Hug Display

Recently, there have been several attempts to improve the force feeling by haptic display. Mueller et al. [6] proposed air-inflatable vest with integrated compressor for presentation of hug over a distance. Air pump inflates the vest and thus generates light pressure around the upper body torso.

Hug display Huggy Pajama is also actuated by the air inflation [7]. The air compressor is placed outside of the vest allowing the usage of more powerful actuator. However, pneumatic actuators possess strong nonlinearity, load dependency, time lag in response (1-2 sec.), and they produce loud noise [6].

Our goal is to develop a wearable haptic display generating the pressure and patterns that are similar to those of a human-human hug. Such device should be lightweight, compact, with low power consumption, comfortable to wear, and aesthetically pleasing.

When people are hugging, they generate pressure on the chest area and on the back of each other by the hands, simultaneously (upper back side of the torso is more frequently touched by the partners). The key feature of the developed HaptiHug is that it physically reproduces the hug pattern similar to that of human-human interaction. The hands for a HaptiHug are sketched from a real human (partner) and made from a soft material so that hugging persons can feel affinity and social presence of each other.

The couple of oppositely rotating motors (Maxon RE 10 1.5 W with gearhead GP 10 A 64:1) are incorporated into the holder placed on the user chest area. The Soft Hands, which are aligned horizontally, contact back of the user. Once 'hug' command is received, couple of motors tense the belt, pressing thus Soft Hands and chest part of the HaptiHug in the direction of human body (Fig. 2). When the movement of the motors stops, the belt rests around the chest snugly. Shoulder straps support the weight of the HaptiHug, so that the user naturally perceives this device as the part of the garment.

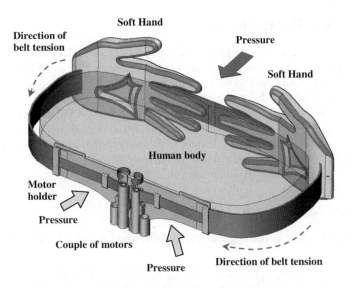

Fig. 2. Structure of the wearable HaptiHug device

The duration and intensity of the hug are controlled by the software in accordance with the emoticon or a keyword, detected from text. For the presentation of a plain hug level (e.g., '(>^_^)>', '{}', '<h>'), a big hug level (e.g., '>:D<', '{{}}'), and a great big hug level (e.g., 'gbh', '{{{}}}'), the different levels of pressure with different durations were applied on the user's back and chest.

The Soft Hands are made from the compliant rubber-sponge material. The contour profile of a Soft Hand is sketched from the male human and has front-face area of 155.6 cm². Two identical pieces of Soft Hand of 5 mm thickness were sandwiched by narrow belt slots and connected by plastic screws. Such structure provides enough flexibility to tightly fit to the human back surface, while being pressed by belt. Moreover, belt can loosely move inside the Soft Hands during tension. The dimensions and structure of Soft Hands are presented in Fig. 3.

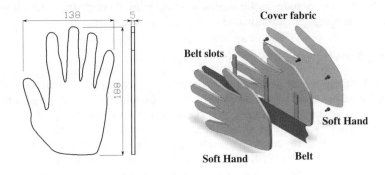

Fig. 3. Left: Soft Hand dimensions. Right: sandwiched structure of Soft Hands.

4   Emotional Haptic Design

Aesthetically pleasing objects appear to the user to be more effective by virtue of their sensual appeal [8]. The designed device is pleasurable to look at and to touch (colorful velvet material was used to decorate the device) and have personalized features (in particular, the Soft Hands in HaptiHug can be sketched from the hands of the real communication partner). We placed great attention on the comfortable wearing of garment. HaptiHug has flexible and intuitive in use system of bucklers and fasteners to enable user to easily adjust the devices to the body shape. Moreover all components of the haptic display are made from compliant and soft materials: rubber-sponge, textile, flexible plastic that makes it comfortable, safe and fun to wear.

5   Social Pseudo-haptic Touch

We developed animation of hug and integrated it into Second Life (Fig. 4).

Fig. 4. Snapshots of hugging animation in Second Life

During the animation the avatars approach and embrace each other by hands. The significance of our idea to realistically reproduce hugging is in integration of active-haptic device HaptiHug and pseudo-haptic touch simulated by hugging animation. Thus, high immersion into the physical contact of partners while hugging is achieved. In [9], the effect of pseudo-haptic feedback on the experiencing force was proved. We expect that hugging animation will also increase the force sensation.

6   Hug Measurement

Since so far there were no attempts to measure the pressure and duration of the hug, we conducted the experiments. A total of 3 pair of subjects (3 males and 3 females) with no previous knowledge about experiment was examined. Their age varied from 24 to 32. They were asked to hug each other three times with three different intensities (plain hug, big hug and great big hug levels). The subject's chest and upper back side were covered with Kinotex tactile sensor measuring the pressure intensity through amount of backscattered light falling on photodetector [10]. The taxels (sensing elements) displaced with 21.5 mm in X and 22 mm in Y direction make up 6x10 array. The Kinotex sensitivity range is from 500 N/m^2 to 8 000 N/m^2. The experimental results (average value of pressure and duration) are listed in Table 1.

Table 1. Experimental findings

	Plain Hug	Big Hug	Great big hug
Pressure on male back side, $[kN/m^2]$	1.4	2.5	5.05
Pressure on female back side, $[kN/m^2]$	1.7	2.9	6.4
Pressure on chest, $[kN/m^2]$	2.3	3.5	5.9
Average duration, sec.	1.98	2.6	3.4

Experimental results shows that males produce more force on the partner back than females. What it is interesting, is that the pressure on the chest changes nonlineary. The probable cause of this is that while experiencing great big hug level humans protect the vitally important part of our body, heart, from overloading. The example of pressure patterns on the back of the user and on the chest area are given in Fig. 5.

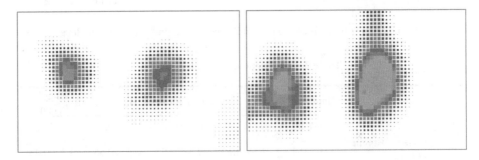

Fig. 5. Left: example of pressure distribution on the back of the user. The highest pressure corresponds to 4800 N/m². Right: example of pressure distribution on the chest of the user. The highest pressure corresponds to 5900 N/m².

While hugging, three phases can be distinguished, i.e., initiation (pressure increases rapidly), steady-state (pressure level is stabilized), and retrieval (pressure decreases rapidly) (Fig. 6). The developed HuptiHug device can achieve the force level of plain hug (generated pressure is bigger comparing with other hug displays). We consider that there is no reason to produce very strong forces (that requires more powerful motors) resulting sometimes in unpleasant sensations. Based on the experimental results we designed the control signals in such a way that the resulting pressure intensity, pattern, and duration are similar to those of human-human hug characteristics. We summarized the technical specifications of the hug displays in Table 2 (**O** means this characteristic is present, – is absent).

Developed HuptiHug is capable of generating strong pressure while being lightweight, and compact. Such features of haptic hug display as visual representation of the partner, social pseudo-haptic touch, and pressure patterns similar to that of human-human interaction, increase the immersion into the physical contact of partners while hugging greatly.

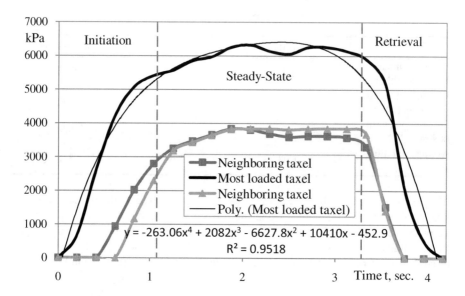

Fig. 6. Example of the pressure plot while people hugging with a big hug level

Table 2. Specifications of the hug displays

	HaptiHug	The Hug	Hug Shirt	Hug vest	Huggy Pajama
Weight	0.146 kg	>1.0 kg	0.160 kg	>2.0 kg	>1.2 kg
Overall sizes Height, m × Width, m	0.1 × 0.4	0.5 × 0.6	0.4 × 0.5	0.4 × 0.55	0.3 × 0.45
Wearable design	O	–	O	O	O
Generated Pressure	2.0 kPa	–	–	0.5 kPa	2.7 kPa
Actuators	DC motors	Vibro-motors	Vibro-motors	Air pump	Air pump
Visual representation of the partner	O	–	–	–	–
Social pseudo-touch	O	–	–	–	–
Based on human-human hug	O	–	–	–	–

7 Conclusions

We demonstrated the HaptiHug (Fig. 7) as the part of the iFeel_IM! system at such conferences as INTETAIN 2009, ACII 2009, ASIAGRAPH 2009, and CHI 2010.

In total more than 300 persons had experienced our system. Subjects enjoyed wearing the HaptiHug. The majority of users reported that this device presented pressure and haptic stimuli in a very realistic manner. The simultaneous observation of hugging animation and experiencing hugging sensation evoked surprise and joy in many

Fig. 7. Demonstration at ASIAGRAPH 2009

participants. The atmosphere between the participants and exhibitors became more relaxing and joyful during HaptiHug demonstration. That proves that HaptiHug was successful at emotion elicitation as well. Also, in spite of users varied greatly in size the device was capable of fitting everyone. In future we will conduct more thorough user study to determine average hug levels, emotional feedback, levels of hugging immersion with and without animation.

References

1. Collier, G.: Emotional Expression. Lawrence Erlbaum Associates Inc., New Jersey (1985)
2. Haans, A., Ijsselsteijn, W.I.: Mediated Social Touch: a Review of Current Research and Future Directions. Virtual Reality 9, 149–159 (2006)
3. DiSalvo, C., Gemperle, F., Forlizzi, J., Montgomery, E.: The Hug: an Exploration of Robotic Form for Intimate Communication. In: 12th IEEE Workshop on Robot and Human Interactive Communication, pp. 403–408. IEEE Press, New York (2003)
4. Hug Shirt. CuteCircuit Company, http://www.cutecircuit.com
5. Haans, A., Nood, C., Ijsselsteijn, W.A.: Investigating Response Similarities Between Real and Mediated Social Touch: a First Test. In: ACM Conference on Human factors in Computing Systems, pp. 2405–2410. ACM Press, New York (2007)
6. Mueller, F.F., Vetere, F., Gibbs, M.R., Kjeldskov, J., Pedell, S., Howard, S.: Hug Over a Distance. In: ACM Conference on Human factors in Computing Systems, pp. 1673–1676. ACM Press, New York (2005)
7. Teh, J.K.S., Cheok, A.D., Peiris, R.L., Choi, Y., Thuong, V., Lai, S.: Haggy Pajama: a Mobile Parent and Child Hugging Communication System. In: International Conference on Interaction Design and Children, pp. 250–257. ACM Press, New York (2008)
8. Norman, D.A.: Emotional Design. Why We Love (or Hate) Everyday Things. Basic Book, New York (2004)
9. Lecuyer, A., Coquillart, S., Kheddar, A., Richard, P., Coiffet, P.: Pseudo-haptic Feedback: Can Isometric Input Devices Simulate Force Feedback? In: IEEE VR, pp. 83–90. IEEE Press, New York (2000)
10. Optic Fiber Tactile Sensor Kinotex. Nitta Corporation, http://www.nitta.co.jp/english/

Physical Contact of Devices:
Utilization of Beats for Interpersonal Communication

Soo-Chul Lim[1], Seung-Chan Kim[1], Jung-Hoon Hwang[2], and Dong-Soo Kwon[1]

[1] Telerobotics & Control Labortory, KAIST, Daejeon, Republic of Korea
{limsc,kimsc}@robot.kaist.ac.kr, kwonds@kaist.ac.kr
[2] Intelligent Robotics Research Center, KETI, Gyeonggi, Republic of Korea
hwangjh@keti.re.kr

Abstract. In this paper, an interpersonal communication method based on tactile beats when devices are established physical contact will be proposed. Tactile beats are a well-known phenomenon that describes frequency modulation occurs when vibrating objects with similar but not same operating frequencies are physically connected. Vibrating signals at each configuration (no contact and contact with same/different frequency) were measured using a laser vibrometer. Preliminary user study revealed that the induced physical tactile stimulus was perceived well by the subjects. As an application, social touch interaction using hand-held devices with differently assigned operating vibration frequencies was described. Mapping the frequency deviation between devices to quantifiable social information, it is expected that the proposed algorithm can be applied for interpersonal communication based on physical contact with enhanced emotional and social experiences.

Keywords: haptic communication, physical contact, tactile beats, social interaction.

1 Introduction

There have been numerous studies on enhancing communication channels for human-computer/human-robot interaction. For example, teleoperation systems and sensory substitution systems were utilized for the extension of direct physical touch. With the support of the visual and auditory senses, which cover a great portion of the communication, many researchers have focused on communication with mediate touch that enables physical interaction through devices in remote locations [1-3]. The established haptic communication channel between touch interfaces was found to be useful for enriching interpersonal communication by complementing another communication channel [1]. These common haptic communication channels connect people with an improved haptic experience. Brave & Dahley [2] stated that *"Physical contact such as handshake and hug is a basic means through which people achieve a sense of connection, indicate intention and express emotion. In close personal relationships, such as family and friends, touch is particularly important as a communicator of affection."* That is, physical contact plays an essential role in our natural perceptual construction from the psychological developmental perspective. Because touch involves social and emotional experiences, it is widely extended to numerous applications. Lover's cups

A.M.L. Kappers et al. (Eds.): EuroHaptics 2010, Part I, LNCS 6191, pp. 348–353, 2010.
© Springer-Verlag Berlin Heidelberg 2010

[4] enable two users to share the feeling of drinking in different places by using cups as the communication interfaces of drinking. For effective communication between the sender and receiver, a *common* or *shared symbolic meaning* should be implied in the social interaction of physical contact. Hapticon [5] shows that a haptic signal can be a robust way to communicate shared meaningful information to a user. In addition to human touch, touch between devices has recently emerged in HCI applications. Peng et. al researched the proximity information between devices. In their research, the relative position measured from the time-of-arrival was utilized for the location-based services [6], such as spanning displays, if contacted. Extending previous proximity-based research, this paper introduces the beat phenomenon between devices that are physically connected for social interaction. Because tactile beats occur only when a specific frequency deviation exists between two different vibrating devices, the device contact can be utilized for device identification. For example, a registered vibrating device can be identified by touching another vibrating device, which has a slightly different operating frequency. Even though carrier frequencies with slight differences are hard to distinguish by users, the beat sensation, which is easily detected, can be utilized for sharing meaning between users who hold a device, simultaneously. Social interaction using established physical contact between devices will be described as an application.

2 Tactile Beats between Devices

Fig. 1 shows the proposed approach to the communicating method with physical contact. Device contact with stimulus of slightly different frequencies causes beats phenomenon in tactile sense that bring out sensation changes. This contact can be applied to touch communication according to the predefined common or shared meaning in the field of the social network services or location based services.

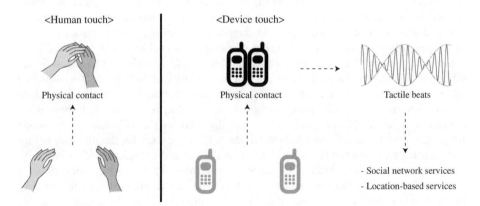

Fig. 1. Overview of the proposed device touch. Like everyday touch between people for interaction, device contact can be also utilized for interaction between devices.

2.1 Beats Phenomenon

The beats are interference between two harmonic motions with frequencies close to one another that produce periodic variations whose rate is the difference between the two frequencies[7]. For example, if

$$x_1(t) = X \sin 2\pi ft$$
$$x_2(t) = X \sin 2\pi (f + \delta f)t \tag{1}$$

where δf is a small quantity; the addition of these motions yields

$$x(t) = x_1(t) + x_2(t) = X[\sin 2\pi ft + \sin 2\pi (f + \delta f)t]. \tag{2}$$

Equation (2) can be rewritten as

$$x(t) = 2X \left[\sin 2\pi \left(f + \frac{\delta f}{2} \right) t \times \sin 2\pi \frac{\delta f}{2} t \right]. \tag{3}$$

Equation (3) shows that two slightly different vibrations create the beats phenomenon. The resulting motion, $x(t)$, represents an approximate sine wave with frequency $(f+\delta f/2)$ and amplitude of envelop building up and dying down between 0 and $2X$ with frequency δf. From Equation (3), the human senses simultaneously perceive the stimuli with the carrier frequency $(f+\delta f/2)$ and the envelope frequency (δf). Human sensation of tactile beats is regardless of a phase offset owing to its physical characteristics.

2.2 Direct Contact of Devices: Utilization of Beats for Communication

People cannot discriminate the difference between two vibrations with slightly different frequencies that are lower than JND for the upper boundary frequency of the reference stimulus [8]. However, when these two vibrations with slightly different frequencies are attached to each other, the alternating constructive and destructive interferences between two stimuli to the skin cause the tactile beats sensation. From the sensation changing, people can perceive whether two stimuli are the same or not.

Fig. 2 shows the schematic figures communicating through direct contact between developed roly-poly interfaces, idealized vibrating signals. The signals acquired from a laser vibrometer (Keyence LC2400A(controller), LC-2430(head)) to measure the vibration of interfaces at each situation. The individual interface is not discriminated by the vibrations difference if one just holds the interfaces when their operating frequencies are slightly different. The graph of Fig. 2(a) is shown when there is no contact between interfaces. And in the case that two interfaces vibrate at the same frequency, people cannot sense the difference in feeling except for the intensity before and after contact between the devices because the vibration frequency of the stimulation is the same. The vibration frequency's pattern is similar to the vibration of a single interface with twofold greater intensity (Fig. 2(b)). However, in the case of meeting two interfaces with the vibrations of a slightly different frequency, people can perceive the difference after the contact because two different vibrations induce tactile beats (Fig. 2(c)). The envelope of the stimulus in the figure clearly shows the frequency and intensity change temporally.

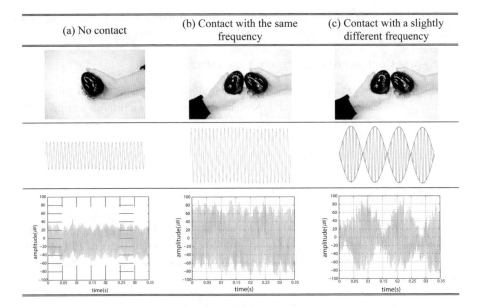

Fig. 2. The idealized vibrating signal and measured signal from a laser vibrometer in each situation

An experiment was conducted to show that humans can feel beats when two devices make contact with slightly different frequencies (Fig.2 (c)). Stimuli consisted of one device that vibrated at 250Hz and another device that vibrated at 254Hz. This induced a 4Hz tactile beats when they are contacted. Vibration based on tactile beats was used to stimulate for 5 seconds. After a 3-second adaptation of the beats, the test stimulus was presented as the same stimulus of the adaptation stimulus for 2 seconds without an interval. The time flow was shown graphically on the monitor screen while the adaptation and test stimulus were presented for 5 seconds, allowing the subject to know the start time of the test. Subjects pressed the keypad of the computer during the test when they perceived an intensity change of the stimulus. Six young subjects, aged 25 to 31 years old, participated in the experiments. The experimental results showed that the subjects felt an intensity change of 4.11±0.21(means±SE) times/second with

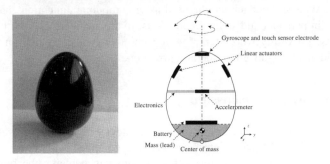

Fig. 3. The developed system and its internal structure. [9]

0.2491±0.0178 second interval. The results show that humans can perceive the beats when the devices establish physical contact with two different operating frequencies.

2.3 System Configuration: Rolypoly Type Interface

Fig. 3 shows the developed system and its internal structure. The system follows the structure of a roly-poly toy. The mechanical structure also facilitates a comfortable and easy control method. The embedded impact type linear vibrator shows a reliable broad frequency response up to 250Hz. Continuous vibration and short tactile pulse can be represented using the linear actuators.[9]

3 Applications

The proposed interaction scheme is based on the fact that a slight frequency difference between devices induces a completely different physical sensation. In this sense, the operating frequency of an actuator can play an important role in characterizing a user's device.

3.1 A Mobile Device with an Assigned Vibration Frequency

Although most vibration actuators are driven under a resonant frequency, slight modulation of the operating frequency is possible according to the application context. Once an operating frequency is assigned to individual devices, physical contact between devices which causes tactile beats can be used in the context of social interaction.

3.2 Social Interaction with Tactile Beats

As described above, different physical vibrations are generated according to the frequency deviation between devices. As users experience different touch feelings with respect to the induced haptic feedback, the proposed interaction method allows users to interact socially with each other in a physical manner. For example, the relative frequency deviation can be mapped to quantifiable social contexts such as posting numbers in microblogs that are related to each other. Although the meaning of the induced vibration can be translated differently in accordance with the interaction context, this type of feedback can be used as visceral communication channel, which is important in personal and social interactions. In this manner, devices that belong to users in close proximity who interact with each other frequently both in the real and virtual world can have different operating frequencies.

4 Conclusion and Discussion

In this study, a tactile beat phenomenon between devices was quantitatively measured using two developed desktop interfaces that are equipped with linear actuators. A major finding in the present study is that humans can perceive the beat vibrations when the devices establish physical contact with two different operating frequencies.

Because human can perceive the beat vibrations, this sensation can be utilized for social touch interaction. Mapping the frequency deviation to quantifiable social information, the proposed algorithm can be applied to social communication. As in the case of the tacton [11], it is expected that tactile information modulated by beats between users can significantly enhance social and emotional experiences by offering a channel for visceral communication. Because the resultant frequency can also be detected by a device itself, the proposed touch interaction can be further extended to location-based services, which have been emerging recently. For future work, the proposed communicating approach will be applied to commercialized handheld devices, such as mobile devices, for social context-based interaction. Also, the psychophysical aspect will be considered to determine the perceptually effective frequency deviations.

Acknowledgment

This work was supported by the IT R&D program of MKE/KEIT, [2009-S-035-01, Contact-free Multipoint Realistic Interaction Technology Development].

References

1. Chang: ComTouch: Design of a Vibrotactile Communication Device. In: Designing interactive systems, DIS 2002, pp. 311–318 (2002)
2. Brave, S., Dahley, A.: in Touch: A Medium for Haptic Interpersonal Communication. In: Human factors in computing systems, pp. 363–364 (1997)
3. Oakley, I., Brewster, S., Gray, P.: Communicating with Feeling. In: Brewster, S., Murray-Smith, R. (eds.) Haptic HCI 2000. LNCS, vol. 2058, pp. 61–68. Springer, Heidelberg (2001)
4. Chung, H., Lee, C.-H.J., Selker, T.: Lover's cups: drinking interfaces as new communication channels. In: CHI 2006, pp. 375–380 (2006)
5. Enriquez, M., MacLean, K., Chita, C.: Haptic Phonemes: Basic Building Blocks of Haptic Communication. In: Multimodal interfaces, ICMI 2006, pp. 302–309 (2006)
6. Peng, C., Shen, G., Zhang, Y., Li, Y., Tan, K.: BeepBeep: A High Accuracy Acoustic Ranging System Using COTS Mobile Devices. In: Embedded networked sensor systems, SenSys 2007, pp. 1–14 (2007)
7. Rao, S.S.: Meachnical Vibration, 3rd edn., pp. 53–55 (1995)
8. Pongrac, H.: Vibrotactile perception: examining the coding of vibrations and the just noticeable difference under various conditions. Multimedia systems 13, 297–307 (2008)
9. Kim, S.C., Han, B.-K., Lim, S.-C., Bianchi, A., Kyung, K.-U., Kwon, D.-S.: Roly-poly: A Haptic Interface with Self-righting Feature. In: EuroHaptics 2010 (to be published, 2010)
10. Dobson, K., boyd, d., Ju, W., Donath, J., Ishii, H.: Creating visceral personal and social interactions in mediated spaces. In: CHI 2001, pp. 151–152 (2001)
11. Brewster, S., Brown, L.M.: Tactons: structured tactile messages for non-visual information display. In: Proceedings of the 5th conference on Australasian user interface, vol. 28, pp. 15–23 (2004)

Tremor Suppression Control
for a Meal-Assist Robot

Ken'ichi Yano*, Kenji Nishiwaki, and Shota Hiramatsu

Dept. of Human and Information Systems, Gifu University,
1-1 Yanagido, Gifu, 501-1193, Japan
yanolab-paper@gifu-u.ac.jp

Abstract. In the near future, a labor shortage will constitute a significant problem in the fields of welfare and nursing care. To solve this problem, researchers are developing rehabilitation and welfare robots such as motion-assist robots and life support robots. The purpose of this study was to develop a meal-assist robot that can help a disabled person with hand tremor. We used a proxy-based sliding-mode control for sensorless admittance control and applied tremor suppression control that uses the resonance of proxy-based sliding control.

Keywords: Assistive robotics, Meal-assist, Sliding mode control.

1 Introduction

Increases in the practical application of robotic and control technology have been seen in the fields of medicine and welfare. Robots to assist disabled and elderly persons who require support in the upper extremities or hands and arms during mealtimes because of the lack of available caregivers are in development. Patients with Parkinson's disease, spinal cord injury or muscular dystrophy, for instance, have difficulty taking their meals. The main symptom of Parkinson's disease patients that makes them candidates for meal assistance is tremor, which is the initial symptom that develops in about 60% of Parkinson's disease patients.

The meal-assist robots HANDY-1 [1], NeaterEater, Winsford Feeder and My Spoon [2] have been developed and put to practical use in past studies. However, many problems remain regarding the practical application of meal-assist robots. For instance, the meal-assist robots developed in the past were mostly fully-automatic, employing a joystick, with food carried to the mouth automatically. For many patients, such as those with Parkinson's disease, who can use their arms even though their arms and hands tremor, a better system would provide body stimulation, allowing the disabled individual to move the body as much as possible, and brain stimulation. Thus, the development of a system that can assist the patient in eating while using the hands is the goal.

Some tremor suppression methods have been already studied. Gonzalez et al. developed a digital filtering algorithm that utilized an optimal equalizer[3]. Riviere et al. have investigated the weighted-frequency Fourier linear combiner for suppressing physiological tremors in microsurgery[4]. Pledie et al. developed the closed-loop human-machine

---

* This work was supported by GIFU & OGAKI Robitics Advanced Medical Cluster.

A.M.L. Kappers et al. (Eds.): EuroHaptics 2010, Part I, LNCS 6191, pp. 354–359, 2010.

system with negative feedback[5]. However, those studies relied on the removal of the tremor signal with a filter and did not suppress the tremor.

In the present study, we developed a novel meal-assist robot named *MARo*[6] and applied a tremor suppression function to the robot using proxy-based sliding mode control (PSMC)[7]. With PSMC, we applied virtual object proxy without mass to sliding-mode control and connected the controlled object with proxy by virtual coupling. Using the new control technique, we achieve virtual coupling to suppress a patient's tremor.

2   Meal-Assist Robot *MARo*

In this study, we employ a newly developed meal-assist robot, as shown in Fig. 1. The robot connects a gripper to the sixth joint through the fifth joint of the patient's hands. Using this method, it is possible to separate the gripper from the robot. The fifth and sixth joints were made into a single free joint that does not have a motor, to maintain low cost and miniaturization. The link lengths are d_1=151.0[mm], a_2=34.7[mm], a_3=92.2[mm], d_3=47.0[mm], d_4=196.5[mm], d_6=55.0[mm].

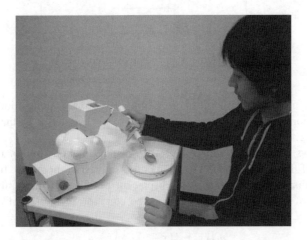

Fig. 1. Meal-Assist Robot; *MARo*

3   Tremor Suppression Using Resonance

In this study, we applied proxy-based sliding mode control(PSMC)[7] to the meal-assist robot. PSMC is the control method by which the operator applies virtual object proxy without mass to sliding-mode control, connected to the controlled object with proxy by the PID control. In the PSMC system, the virtual proxy follows by sliding-mode control to a target trajectory P_d. The switching hyperplane of the sliding-mode control is set to the value obtained from the position error from the target trajectory to the end position and time constant H.

Virtual coupling of PSMC is resonated to suppress the tremor actively. The output torque of the PSMC is calculated from the present end-effector position, target position and position of the virtual mass. When the tremor is input to the end-effector of the meal-assist robot, the virtual coupling is resonated in the tremor frequency. Then, the proxy vibrates more than the tremor of the end-effector, and P_s increases. Herewith, the trajectory error increases and the force that tries to return the robot to a target trajectory occurs by sliding-mode control. Because the force direction is opposite of where the proxy was pushed, the force is added to the end-effector at the opposite phase of the user's tremor. As a result, the tremor can be suppressed. The conceptual diagram of tremor suppression using resonance is shown in Fig. 2.

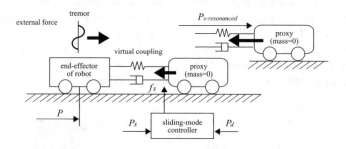

Fig. 2. Tremor suppression using resonance

Because the meal-assist robot is operated directly by manual operation, the effect of the user's tremor is received directly. The system forces oscillation by the displacement shown in Fig. 3.

Fig. 3 shows a system in which the forced displacement as tremor is input to the end-effector of the robot and the vibration is transmitted to the proxy. In the figure, u is the forced displacement and x is the displacement of m_2. At this time, the relative displacement of m_2 to m_1 becomes $x - u$. The equation of motion of a proxy m_2 is expressed as

$$m_2\ddot{x} = -k(x - u) - c(\dot{x} - \dot{u}) \tag{1}$$

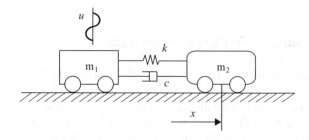

Fig. 3. Forced vibration by the displacement

where k is the coefficient of stiffness and c is the coefficient of viscous damping. x_r is defined as

$$x - u = x_r \tag{2}$$

If (2) is substituted for (1), we have the following:

$$m_2\ddot{x}_r + c\dot{x}_r + kx_r = -m_2\ddot{u} \tag{3}$$

If $u(t)$ is given, the right-hand side of (3) is decided. $u(t)$ can be shown as cyclic motion because of the tremor. (3) becomes

$$m_2\ddot{x}_r + c\dot{x}_r + kx_r = m_2 a\omega^2 \sin \omega t \tag{4}$$

where

$$2\mu = \frac{c}{m}, \quad p = \sqrt{\frac{k}{m}} \tag{5}$$

Therefore, the expression of the forced vibration can be shown as follows:

$$x_r = A_r \sin(\omega t - \beta) \tag{6}$$

$$A_r = \frac{a\omega^2}{\sqrt{(p^2 - \omega^2)^2 + 4\mu^2\omega^2}} = \frac{a\omega^2/p^2}{(1 - \omega^2/p^2)^2 + (2\xi\omega/p)^2} \tag{7}$$

$$\tan\beta = \frac{2\mu\omega}{p^2 - \omega^2} = \frac{2\xi\omega/p}{1 - \omega^2/p^2} \tag{8}$$

ξ is designated as a parameter. When $\omega \ll p$, A_r becomes $x \simeq u$. m_2 moves almost as well as m_1. The vibration of m increases as ω approaches p when ξ is small, and the resonance is generated by reaching the maximum value. When ξ is larger than $1/\sqrt{2}$, the maximum value does not occur. When $\omega \gg p$, since $\alpha \simeq 180$ and $\beta \simeq 180$, A_r becomes

$$x_r \simeq -a \sin \omega t \tag{9}$$

Therefore,

$$x = x_r + u \simeq 0 \tag{10}$$

Only m_1 moves by u, because m_2 is almost at a resting state. Because each displacement is shown by (7), the transmission rate of displacement is shown as follows:

$$T_A = A/a = \frac{\sqrt{1 + (2\xi\omega/p)^2}}{\sqrt{(1 - \frac{\omega^2}{p^2})^2 + (2\xi\frac{\omega}{p})^2}} \tag{11}$$

As above, resonance by displacement is generated when p approaches ω, and transmission rate T_A is decided by ξ, as follows:

$$k = mp^2 = m\omega^2, \quad c = 2\mu m = 2m\xi\omega \tag{12}$$

4   Experimental Results

We conducted experiments to test the effectiveness of the proposed technique using the meal-assist robot *MARo*. In the experiments, an artificial tremor was added by having an operator hold the end-effector. We applied two control methods, PID control and PSMC designed in consideration of resonance frequency, to the meal-assist robot. In addition, to avoid having tremor frequency in the target trajectory, we used a notch filter in each experiment, with the tremor frequency set to 3.0 [Hz], and the input tremor was also set to about 3.0 [Hz]. The experimental result by a PID controller is shown in Fig. 4.

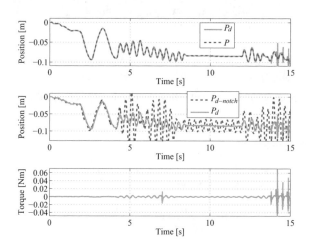

Fig. 4. Experimental result of PID control

In the figures, P_d is the target trajectory of PSMC, P is the end-effector position of *MARo* and $P_{d-notch}$ is the trajectory before passing the notch filter in the trajectory generated from sensorless admittance. The bottom graph in the figure shows the necessary torque to the end-effector. As shown in the middle graph, in the experiment with the PID control using a notch filter, $P_{d-notch}$ continued vibrating in the part where P_d was not vibrating.

Finally, the experimental result of PSMC that resonated a virtual coupling to a given tremor frequency is shown in Fig. 5, where the rate of transmissibility, T_A, was set to $\xi = 0.4$ in consideration of the emanation of the proxy. The resonance frequency was 3.0[Hz] as was the tremor frequency in the notch filter. The PSMC was set in all 3-direction.

In the case of tremor suppression using resonance, the proxy resonates and the end-effector torque is output with the antiphase of tremor frequency by the resonance. We found that tremor suppression was clearly realized. In addition, we found that the end-effector position did not emanate to the input of another frequency.

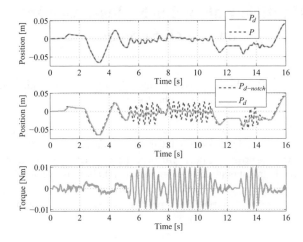

Fig. 5. Experimental result of resonance PSMC

5   Conclusions

In this study, we applied PSMC using resonance to the self-supportive meal-assist robot *MARo*. We were able to construct a system that allowed the robot to assist a user to eat without spilling food even if the user suffered from tremor. If this meal-assist robot can be put to practical use, the caregivers' load could be reduced and one cause of daily stress for disabled persons could be eliminated, heightening quality of life for this population.

References

1. Whittaker, M.: Handy-1 Robotic Aid to Eating:A Study in Social Impact. In: Proc. of RESNA Int., vol. 92, pp. 589–594 (1992)
2. Soyama, R., Ishii, S., Fukase, A.: 8 Selectable Operating Interfaces of the Meal-Assistance Device "My Spoon". In: Advances in Rehabilitation Robotics, pp. 155–163 (2004)
3. Gonzalez, J., Heredia, E., Rahman, T., Barner, K., Arce, G.: Filtering involuntary motion of people with tremor disability using optimal equalization. In: Proc. IEEE Int. Conf. on Systems, Man and Cybernetics, vol. 3, pp. 2402–2407 (1995)
4. Riviere, C.N., Ang, W., Khosla, P.: Toward Active Tremor Canceling in Handheld Microsurgical Instruments. IEEE Trans. on Robotics and Automation 15, 793–800 (2003)
5. Pledgie, S., Barner, K., Agrawal, S., Rahman, T.: Tremor suppression through impedance control. IEEE. Trans. on Rehabilitation and Engineering 121(11), 2127–2134 (1998)
6. Nishiwaki, K., Yano, K.: Variable Impedance Control of Meal Assistance Robot Using Potential Method. In: Proc. of IEEE IROS, pp. 3242–3247 (2008)
7. kikuue, R., Fujimoto, H.: Proxy-Based Sliding Mode Control For Accurate and Safe Position Control. In: Proc. of IEEE ICRA, pp. 25–30 (2006)

Reflective Haptics: Enhancing Stylus-Based Interactions on Touch Screens

Götz Wintergerst[1], Ron Jagodzinski[1], Fabian Hemmert[2], Alexander Müller[2], and Gesche Joost[2]

[1] HfG Schwäbisch Gmünd, Hochschule für Gestaltung, Rektor-Klaus-Straße 100, 73525 Schwäbisch Gmünd, Germany
{goetz.wintergerst,ron.jagodzinski}@hfg-gmuend.de
[2] Deutsche Telekom Laboratories, Design Research Lab, Ernst-Reuter-Platz 7, 10587 Berlin, Germany
{fabian.hemmert,a.mueller,gesche.joost}@telekom.de

Abstract. In this paper, we introduce the prototype of a low cost haptically augmented stylus for pen computing on touch screens. The stylus supports human-computer interaction through a dynamic haptic feedback. This reflective feedback is generated by a magnetically operated brake system. The feedback actuator is integrated in the stylus. Therefore, the pen supports the use of multiple styli on a single touch screen. The pen provides a broad scale of feedback – especially for the display of haptic surface cues. Hence, it is predestined for stroke gestures, as they are commonly used in crossing-based pen interfaces.

Keywords: stylus, pen computing, haptics, interface, HCI, haptic feedback, magnetic, brake, crossing-based interface.

1 Introduction

Touch screens are increasingly important for human-computer interaction systems. They can be found in various electronic devices, ranging from large tabletop interfaces to small mobile phones. One reason for this importance is the intuitive access to digital content that they provide. By joining the locations of input and output, they enable the user to manipulate digital content at the same spot where it is displayed. This joint location can strengthen the connection between action and reaction. Yet, there are still some limitations to these technologies: for example, the occlusion of content by the finger, called the "fat finger problem". Especially on small screens, as they are used in PDAs or mobile phones, this is a emergent issue. There are several software-based solutions for this problem, such as the "Shift" system [1]. By shifting the covered interaction area besides or above the users fingertip, the occlued information is moved into a visible area. However, this shift is occluding other parts of the interface, and is thus separating the position of input and output. Another solution is the use of a stylus to minimize the contact area and therefore the occlusion of content. Generally, by touching objects – for example, the key of a keyboard – the user has to cover the contact area, but still receives haptic information about their action. Since the perceived haptic feedback of a touch screen is limited to the properties of the

A.M.L. Kappers et al. (Eds.): EuroHaptics 2010, Part I, LNCS 6191, pp. 360–366, 2010.

screen itself and does not correspond to the properties of the virtual content, the user receives no distinct information about their actions.

According to Wigdor et al., [2], this feedback ambiguity can reduce a user's confidence in a device. Therefore, a context-corresponding haptic feedback can improve the touch screen interaction with respect to speed and accuracy. Brewster et al. [3] confirm that haptic feedback can significantly improve the performance of text entry tasks on a touch screen. In order to solve these inherent problems, we developed a simple and low cost stylus-based interface that provides a wide range of haptic feedback. We integrated a feedback-actuator into this pen which cannot only be applied to any kind of touch screen, but that also supports multi-user situations. This setup enables the use of multiple pens on one screen, which is important for multi-user applications.

2 Related Work

In recent developments, haptically enhanced pen interfaces have become an active field of research. The "Haptic Pen" by Lee et al. [4] is a low-cost device that generates a haptic feedback through solenoid-based actuation. In combination with a pressure-sensitive tip, it allows a variety of haptic click feedback, for the interaction with point and click GUIs. Another approach is the "Ubi-Pen" by Kyung and Lee [5]. It combines a compact tactile display for texture simulation and a pancake motor that provides vibration and texture stimuli.

Both prototypes – as well as the system presented in this paper – are designed for being used on touch screens. In contrast to these two systems, we focus on the display of lateral forces, as they appear in stroke gestures. In 2004, Poupyrev et al. [6] conducted a study about haptic feedback for pen computing in which they argued that most users prefer haptic feedback in combination with an active input gesture. They presume that this fact refers to Gibson's active touch paradigm [7]. Forlines et al. [8] confirm that tactile feedback improves selection times, especially for gesture-based crossing tasks.

3 Pen Prototype Using Reflective Haptics

One possibility to provide a realistic feedback in two dimensional stroking gestures is increasing the force that a user has to apply, dragging a stylus across a surface and therefore simulating a higher friction of the virtual content. In order to display such a force, we developed a pen setup that is similar to a conventional ball pen. It consists of three functional components: A high-precision steel ball, an electromagnetic coil and a pen housing (Fig. 1).

When the pen is moved over the touch screen surface the steel ball is rolled in consequence. The steel ball is partly guided by the electromagnetic coil. When voltage is applied to the coil, it magnetically attracts the steel ball and the dynamic friction between these two parts increases. As a result of a higher friction between these two parts, it is more difficult to spin the steel ball. Thus, the user has to apply a greater force in order to move the stylus. To ensure that the friction between the steel ball and the touch screen surface is high enough, we applied a soft PVC film to the touch screen (Fig. 2).

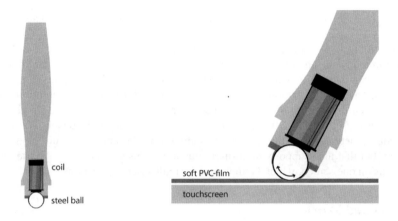

Fig. 1. Pen setup   Fig. 2. Setup of screen, PVC film and pen

We developed a series of different prototypes (Fig. 3), in which we tested different steel ball diameters and electromagnets of different strengths and sizes (Fig. 4 and Table 1). First informal evaluations showed that the usability of the stylus is depending on its size and weight. The final version displayed a suitable relation between friction actuation and stylus size and weight.

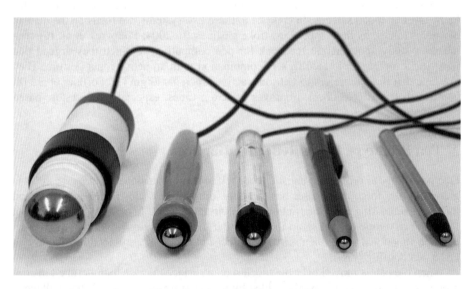

Fig. 3. Series of different prototypes

The operating strength of the electromagnetic coil is controlled by an ATMel AT-Mega328 attached to an Arduino development board. The generation of haptic effects is based on the tracking position of a 3M resistive touch sensor. These positions are relayed via USB to the Personal Computer for further processing. After calculating

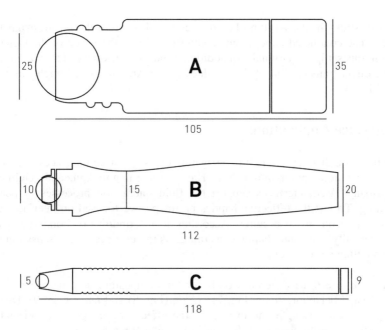

Fig. 4. Technical drawing of the tested prototypes

Table 1. Measurements of the different prototypes

	Prototype A	Prototype B	Prototype C
Body length	105 mm	112 mm	118 mm
Body diameter	35 mm	15 mm	9 mm
Pen weight	265 g	20 g	10 g
Steel ball diameter	25 mm	10 mm	5 mm

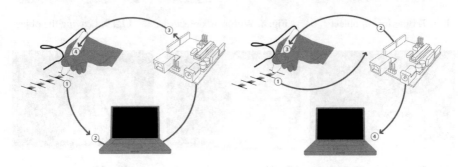

Fig. 5. Current signal processing   **Fig. 6.** Enhanced signal processing

the effect strength, the Arduino board is assigned to drive the electromagnetic coil (Fig. 5). The conducted experiments demonstrated that the speed of the signal processing in this setup is marginal. An additional motion tracking system within the pen, and the direct transmission of these values to the Arduino board might improve the setup (Fig. 6).

4 Interface Applications

There has been distinct research investigating crossing-based interfaces as an alternative to conventional point-and-click interfaces. According to Apitz and Guimbretière [9], crossing-based interfaces support the fluid interaction processes of pen-based computing. To test the reflective haptics prototype, we focused on interface samples that are based on stroke gestures. According to the findings of Poupyrev et al. [6], users especially appreciate haptic constraints, as the user receives a sensation similar to a pen hitting a groove or guide.

Snap: There are three different events for the composition and representation of a virtual "snap" behavior: *enter* (Fig. 7), *within* (Fig. 8) and *leave* (Fig. 9). Due to the varying magnetic strength and durability, the effect can be specified. Virtual edges can therefore be differentiated as well as virtual object mass.

Guide: The perception of guidelines – as they are used in common drawing programs – can be assisted, through the raise of resistance for a short period or time (Fig. 10).

Drag: The mass of a virtual object can be simulated via constant friction, which is a distinctive criterion of their individual characteristic (Fig. 11).

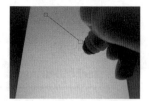

Fig. 7. Entering an object   **Fig. 8.** Within an object   **Fig. 9.** Leaving the object

Fig. 10. Display of guidelines   **Fig. 11.** Variable object mass   **Fig. 12.** Drawing task

Draw: The process of free drawing can be enhanced by adding haptic information. Constant friction increases not only the accuracy of the gestures, but also provides some information about the simulated paint brush (Fig. 12).

5 Conclusion and Future Work

First evaluations of the different reflective haptic pen prototypes showed promising results concerning the haptic support of stroke gestures. Most participants were convinced by the overall performance of the pen and its implementation with crossing-based interfaces. Prototype A received the best results regarding the effect strength but was perceived as beeing too big and too heavy. Prototype B showed a suitable relation between size and effect-strength. Prototype C received the best ratings concerning its size and weight, but the haptic effect was too weak to be differentiated from the basic friction of the steel ball. In most cases, the participants assigned the haptic sensation to the visually displayed surface and *not* to the stylus. An exception was the guideline interface sample (Fig. 10) where the effect of rendering delay became obvious. Therefore, the improvement of the signal rendering seems to be a goal worthwhile to follow-up on in the near future. By integrating motion tracking into the stylus – in combination with the location tracking of the touch screen – a faster signal processing could be achieved. In order to explore how reflective haptic feedback can improve the interaction process for different applications, further studies need to be conducted. For the generation of a pressure-dependent feedback, we also plan to integrate a pressure sensor in the setup. To meet the demands of mobile applications, we intent to minimize the existing setup and work towards a wireless version of the pen.

Acknowledgments. This work has been supported by Deutsche Telekom Laboratories, Ernst Reuter Platz 7, 10587 Berlin, Germany.

References

1. Vogel, D., Baudisch, P.: Shift: A Technique for Operating Pen-Based Interfaces Using Touch. In: Proceedings of the CHI 2007 conference, pp. 657–666 (2007)
2. Widgor, D., Williams, S., Cronin, M., Levyl, R., White, K., Mazeevl, M., Benko, H.: Ripples: Utilizing Per-Contact Visualizations to Improve User Interaction with Touch Display. In: Proceedings of the 22nd Annual ACM Symposium on User Interface Software and Technology (2009)
3. Brewster, S., Chohan, F., Brown, L.: Tactile Feedback for Mobile Interactions. In: Proceedings of the SIGCHI conference on Human factors in computing systems, pp. 159–162 (2007)
4. Lee, J.C., Dietz, P.H., Leigh, D., Yerazunis, W.S., Hudson, S.E.: Haptic Pen: A Tactile Feedback Stylus for Touch Screens. In: Proceedings of the SIGCHI conference on Human Factors in computing systems (CHI 2004), pp. 291–294. ACM Press, New York (2004)
5. Kyung, K.U., Lee, J.Y.: Design and Applications of a Pen-Like Haptic Interface with Texture and Vibrotactile Display. IEEE Computer Graphics and Applications (2008)

6. Poupyrev, I., Okabe, M., Maruyama, S.: Haptic feedback for pen computing: directions and strategies. In: Proceedings of the CHI 2004 conference, Extendet Abstracts. ACM Press, New York (2004)
7. Gibson, J.J.: Observations on active touch. Psychological Review 69(6), 477–491 (1962)
8. Forelines, C., Balakrishnan, R.: Evaluating tactile feedback and direct vs. indirect stylus input in pointing and crossing selection tasks. In: Proceedings of SIGCHI, pp. 1563–1572. ACM Press, New York (2008)
9. Apitz, G., Guimbretière, F.: CrossY: a crossing-based drawing application. In: ACM UIST Symposium on User Interface Software and Technology, pp. 3–12 (2004)

A Novel Tactile Sensor for Detecting Lumps in Breast Tissue

Mehmet Ayyildiz [1], Burak Guclu [2], Mustafa Z. Yildiz [2], and Cagatay Basdogan [1]

[1] College of Engineering, Koc University, Istanbul, 34450 Turkey
[2] Biomedical Engineering Institute, Boğaziçi University, Istanbul, 34684 Turkey
mayyildiz@ku.edu.tr, burak.guclu@boun.edu.tr,
mustafa.yildiz@boun.edu.tr, cbasdogan@ku.edu.tr

Abstract. We developed a compact tactile sensor in order to guide the clinician or the self-user for non-invasive detection of lumps. The new design has an advantage over the existing discrete tactile sensors and detection methods by efficiently sensing force distribution over an area without any side effects. The sensor consists of 10×10 infrared emitter-detector pairs, a silicon-rubber elastic pad, and a contoured tactile interface (25x21 moving pins) for palpating three-dimensional objects. To demonstrate the practical use of the sensor, first a cylindrical tissue-like silicon phantom was prepared, then a 13 mm diameter rigid spherical object was placed at varying depths of 0-20 mm to simulate cancerous lumps in breast tissue, and finally the tactile sensor was systematically pressed on the phantom to successfully detect the lumps for compression depths of 10-24 mm. The location and the estimated radius of each lump were calculated from the recorded tactile images.

Keywords: Optical array sensor, lump detection, breast cancer, tactile mapping, artificial palpation, haptics.

1   Introduction

Cancer, a foremost cause of death worldwide, is accounted for 7.4 million deaths (around 13% of all deaths) in 2004. [1] In Europe, 3,191,600 cancer diagnoses (excluding nonmelanoma skin cancers) and 1,703,000 deaths in consequence of cancer were recorded in 2006. Breast cancer was the most widespread type of all the cancer cases (a total of 429,900 cases account for 13.5%). [2] Since the incidence rate of breast cancer is significantly high, early detection becomes a vital issue. However, the majority of the people in developing countries have insufficient access to screening and diagnostic medical equipment for the detection. [3] Although various sensing methods and devices have been developed, only a few has been accepted for standard clinical use. Tactile imaging is one of the potential methods to address the needs in breast cancer screening and diagnostics cost-effectively. [4] Mammography, one of the most popular diagnostic techniques in breast examination is unable to examine breast tissue near the chest wall and axilla. Palpation complements mammography by finding lumps which are the most common symptoms of breast cancer [5]. It was also found that as many as 12-15 % of breast cancers that were detected by physical

A.M.L. Kappers et al. (Eds.): EuroHaptics 2010, Part I, LNCS 6191, pp. 367–372, 2010.
© Springer-Verlag Berlin Heidelberg 2010

examination were not apparent on mammograms. [5-7] In conventional palpation, hands are used to evaluate the location, size, shape, and stiffness of breast tissue. However, it is not possible to obtain quantitative, objective and firm information in traditional hand palpation. [8-10] There are more quantitative methods, but they have some disadvantages. In X-ray computed tomography, excessive exposure to radiation creates an additional risk of cancer. [11] Likewise, magnetic resonance imaging (MRI) generates a powerful magnetic field and hence orthopedic implants, materials or devices in the body of patient or in the environment may cause hazardous situations. [12] In this study, a tactile sensor was developed for the quantitative assessment of lumps in soft tissue noninvasively. The proposed approach has no side effects and unlike in other diagnostic techniques mentioned above, the tactile sensor can be used at home for self-examination. Additionally, during the neoadjuvant chemotheraphy, the current design can provide regular information about the response of the patient to the treatment. Here, we present the design details of our system and the initial results of the lump detection experiments performed with a tissue-like silicon phantom.

2   Materials and Methods

2.1   Tactile Sensor and Processor Module

The tactile sensor consisted of infrared emitter-detector pairs (QRD1313, Reflective Object Sensor; Fairchild Semiconductor) arranged in a 10×10 array. The entire sensor was housed in an aluminum casing with a square base (Fig. 1). The side length of the square base is 9.2 cm, and the height of sensor is 3.0 cm. The sensor elements were covered by silicon-rubber tactile pad with outer surface dyed in black to block ambient light. The IR light rays emitted from the LEDs reflect off from the white inner surface of the rubber pad and their intensity is measured by the detectors. This reflection is modulated by force applied to the pad's outer surface, which is deflected towards the sensor element with the mechanical effect of the force. The force was transmitted from the palpation object to the pad via rigid pins which conformed to the contour of the object. The processing module received light-intensity data from each sensor element and transmitted this data array via a single analog channel by using

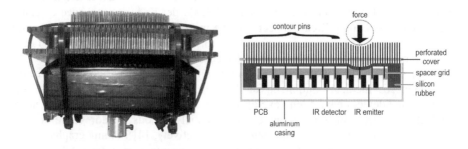

Fig. 1. a. Our tactile sensor. **b.** Cross section of the tactile sensor.

time-division multiplexing (TDM). The output from the entire array took approximately 10.9 ms; and therefore, the theoretical limit for the scan rate is 91.7 Hz in the presented design. The beginning of each packet cycle was signaled by a synchronization pulse. The processing module also amplified the multiplexed data and applied offset shifting to match the input range of the data-acquisition system.

2.2 Data Acquisition and Calibration

The sensor data was acquired by a 16-bit ADC card (NI6034; National Instruments) connected to a PC. The sampling rate was 100 kHz. This yielded 10-11 data points for each sensor element in every multiplexing cycle. Each sensor element was calibrated in the range of 0-5 N forces. The calibration was performed by a micromanipulator (WPI) and a digital balance (Kern). A software code in C language was developed in Visual C++ 6.0, (Microsoft) for sensor calibration, offset nulling, reading sensor array data, spatial interpolation, and outputting interpolated data. The sensor data was spatially interpolated to give an output array of 100 by 100 elements. The spatial interpolation was performed successively along the x- and y-dimensions by up-sampling and then low-pass filtering to remove undesired spectral images. The low-pass filter was a 29th-order digital FIR filter designed with Kaiser Window (beta: 5), and it could achieve 65-dB attenuation in the stop band. The spatial cutoff frequency was 5 cycles per linear length of the tactile membrane (i.e. 0.82 cycles/cm). The scan rate achieved by the compiled program was 33 Hz.

2.3 Phantom Experiments and Analyses

Lump detection experiments were conducted by a compression device consists of a moving shuttle on a power screw driven by a step motor (Fig. 2). Tactile array sensor was attached to the moving shuttle, which compressed a tissue-like cylindrical silicone phantom to varying depths of 10, 15, 20, and 24 mm. The Young's modulus of the silicon sample was measured as 44 kPa by compressing the sample slowly (rate: 0.5 mm/s) up to 20% strain. A rigid marble sphere having a radius of 6.5 mm was embedded into the silicon phantom (Fig. 3) at varying depths of 0, 4, 8, 12, 16, 20 mm to simulate a cancerous lump in a soft tissue. For each depth, the compression experiment was repeated 10 times. Additionally, 10 control measurements were performed at each compression depth without the simulated lump. The statistical differences between the interpolated sensor data and the control data were tested by Bonferroni-corrected two-sample t-test. To plot the sensor images, only the force values at pixels which were significantly different than that of the control experiments were selected and used in color coding (Fig. 4). Lump parameters were calculated based on the image data. Specifically, the peak force, and its pixel coordinates, the coordinates of the force centroid of the lump, and the estimated lump radius were all determined with respect to the control data. The lump radius was defined as the average distance between the pixel coordinates of the force centroid and the pixel coordinates which had force values greater than one tenth of the peak force.

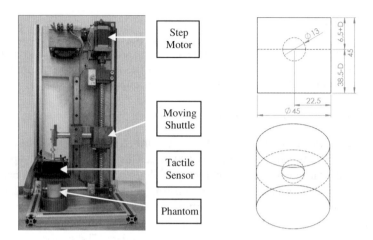

Fig. 2. The experimental set-up

Fig. 3. The silicon phantom and definition of depth (D) in our experiments

3 Results

Fig. 5 shows the peak force read by the tactile array versus the depth of the lump with the compression depth of the tactile sensor used as an additional control parameter. As the depth of the simulated lump increases, the peak force decreases. However, peak forces at 20 mm lump depth are greater than those at 16 mm, because the lumps at 20 mm are closer to the bottom surface, which acts as a boundary and increases the magnitude of the peak forces. The same figure also suggests that better detection of the lump is achieved at higher compression depths. The x and the y coordinates of the peak force detected by the tactile sensor with respect to the control data and the force centroid estimated from the distributed differential force response are plotted for the

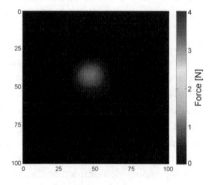

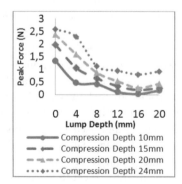

Fig. 4. An image of interpolated sensor data. The simulated lump was at 4 mm depth and the compression depth was 15 mm.

Fig. 5. The peak force detected by the tactile sensor versus the lump depth for the different compression depths of the silicon phantom

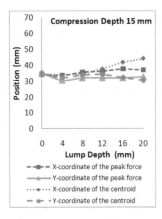

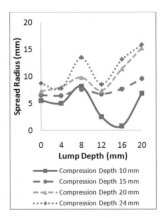

Fig. 6. The position of the peak force and the force centroid for the different lump depths

Fig. 7. The spread radius of the simulated lump versus the lump depth

different lump depths in Fig. 6. As shown in the figure, the results are highly consistent. Furthermore, Fig. 7 shows that the spread radius of the simulated lump increases as the silicon phantom is compressed more, exciding the ideal value of 6.5 mm (radius of the spherical marble placed into the silicon) for the lump depths greater than 12 mm. This is again due to the influence of the ground reaction forces caused by the lower boundary (bottom surface) of the silicon phantom.

4 Conclusion and Future Work

The aim of this study was to develop a prototype tactile array sensor which can be used by clinicians and home user to detect lumps in soft breast tissue. To evaluate the hardware, software and computational performance of the sensor, some preliminary compression experiments were performed with a tissue-like silicon phantom and a small spherical rigid object, imitating a cancerous lump, placed inside the phantom at various depths. The tactile sensor successfully detected all the lumps placed at the different depths, but for deeper lumps, more compression of the silicon phantom was required. However, as the compression depth was increased, the boundary conditions affected the force response of the tactile sensor. Based on the experimental results, we determined the optimum compression depth as 15 mm for the accurate detection of the lumps placed at varying depths (0 to 20 mm) in this study. In the future, we plan to perform more experiments to characterize the static and dynamic performance of the tactile array and test the device on patients with breast cancer and compare the results with those acquired by conventional methods.

References

1. Organization, W. H. World Health Statistics 2009. World Health Organization, Geneva (2009)
2. Ferlay, J., Autier, P., Boniol, M., Heanue, M., Colombet, M., Boyle, P.: Estimates of the cancer incidence and mortality in Europe in 2006. Ann Oncol. 18(3), 581–592 (2007)

3. Sarvazyan, A., Egorov, V.: Cost-Effective Screening for Breast Cancer Worldwide: Current State and Future Directions. Breast Cancer: Basic and Clinical Research, 91–99 (2008)

4. Lang, P.: Optical Tactile Sensor for Medical Palpation. In: The Thirty-Fourth London District Science and Technology Conference, pp. 1–5 (March 2004)

5. Wang, Y., Nguyen, C., Srikanchana, R., Geng, Z., Freedman, M.T.: Tactile Mapping of Palpable Abnormalities for Breast Cancer Diagnosis. In: Proc. of the Int. Conf. on Robotics and Automation, pp. 1305–1309 (May 1999)

6. Zeng, J., Wang, Y., Freedman, M.T., Mun, S.K.: Finger Tracking for Breast Palpation Quantification using Color Image Features. SPIE J. of Opt. Eng. 36(12), 3455–3461 (1997)

7. Haagensen, C.D.: Diseases of the Breast, 3rd edn. Saunders, Philadelphia (1986)

8. Kitagawa, M., Okamura, A.M., Bertha, B.T., Gott, V.L., Baumgartner, W.A.: Analysis of Suture Manipulation Forces for Teleoperation with Force Feedback. In: Dohi, T., Kikinis, R. (eds.) MICCAI 2002. LNCS, vol. 2488, pp. 155–162. Springer, Heidelberg (2002)

9. Ohtsuka, T., Furuse, A., Kohno, T., Nakajima, J., Yagyu, K., Omata, S.: New Tactile Sensor Techniques for Localization of Pulmonary Nodules. International Surgery 82, 12–14 (1997)

10. Wellman, P.S., Dalton, E.P., Krag, D., Kern, K.A., Howe, R.D.: Tactile Imaging of Breast Masses: First Clinical Report. Archives of Surgery 136, 204–208 (2001)

11. Carmichael, A., Sami, A., Dixon, J.: Breast cancer risk among the survivors of atomic bomb and patients exposed to therapeutic ionising radiation. European Journal of Surgical Oncology 29(5), 475–479

12. Shellock, F.G.: Biomedical Implants and Devices: Assessment of Magnetic Field Interactions with a 3.0-Tesla MR System. Journal Of Magnetic Resonance Imaging (2002)

Tactile Sensation Imaging for Artificial Palpation

Jong-Ha Lee[1], Chang-Hee Won[1], Kaiguo Yan[2], Yan Yu[2], and Lydia Liao[3]

[1] Control, Sensor, Network, and Perception (CSNAP) Laboratory, Temple University,
Philadelphia, PA 19040, USA
{jong,cwon}@temple.edu
[2] Department of Radiation Oncology, Thomas Jefferson University Hospital,
Philadelphia, PA 19107, USA
{kaiguo.yan,yan.yu}@jeffersonhospital.org
[3] Department of Radiology, Cooper University Hospital,
Voorhees, NJ 08043, USA
{liao-lydia}@cooperhealth.edu

Abstract. In this paper we investigated a novel tactile sensation imaging method using a flexible, transparent waveguide and the total internal reflection principle. The developed sensor is used to detect and identify inclusions within tissues. To test the performance of the proposed sensor, a realistic tissue phantom with hard inclusions (tumor models) is developed. The proposed tactile imaging sensor estimated the inclusion diameter within 4.09% and the inclusion depth within 7.55%.

Keywords: Tactile Sensation, Tactile Display, Haptic, Inclusion Detection.

1 Introduction

Diagnosing early formation of tumors or lumps, particularly those caused by cancer, has been a challenging problem. To help physicians detect tumor more efficiently, various imaging techniques with different imaging modalities such as computer tomography, ultrasonic imaging, nuclear magnetic resonance imaging, and x-rays have been developed [1], [2]. However, each of these techniques has limitations, including the exposure to radiation, excessive costs, and complexity of machinery. Artificial tactile sensors are a valuable non-invasive tool for the medical society, where physicians use tactile sensation to identify malignant tissue [3], [4]. Traditionally physicians have used palpation to detect breast or prostate tumors, which is based on the observation that the tissue abnormalities are usually associated with localized changes in mechanical properties such as stiffness [5]. An artificial tactile sensor can accurately quantify and record the tactile sensation of benign and malignant regions.

In this paper, we present a newly designed tactile imaging sensor to detect or locate sub-surface inclusions such as tumors or lumps. Polydimethylsiloxane (PDMS) is used to make a multi-layer optical waveguide as a sensing probe. The mechanical properties of each layer have emulated the human finger layers to maximize the touch sensitivity. In our sensor, total internal reflection principle is utilized to obtain the high resolution of the tactile image. A force applied to an elastic waveguide, while light passes through

A.M.L. Kappers et al. (Eds.): EuroHaptics 2010, Part I, LNCS 6191, pp. 373–378, 2010.

it, causes change in the critical angle of internally reflected light. This results in dif-
fused light outside the waveguide that is captured by a camera. The sensitivity and the
resolution of the proposed sensor are controlled by the size of the waveguide and the
light source intensity.

This paper is organized as follows: Section 2 discusses the proposed sensor design
and sensing principle. Section 3 presents the experimental results for inclusion detection
in a phantom. Finally, Section 4 presents the conclusions and discusses the future work.

2   Tactile Imaging Sensor Design and Sensing Principle

In this section, we present the design concept and sensing principle of the proposed
sensor in detail.

2.1   Tactile Imaging Sensor Design

Fig. 1(a) shows the schematic of the tactile imaging sensor. The sensor comprises of an
optical waveguide unit, a light source unit, a light coupling unit, a camera unit, and a
computer unit.

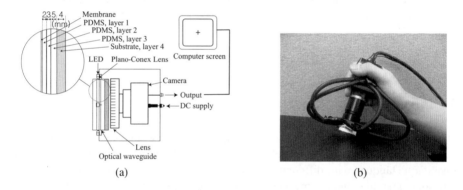

(a)   (b)

Fig. 1. (a) The schematic of the tactile imaging sensor. (b) The tactile imaging sensor.

The optical waveguide is the main sensing probe. It is composed of three polydimethylsiloxane (PDMS, $Si(CH_3)_2$) layers, which is a high performance silicone elas-
tomer [6]. The elastic modulus of each PDMS layer is matched as the modulus values
of epidermis (1.4×10^5 Pa), dermis (8.0×10^4 Pa) and subcutanea (3.4×10^4 Pa) of a human fingertip to realize the sensitivity to the level of the human touch sensation [7].
The digital imager is a mono-cooled complementary camera with 4.65 μm $\times$ 4.65 μm
individual pixel size. The maximum lens resolution is 1392 μm (H) $\times$ 1042 μm (V)
with 60° view angle. The camera is placed below an optical waveguide. A borosilicate
glass plate is placed as a substrate between camera and optical waveguide to sustain the
waveguide without losing camera resolution. The glass plate emulates the bone in the
human fingertip. The internal light source is a micro-LED with a diameter of 1.8 mm.

There are four LEDs used on four sides of the waveguide to provide enough illumination. The direction and incident angle of the LED light have been calibrated with the acceptance angle and it is discussed in the next section. Fig. 1(b) shows the integrated tactile imaging sensor.

2.2 Sensing Principle

The tactile imaging sensor is developed based on the optical phenomenon known as the total internal reflection (TIR) principle of light in a multi-layer optical waveguide. To maintain the light in a waveguide, the critical angle and the acceptance angle of light are analyzed using the geometric optics approximation. This allows determining the direction of the light source illumination.

Consider light trapped inside the multi-layer waveguide in the geometry as shown in Fig. 2. As a result of Snell's Law, the light propagation angle γ_i, $i = 0,1,2,3,4$ are bound by the following relations:

$$n_{i+1}\sin\gamma_{i+1} = n_i\sin\gamma_i, \tag{1}$$

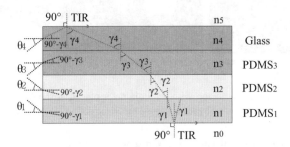

Fig. 2. Graphic representation of light propagation as a ray, propagating in the waveguide

Here n_0 and n_5 are the refractive indices of air $n_0 = n_5 = 1$. The critical TIR angles γ_1 and γ_4 are achieved when $\gamma_0 = \gamma_5 = 90^o$ at the boundaries with air. Light propagating in the waveguide with angles γ_1, γ_2, γ_3, γ_4 or higher in their respective layers will remain trapped inside the waveguide. The critical angle indicates the minimum propagation angle. To make the propagation angle above the critical angle, the acceptance angle of light source has been calculated.

The acceptance angle θ_i is the maximum angle, under which the light directed into the waveguide remains trapped inside it. The propagation angle γ_i are related to the acceptance angle θ_i by the same Snell's law:

$$\sin\theta_i = n_i\sin(90^o - \gamma_i) = n_i\cos\gamma_i. \tag{2}$$

Further, transforming Eq. (2), we obtain

$$\sin\theta_i = n_i\cos\gamma_i = n_i(1 - \sin^2\gamma_i)^{1/2} = (n_i^2 - n_i^2\sin^2\gamma_i)^{1/2}. \tag{3}$$

But as follows from Eq. (1), all $n_i\sin\gamma_i$ are equal to n_0, which is equal to 1 for air. Therefore, we finally have

$$\theta_i = \text{asin}[(n_i^2 - 1)^{1/2}]. \tag{4}$$

Light, incident on layer i under the acceptance angle θ_i, will be trapped inside the waveguide.

In the current design, the refractive index of each PDMS layer and glass plate are measured approximately as 1.41, 1.40, 1.39, 1.38 and the acceptance angles θ_i are calculated as $\theta_1 = 83.73^o$, $\theta_2 = 78.46^o$, $\theta_3 = 74.89^o$, and $\theta_4 = 71.98^o$. Thus for the TIR in the waveguide, the spatial radiation pattern of LED light with the angle less than $71.98^o \times 2 = 143.96^o$ has been chosen and placed to inject the light.

3   Inclusion Detection Experiments

In this section, we performed the inclusion detection experiments using the tactile imaging sensor.

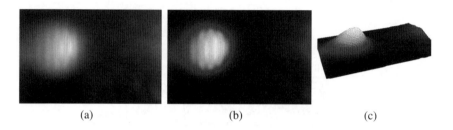

(a)   (b)   (c)

Fig. 3. The tactile image of inclusion with 3.29 diameter placed at the 4.2 mm depth. (a) Grey scale tactile image, (b) Color visualization, (c) 3-D reconstruction.

3.1   Empirical Equation of Inclusion Characterization

For the experiments, a tissue phantom with embedded hard inclusions (simulated tumor) has been developed. The phantom was made of a silicone composite having Young's modulus of approximately 5 $\sim$ 10kPa. To find the relation between tactile image and inclusion size, total of nine inclusions with different diameters were placed below the surface of the phantom. The inclusion was made using another silicone composite, the stiffness of which was much higher (300 $\sim$ 500kPa) than the surrounding tissue phantom. The depth of each inclusion was 4.2 mm. To find the relation between tactile image and inclusion depth, eight inclusions were placed in the tissue phantom with varying depth. The diameter of each inclusion was 5.15 mm. The tactile images of each inclusion were obtained under the normal force of between 10 mN and 20 mN.

Fig. 3 shows a sample tactile image of inclusion with 3.29 mm diameter placed at the 4.2 mm depth. Figs. 4(a) and 4(b) represent the integrated pixel value of tactile images along the diameter and depth of the inclusions. The curve fitting method was used with these empirical measurements.

$$P_1 = (1.0 \times 10^7)[1.0 \times 10^{-3}D + 1.21], \tag{5}$$

$$P_2 = (-1.0 \times 10^7)[4.1 \times 10^{-2}H - 2.06]. \tag{6}$$

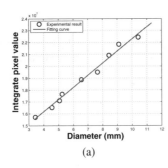 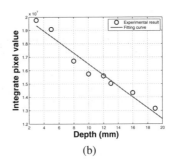

(a)   (b)

Fig. 4. (a) Diameter versus integrated pixel value of tactile image. (b) Depth versus integrated pixel value of tactile image.

where D is the inclusion diameter and H is the inclusion depth. P_1 and P_2 are the integrated pixel value for different inclusion diameter D and depth H. Eqs. (5) and (6) will vary with the thickness and the modulus of the surrounding tissue sample.

3.2 Inclusion Diameter and Depth Estimation

The inclusion parameter estimations (i.e. diameter and depth) based on the obtained tactile image can be formulated as an inversion problem. In our case, the integrated pixel value of tactile image is taken as input for the problem. For the inclusion diameter estimation experiments, two new inclusions were embedded into the tissue with the same depths of 4.2 mm. After obtaining the tactile images, the diameters have been estimated using Eq. (5). Similarly, for the depth estimation experiments, another two inclusions with the same diameters of 5.15 mm have been embedded and the depths have been estimated using Eq. (6). The results are shown in Table 1 and 2. The tactile imaging sensor estimated the inclusion diameter within 4.09% and the inclusion depth within 7.55%. So far we have determined either the diameter or the depth of the inclusions. The next step is to determine both diameter and depth based on one tactile image.

Table 1. Inclusion Diameter Estimation

	Truth	**Estimate**	**Error**
Inclusion 1	4.91 mm	4.76 mm	3.05 %
Inclusion 2	6.35 mm	6.61 mm	4.09 %

Table 2. Inclusion Depth Estimation

	Truth	**Estimate**	**Error**
Inclusion 3	9.01 mm	9.59 mm	7.55 %
Inclusion 4	15.11 mm	14.71 mm	2.65 %

4   Conclusions

In this paper, a new tactile sensation imaging method for artificial palpation is proposed and experimentally evaluated. To increase the sensitivity of touch, an optical waveguide consisting of three different elastic moduli of PDMS is fabricated as the sensing probe. The experimental results show that the proposed sensor successfully identifies inclusion diameter and depth from the tactile images.

References

1. Sojaku, H., Seto, H., Iwai, H., Kitazawa, S., Fukushima, W., Saito, K.: Detection of Incidental Breast Tumors by Noncontrast Spiral Computed Tomography of the Chest. Radiat. Med. 3, 780–782 (2008)
2. Gentle, C.R.: Mammobarography: A Possible Method of Mass Breast Screening. J. Biomech. Eng. 10, 124–126 (1998)
3. Wellman, P.S., Dalton, E.P., Krag, D., Kern, K.A., Howe, R.D.: Tactile Imaging of Breast Masses. Arch. Sur. 136, 204–208 (2001)
4. Howe, R.D., Matsuoka, Y.: Robotics for Surgery. Annual Review of Biomedical Engineering 1, 211–240 (1999)
5. Krouskop, T.A., Wheeler, T.B., Kallel, F., Garra, B.S., Hall, T.: Elastic Moduli of Breast and Prostate Tissues under Compression. Ultrason. Imaging 20, 260–274 (1998)
6. Chang-Yen, D.A., Eich, R.K., Gale, B.K.: A Monolithic PDMS Waveguide System Fabricated using Soft-lithography Techniques. J. Light. Tech. 23, 2088–2093 (2005)
7. Kandel, E., Schwartz, J., Jessell, T.: Principles of Neural Science. McGraw-Hill Medical, New York (2000)

Improving Vehicular Window Control with Haptic and Visual Feedback

David Racine, John Holmen, Mehrdad Hosseini Zadeh, and Mark Thompson

The Electrical and Computer Engineering Department, Kettering University
{raci8908,holm5073,mzadeh,mthompso}@kettering.edu

Abstract. When paired with a user-friendly GUI, a haptic-enabled rotary control knob provides a convenient and easy to use interface to control vehicle instrumentation. Such a haptic knob helps to reduce distractions on the driver. As a result, driver safety and performance is increased. Means of integrating current window control systems within such a knob is examined through human factors studies. The effects of varying forces on a knob are also investigated to further increase accuracy and performance during window selection. Results show that when forces are applied to the knob, drivers are better able to maintain control of the simulated vehicle while selecting a window.

Keywords: haptics, force-feedback, centralized rotary control knob, window control, driving simulator.

1 Introduction

Current window control systems do not provide a single control point incorporating force feedback. By utilizing a single haptic-enabled rotary control knob, it is possible for current window control systems to be simplified, maximizing instrumentation ease of use. Such a knob has the ability to increase driving and task performance by utilizing senses least used during driving (e.g. touch) [1,4,5]. This performance increase is attributed to the reduction of errors and time spent performing the task. Most importantly, such instrumentation control devices reduce the likelihood of an accident [1].

In recent years, several major automotive manufacturers have incorporated the control of vehicle instrumentation into a single rotary control knob supported by a Graphical User Interface (GUI) [7,8,10,12,13]. Such a knob has the ability to provide a driver with quick and easy access to instrumentation functionality [2,5-8,12,13]. Additionally, it has the ability to effectively deliver information to the driver when paired with force feedback [9]. This allows primary focus to remain on driving, increasing the safety of the driver [1,5]. For optimum performance, it is desirable for the rotary knob to operate consistently and free of torque variations or noise due to manufacturing tolerances [14]. Examples of such instrumentation control devices include the Multi Media Interface (MMI) offered by Audi [7], the iDrive control system offered by BMW [8], the COMAND control system offered by Mercedes-Benz [12], and advanced control panels offered by Visteon [13]. However, these devices fail to incorporate both controlled force feedback and control of the windows.

A.M.L. Kappers et al. (Eds.): EuroHaptics 2010, Part I, LNCS 6191, pp. 379–384, 2010.

In this paper, we investigate the simplification of controlling windows within a vehicle by utilizing a haptic-enabled rotary control knob and visual feedback. Accordingly, we designed and constructed a haptic knob and GUI for experimentation. The resulting device allows a user to select a window and control its position. Human factors studies were then conducted to examine the effects of integrating window selection into an instrumentation control device such as iDrive. Using this device in conjunction with a driving simulator, the following two hypotheses were tested:

> H_1: Adding haptics to a rotary control knob reduces driver distraction while selecting a window by allowing focus to remain on the road.
>
> H_2: Varying forces on a haptic-enabled rotary control knob enables the driver to more accurately select windows.

Two tests were designed to evaluate the above hypotheses. Test 1 catered to evaluating H_1, while Test 2 catered to H_2. These tests are explained in greater detail in the next section.

2   Experimental Setup and Procedure

Experiments were conducted with the assistance of a driving simulator to recreate the act of driving, as shown in Fig. 1. The driving simulator consisted of a seat, force-feedback steering wheel, gas and brake pedals, a display for the driving task, a display for the window selection task, and the haptic knob placed within reach of the right hand.

Fig. 1. Subject selecting a window while driving

In the driving simulator, subjects are presented with a virtual car interior and scene. The driving scene was a circuit complete with a gray road and surrounding green area to simulate grass. Subjects are also provided with their current speed in a place consistent with where a speedometer would be.

The GUI supporting the haptic knob can be seen in Fig. 2. The left picture displays the window selection screen and the right displays the window position screen.

However, subjects will only be presented with Window Selection screen as this paper does not focus on controlling window position. This screen associates a numbered LED indicator with a window such that 1 represents the driver front window, 2 represents the passenger front window, and so on. Using this association, each window is selectable within a unique range of 90 degrees of knob rotation.

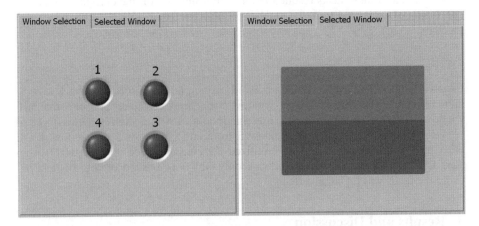

Fig. 2. Screenshot depicting the GUI supporting the haptic-enabled rotary control knob

Using this setup, two tests were performed. Test 1 was conducted to show that by adding forces on the knob, drivers are better able to select a window and maintain control of the simulated car. Expanding on Test 1, Test 2 was used to investigate the effect of using varying levels of force to more accurately select a specific window. This test is conducted to alert the user that they have selected a favorite window, e.g. a window most often used or user specified. This discriminating force also provides a known "landmark" to the user.

Utilizing this experimental platform, 10 healthy right-handed drivers (7 male, 3 female) between the ages of 16 and 55, completed both Test 1 and 2 as follows:

Test 1

In Test 1, haptic feedback was generated for the Window Select screen by generating a "constant force" that must be overcome to reach the next window. This constant force opposes the subjects movement when approaching the boundary between two windows. However, once the subject exceeds this boundary between windows an attracting force attracts the subject to the next window. A uniform level of controlled force feedback was generated between each window boundary. This controlled force feedback exerts a force of 0.83±0.01 N on the subject's hand. This force measurement was obtained using a force sensor with a resolution of ±0.01N. During this test, subjects are randomly exposed to three situations:

1) Window selection with visual feedback only.
2) Window selection with haptic feedback only.
3) Window selection with haptic and visual feedback.

Each condition consisted of 15 trials where each subject was told what window number they were currently on and what window number they should navigate to. The navigation technique was left for the driver to decide be it clockwise or counterclockwise. While the experiment was in session, the subjects were asked to maintain a speed range, stay within the virtual road and navigate to the dictated window. Failure to perform all of these tasks resulted in an overall mistake for the current trial. At the conclusion of each condition, the number of mistakes for all 15 trials was then added together.

Test 2

Expanding upon Test 1, Test 2 incorporated varying levels of force feedback to window selection. The force between window boundaries remained constant for each window in Test 1. However, Test 2 presented the user with a slightly higher force of 1.34±0.02N when navigating to window 3 from either window 2 or window 4. All other navigation scenarios in Test 2 utilized the constant force of 0.83±0.01N from Test 1. The condition of visual feedback only was not revisited during this test because the focus was on haptic effects.

3   Results and Discussion

The number of mistakes made during each trial was utilized to determine the average percentage of execution without a mistake as shown in Fig. 3. It can be seen that the condition with visual feedback only generated the most mistakes. As force-feedback was introduced, this percentage dramatically increases.

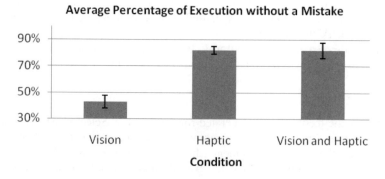

Fig. 3. Percentage of execution without a mistake for each condition for Test 1

A one-way ANOVA was conducted and the results confirm the hypothesis, H_1, in favor over the null hypothesis ($F(2,18) = 101.39$; $p=0.0098$), showing that adding haptics to a control knob reduces driver distraction while selecting a window. A post hoc test was conducted to determine between which two conditions the greater difference lies. The results of a one-way ANOVA analysis, show that the biggest difference was between the conditions Vision and Haptic ($F(1,9) = 3.61$; $p = 0.000003$). A large difference also exists between the conditions Vision and Vision & Haptic ($F(1,9) = 48.27$; $p = 0.0001$). Thus, haptics has a dominant effect when compared to only vision.

The results of Test 2 can be seen in Fig. 4, which draws a comparison between the conditions Haptics and Vision & Haptics of both Test 1 and 2. These results show that adding force discrimination on window 3 enables the user to make fewer mistakes compared to the constant force of Test 1. The initial results seem to support the hypothesis, H_2, that varying forces on a haptic knob enables the driver to be more accurate while selecting windows. However, after conducting a one-way ANOVA on the Vision and Haptic condition from Test 1 and 2 it was clear that more data was needed to determine if these results are approaching significance ($F(1,9) = 2.14$; $p = 0.1773$).

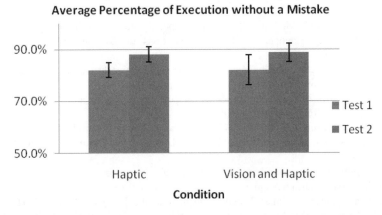

Fig. 4. Percentage of execution without a mistake for Haptic and Haptic & Vision conditions for Tests 1 and 2

In addition to objective testing, each subject was then asked their opinion on integrating window control into such a centralized knob. The ten subjects unanimously thought it was a good idea. Furthermore, many subjects also voluntarily stated that it was much easier to maintain control of the vehicle and switch windows while forces were being applied to the knob.

4   Conclusions and Future Work

One purpose of this study was to investigate the possibility of integrating window control into a haptic centralized rotary knob for the purpose of reducing driver distraction. In addition to reducing driver distraction, another purpose of this study was to increase window selection accuracy and further reduce distraction through the use of varying forces.

In observance of the obtained results, it was strongly confirmed that in regards to integrating window control into a centralized knob, the addition of forces has the ability to increase driver performance by allowing focus to remain on the road. Also the effect of varying the forces on the knob showed to have a positive result on how well the subject performed the window selection task.

Future work includes conducting more trials to determine if varying forces on the knob are approaching significance in regards to driver accuracy. We also need to conduct human factors studies to investigate the effects of introducing haptics for the purpose of controlling the position of windows.

References

1. MacLean, Hasser, Chu: Driving with Programmable Haptic Feedback: Design Scenarios and Contextual Evaluation. Submitted to UIST (2001)
2. Badescu, Wampler, Mavroidis: Rotary Haptic Knob for Vehicular Instrument Controls. In: Proceedings of the 10th Symp. On Haptic Interfaces For Virtual Environments & Teleoperator Systems (2002)
3. Hannaford, Wood, McAffee, Zak: Performance Evaluation of a Six-Axis Generalized Force-Reflecting Teleoperator. IEEE Transactions on Systems, Man, and Cybernetics 21(3) (May/June 1991)
4. Swindells, MacLean, Booth, Meitner: Exploring Affective Design for Physical Controls. In: CHI 2007 Proceedings on Emotion and Empathy (2007)
5. Hjelm : Haptics in Cars, Univerisity of Tampere Seminar on Haptic Communication and Interaction in Mobile Contexts (2008)
6. Vitrani, Nikitczuk, Morel, Mavroidis, Weinberg: Torque Control of Electrorehological Fluidic Resistive Actuators for Haptic Vehicular Instrument Controls. In: ASME, vol. 128 (June 2006)
7. Audi Multi Media Interface, http://www.audiusa.com
8. BMW iDrive Control System, http://www.bmw.com
9. MacLean, Roderick: Smart Tangible Displays in the Everyday World: A Haptic Door Knob. In: Proc. IEEE/ASME Intl. Conf. on Advanced Intelligent Mechatronics, AIM 1999 (1999)
10. Audi A8/S8 Quick Reference Guide, http://www.audiusa.com
11. Enriquez, MacLean, Chita: Haptic Phonemes: Basic Buildin Blocks of Haptic Communication. In: IMCI 2006 (2006)
12. Mercedes S-Class Rotary COMAND Controller, http://www.immersion.com
13. Advanced Control Panels from Visteon, http://www.immersion.com
14. Tan, Yang, Pizlo, Buttolo, Johnston: Manual Detection of Spatial and Temporal Torque Variation through a Rotary Switch. IEEE Transactions on Haptics 1(2) (July/December 2008)

Gesture Recognition in the Haptic Creature

Jonathan Chang, Karon MacLean, and Steve Yohanan

Department of Computer Science, University of British Columbia
2366 Main Mall, Vancouver, B.C., V6N 2K6, Canada
jchang86@interchange.ubc.ca, {maclean,yohanan}@cs.ubc.ca

Abstract. Touch is an important but poorly studied aspect of emotional communication. With the *Haptic Creature* we are investigating fundamentals of affective touch. This small robot senses the world solely by being touched via a force-sensing resistor network, and communicates its internal state via purring, stiffening its ears and modulating its breathing and pulse. We describe the Creature's first-generation gesture recognition engine, analyze its results, and specify its next iteration. In the region of highest sensor density, four gestures were differentiated with an average of 77% accuracy. Error patterns suggest that sensor deficiency rather than algorithm pose current performance limits.

Keywords: Affect, touch sensing, human-robot interaction, gesture recognition.

1 Introduction

Affective touch communicates or evokes emotion. In the Haptic Creature project we are investigating affective touch in social human-robot interactions, to identify its physical traits for eventual applications such as therapy and companionship. Our immediate goals are the display and recognition of affective touch by human and machine, as well as the interactive touch dynamics that can develop between them [1].

We are leveraging research in human-animal interaction with a robotic creature that mimics a small animal sitting on a person's lap (Fig. 1). The Haptic Creature interacts entirely through touch by breathing, purring and stiffening its ears in response to the user's touch. We use an animal platform to avoid confounding factors in human-human social touching such as gender, social status and culture. With studies now in progress we are exploring essential traits of this form of touch, and mechatronics and computation needed to support them. What touch gestures do humans most naturally use to express specific emotions? What is required to *elicit* (form factor, surface textures, movements) and recognize them (sensing, modeling)?

This paper describes our first-generation Gesture Recognition Engine (GRE), an essential part of a platform that will help us answer these questions.

1.1 Background

Social touch. Our interest in affective touch is informed by studies of human-to-human social touch. Hertenstein et al examined touch-only communication of specified emotions between strangers, and identified the specific tactile behaviors used [2].

A.M.L. Kappers et al. (Eds.): EuroHaptics 2010, Part I, LNCS 6191, pp. 385–391, 2010.

Fig. 1. The Haptic Creature and its sensors. CCW from top left: (a) with furry skin; (b) fiber-glass shell and touch sensors; (c) touch sensor mapping to region, flattened; black squares indicate underbelly, and gray indicate lower sides.

Participants transmitted emotional meanings (anger, fear, disgust, love, gratitude, and sympathy) with accuracy rates of 48-83%/chance=25%), comparable to performance observed for facial displays and vocal communication.

To illuminate how touch is used for communication in real-life settings, Jones and Yarbrough asked participants to record details of touch-based social interactions and context in their daily lives; then segmented these touches into 12 distinct categories of meaning such as inclusion, sexual interest, compliance or playful aggression. For example, attention-getting usually involved "spot touches" by the initiator's hand on a non-vulnerable body part of the recipient [3]. While many questions remain and re-sults such as these are almost certainly culturally specific, they confirm the impor-tance of touch as a communicative medium and reveal key social mechanisms.

Human Robot Interaction and Touch. Current trends in human-robot interaction (HRI) are represented in Dautenhahn's survey of social and interactive skills needed for robots to be socially intelligent companions or therapeutic agents [4]. Touchability has been a part of a several HRI platforms, beginning with Paro [5].

Using a teddy bear with 56 capacitive touch sensors, Knight et al distinguish "touch subgestures" (low level touches such as *pet, stroke, pat* and *hold*) and "sym-bolic gestures" (location-dependent, with contextual social meaning such as, for this teddy bear model, *feeding, rocking, hug, head-pat* etc) [6]. Touch subtypes are in-ferred with classifiers (e.g. average sensor value, number of sensors active, spatial distributions), and symbolic gestures with priority logic relying on location filters. Training data files collected on 4 subgestures from one user produced distinctive variable profiles, but results are not reported for subgesture recognition rate, nor real-time interactive configuration discussed.

Our Approach. The Haptic Creature platform is designed for purely haptic bidirectional interaction, and takes a deliberately non-representational physical form [1]. Our GRE uses a probabilistic Markovian model with architectural similarities to [6]; the Creature has been assessed in an operational setup for recognition success of gestures analogous to [6]'s "subgesture" class. The GRE is a component of a physically interactive system, mandating eventual realtime performance and a modular, scalable structure able to concurrently evaluate multiple candidate gestures of different durations and urgencies. These recognized gestures guide the Creature's emotion model and physical behavior, which is being independently developed.

1.2 Mechatronic Description

The Haptic Creature's mechatronics are designed to produce organic, coordinated behavior with a minimalist zoomorphism that suggests animal traits while avoiding replication of a single real animal. The robot is clothed with faux fur on a fiberglass shell which supports 56 Interlink™ force sensing resistors (Fig. 1(a-b)).

Fig. 1(c) shows the sensor mapping to the touch regions of interest in the GRE, with 47 round (0.5") and 9 square (1.5"); because FSR sensitivity drops in bending, small sensors were used in higher curvature regions. FSRs are spaced on ~2" centers (average), front to back and left to right, but with variations primarily dictated by curvature. Each ear bulb has two sensors, on the front and outer side.

The Creature's display features are described in [7]. The stiffness of two inflation bulb "ears" are individually controlled by out-take valves. The Creature purrs through an offset weight attached to a motor shaft spinning under modulated motor control, and simulates breathing via a servo that displaces the articulated breastplate.

1.3 System Goals and Proof of Concept

The GRE must eventually identify and differentiate 10-20 affectively significant gestures (not emotions), varying in aspects such as duration, localization, and temporal/spatial force profile. It must do this in realtime: "sharp" gestures (e.g. poke or slap) within a few milliseconds, and gentle, slow touches over a longer period.

Perfect GRE accuracy is unlikely to be feasible given the imprecision found even with people touching people. We have provisionally estimated a useable accuracy target of 75% / chance=25% (to be confirmed in later experimental stages), and have prioritized understanding affective gesture classes and correctly identifying them. Accuracy will always be best when the GRE is individually tuned, just as we best understand touches from familiar living touch-partners, such as a family member or a pet. Personal customization of the GRE is impractical for our short-term purposes, although it may be helpful for applications where the Creature will work in a dedicated partnership.

The GRE version described is a proof of concept, which we assess for feasibility of general approach. To that end, we consider (a) best-case results, which show what is possible and help distinguish mechatronic and algorithmic causes; and (b) analyze lesser results and (c) discuss the algorithm's scalability.

2 The Creature Gesture Recognition Engine

The GRE is a software system for recognizing atomic user actions through touch sensor activations. It extracts key features from the data, after normalization and averaging to deduce user intention. As a part of the overall Haptic Creature system, the mechanisms that exist within the GRE represent the Creature's internal disposition towards various kinds of touch. Just as a sensitive person may mistake your pat for a slap, the GRE's internal values may be tuned to be more or less sensitive.

The GRE passes its estimate of the most likely recent gesture to the Haptic Creature's "emoter", which determines a *response* to the identified gesture. Whereas the GRE is tunable in classification sensitivity, the emoter encodes higher-level strategies, e.g. mirroring an emotion versus provoking an emotion change in the user.

2.1 GRE Description

The Java-based GRE version described here is built with Markovian principles in mind, but in its current stage it more resembles a deterministic decision tree. The GRE can map inputs of a certain domain to outputs of another discrete domain with error probability calculations [8]. It maps the sensor array data to various gestures that caused the patterns in the sensor array, and makes error inferences based on deviations from the set gesture definitions. In Markovian terminology, the gestures represent the "state of the world", the sensory array is the "observation", and the GRE is the "agent".

The sensor array (56 10-bit values) generates an extremely large raw data stream, currently sampled at 15 Hz following Nyquist criteria applied to anticipated traversal and tapping rates (much higher sample rates are possible), and with it the danger of temporally missing quick touches altogether. To handle this stream, we created "features" [8] which extract key data properties. These can be thought of as key statistics (peak activation, average activation, points of contact, etc.) that summarize the raw data to ease processing.

Features employed in the current evaluation (Table 1) were chosen pragmatically, based on greatest accuracy for the gestures targeted below. Additional features still in development are *gesture vector* (direction and intensity of the activated sensors); and *centroid movement* (movement of an activation patch's centroid over time). Less helpful to date are *peak activation area, peak movement, median and quartile activation and area*, and *centroid activation* (the level of activation at the centroid).

Table 1. Feature values used and their levels.

Feature	Description
Average Area [0-56]	All sensor readings across all frames *[no sensors activated – all sensors activated for all frames]*
Average Activation [0-65535]	Average number of sensors activated / frame, regardless of pressure *[no activation – all sensors activated to maximum for all frames]*
Peak Activation [0-65535]	Highest value any sensor achieved during a gesture capture *[no activation – all sensors maximally activated for at least one frame]*
Movement Index [0-56]	Quantifies adjacent activity *[no sensors exhibited neighboring activation in previous frame – every sensor's neighbour was activated in the previous frame for all frames]*

Currently, the GRE algorithm calculates features based on available data and evaluates them in various combinations. We use exclusion sets to further tailor the feature behavior to the idiosyncrasies of the platform (de-emphasize known low-probability or commonly misinterpreted gestures and increase likelihood of recognizing common patterns) in a manner similar to a deterministic decision tree. For example, should the average area be large, and there is a high value for average and peak activation, the system may be inclined to recognize a slap – as long as there was a low degree of movement. The use of features refined by exclusion sets has the potential of greater effectiveness than a more purely feature-based approach, but is also somewhat more complex and platform-specific.

While the current GRE is resembles a deterministic decision tree, its next realtime event-based version will introduce probabilistic factors based on previous values of features and gesture probability calculations. A principal advantage of a stochastic (and properly Markovian) GRE is its additional ability to determine gesture output probabilities based on recent past recognitions. For example, if the system has seen several "strokes", a stochastic GRE could on a historical basis be more likely to infer that the current gesture is also a stroke. This characteristic is likely to increase recognition accuracy because it approximates human tendencies in this context, typified by repetitive gestural touch driven by an emotional state that tends to change slowly.

The GRE is most similar to the system described in Knight et al [6], but the contrast is revealed in the systematic differences of the recognized gestures; Knight's gestures are defined primarily by localization – "head-pat", "foot-rub", "side-tickle". In Knight's algorithm, gesture candidates are *first* selected based on location, then subgestures more similar to ours (but not "stroke", the most difficult due to low force activations) are excluded using decision tree logic. In the GRE, the decision tree produces a gesture output from a variety of non-locale-based features. Location is a property of gestures (e.g. a *stroke* that occurred on the back) as opposed to its most defining characteristic (e.g. a side tickle). This leads to different approaches in recognition – more aggressive inferences based on location versus the GRE's reliance on nuanced sensor data. Knight's locale-based gestures and the approach that enables them are relevant in the specific context of an anthropomorphized bear, whereas we sought more general definitions. As well, we infer that Knight's capacitive sensors offer greater resolution and density than the FSRs used here; that is, our algorithm had to operate in a more sparse data environment. Finally, our approach is directed by a near-term need to use Markovian (history-based) processes, whereas other works do not appear to be moving in this direction.

2.2 Current Capabilities

We selected four gestures on the body (*stroke*, *slap*, *poke*, and *pat*) and three on the ears (*pinch*, *pat*, and *squeeze*) as most relevant to the Creature project's goals of studying emotional touch, and required for it to serve as a study platform. Behavioral literature indicates that they are crucial in a context of human-pet or human-child interaction, whereas other important gestures – e.g. *hug* – are not afforded by the robot's lap-situated form. These gestures were not selected for recognition ease.

The GRE is currently tuned to detect these gestures out of a 30-50 frame sequence collected from a fur-covered Creature held on the user's lap. To focus on recognition,

Table 2. Accuracy and error results

a. **Overall accuracy** (w/o uninformative files)

	Pat	Stroke	Slap	Poke	*Avg*
Snout	0%		100%	67%	*56%*
Front	67%	40%	100%	100%	*77%*
Back	25%	17%	0%	50%	*23%*
Rump	0%		0%	50%	*17%*
Side	0%	33%		0%	*11%*

b. **Errors**: % of captures that are *uninformative*

	Pat	Stroke	Slap	Poke	*Avg*
Snout	67%	100%	0%	0%	*42%*
Front	0%	0%	0%	0%	*0%*
Back	20%	0%	80%	67%	*42%*
Rump	0%	100%	20%	0%	*30%*
Side	0%	0%	100%	80%	*45%*

c. **Errors**: % of captures that are *inconclusive*

	Pat	Stroke	Slap	Poke	*Avg*
Snout	0%		0%	0%	*0%*
Front	33%	0%	0%	0%	*8%*
Back	40%	17%	20%	0%	*19%*
Rump	75%		80%	50%	*68%*
Side	100%	0%		0%	*33%*

actuation was turned off for these samples. At present, the GRE uses the entire 2-4 second history for classification, but has the ability to selectively process a shorter time-window (necessary in realtime where multiple concurrent GRE processes must examine varying window lengths to detect gestures of different duration). The current single-process GRE can process a data stream continuously, by defining a fixed-length window that moves along the stream's timeline. The feature values used for the results shown here are listed in Table 1.

Table 2(a) lists recognition success rates for this GRE version from a single user for body-based (non-ear) gestures, while (b-c) show error sources. We indicate where the gesture was applied; classification does not currently indicate area, although this is a minor extension.

In Table 2(b-c), where small numbers are good, we define *uninformative data* as samples that exhibited only rest activity, i.e. no activation, generally because the regional sensors were too sparse or insensitive to the lightness of the touch. *Inconclusive data* are samples that exhibited some consistency in non-rest activity that the engine is unable to classify, yet. Gray cells with no value indicate erratic data collected for that region and gesture type, indicating sensor difficulties in snout, rump and side that are exacerbated by the gesture type (stroke, with low force activations; and the very brief slap). Side sensitivity was impacted by loose fur accommodating rib expansion.

The Creature's Front, with the highest and most sensitive coverage due to its low curvature (permitting larger sensors and less bending) produced the highest average recognition rate of 77% (chance=25%), a value which meets our provisional goal of 75% but needs to be verified for usability in interactive contexts.

The remaining areas revealed recognition or sensing difficulties for several region/touch combinations. We interpret *inconclusive* data rates in Table 2(c) as situations with strong potential to be solved with improved features (more, and better optimized), with visually identifiable patterns. With current sensors, the Rump region will be the primary beneficiary of such improvement.

To determine whether *uninformative* data rates of Table 2(b) are a hardware problem, it is useful to consider the pattern of GRE misclassifications. Without space for a full confusion matrix, we summarize. *Pat⇔Slap* is the most common, a response to variable sensor sensitivity and positioning. *Slap⇒Poke* is a common unidirectional confusion, occurring when a slap hits too-few sensors. *Pat* or *Poke⇒ No Detection* is a too-light pat or a poke that misses a sensor altogether. Finally, *Stroke⇒Pat*, while rare, occurs when only part of a stroke is registered. Together, these patterns confirm a diagnosis of sensor rather than algorithmic weakness.

3 Conclusions and Future Work

In conclusion, we have described a first version of a generalizable engine for recognizing affective touch gestures, embodied in a fully functional, physically animated robot creature, constructed as the fundamental module of a multi-threaded, realtime gesture processor. Our initial assessment shows that the GRE algorithm meets bandwidth and provisional accuracy targets for our experimental purposes when the sensor coverage is adequately dense and sensitive; weaker performance in other areas known to suffer from poorer sensor quality is consistent with the interpretation that sensor network design rather than algorithm poses our current performance bottleneck, and thus is our most immediate target.

In addition to improved sensor system design, our next steps are to move to fully realtime processing by (a) implementing event-driven data stream processing through tying the GRE to an already-existent data event recognizer; and (b) parallelizing multiple moving-window GRE processes to support concurrent consideration of gestures of varying duration. To support more powerful functions in the downstream Emoter module, we will (c) localize gestures, through either logic changes in each of the feature calculator functions or adding a function that weighs relative activation average by per region. Finally, we will fully integrate the GRE with the larger Creature interactive system, as described in [1].

References

1. Yohanan, S., MacLean, K.E.: The Haptic Creature Project: Social Human-Robot Interaction through Affective Touch. In: Proc. of The Reign of Katz and Dogz, 2nd AISB Symp on the Role of Virtual Creatures in a Computerised Society (AISB 2008), Aberdeen, UK, pp. 7–11 (2008)
2. Hertenstein, M.J., Keltner, D., App, B., Bulleit, B., Jaskolka, A.: Touch Communicates Distinct Emotions. Emotion 6, 528–533 (2006)
3. Jones, S.E., Yarbrough, A.E.: A Naturalistic Study of the Meanings of Touch. Communications Monographs 52(1), 19–58 (1985)
4. Dautenhahn, K.: Socially Intelligent Robots: Dimensions of Human–Robot Interaction. Phil. Trans. of the Royal Soc. B: Bio. Sci. 362(1480), 679–704 (2007)
5. Mitsui, T., Shibata, T., Wada, K., Touda, A., Tanie, K.: Psychophysiological Effects by Interaction with Mental Commit Robot. J. of Robotics and Mechatronics 14(1), 13–19 (2002)
6. Knight, H., Toscano, R., Stiehl, W.D., Chang, A., Wang, Y., Breazeal, C.: Real-Time Social Touch Gesture Recognition for Sensate Robots. In: Proc. of IEEE/RSJ Int'l. Conf. on Intelligent Robots and Systems (IROS 2009), St. Louis (2009)
7. Yohanan, S., MacLean, K.E.: A Tool to Study Affective Touch: Goals and Design of the Haptic Creature. In: Proc. of ACM Conf. on Human Factors in Computing Systems (CHI 2009), Works in Progress, pp. 4153–4158 (2009)
8. Russell, S., Norvig, P.: Artificial Intelligence: A Modern Approach. Prentice Hall, New Jersey (2009)

Author Index

Printing: Mercedes-Druck, Berlin
Binding: Stein+Lehmann, Berlin